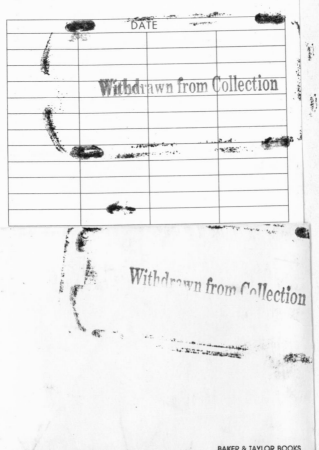

Essays in
Zen Buddhism

(First Series)

DAISETZ TEITARO SUZUKI

Grove Weidenfeld
New York

Published by Grove Weidenfeld
A division of Grove Press, Inc.
841 Broadway
New York, NY 10003-4793

This volume was first published in 1949 by Rider & Company, London, England.

Library of Congress Catalog Card Number 61-11477
ISBN 0-8021-5118-3

Manufactured in the United States of America

Printed on acid-free paper

First Evergreen Edition 1961

20 19 18 17 16

CONTENTS

ILLUSTRATIONS

(Between pages 192 *and* 193*)*

EDITOR'S FOREWORD

Daisetz Teitaro Suzuki, d.litt., Professor of Buddhist Philosophy in the Otani University, Kyoto, was born in 1869. He is probably now the greatest living authority on Buddhist philosophy, and is certainly the greatest authority on Zen Buddhism. His major works in English on the subject of Buddhism number a dozen or more, and of his works in Japanese as yet unknown to the West there are at least eighteen. He is, moreover, as a chronological bibliography of books on Zen in English clearly shows, the pioneer teacher of the subject outside Japan, for except for Kaiten Nukariya's *Religion of the Samurai* (Luzac and Co., 1913) nothing was known of Zen as a living experience, save to the readers of *The Eastern Buddhist* (1921–1939) until the publication of *Essays in Zen Buddhism* (Volume I) in 1927.

Dr. Suzuki writes with authority. Not only has he studied original works in Sanskrit, Pali, Chinese and Japanese, but he has an up-to-date knowledge of Western thought in German and French as well as in the English, which he speaks and writes so fluently. He is, moreover, more than a scholar: he is a Buddhist. Though not a priest of any Buddhist sect, he is honoured in every temple in Japan, for his knowledge of spiritual things, as all who have sat at his feet bear witness, is direct and profound. When he speaks of the higher stages of consciousness he speaks as a man who dwells therein, and the impression he makes on those who enter the fringes of his mind is that of a man who seeks for the intellectual symbols wherewith to describe a state of awareness which lies indeed 'beyond the intellect'.

To those unable to sit at the feet of the Master his writings must be a substitute. All these, however, were out of print in England by 1940, and all remaining stocks in Japan were destroyed in the fire which consumed three quarters of Tokyo in 1945. When, therefore, I reached Japan in 1946, I arranged with the author for the Buddhist Society, London—my wife and myself as its nominees—to begin the publication of his Collected Works, reprinting the old favourites, and printing as fast as possible translations of the many new works which the Professor, self-immured in his house at Kyoto, had written during the war.

This undertaking, however, was beyond the powers of the Buddhist Society, and we therefore secured the assistance of Rider and Co., who, backed by the vast resources of the House of Hutchinson, can honour the needs of such a considerable task.

Of Zen itself I need say nothing here, but the increasing sale of books on the subject, such as *The Spirit of Zen* by Alan Watts (Murray) and the series of original translations of Chinese Zen Scriptures and other works published by the Buddhist Society, prove that the interest of the West is rising rapidly. Zen, however, is a subject extremely easy to misunderstand, and it is therefore important that the words of a qualified Master should come readily to hand.

CHRISTMAS HUMPHREYS
President of the Buddhist Society, London

PREFACE

THE most fruitful growth of Buddhism in the Far East has resulted in the development of Zen and Shin. Zen attained its maturity in China and Shin in Japan. The vigour and vitality which Buddhism still has after more than two thousand years of history will be realized when one comes in contact with these two branches of Buddhism. The one appeals to the inmost religious consciousness of mankind, while the other touches the intellectual and practical aspects of the Oriental mind, which is more intuitive than discursive, more mystical than logical. If Zen is the ultra 'self-power' wing of Buddhism, Shin represents the other extreme wing known as the 'other-power', and these two extremes are synthesized in the enlightened Buddha-consciousness.

Since the publication of my short note on Zen Buddhism in the *Journal of the Pāli Text Society*, 1907, nothing of importance has been published in English on the subject except Professor Kwaiten Nukariya's *Religion of the Samurai*, 1913. In fact, even in Japanese or Chinese, this branch of Buddhism has received very slight attention from modern writers of Buddhism. This is due to the peculiar difficulties which accompany the study of it. The 'Goroku' (sayings) is the only literary form in which Zen expresses itself; and to understand it requires some special practical training in Zen, for mere knowledge of the Chinese, classical and historical, is far from being enough; even with the masterly understanding of the philosophy of general Buddhism, Zen is found quite hard to fathom. Some of such scholars sometimes try to explain the truth and development of Zen, but they sadly fail to do justice to the subject.

On the other hand, the Zen masters so called are unable to present their understanding in the light of modern thought. Their most intellectually productive years are spent in the Meditation Hall, and when they successfully graduate from it they are looked up to as adepts thoroughly versed in the ko-ans. So far so good; but, unfortunately from the scholarly point of view, they remain contented with this, and do not show any lively intellectual interest in the psychology and philosophy of Zen. Thus Zen is left to lie quietly sealed up in the 'Sayings' of the masters and in the technical study of the koans; it is thus incapacitated to walk out of the seclusion of the cloisters.

Of course, great mistake it would be if one should ever take the notion even for a moment that Zen could be mastered from its philosophical presentation or its psychological description; but this ought not to mean that Zen is not to be intelligently approached or to be made somewhat accessible by our ordinary means of reasoning. I need not mention that my attempts in the following pages are anything but adequate for the rational treatment of the subject. But as a tentative experiment to present Zen from our common-sense point of view and as a direct lineage of Buddhist faith as first proclaimed, or rather realized, by the Buddha, I hope I have worked towards removing some of the difficulties usually besetting us in the mastery of Zen thought. How far I have succeeded or how utterly I have failed—this is naturally for the reader to judge.

The book is a collection of the Essays originally published in *The Eastern Buddhist*, except one on the 'History of Zen Buddhism' which was written specially for this volume; but all of them have been thoroughly revised and in some parts entirely rewritten and new chapters added. The book will be followed by a second series of Essays before long, in which some more of the important points in the constitution of Zen will be treated.

The publication of these Essays in book form is principally due to the most liberal encouragement, both material and moral, of Mr. Yakichi Ataka, of Osaka, who is an old friend of the author's and who has not forgotten the pledge half seriously and half dreamily made in our youthful days.

The author also owes a great deal to his wife in the preparation and revision of the MS., without which the book would have shown many more imperfections than it does now in various ways.

Lastly, in sending this humble work, not written in the author's native tongue, out to the world, he cannot help thinking of his late teacher in Zen, Soyen Shaku, of Engakuji, Kamakura, with regret that his life had not been spared for several years yet, not only for the sake of Japanese Buddhism but for many of his lamenting friends. This is the seventh autumn for the maple-trees to scatter their crimson leaves over his grave at Matsuga-oka. Might his spirit not for once be awakened from deep meditation and criticize the book now before the reader!

DAISETZ TEITARO SUZUKI.

Kyoto, October, 1926.

INTRODUCTION[1]

Zen in its essence is the art of seeing into the nature of one's own being, and it points the way from bondage to freedom. By making us drink right from the fountain of life, it liberates us from all the yokes under which we finite beings are usually suffering in this world. We can say that Zen liberates all the energies properly and naturally stored in each of us, which are in ordinary circumstances cramped and distorted so that they find no adequate channel for activity.

This body of ours is something like an electric battery in which a mysterious power latently lies. When this power is not properly brought into operation, it either grows mouldy and withers away or is warped and expresses itself abnormally. It is the object of Zen, therefore, to save us from going crazy or being crippled. This is what I mean by freedom, giving free play to all the creative and benevolent impulses inherently lying in our hearts. Generally, we are blind to this fact, that we are in possession of all the necessary faculties that will make us happy and loving towards one another. All the struggles that we see around us come from this ignorance. Zen, therefore, wants us to open a 'third eye', as Buddhists call it, to the hitherto un-dreamed-of region shut away from us through our own ignorance. When the cloud of ignorance disappears, the infinity of the heavens is manifested, where we see for the first time into the nature of our own being. We now know the signification of life, we know that it is not blind striving nor is it a mere display of brutal forces, but that while we know not definitely what the ultimate purport of life is,

[1] One of the popular lectures prepared by the author for students of Buddhism, 1911. It was first published in *The Eastern Buddhist*, under the title, 'Zen Buddhism as Purifier and Liberator of Life'. Since it treats of Zen in its general aspect, I have decided to make it serve as Introduction to this book.

there is something in it that makes us feel infinitely blessed in the living of it and remain quite contented with it in all its evolution, without raising questions or entertaining pessimistic doubts.

When we are full of vitality and not yet awakened to the knowledge of life, we cannot comprehend the seriousness of all the conflicts involved in it which are apparently for the moment in a state of quiescence. But sooner or later the time will come when we have to face life squarely and solve its most perplexing and most pressing riddles. Says Confucius, 'At fifteen my mind was directed to study, and at thirty I knew where to stand.' This is one of the wisest sayings of the Chinese sage. Psychologists will all agree to this statement of his; for, generally speaking, fifteen is about the age youth begins to look around seriously and inquire into the meaning of life. All the spiritual powers until now securely hidden in the subconscious part of the mind break out almost simultaneously. And when this breaking out is too precipitous and violent, the mind may lose its balance more or less permanently; in fact, so many cases of nervous prostration reported during adolescence are chiefly due to this loss of the mental equilibrium. In most cases the effect is not very grave and the crisis may pass without leaving deep marks. But in some characters, either through their inherent tendencies or on account of the influence of environment upon their plastic constitution, the spiritual awakening stirs them up to the very depths of their personality. This is the time you will be asked to choose between the 'Everlasting No' and the 'Everlasting Yea'. This choosing is what Confucius means by 'study'; it is not studying the classics, but deeply delving into the mysteries of life.

Normally, the outcome of the struggle is the 'Everlasting Yea', or 'Let thy will be done'; for life is after all a form of affirmation, however negatively it might be conceived by the pessimists. But we cannot deny the fact that there are many things in this world which will turn our too sensitive minds towards the other direction and make us exclaim with

Andreyev in *The Life of Man*: 'I curse everything that you have given. I curse the day on which I was born. I curse the day on which I shall die. I curse the whole of my life. I fling everything back at your cruel face, senseless Fate! Be accursed, be forever accursed! With my curses I conquer you. What else can you do to me? . . . With my last thought I will shout into your asinine ears: Be accursed, be accursed!' This is a terrible indictment of life, it is a complete negation of life, it is a most dismal picture of the destiny of man on earth. 'Leaving no trace' is quite true, for we know nothing of our future except that we all pass away, including the very earth from which we have come. There are certainly things justifying pessimism.

Life, as most of us live it, is suffering. There is no denying the fact. As long as life is a form of struggle, it cannot be anything but pain. Does not a struggle mean the impact of two conflicting forces, each trying to get the upper hand of the other? If the battle is lost, the outcome is death, and death is the fearsomest thing in the world. Even when death is conquered, one is left alone, and the loneliness is sometimes more unbearable than the struggle itself. One may not be conscious of all this, and may go on indulging in those momentary pleasures that are afforded by the senses. But this being unconscious does not in the least alter the facts of life. However insistently the blind may deny the existence of the sun, they cannot annihilate it. The tropical heat will mercilessly scorch them, and if they do not take proper care they will all be wiped away from the surface of the earth.

The Buddha was perfectly right when he propounded his 'Fourfold Noble Truth', the first of which is that life is pain. Did not everyone of us come to this world screaming and in a way protesting? To come out into cold and prohibitive surroundings after a soft, warm motherly womb was surely a painful incident, to say the least. Growth is always attended with pain. Teething is more or less a painful process. Puberty is usually accompanied by a mental as well as a physical disturbance. The growth of the organism called society is also marked with painful cataclysms, and we are at present witnessing one of its birth-throes. We may calmly reason and say that this is all inevitable, that inasmuch as every reconstruction means the destruction of the old regime, we cannot help going through a painful operation. But this cold intellectual analysis does not alleviate whatever harrowing feelings we have to undergo. The pain heartlessly inflicted on our nerves is ineradicable. Life is, after all arguing, a painful struggle.

This, however, is providential. For the more you suffer the deeper grows your character, and with the deepening of your character you read the more penetratingly into the secrets of life. All great artists, all great religious leaders, and all great social reformers have come out of the intensest struggles which they fought bravely, quite frequently in tears and with bleeding hearts. Unless you eat your bread in sorrow, you cannot taste of real life. Mencius is right when he says that when Heaven wants to perfect a great man it tries him in every possible way until he comes out triumphantly from all his painful experiences.

To me Oscar Wilde seems always posing or striving for an effect; he may be a great artist, but there is something in him that turns me away from him. Yet he exclaims in his *De Profundis*: 'During the last few months I have, after terrible difficulties and struggles, been able to comprehend some of the lessons hidden in the heart of pain. Clergymen and people who use phrases without wisdom sometimes talk of suffering as a mystery. It is really a revelation. One discerns things one never discerned before. One approaches the whole of history from a different standpoint.' You will observe here what sanctifying effects his prison life produced on his character. If he had had to go through a similar trial in the beginning of his career, he might have been able to produce far greater works than those we have of him at present.

We are too ego-centred. The ego-shell in which we live is the hardest thing to outgrow. We seem to carry it all the time from childhood up to the time we finally pass away.

We are, however, given many chances to break through this shell, and the first and greatest of them is when we reach adolescence. This is the first time the ego really comes to recognize the 'other'. I mean the awakening of sexual love. An ego, entire and undivided, now begins to feel a sort of split in itself. Love hitherto dormant deep in his heart lifts its head and causes a great commotion in it. For the love now stirred demands at once the assertion of the ego and its annihilation. Love makes the ego lose itself in the object it loves, and yet at the same time it wants to have the object as its own. This is a contradiction, and a great tragedy of life. This elemental feeling must be one of the divine agencies whereby man is urged to advance in his upward walk. God gives tragedies to perfect man. The greatest bulk of literature ever produced in this world is but the harping on the same string of love, and we never seem to grow weary of it. But this is not the topic we are concerned with here. What I want to emphasize in this connection is this: that through the awakening of love we get a glimpse into the infinity of things, and that this glimpse urges youth to Romanticism or to Rationalism according to his temperament and environment and education.

When the ego-shell is broken and the 'other' is taken into its own body, we can say that the ego has denied itself or that the ego has taken its first steps towards the infinite. Religiously, here ensues an intense struggle between the finite and the infinite, between the intellect and a higher power, or, more plainly, between the flesh and the spirit. This is the problem of problems that has driven many a youth into the hands of Satan. When a grown-up man looks back to these youthful days he cannot but feel a sort of shudder going through his entire frame. The struggle to be fought in sincerity may go on up to the age of thirty, when Confucius states that he knew where to stand. The religious consciousness is now fully awakened, and all the possible ways of escaping from the struggle or bringing it to an end are most earnestly sought in every direction. Books are read, lectures are attended, sermons are greedily taken in, and various religious exercises or disciplines are tried. And naturally Zen too comes to be inquired into.

How does Zen solve the problem of problems?

In the first place, Zen proposes its solution by directly appealing to facts of personal experience and not to book-knowledge. The nature of one's own being where apparently rages the struggle between the finite and the infinite is to be grasped by a higher faculty than the intellect. For Zen says it is the latter that first made us raise the question which it could not answer by itself, and that therefore it is to be put aside to make room for something higher and more enlightening. For the intellect has a peculiarly disquieting quality in it. Though it raises questions enough to disturb the serenity of the mind, it is too frequently unable to give satisfactory answers to them. It upsets the blissful peace of ignorance and yet it does not restore the former state of things by offering something else. Because it points out ignorance, it is often considered illuminating, whereas the fact is that it disturbs, not necessarily always bringing light on its path. It is not final, it waits for something higher than itself for the solution of all the questions it will raise regardless of consequences. If it were able to bring a new order into the disturbance and settle it once for all, there would have been no need for philosophy after it had been first systematized by a great thinker, by an Aristotle or by a Hegel. But the history of thought proves that each new structure raised by a man of extraordinary intellect is sure to be pulled down by the succeeding ones. This constant pulling down and building up is all right as far as philosophy itself is concerned; for the inherent nature of the intellect, as I take it, demands it and we cannot put a stop to the progress of philosophical inquiries any more than to our breathing. But when it comes to the question of life itself we cannot wait for the ultimate solution to be offered by the intellect, even if it could do so. We cannot suspend even for a moment our life-activity for philosophy to unravel its mysteries. Let the mysteries remain as they are, but live we must. The hungry cannot wait until a complete analysis of food is obtained and the nourishing value of each element is determined. For the dead the scientific knowledge of food will be of no use whatever. Zen therefore does not rely on the intellect for the solution of its deepest problems.

By personal experience it is meant to get at the fact at first hand and not through any intermediary, whatever this may be. Its favourite analogy is: to point at the moon a finger is needed, but woe to those who take the finger for the moon; a basket is welcome to carry our fish home, but when the fish are safely on the table why should we eternally bother ourselves with the basket? Here stands the fact, and let us grasp it with the naked hands lest it should slip away—this is what Zen proposes to do. As nature abhors a vacuum, Zen abhors anything coming between the fact and ourselves. According to Zen there is no struggle in the fact itself such as between the finite and the infinite, between the flesh and the spirit. These are idle distinctions fictitiously designed by the intellect for its own interest. Those who take them too seriously or those who try to read them into the very fact of life are those who take the finger for the moon. When we are hungry we eat; when we are sleepy we lay ourselves down; and where does the infinite or the finite come in here? Are not we complete in ourselves and each in himself? Life as it is lived suffices. It is only when the disquieting intellect steps in and tries to murder it that we stop to live and imagine ourselves to be short of or in something. Let the intellect alone, it has its usefulness in its proper sphere, but let it not interfere with the flowing of the life-stream. If you are at all tempted to look into it, do so while letting it flow. The fact of flowing must under no circumstances be arrested or meddled with; for the moment your hands are dipped into it, its transparency is disturbed, it ceases to reflect your image which you have had from the very beginning and will continue to have to the end of time.

Almost corresponding to the 'Four Maxims' of the Nichiren Sect, Zen has its own four statements:

'A special transmission outside the Scriptures;
No dependence upon words and letters;
Direct pointing to the soul of man;
Seeing into one's nature and the attainment of
Buddhahood.'[1]

This sums up all that is claimed by Zen as religion. Of course we must not forget that there is a historical background to this bold pronunciamento. At the time of the introduction of Zen into China, most of the Buddhists were addicted to the discussion of highly metaphysical questions, or satisfied with the merely observing of the ethical precepts laid down by the Buddha or with the leading of a lethargic life entirely absorbed in the contemplation of the evanescence of things worldly. They all missed apprehending the great fact of life itself, which flows altogether outside of these vain exercises of the intellect or of the imagination. Bodhidharma and his successors recognized this pitiful state of affairs. Hence their proclamation of 'The Four Great Statements' of Zen as above cited. In a word, they mean that Zen has its own way of pointing to the nature of one's own being, and that when this is done one attains to Buddhahood, in which all the contradictions and disturbances caused by the intellect are entirely harmonized in a unity of higher order.

For this reason Zen never explains but indicates, it does not appeal to circumlocution, nor does it generalize. It always deals with facts, concrete and tangible. Logically considered, Zen may be full of contradictions and repetitions. But as it stands above all things, it goes serenely on its own way. As a Zen master aptly puts it, 'carrying his home-made cane on the shoulder, he goes right on among the mountains one rising above another.' It does not challenge logic, it simply walks its path of facts, leaving all the rest to their own fates. It is only when logic neglecting its proper functions tries to step into the track of Zen

---

[1] See also the Essay entitled 'History of Zen Buddhism', p. 163 *ff.*

that it loudly proclaims its principles and forcibly drives
out the intruder. Zen is not an enemy of anything. There
is no reason why it should antagonize the intellect which
may sometimes be utilized for the cause of Zen itself. To
show some examples of Zen's direct dealing with the fundamental facts of existence, the following are selected:

Rinzai[1] (Lin-chi) once delivered a sermon, saying: 'Over
a mass of reddish flesh there sits a true man who has no
title; he is all the time coming in and out from your sense-
organs. If you have not yet testified to the fact, Look!
Look!' A monk came forward and asked, 'Who is this true
man of no title?' Rinzai came right down from his straw
chair and taking hold of the monk exclaimed: 'Speak!
Speak!' The monk remained irresolute, not knowing what
to say, whereupon the master, letting him go, remarked,
'What worthless stuff is this true man of no title!' Rinzai
then went straight back to his room.

Rinzai was noted for his 'rough' and direct treatment of
his disciples. He never liked those roundabout dealings
which generally characterized the methods of a lukewarm
master. He must have got this directness from his own
teacher Ōbaku (Huang-po), by whom he was struck
three times for asking what the fundamental principle of
Buddhism was. It goes without saying that Zen has nothing
to do with mere striking or roughly shaking the questioner.
If you take this as constituting the essentials of Zen, you
would commit the same gross error as one who took the
finger for the moon. As in everything else, but most particularly in Zen, all its outward manifestations or demonstrations must never be regarded as final. They just indicate the way where to look for the facts. Therefore these
indicators are important, we cannot do well without them.
But once caught in them, which are like entangling meshes,
we are doomed; for Zen can never be comprehended. Some
may think Zen is always trying to catch you in the net of
logic or by the snare of words. If you once slip your steps,
you are bound for eternal damnation, you will never get to

[1] The founder of the Rinzai School of Zen Buddhism, died 867.

freedom, for which your hearts are so burning. Therefore, Rinzai grasps with his naked hands what is directly presented to us all. If a third eye of ours is opened undimmed, we shall know in a most unmistakable manner where Rinzai is driving us. We have first of all to get into the very spirit of the master and interview the inner man right there. No amount of wordy explanations will ever lead us into the nature of our own selves. The more you explain, the further it runs away from you. It is like trying to get hold of your own shadow. You run after it and it runs with you at the identical rate of speed. When you realize it, you read deep into the spirit of Rinzai or Ōbaku, and their real kindheartedness will begin to be appreciated.

Ummon[1] (Yün-mên) was another great master of Zen at the end of the T'ang dynasty. He had to lose one of his legs in order to get an insight into the life-principle from which the whole universe takes rise, including his own humble existence. He had to visit his teacher Bokuju (Mu-chou), who was a senior disciple of Rinzai under Ōbaku, three times before he was admitted to see him. The master asked, 'Who are you?' 'I am Bun-yen (Wên-yen),' answered the monk. (Bun-yen was his name, while Ummon was the name of the monastery where he was settled later.) When the truth-seeking monk was allowed to go inside the gate, the master took hold of him by the chest and demanded: 'Speak! Speak!' Ummon hesitated, whereupon the master pushed him out of the gate, saying, 'Oh, you good-for-nothing fellow!'[2] While the gate was hastily shut, one of Ummon's legs was caught and broken. The intense pain resulting from this apparently awakened the poor fellow to the greatest fact of life. He was no more a solicitous, pity-begging monk; the realization now gained paid more than enough for the loss of his leg. He was not, however, a solitary instance in this respect, there were many such in the history of Zen who were willing to sacrifice a part of the body for the truth. Says Confucius, 'If a man under-

---

[1] The founder of the Ummon School of Zen Buddhism, died 996.
[2] Literally, an old clumsy gimlet of the Ch'in dynasty.

stands the Tao in the morning, it is well with him even when he dies in the evening.' Some would feel indeed that truth is of more value than mere living, mere vegetative or animal living. But in the world, alas, there are so many living corpses wallowing in the mud of ignorance and sensuality.

This is where Zen is most difficult to understand. Why this sarcastic vituperation? Why this seeming heartlessness? What fault had Ummon to deserve the loss of his leg? He was a poor truth-seeking monk, earnestly anxious to get enlightenment from the master. Was it really necessary for the latter from his way of understanding Zen to shut him out three times, and when the gate was half opened to close it again so violently, so inhumanly? Was this the truth of Buddhism Ummon was so eager to get? But the outcome of all this singularly was what was desired by both of them. As to the master, he was satisfied to see the disciple attain an insight into the secrets of his being; and as regards the disciple he was most grateful for all that was done to him. Evidently, Zen is the most irrational, inconceivable thing in the world. And this is why I said before that Zen was not subject to logical analysis or to intellectual treatment. It must be directly and personally experienced by each of us in his inner spirit. Just as two stainless mirrors reflect each other, the fact and our own spirits must stand facing each other with no intervening agents. When this is done we are able to seize upon the living, pulsating fact itself.

Freedom is an empty word until then. The first object was to escape the bondage in which all finite beings find themselves, but if we do not cut asunder the very chain of ignorance with which we are bound hands and feet, where shall we look for deliverance? And this chain of ignorance is wrought of nothing else but the intellect and sensuous infatuation, which cling tightly to every thought we may have, to every feeling we may entertain. They are hard to get. rid of, they are like wet clothes as is aptly expressed by the Zen masters. 'We are born free and equal.' Whatever this may mean socially or politically, Zen maintains that it is absolutely true in the spiritual domain, and that all the fetters and manacles we seem to be carrying about ourselves are put on later through ignorance of the true condition of existence. All the treatments, sometimes literary and sometimes physical, which are most liberally and kindheartedly given by the masters to inquiring souls, are intended to get them back to the original state of freedom. And this is never really realized until we once personally experience it through our own efforts, independent of any ideational representation. The ultimate standpoint of Zen, therefore, is that we have been led astray through ignorance to find a split in our own being, that there was from the very beginning no need for a struggle between the finite and the infinite, that the peace we are seeking so eagerly after has been there all the time. Sotoba (Su Tung-p'o), the noted Chinese poet and statesman, expresses the idea in the following verse:

> 'Misty rain on Mount Lu,
> And waves surging in Che-chiang;
> When you have not yet been there,
> Many a regret surely you have;
> But once there and homeward you wend,
> And how matter-of-fact things look!
> Misty rain on Mount Lu,
> And waves surging in Che-chiang.'

This is what is also asserted by Seigen Ishin (Ch'ing-yüan Wei-hsin), according to whom, 'Before a man studies Zen, to him mountains are mountains and waters are waters; after he gets an insight into the truth of Zen through the instruction of a good master, mountains to him are not mountains and waters are not waters; but after this when he really attains to the abode of rest, mountains are once more mountains and waters are waters.'

Bokuju (Mu-chou), who lived in the latter half of the ninth century, was once asked, 'We have to dress and eat every day, and how can we escape from all that?' The master replied, 'We dress, we eat.' 'I do not understand you,' said the questioner. 'If you don't understand put your dress on and eat your food.'

Zen always deals in concrete facts and does not indulge in generalizations. And I do not wish to add unnecessary legs to the painted snake, but if I try to waste my philosophical comments on Bokuju, I may say this: We are all finite, we cannot live out of time and space; inasmuch as we are earth-created, there is no way to grasp the infinite, how can we deliver ourselves from the limitations of existence? This is perhaps the idea put in the first question of the monk, to which the master replies: Salvation must be sought in the finite itself, there is nothing infinite apart from finite things; if you seek something transcendental, that will cut you off from this world of relativity, which is the same thing as the annihilation of yourself. You do not want salvation at the cost of your own existence. If so, drink and eat, and find your way of freedom in this drinking and eating. This was too much for the questioner, who, therefore, confessed himself as not understanding the meaning of the master. Therefore, the latter continued: Whether you understand or not, just the same go on living in the finite, with the finite; for you die if you stop eating and keeping yourself warm on account of your aspiration for the infinite. No matter how you struggle, Nirvāṇa is to be sought in the midst of Saṁsāra (birth-and-death). Whether an enlightened Zen master or an ignoramus of the first degree, neither can escape the so-called laws of nature. When the stomach is empty, both are hungry; when it snows, both have to put on an extra flannel. I do not, however, mean that they are both material existences, but they are what they are, regardless of their conditions of spiritual development. As the Buddhist scriptures have it, the darkness of the cave itself turns into enlightenment when a torch of spiritual insight burns. It is not that a thing called darkness is first taken out and another thing known by the name of enlightenment is carried in later, but that enlightenment and darkness are substantially one and the same thing from the very beginning; the change from the one to the other has taken place only inwardly or subjectively. Therefore the finite is the infinite, and *vice versa*. These are not two separate things, though we are compelled to conceive them so, intellectually. This is the idea, logically interpreted, perhaps contained in Bokuju's answer given to the monk. The mistake consists in our splitting into two what is really and absolutely one. Is not life one as we live it, which we cut to pieces by recklessly applying the murderous knife of intellectual surgery?

On being requested by the monks to deliver a sermon, Hyakujo Nehan (Pai-chang Nieh-p'an) told them to work on the farm, after which he would give them a talk on the great subject of Buddhism. They did as they were told, and came to the master for a sermon, when the latter, without saying a word, merely extended his open arms towards the monks. Perhaps there is after all nothing mysterious in Zen. Everything is open to your full view. If you eat your food and keep yourself cleanly dressed and work on the farm to raise your rice or vegetables, you are doing all that is required of you on this earth, and the infinite is realized in you. How realized? When Bokuju was asked what Zen was he recited a Sanskrit phrase from a Sūtra, 'Mahāprajñāpāramitā!' (in Japanese, *Makahannyaharamii!*). The inquirer acknowledged his inability to understand the purport of the strange phrase, and the master put a comment on it, saying:

'My robe is all worn out after so many years' usage.
And parts of it in shreds loosely hanging have been
blown away to the clouds.'

Is the infinite after all such a poverty-stricken mendicant? Whatever this is, there is one thing in this connection which we can never afford to lose sight of—that is, the peace or poverty (for peace is only possible in poverty) is obtained after a fierce battle fought with the entire strength of your personality. A contentment gleaned from idleness or from a *laissez-faire* attitude of mind is a thing most to be

abhorred. There is no Zen in this, but sloth and mere vege-
tation. The battle must rage in its full vigour and mascu-
linity. Without it, whatever peace that obtains is a simula-
crum, and it has no deep foundation; the first storm it may
encounter will crush it to the ground. Zen is quite emphatic
in this. Certainly, the moral virility to be found in Zen,
apart from its mystic flight, comes from the fighting of the
battle of life courageously and undauntedly.

From the ethical point of view, therefore, Zen may be
considered a discipline aiming at the reconstruction of
character. Our ordinary life only touches the fringe of personality, it does not cause a commotion in the deepest
parts of the soul. Even when the religious consciousness is
awakened, most of us lightly pass over it so as to leave no
marks of a bitter fighting on the soul. We are thus made to
live on the superficiality of things. We may be clever,
bright, and all that, but what we produce lacks depth,
sincerity, and does not appeal to the inmost feelings. Some
are utterly unable to create anything except makeshifts
or imitations betraying their shallowness of character and
want of spiritual experience. While Zen is primarily religious, it also moulds our moral character. It may be better
to say that a deep spiritual experience is bound to effect a
change in the moral structure of one's personality.

How is this so?

The truth of Zen is such that when we want to comprehend it penetratingly we have to go through with a great
struggle, sometimes very long and exacting constant
vigilance. To be disciplined in Zen is no easy task. A Zen
master once remarked that the life of a monk can be
attained only by a man of great moral strength, and that
even a minister of the State cannot expect to become a
successful monk. (Let us remark here that in China to be
a minister of the State was considered to be the greatest
achievement a man could ever hope for in this world.) Not
that a monkish life requires the austere practice of asceticism
but that it implies the elevation of one's spiritual powers
to their highest notch. All the utterances or activities of the

27

great Zen masters have come from this elevation. They are not intended to be enigmatic or driving us to confusion. They are the overflowing of a soul filled with deep experiences. Therefore, unless we are ourselves elevated to the same height as the masters, we cannot gain the same commanding views of life. Says Ruskin: 'And be sure also, if the author is worth anything, that you will not get at his meaning all at once—nay, that at his whole meaning you will not for a long time arrive in any wise. Not that he does not say what he means, and in strong words, too; but he cannot say it all and what is more strange, will not, but in a hidden way and in parable, in order that he may be sure you want it. I cannot see quite the reason of this, nor analyse that cruel reticence in the breasts of wise men which makes them always hide their deeper thought. They do not give it you by way of help, but of reward, and will make themselves sure that you deserve it before they allow you to reach it.' And this key to the royal treasury of wisdom is given us only after patient and painful moral struggle.

The mind is ordinarily chock full with all kinds of intellectual nonsense and passional rubbish. They are of course useful in their own ways in our daily life. There is no denying that. But it is chiefly because of these accumulations that we are made miserable and groan under the feeling of bondage. Each time we want to make a movement, they fetter us, they choke us, and cast a heavy veil over our spiritual horizon. We feel as if we are constantly living under restraint. We long for naturalness and freedom, yet we do not seem to attain them. The Zen masters know this, for they have gone through with the same experiences once. They want to have us get rid of all these wearisome burdens which we really do not have to carry in order to live a life of truth and enlightenment. Thus they utter a few words and demonstrate with action that, when rightly comprehended, will deliver us from the oppression and tyranny of these intellectual accumulations. But the comprehension does not come to us so easily. Being so long accustomed to the oppression, the mental inertia becomes hard to remove. In fact it has gone down deep into the roots of our own being, and the whole structure of personality is to be overturned. The process of reconstruction is stained with tears and blood. But the height the great masters have climbed cannot otherwise be reached; the truth of Zen can never be attained unless it is attacked with the full force of personality. The passage is strewn with thistles and brambles, and the climb is slippery in the extreme. It is no pastime but the most serious task in life; no idlers will ever dare attempt it. It is indeed a moral anvil on which your character is hammered and hammered. To the question, 'What is Zen?' a master gave this answer, 'Boiling oil over a blazing fire.' This scorching experience we have to go through with before Zen smiles on us and says, 'Here is your home.'

One of these utterances by the Zen masters that will stir a revolution in our minds is this: Hōkoji (P'ang-yün), formerly a Confucian, asked Baso (Ma-tsu, –788), 'What kind of man is he who does not keep company with any thing?' Replied the master, 'I will tell you when you have swallowed up in one draught all the waters in the West River.' What an irrelevant reply to the most serious question one can ever raise in the history of thought! It sounds almost sacrilegious when we know how many souls there are who go down under the weight of this question. But Baso's earnestness leaves no room for doubt, as is quite well known to all the students of Zen. In fact, the rise of Zen after the sixth patriarch, Hui-nêng, was due to the brilliant career of Baso, under whom there arose more than eighty fully qualified masters, and Hōkoji, who was one of the foremost lay disciples of Zen, earned a well-deserved reputation as the Vimalakīrti of Chinese Buddhism. A talk between two such veteran Zen masters could not be an idle sport. However easy and even careless it may appear, there is hidden in it a most precious gem in the literature of Zen. We do not know how many students of Zen were made to sweat and cry in tears because of the inscrutability of this statement of Baso's.

To give another instance: a monk asked the master Shin of Chōsa (Chang-sha Ching-ch'ên), 'Where has Nansen (Nan-ch'üan) gone after his death?' Replied the master, 'When Sekitō (Shih-t'ou) was still in the order of young novitiates, he saw the sixth patriarch.' 'I am not asking about the young novitiate. What I wish to know is, where is Nansen gone after his death?' 'As to that,' said the master, 'it makes one think.'

The immortality of the soul is another big question. The history of religion is built upon this one question, one may almost say. Everybody wants to know about life after death. Where do we go when we pass away from this earth? Is there really another life? Or is the end of this the end of all? While there may be many who do not worry themselves as to the ultimate significance of the solitary, 'companionless' One, there are none perhaps who have not once at least in their lives asked themselves concerning their destiny after death. Whether Sekitō when young saw the sixth patriarch or not does not seem to have any inherent connection with the departure of Nansen. The latter was the teacher of Chōsa, and naturally the monk asked him whither the teacher finally passed. Chōsa's answer is no answer, judged by the ordinary rules of logic. Hence the second question, but still a sort of equivocation from the lips of the master. What does this 'making one think' explain? From this it is apparent that Zen is one thing and logic another. When we fail to make this distinction and expect of Zen to give us something logically consistent and intellectually illuminating, we altogether misinterpret the signification of Zen. Did I not state in the beginning that Zen deals with facts and not with generalizations? And this is the very point where Zen goes straight down to the foundations of personality. The intellect ordinarily does not lead us there, for we do not live in the intellect, but in the will. Brother Lawrence speaks the truth when he says (*The Practice of the Presence of God*), 'that we ought to make a great difference between the acts of the understanding and those of the will: that the first were comparatively of little value, and the others, all'.

Zen literature is all brim full of such statements, which seem to have been uttered so casually, so innocently, but those who actually know what Zen is will testify to the fact that all these utterances dropped so naturally from the lips of the masters are like deadly poisons, that when they are once taken in they cause such a violent pain as to make one's intestines wriggle nine times and more, as the Chinese would express it. But it is only after such pain and turbulence that all the internal impurities are purged and one is born with quite a new outlook on life. It is strange that Zen grows intelligible when these mental struggles are gone through. But the fact is that Zen is an experience actual and personal, and not a knowledge to be gained by analysis or comparison. 'Do not talk poetry except to a poet; only the sick know how to sympathize with the sick.' This explains the whole situation. Our minds are to be so matured as to be in tune with those of the masters. Let this be accomplished, and when one string is struck, the other will inevitably respond. Harmonious notes always result from the sympathetic resonance of two or more chords. And what Zen does for us is to prepare our minds to be yielding and appreciative recipients of old masters. In other words, psychologically Zen releases whatever energies we may have in store, of which we are not conscious in ordinary circumstances.

Some say that Zen is self-suggestion. But this does not explain anything. When the word 'Yamato-damashi' is mentioned it seems to awaken in most Japanese a fervent patriotic passion. The children are taught to respect the flag of the rising sun, and when the soldiers come in front of the regimental colours they involuntarily salute. When a boy is reproached for not acting like a little samurai, and with disgracing the name of his ancestor, he at once musters his courage and will resist temptations. All these ideas are energy-releasing ideas for the Japanese, and this release, according to some psychologists, is self-suggestion. Social conventions and imitative instincts may also be regarded as self-suggestions. So is moral discipline. An example is given to the students to follow or imitate it. The idea gradually takes root in them through suggestion, and they finally come to act as if it were their own. Self-suggestion is a barren theory, it does not explain anything. When they say that Zen is self-suggestion, do we get any clearer idea of Zen? Some think it scientific to call certain phenomena by a term newly come into fashion, and rest satisfied with it as if they disposed of them in an illuminating way. The study of Zen must be taken up by the profounder psychologists.

Some think that there is still an unknown region in our consciousness which has not yet been thoroughly and systematically explored. It is sometimes called the Unconscious or the Subconscious. This is a territory filled with dark images, and naturally most scientists are afraid of treading upon it. But this must not be taken as denying the fact of its existence. Just as our ordinary field of consciousness is filled with all possible kinds of images, beneficial and harmful, systematic and confusing, clear and obscure, forcefully assertive and weakly fading; so is the Subconscious a storehouse of every form of occultism or mysticism, understanding by the term all that is known as latent or abnormal or psychic or spiritualistic. The power to see into the nature of one's own being may lie also hidden there, and what Zen awakens in our consciousness may be that. At any rate, the masters speak figuratively of the opening of a third eye. 'Satori' is the popular name given to this opening or awakening.

How is this to be effected?

By meditating on those utterances or actions that are directly poured out from the inner region undimmed by the intellect or the imagination, and that are calculated successfully to exterminate all the turmoils arising from ignorance and confusion.[1]

---

[1] Zen has its own way of practising meditations so called, for the Zen methods are to be distinguished from what is popularly or Hinayanistically understood by the term. Zen has nothing to do with mere quietism or losing oneself in trance. I may have an occasion to speak more about the subject elsewhere.

It may be interesting to readers in this connection to get acquainted with some of the methods[1] used by the masters in order to open the spiritual eye of the disciple. It is natural that they frequently make use of the various religious insignia which they carry when going out to the Hall of the Dharma. Such are generally the 'hossu',[2] 'shippe',[3] 'nyoi',[4] or 'shujvo' (or a staff). The last-mentioned seems to have been the most favourite instrument used in the demonstration of the truth of Zen. Let me cite some examples of its use.

According to Yeryō (Hui-lêng), of Chōkei (Chang-ch'ing), 'when one knows what that staff is, one's life study of Zen comes to an end'. This reminds us of Tennyson's flower in the crannied wall. For when we understand the reason of the staff, we know 'what God and man is'; that is to say, we get an insight into the nature of our own being, and this insight finally puts a stop to all the doubts and hankerings that have upset our mental tranquillity. The significance of the staff in Zen can thus readily be comprehended.

Yesei (Hui-ch'ing), of Bashō (Pa-chiao), probably of the tenth century, once made the following declaration: 'When you have a staff, I will give you one; when you have none, I will take it away from you.' This is one of the most characteristic statements of Zen, but later Bokitsu (Mu-chi), of Daiyi (Ta-wei), was bold enough to challenge this by saying what directly contradicts it, viz: 'As to myself, I differ from him. When you have a staff, I will take it away from you; and when you have none, I will give you one. This is my statement. Can you make use of the staff? or can you not? If you can, Tokusan (Tê-shan) will be your vanguard and Rinzai (Lin-chi) your rearguard. But if you cannot, let it be restored to its original master.'

A monk approached Bokuju and said, 'What is the

[1] See also the Essay entitled, 'Practical Methods of Zen Instruction'.
[2] Originally a mosquito driver in India.
[3] A bamboo stick a few feet long.
[4] Also a stick or baton fancifully shaped and made of all kinds of material. It means literally 'as one wishes or thinks' (*cinta*, in Sanskrit).

33

statement surpassing [the wisdom of] all Buddhas and Patriarchs?' The master instantly held forth his staff before the congregation, and said, 'I call this a staff, and what do you call it?' The monk who asked the question uttered not a word. The master holding it out again said, 'A statement surpassing [the wisdom of] all Buddhas and Patriarchs— was that not your question, O monk?'

Those who carelessly go over such remarks as Bokuju's may regard them as quite nonsensical. Whether the stick is called a staff or not it does not seem to matter very much, as far as the divine wisdom surpassing the limits of our knowledge is concerned. But the one made by Ummon, another great master of Zen, is perhaps more accessible. He also once lifted his staff before a congregation and re-marked: 'In the scriptures we read that the ignorant take this for a real thing, the Hinayanists resolve it into a nonentity, the Pratyekabuddhas regard it as a hallucination, while the Bodhisattvas admit its apparent reality, which is, however, essentially empty.' 'But,' continued the master, 'monks, you simply call it a staff when you see one. Walk or sit as you will, but do not stand irresolute.'

The same old insignificant staff and yet more mystical statements from Ummon. One day his announcement was, 'My staff has turned into a dragon, and it has swallowed up the whole universe; where would the great earth with its mountains and rivers be?' On another occasion, Ummon, quoting an ancient Buddhist philosopher who said 'Knock at the emptiness of space and you hear a voice; strike a piece of wood and there is no sound,' took out his staff and, striking space, cried, 'Oh, how it hurts!' Then tapping at the board, he asked, 'Any noise?' A monk responded, 'Yes, there is a noise.'[1] Thereupon the master exclaimed, 'Oh you ignoramus!'

If I go on like this there will be no end. So I stop, but

[1] This reminds one of the remarks made by the master Ten (Chan), of Hofuku (Pao-fu), who, seeing a monk approach, took up his staff and struck a pillar, and then the monk. When the monk naturally cried with pain, said the master, 'How is it that this does not get hurt?'

expect some of you to ask me the following questions:
'Have these utterances anything to do with one's seeing
into the nature of one's being? Is there any relationship
possible between those apparently nonsensical talks about
the staff and the all-important problem of the reality of
life?'

In answer I append these two passages, one from Jimyo
(T'zu-ming) and the other from Yengo (Yüan-wu): In one
of his sermons, Jimyo said: 'As soon as one particle of dust
is raised, the great earth manifests itself there in its entirety.
In one lion are revealed millions of lions, and in millions
of lions is revealed one lion. Thousands and thousands of
them there are indeed, but know ye just one, one only.'
So saying he lifted up his staff, and continued, 'Here is my
own staff, and where is that one lion?' Bursting out into a
'Kwatz' (*hê*), he set the staff down, and left the pulpit.

In the *Hekigan* (Pi-yen-lu),[1] Yengo expresses the same
idea in his introductory remark to the 'one-finger Zen' of
Gutei (*Chuk-chih i chih t'ou ch'an*)[2]:

.   .   .   .   .

[1] *Hekiganshu* is a collection of one hundred 'cases' with Secchō's
(Hsüeh-tou's) poetical comments and Yengo's partly explanatory and
partly critical annotations. The book was brought to Japan during the
Kamakura era, and ever since it is one of the most important text-books
of Zen, especially for the followers of the Rinzai school.

[2] Gutei was a disciple of Tenryu (T'ien-lung), probably towards the
end of the T'ang dynasty. While he was first residing in a small temple,
he had a visit from a travelling nun, who came right into the temple
without removing her headgear. Carrying her staff with her, she went
three times around the meditation chair in which Gutei was sitting. Then
she said to him, 'Say a word of Zen, and I shall take off my hat.' She
repeated this three times, but Gutei did not know what to say. When the
nun was about to depart, Gutei suggested, 'It is growing late, and why
not stay here overnight?' Jissai (Shih-chi), which was the name of the
nun, said, 'If you say a word of Zen, I shall stay.' As he was still unable
to say a word, she left.

This was a terrible blow to poor Gutei, who pitifully sighed: 'While
I have the form of a man, I seem not to have any manly stamina!' He
then resolved to study and master Zen. When he was about to start on
his Zen 'wanderings', he had a vision of the mountain god who told
him not to go away from his temple, for a Bodhisattva in flesh would be
coming here before long and enlighten him in the truth of Zen. Surely
enough a Zen master called Tenryu (T'ien-lung) appeared the following

'One particle of dust is raised and the great earth lies therein; one flower blooms and the universe rises with it. But where should our eye be fixed when the dust is not yet stirred and the flower has not yet bloomed? Therefore, it is said that, like cutting a bundle of thread, one cut cuts all asunder; again like dyeing a bundle of thread, one dyeing dyes all in the same colour. Now yourself get out of all the entangling relations and rip them up to pieces, but do not lose track of your inner treasure; for it is through this that the high and the low universally responding and the advanced and the backward making no distinction, each manifests itself in full perfection.'

The foregoing sketch of Zen I hope will give the reader a general, though necessarily vague, idea of Zen as it is and has been taught in the Far East for more than one thousand years. In what follows I will try first to seek the origin of Zen in the spiritual enlightenment itself of the Buddha; for Zen has been frequently criticized for deviating too far from what is popularly understood to be the teaching of the Buddha as it is recorded, especially in the Āgamas or Nikāyas. While Zen, as it is, is no doubt the native product of the Chinese mind, the line of its development must be traced back to the personal experience of the Indian founder himself. Unless this is understood in connection with the psychological characteristics of the people, the growth of Zen among the Chinese Buddhists would be unintelligible. Zen is, after all, one of the Mahāyāna schools of Buddhism

day. Gutei told the master all about the humiliating experience of the previous day and his firm resolution to attain the secrets of Zen. Tenryu just lifted one of his fingers and said nothing. This, however, was enough to open Gutei's mind at once to the ultimate meaning of Zen, and it is said that ever since Gutei did or said nothing but just hold up a finger to all the questions that might be asked of him concerning Zen.

There was a boy in his temple, who seeing the master's trick imitated him when the boy himself was asked about what kind of preaching his master generally practised. When the boy told the master about it show-ing his lifted little finger, the master cut it right off with a knife. The boy ran away screaming in pain, when Gutei called him back. The boy turned back, the master lifted his own finger, and the boy instantly realized the meaning of the 'one-finger Zen' of Tenryu as well as Gutei.

shorn of its Indian garb. Next I have tried to write a history of Zen in China after Bodhi-Dharma, who is the real author of the school. Zen was quietly matured and transmitted by the five successive patriarchs so-called after the passing of the first propagator from India. When Hui-nêng, the sixth patriarch, began to teach the gospel of Zen Buddhism, it was no more Indian but thoroughly Chinese, and what we call Zen now in the form as we have it dates from him. The course thus definitely given shape by the sixth patriarch to the development of Zen in China gained its strength not only in volume but in content by the masterful handling of it by the spiritual descendants of Hui-nêng. The first section of the Chinese history of Zen therefore naturally closes with him. As the central fact of Zen lies in the attainment of 'Satori' or the opening of a spiritual eye, I have next dwelt upon the subject. The treatment is somewhat popular, for the main idea is to present the fact that there is such a thing as an intuitional understanding of the truth of Zen, which is 'satori', and also to illustrate the uniqueness of 'satori' as experienced by Zen devotees. When we understand the significance of 'satori' in Zen, we may logically wish to know something about the methods whereby the masters contrive to bring about such a revolutionary experience, more or less noetic, in the minds of the students. Some of the practical Zen methods resorted to by the masters are classified under a certain number of headings, but in this classification I have not attempted to be thoroughly exhaustive here. The Meditation Hall is an institution quite peculiar to Zen Buddhism, and those who want to know something about Zen and its educational system cannot afford to ignore the subject. This unique organ of Zen Buddhism, however, has never been described before. The reader I hope will find here a subject interesting enough for his thorough investigation. While Zen claims to be the 'ultra-abrupt' wing of Buddhism, it has a well-marked gradation in its progress towards the ultimate goal. Hence the concluding chapter on 'The Ten Cowherding Pictures'.

There are many more topics with which one ought to be acquainted in the study of Zen Buddhism, and some of them, considered by the author the more important, will be treated in the second series of the Essays.

Foreword

Before I proceed to the discussion of the main idea of
this essay, which is to consider Zen the Chinese way of
applying the doctrine of Enlightenment in our practical
life, I wish to make some preliminary remarks concerning
the attitude of some Zen critics and thereby to define the
position of Zen in the general body of Buddhism. According to them Zen Buddhism is not Buddhism; it is something
quite foreign to the spirit of Buddhism, and is one of those
aberrations which we often see growing up in the history
of any religion. Zen is thus, they think, an abnormality
prevailing among the people whose thought and feeling
flow along a channel different from the main current of
Buddhist thought. Whether this allegation is true or not
will be decided, on the one hand, when we understand what
is really the essence or genuine spirit of Buddhism, and, on
the other, when we know the exact status of Zen doctrine
in regard to the ruling ideas of Buddhism as they are
accepted in the Far East. It may also be desirable to know
something about the development of religious experience in
general. When we are not prepared thoroughly to understand these questions in the light of the history and philosophy of religion, we may come dogmatically to assert that
Zen is not Buddhism just because it looks so different on its
surface from what some people with a certain set of pre-
conceived notions consider Buddhism to be. The statement
of my position as regards these points will therefore pave the
way to the development of the principal thesis.

Superficially, indeed, there is something in Zen so bizarre
and even irrational as to frighten the pious literary followers

of the so-called primitive Buddhism and to make them declare that Zen is not Buddhism but a Chinese anomaly of
it. What, for instance, would they really make out of such
statements as follows: In the *Sayings of Nan-ch'üan* we read
that, when T'sui, governor of Ch'i District, asked the fifth
patriarch of the Zen sect—that is, Hung-jên—how it was
that while he had five hundred followers, Hui-nêng, in
preference to all others, was singled out to be given the
orthodox robe of transmission as the sixth patriarch, the
fifth patriarch replied: 'Four hundred and ninety-nine out
of my disciples understand well what Buddhism is, except
one Hui-nêng. He is a man not be measured by an ordinary
standard. Hence the robe of faith was handed over to him.'
On this comments Nan-ch'üan: 'In the age of Void there
are no words whatever; as soon as the Buddha appears on
earth, words come into existence, hence our clinging to
signs. . . . And thus as we now so firmly take hold of words,
we limit ourselves in various ways, while in the Great Way
there are absolutely no such things as ignorance or holiness.
Everything that has a name thereby limits itself. Therefore,
the old master of Chiang-hsi declared that "it is neither
mind, nor Buddha, nor a thing". It was in this way that he
wished to guide his followers, while these days they vainly
endeavour to experience the Great Way by hypostatizing
such an entity as mind. If the Way could be mastered in this
manner, it would be well for them to wait until the appearance of Maitreya Buddha [which is said to be at the end
of the world] and then to awaken the enlightenment-
thought. How could such ones ever hope for spiritual freedom? Under the fifth patriarch, all of his five hundred
disciples, except one Hui-nêng, understood Buddhism well.
The lay-disciple, Nêng, was quite unique in this respect, for
he did not at all understand Buddhism.[1] He understood the Way
only and no other thing.'

These are not very extraordinary statements in Zen, but

[1] Compare this with the statement made by the sixth patriarch himself when he was asked how it was that he came to succeed the fifth
patriarch, 'Because I do not understand Buddhism'. Let me also cite
a passage from the *Kena-Upanishad*, in which the readers may find a

to most of the Zen critics they must spell abomination. Buddhism is flatly denied, and its knowledge is regarded not to be indispensable to the mastery of Zen, the Great Way, which on the contrary is more or less identified with the negation of Buddhism. How is this? In the following pages an attempt is made to answer this question.

The Life and Spirit of Buddhism

To make this point clear and to justify the claim for Zen that it transmits the essence of Buddhism and not its formulated articles of faith as are recorded in letters, it is necessary to strip the spirit of Buddhism of all its outer casings and appendages, which, hindering the working of its original life-force, are apt to make us take the unessential for the essential. We know that the acorn is so different from the oak, but as long as there is a continuation of growth their identity is a logical conclusion. To see really into the nature of the acorn is to trace an uninterrupted development through its various historical stages. When the seed remains a seed and means nothing more, there is no life in it; it is a finished piece of work and, except as an object of historical curiosity, it has no value whatever in our religious experience. In like manner, to determine the nature of Buddhism we must go along its whole line of development and see what are the healthiest and most vital germs in it which have brought it to the present state of maturity. When this is done we shall see in what manner Zen is to be recognized as one of the various phases of Buddhism and, in fact, as the most essential factor in it.

singular coincidence between the Brahman seer and those Zen masters, not only in thought but in the way it is expressed:

'It is conceived of by him by whom it is not conceived of;
He by whom It is conceived of, knows It not.
It is not understood by those who understand It;
It is understood by those who understand It not.'

Lao-tzŭ, founder of Taoist mysticism, breathes the same spirit when he says: 'He who knows it speaks not, he who speaks knows not.'

To comprehend fully, therefore, the constitution of any existent religion that has a long history, it is advisable to separate its founder from his teaching, as a most powerful determinant in the development of the latter. By this I mean, in the first place, that the founder so called had in the beginning no idea of being the founder of any religious system which would later grow up in his name; in the second that to his disciples, while he was yet alive, his personality was not regarded as independent of his teaching, at least as far as they were conscious of the fact; in the third that what was unconsciously working in their minds as regards the nature of their master's personality came out in the foreground after his passing with all the possible intensity that had been latently gaining strength within them, and lastly, that the personality of the founder grew up in his disciples' minds so powerful as to make itself the very nucleus of his teaching; that is to say, the latter was made to serve as explanation of the meaning of the former.

It is a great mistake to think that any existent religious system was handed down to posterity by its founder as the fully matured product of his mind, and, therefore, that what the followers had to do with their religious founder and his teaching was to embrace both the founder and his teaching as sacred heritage—a treasure not to be profaned by the content of their individual spiritual experience. For this view fails to take into consideration what our spiritual life is and petrifies religion to its very core. This static conservatism, however, is always opposed by a progressive party which looks at a religious system from a dynamic point of view. And these two forces which are seen conflicting against each other in every field of human activity weave out the history of religion as in other cases. In fact history is the record of these struggles everywhere. But the very fact that there are such struggles in religion shows that they are here to some purpose and that religion is a living force; for they gradually bring to light the hidden implications of the original faith and enrich it in a manner undreamed of in the beginning. This takes place not only with regard to the personality of the founder but with regard to his teaching, and the result is an astounding complexity or rather confusion which sometimes prevents us from properly seeing into the constitution of a living religious system.

While the founder was still walking among his followers and disciples, the latter did not distinguish between the person of their leader and his teaching; for the teaching was realized in the person and the person was livingly explained in the teaching. To embrace the teaching was to follow his steps—that is, to believe in him. His presence among them was enough to inspire them and convince them of the truth of his teaching. They might not have comprehended it thoroughly, but his authoritative way of presenting it left in their hearts no shadow of doubt as to its truth and eternal value. So long as he lived among them and spoke to them his teaching and his person appealed to them as an individual unity. Even when they retired into a solitary place and meditated on the truth of his teaching, which they did as a form of spiritual discipline, the image of his person was always before their mental eyes.

But things went differently when his stately and inspiring personality was no more seen in the flesh. His teaching was still there, his followers could recite it perfectly from memory, but its personal connection with the author was lost, the living chain which solidly united him and his doctrine as one was for ever broken. When they reflected on the truth of the doctrine, they could not help thinking of their teacher as a soul far deeper and nobler than themselves. The similarities that were, either consciously or unconsciously, recognized as existing in various forms between leader and disciple gradually vanished, and as they vanished, the other side—that is, that which made him so distinctly different from his followers—came to assert itself all the more emphatically and irresistibly. The result was the conviction that he must have come from quite a unique spiritual source. The process of deification thus constantly went on until, some centuries after the death of the Master, he became a direct manifestation of the Supreme Being himself—in fact, he was the Highest One in the flesh, in him there was a divine humanity in perfect realization. He was Son of God or the Buddha and the Redeemer of the world. He will then be considered by himself independently of his teaching; he will occupy the centre of interest in the eyes of his followers. The teaching is of course important, but mainly as having come from the mouth of such an exalted spirit, and not necessarily as containing the truth of love or Enlightenment. Indeed, the teaching is to be interpreted in the light of the teacher's divine personality. The latter now predominates over the whole system; he is the centre whence radiate the rays of Enlightenment, salvation is only possible in believing in him as saviour.[1]

Around this personality or this divine nature there will now grow various systems of philosophy essentially based on his own teaching, but more or less modified according to the spiritual experiences of the disciples. This would perhaps never have taken place if the personality of the founder were not such as to stir up the deep religious feelings in the hearts of his followers, which is to say, what most attracted the latter to the teaching was not primarily the teaching itself but that which gave life to it, and without which it would never have been what it was. We are not always convinced of the truth of a statement because it is so logically advanced, but mainly because there is an inspiring life-impulse running through it. We are first struck

---

[1] The conception of Dharmakāya apart from the physical body (rūpakāya) of the Buddha was logically inevitable, as we read in the Ekottara-Āgama, XLIV, 'The Life of the Śākyamuni-Buddha is extremely long, the reason is that while his physical body enters into Nirvāṇa, his Law-body exists.' But the Dharmakāya could not be made to function directly upon suffering souls, as it was too abstract and transcendental; they wanted something more concrete and tangible towards which they could feel personally intimate. Hence the conception of another Buddha-body—that is, Sambhogakāya-Buddha or Vipākaja-Buddha, completing the dogma of the Triple Body (Trikāya).

with it and later try to verify its truth. The understanding is needed, but this alone will never move us to risk the fate of our souls.

One of the greatest religious souls in Japan once confessed,[1] 'I do not care whether I go to hell or elsewhere, but because my old master taught me to invoke the name of the Buddha, I practise the teaching.' This was not a blind acceptance of the master, in whom there was something deeply appealing to one's soul, and the disciple embraced this something with his whole being. Mere logic never moves us; there must be something transcending the intellect. When Paul insisted that 'if Christ be not raised, your faith is vain; ye are yet in your sins', he was not appealing to our logical idea of things, but to our spiritual yearnings. It did not matter whether things existed as facts of chronological history or not, the vital concern of ours was the fulfilment of our inmost inspirations; even so-called objective facts could be so moulded as to yield the best result to the requirements of our spiritual life. The personality of the founder of any religious system that has survived through centuries of growth must have had all the qualities that fully meet such spiritual requirements. As soon as the person and his teaching are separated after his own passing in the religious consciousness of his followers, if he was sufficiently great, he will at once occupy the centre of their spiritual interest and all his teachings will be made to explain this fact in various ways.

To state it more concretely, how much Christianity, for instance, as we have it today is the teaching of Christ himself? and how much of it is the contribution of Paul,

[1] The absolute faith Shinran had in the teaching of Hōnen as is evidenced in this quotation proves that the Shin sect is the result of Shinran's inner experience and not the reasoned product of his philosophy. His experience came first, and to explain it to himself as well as to communicate it to others, he resorted to various Sūtras for verification. *The Teaching, Practice, Faith, and Attainment* was thus written by him giving an intellectual and scriptural foundation to the Shin-shu faith. In religion, as in other affairs of human life, belief precedes reasoning. It is important not to forget this fact when tracing the development of ideas.

John, Peter, Augustine, and even Aristotle? The magnificent structure of Christian dogmatics is the work of Christian faith as has been experienced successively by its leaders; it is not the work of one person, even of Christ. For dogmatics is not necessarily always concerned with historical facts which are rather secondary in importance compared with the religious truth of Christianity: the latter is what ought to be rather than what is or what was. It aims at the establishment of what is universally valid, which is not to be jeopardized by the fact or nonfact of historical elements as is maintained by some of the modern exponents of Christian dogmatics. Whether Christ really claimed to be the Messiah or not is a great historical discussion still unsettled among Christian theologians. Some say that it does not make any difference as far as Christian faith is concerned whether or not Christ claimed to be the Messiah. In spite of all such theological difficulties, Christ is the centre of Christianity. The Christian edifice is built around the person of Jesus. Buddhists may accept some of his teachings and sympathize with the content of his religious experience, but so long as they do not cherish any faith in Jesus as 'Christ' or Lord, they are not Christians.

Christianity is therefore constituted not only with the teaching of Jesus himself but with all the dogmatical and speculative interpretations concerning the personality of Jesus and his doctrine that have accumulated ever since the death of the founder. In other words, Christ did not found the religious system known by his name, but he was made its founder by his followers. If he were still among them, it is highly improbable that he would sanction all the theories, beliefs, and practices which are now imposed upon self-styled Christians. If he were asked whether their learned dogmatics were his religion, he might not know how to answer. He would in all likelihood profess complete ignorance of all the philosophical subtleties of Christian theology of the present day. But from the modern Christians' point of view they will most definitely assure us that their religion is to be referred to 'a unitary starting point and to an original basic character', which is Jesus as Christ, and that whatever manifold constructions and transformations that were experienced in the body of their religion did not interfere with their specific Christ-faith. They are Christians just as much as the brethren of their primitive community were; for there is an historical continuation of the same faith all along its growth and development which is its inner necessity. To regard the form of culture of a particular time as something sacred, and to be transmitted for ever as such is to suppress our spiritual yearnings after eternal validity. This I believe is the position taken up by progressive modern Christians.

How about progressive modern Buddhists then in regard to their attitude towards Buddhist faith constituting the essence of Buddhism? How is the Buddha conceived by his disciples? What is the nature and value of Buddhahood? When Buddhism is defined merely as the teaching of the Buddha, does it explain the life of Buddhism as it moves on through the course of history? Is not the life of Buddhism the unfolding of the inner spiritual life of the Buddha himself rather than his exposition of it, which is recorded as the Dharma in Buddhist literature? Is there not something in the wordy teaching of the Buddha, which gives life to it and which lieth underneath all the arguments and controversies characterizing the history of Buddhism throughout Asia? This life is what progressive Buddhists endeavour to lay hands on.

It is therefore not quite in accordance with the life and teaching of the Buddha to regard Buddhism merely as a system of religious doctrines and practices established by the Buddha himself; for it is more than that, and comprises as its most important constituent elements all the experiences and speculations of the Buddha's followers, especially concerning the personality of their master and his relations to his own doctrine. Buddhism did not come out of the Buddha's mind fully armed, as did Minerva from Jupiter. The theory of a perfect Buddhism from the beginning is the static view of it, and cuts it short from its continuous and never-ceasing growth. Our religious experience transcends the limitations of time, and its ever-expanding content requires a more vital form which will grow without doing violence to itself. Inasmuch as Buddhism is a living religion and not an historical mummy stuffed with dead and functionless materials, it must be able to absorb and assimilate all that is helpful to its growth. This is the most natural thing for any organism endowed with life. And this life may be traceable under divergent forms and constructions.

According to scholars of Pali Buddhism and of the Āgama literature, all that the Buddha taught, as far as his systematic teaching went, seems to be summed up by the Fourfold Noble Truth, the Twelvefold Chain of Causation, the Eightfold Path of Righteous Living, and the doctrine of Non-ego (*Anātman*) and Nirvāṇa. If this was the case, what we call primitive Buddhism was quite a simple affair when its doctrinal aspect alone is considered. There was nothing very promising in these doctrines that would eventually build up a magnificent structure to be known as Buddhism, comprising both the Hīnāyana and the Mahāyāna. When we wish to understand Buddhism thoroughly we must dive deep into its bottom where lies its living spirit. Those that are satisfied with a superficial view of its dogmatical aspect are apt to let go the spirit which will truly explain the inner life of Buddhism. To some of the Buddha's immediate disciples the deeper things in his teachings failed to appeal, or they were not conscious of the real spiritual forces which moved them towards their Master. We must look underneath if we want to come in contact with the ever-growing life-impetus of Buddhism. However great the Buddha was, he could not convert a jackal into a lion, nor could a jackal comprehend the Buddha above his beastly nature. As the later Buddhists state, a Buddha alone understands another Buddha; when our subjective life is not raised to the same level as the Buddha's, many things that go to make up his inner life escape us; we cannot live in any other world than our own.[1] Therefore, if the primitive Buddhists read so much in the life of their Master as is recorded in their writings, and no more, this does not prove that everything belonging to the Buddha has thereby been exhausted. There were probably other Buddhists who penetrated deeper into his life, as their own inner consciousness had a richer content. The history of religion thus becomes the history of our own spiritual unfolding. Buddhism must be conceived biologically, so to speak, and not mechanically. When we take this attitude, even the doctrine of the Fourfold Noble Truth becomes pregnant with yet deeper truths.

The Buddha was not a metaphysician and naturally avoided discussing such subjects as were strictly theoretical and had no practical bearing on the attainment of Nirvāṇa. He might have had his own views on those philosophical problems that at the time engaged Indian minds. But like other religious leaders his chief interest was in the practical

[1] This was very well understood by the Buddha himself when he first attained Enlightenment; he knew that what he realized in his enlightened state of mind could not be imparted to others, and that if it were imparted they could not understand it. This was the reason why he, in the beginning of his religious career, expressed the desire to enter into Nirvāna without trying to revolve the Wheel of the Dharma. We read in one of the Sūtras belonging to the Āgama class of Buddhist literature, which is entitled *Sūtra on the Cause and Effect in the Past and Present* (fas. II.): 'My original vows are fulfilled, the Dharma [or Truth] I have attained is too deep for the understanding. A Buddha alone is able to understand what is in the mind of another Buddha. In this age of the Five Taints (*pañca-kashāyā*), all beings are enveloped in greed, anger, folly, falsehood, arrogance, and flattery; they have few blessings and are stupid and have no understanding to comprehend the Dharma I have attained. Even if I make the Dharma-Wheel revolve, they would surely be confused and incapable of accepting it. They may on the contrary indulge in defamation, and, thereby falling into the evil paths, suffer all kinds of pain. It is best for me to remain quiet and enter into Nirvāṇa.' In the *Sūtra on the Story of the Discipline*, which is considered an earlier translation of the preceding text and was rendered into Chinese by an Indian Buddhist scholar, Ta-li and a Tibetan, Mangsiang, in A.D. 197, no reference is yet made to the Buddha's resolution to keep silent about his Enlightenment, only that what he attained was all-knowledge which was beyond the understanding and could not be explained, as its height was unscalable and its depth unfathomable, 'containing the whole universe in it and yet penetrating into the unpenetrable'. . . . Cf. the *Mahāpadāna Suttanta* (Dīgha Nikāya, XIV), and the *Ariyapariyesana Suttam* (Majjhima, XXVI).

result of speculation and not in speculation as such. He was too busy in trying to get rid of the poisonous arrow that had pierced the flesh, he had no desire to inquire into the history, object, and constitution of the arrow; for life was too short for that. He thus took the world as it was; that is, he interpreted it as it appeared to his religious insight and according to his own valuation. He did not intend to go any further. He called his way of looking at the world and life 'Dharma', a very comprehensive and flexible term, though it was not a term first used by the Buddha; for it had been in vogue some time prior to him, mainly in the sense of ritual and law, but the Buddha gave it a deeper spiritual signification.

That the Buddha was practical and not metaphysical may be seen from the criticism which was hurled at him by his opponents: 'As Gautama is always found alone sitting in an empty room, he has lost his wisdom. . . . Even Śāriputra, who is the wisest and best disciple of his, is like a babe, so stupid and without eloquence.'[1] Here however lies the seed of a future development. If the Buddha had been given up to theorizing his teaching never could be expected to grow. Speculation may be deep and subtle, but if it has no spiritual life in it its possibilities are soon exhausted. The Dharma was ever maturing, because it was mysteriously creative.

The Buddha evidently had quite a pragmatic conception of the intellect and left many philosophical problems unsolved as unnecessary for the attainment of the final goal of life. This was quite natural with him. Whilst he was still alive among his disciples, he was the living illustration of all that was implied in his doctrine. The Dharma was manifest in him in all its vital aspects, and there was no need to indulge in idle speculation as to the ultimate meaning of such concepts as Dharma, Nirvāṇa, Ātman (ego), Karma, Bodhi (enlightenment), etc. The Buddha's personality was the key to the solution of all these. The disciples were not fully aware of the significance of this fact. When they

[1] Cf. Saṁyukta Āgama (Chinese), Fas. XXXII.

thought they understood the Dharma, they did not know that this understanding was really taking refuge in the Buddha. His presence somehow had a pacifying and satisfying effect on whatever spiritual anguish they had; they felt as if they were securely embraced in the arms of a loving, consoling mother; to them the Buddha was really such.[1] Therefore, they had no need to press the Buddha very hard to enlighten them on many of the philosophical problems that they might have grown conscious of. They were easily reconciled in this respect to the Buddha's unwillingness to take them into the heart of metaphysics. But at the same time this left much room for the later Buddhists to develop their own theories not only as to the teaching of the Buddha but mainly as to its relation to his personality.

The Buddha's entrance into Nirvāṇa meant to his

[1] That the personality of the Buddha was an object of admiration and worship as much as, or perhaps more than, his extraordinary intellectual attributes, is gleaned throughout the Āgama literature. To quote one or two instances: 'When Subha-Manāva Todeyyaputta saw the Blessed One sitting in the woods, the Brahman was struck with the beautiful serenity of his personality which most radiantly shone like the moon among the stars; his features were perfect, glowing like a golden mountain; his dignity was majestic with all his senses under perfect control, so tranquil and free from all beclouding passions, and so absolutely calm with his mind subdued and quietly disciplined.' (The Middle Āgama, fas. XXXVIII.) This admiration of his personality later developed into the deification of his being, and all the evils moral and physical were supposed to be warded off if one thought of him or his virtues. 'When those beings who practised evil deeds with their bodies, mouths, or minds, think of the merits of the Tathagata at the moment of their deaths, they would be kept away from the three evil paths and born in the heavens; even the vilest would be born in the heavens.' (The Ekottara-Āgama, fas. XXXII.) 'Wherever Śramaṇa Gautama appears, no evil spirits or demons can approach him; therefore let us invite him here and all those evil gods [who have been harassing us] would by themselves take to their heels.' (Loc. cit.) It was quite natural for the Buddhists that they later made the Buddha the first object of Recollection (smṛti), which, they thought, would keep their minds from wandering away and help them realize the final aim of the Buddhist life. These statements plainly demonstrate that while on the one hand the teaching of the Buddha was accepted by his followers as the Dharma beautiful in the beginning, beautiful in the middle, and beautiful in the end, his person was on the other hand regarded as filled with miraculous powers and divine virtues, so that his mere presence was enough to create a most auspicious atmosphere not only spiritually but materially.

disciples the loss of the World-Light,[1] through which they had such an illuminating view of things. The Dharma was there, and in it they tried to see the Buddha as they were instructed by him, but it had no enlivening effect on them as before; the moral precepts consisting of many rules were regularly observed in the Brotherhood, but the authoritativeness of these regulations was missed somehow. They retired into a quietude and meditated on the teaching of the Master, but the meditation was not quite so life-giving and satisfying because they were ever assailed by doubts, and, as a natural consequence, their intellectual activities were resumed. Everything was now to be explained to the full extent of the reasoning faculty. The metaphysician began to assert himself against the simple-hearted devotion of the disciple. What had been accepted as an authoritative injunction from the mouth of the Buddha was now to be examined as a subject of philosophical discussion. Two factions were ready to divide the field with each other, and radicalism was opposed to conservatism and between the two wings there were arranged schools of various tendencies. The Sthaviras were pitted against the Mahāsaṁghikas, with twenty or more different schools representing various grades of diversity.[2]

We cannot, however, exclude from the body of Buddhism all the divergent views on the Buddha and his teaching as something foreign and not belonging to the constituent elements of Buddhism. For these views are exactly

[1] When the Buddha entered Nirvāna, the monks cried, 'Too soon has the Tathāgata passed away, too soon has the World-honoured One passed away, too soon has the Great Law died out; all beings are for ever left to misery; for the Eye of the World is gone.' Their lamentation was beyond description, they lay on the ground like great trees with roots, stems, and branches all torn and broken to pieces, they rolled and wriggled like a slain snake. Such excessive expressions of grief were quite natural for those Buddhists whose hearts were directed towards the personality of their master more than towards his sane and rationalistic teachings. Cf. the Pali *Parinibbāna-suttanta*.

[2] For a more or less detailed account of the various Buddhist schools that came up within a few centuries after the Buddha, see Vasumitra's *Samayabhedo-paracana-cakra*. Professor Suisai Funahashi recently published an excellent commentary on this book.

what support the frame of Buddhism, and without them the frame itself will be a non-entity altogether. The error with most critics of any existent religion with a long history of development is to conceive it as a completed system which is to be accepted as such, while the fact is that anything organic and spiritual—and we consider religion such —has no geometrical outline which can be traced on paper by ruler and compass. It refuses to be objectively defined, for this will be setting a limit to the growth of its spirit. Thus to know what Buddhism is will be to get into the life of Buddhism and to understand it from the inside as it unfolds itself objectively in history. Therefore, the definition of Buddhism must be that of the life-force which carries forward a spiritual movement called Buddhism. All these doctrines, controversies, constructions, and interpretations that were offered after the Buddha's death as regards his person, life, and teaching were what essentially constituted the life of Indian Buddhism, and without these there could be no spiritual activity to be known as Buddhism.

In a word, what constituted the life and spirit of Buddhism is nothing else than the inner life and spirit of the Buddha himself; Buddhism is the structure erected around the inmost consciousness of its founder. The style and material of the outer structure may vary as history moves forward, but the inner meaning of Buddhahood which supports the whole edifice remains the same and ever living. While on earth the Buddha tried to make it intelligible in accordance with the capacities of his immediate followers; that is to say, the latter did their best to comprehend the deeper significance of the various discourses of their master, in which he pointed the way to final deliverance. As we are told, the Buddha discoursed 'with one voice',[1] but this was interpreted and understood by his

[1] Cf. *The Sukhāvatī-vyūha* (edited by Max Muller and B. Nanjio), p. 7, where we have: 'Buddhasvaro anantaghoshah'; that is, the Buddha's voice is of infinite sounds. See also the *Saddharma-puṇḍarīka* (p. 128), where we read: 'Savareṇa caikena vadāmi dharmam'—I preach the law with one voice. The parable of the water of one taste (*ekarasam vāri*), variously producing herbs, shrubs, and others, is very well known among the Mahāyānists.

devotees in as manifold manners as possible. This was inevitable, for we have each our own inner experience which is to be explained in terms of our own creation, naturally varying in depth and breadth. In most cases these so-called individual inner experiences, however, may not be so deep and forceful as to demand absolutely original phraseology, but may remain satisfied with new interpretations of the old terms—once brought into use by an ancient original spiritual leader. And this is the way every great historical religion grows enriched in its contents or ideas. In some cases this enrichment may mean the overgrowth of superstructures ending in a complete burial of the original spirit. This is where critical judgment is needed, but otherwise we must not forget to recognize the living principle still in activity. In the case of Buddhism we must not neglect to read the inner life of the Buddha himself asserting itself in the history of a religious system designated after his name. The claim of the Zen followers that they are transmitting the essence of Buddhism is based on their belief that Zen takes hold of the enlivening spirit of the Buddha, stripped of all its historical and doctrinal garments.

Some Vital Problems of Buddhism

To the earlier Buddhists the problem did not present itself in this light; that is to say, they did not realize that the centre of all their dogmatics and controversies was to ascertain the real inner life of the Buddha, which constituted their active faith in the Buddha and his teaching. Without exactly knowing why, they first entertained, after the passing of the Buddha, a strong desire to speculate on the nature of his personality. They had no power to check the constant and insistent cry of this desire brimming over in their inmost hearts. What constituted Buddhahood? What was the essence of Buddhahood? Questions like these assailed them one after another, and among those there were the following which stood out more prominently as they were more vitally interesting. They were those concerned with the Enlightenment of the Buddha, his entrance into Nirvāṇa, his former life as a Bodhisattva (that is, as one capable of Enlightenment), and his teaching as viewed from their way of understanding the Buddha. Thus his teaching ceased to be considered independently of its author, the truth of the teaching was so organically connected with the Buddha's personality, the Dharma was to be believed because it was the very embodiment of Buddhahood, and not necessarily because it was so logically consistent or philosophically tenable. The Buddha was the key to the truth of Buddhism.

When attention thus centres in the person of the Buddha as the author of the Dharma, the question of his inner experience known as Enlightenment becomes the most vital one. Without this experience the Buddha could not be called a Buddha; in fact, the term 'Buddha', the Enlightened One, was his own making. If a man understands what enlightenment is or really experiences it in himself, he knows the whole secret of the Buddha's superhuman nature and with it the riddle of life and the world. The ·essence of Buddhism must then lie in the Doctrine of Perfect Enlightenment. In the enlightened mind of the Buddha there were many things which he did not, and could not, divulge to his disciples. When he refused to answer metaphysical questions, it was not because the minds of the questioners were not developed enough to comprehend the full implications of them. If, however, the Buddhists really desired to know their master, and his teaching, they had to study the secrets of Enlightenment. As they had no living master now they had to solve the problems by themselves if they could, and they were never tired of exhausting their intellectual ingenuity on them. Various theories were then advanced, and Buddhism grew richer in content, it came to reflect something eternally valid besides mere personal teaching of an individual. It ceased to be a thing merely historical, but a system ever living, growing, and energy-imparting. Various Mahāyāna Sūtras and Shastras were produced to develop various aspects of the content of Enlightenment as realized by the Buddha. Some of them were speculative, others mystical, and still others ethical and practical. In the idea of Enlightenment was thus focused all Buddhist thought.

Nirvāṇa as the ideal of Buddhist life next engaged the serious attention of Buddhist philosophers. Was it an annihilation of existence, or that of passions or desires, or the dispelling of ignorance, or a state of egolessness? Did the Buddha really enter into a state of utter extinction leaving all sentient beings to their own fate? Did the love he showed to his followers vanish with his passing? Would he not come back among them in order to guide them, to enlighten them, to listen to their spiritual anguish? The value of such a grand personality as the Buddha could not perish with his physical existence, it ought to remain with us for ever as a thing of eternal validity. How could this notion be reconciled with the annihilation theory of Nirvāṇa so prevalent among the personal disciples of the Buddha? When history conflicts with our idea of value, can it not be interpreted to the satisfaction of our religious yearnings? What is the objective authority of 'facts' if not supported by an inwardly grounded authority? Varieties of interpretation are then set forth in the Mahāyāna texts as to the implications of Nirvāṇa and other cognate conceptions to be found in the 'original' teaching of the Buddha.[1]

What is the relationship between Enlightenment and Nirvāṇa? How did Buddhists come to realize Arhatship? What convinced them of their attainment? Is the Enlightenment of an Arhat the same as that of the Buddha? To answer these questions and many others in close connection

[1] Here we find the justification of a 'mystic' interpretation of the sacred books of any religion. The Swedenborgian doctrine of Correspondence thus grows illuminating. The philosophy of Shingon mysticism somewhat reflects the idea of correspondence, though naturally it is based on a different set of philosophical ideas. Varieties of interpretation are always possible in anything not only because of the presence of the subjective elements in every judgment, but because of infinite complications of objective relationship.

with them was the task imposed upon various schools of Hīnayāna and Mahāyāna Buddhism. While they quarrelled much, they never forgot that they were all Buddhists and whatever interpretations they gave to these problems they were faithful to their Buddhist experience. They were firmly attached to the founder of their religion and only wished to get thoroughly intimate with the faith and teaching as first promulgated by the Buddha. Some of them were naturally more conservative and wished to submit to the orthodox and traditional way of understanding the Dharma; but there were others, as in every field of human life, whose inner experience meant more to them, and to harmonize this with the traditional authority they resorted to metaphysics to its fullest extent. Their efforts, there is no doubt, were honest and sincere, and when they thought they solved the difficulties or contradictions they were satisfied inwardly as well as intellectually. In fact they had no other means of egress from the spiritual impasse in which they found themselves through the natural and inevitable growth of their inmost life. This was the way Buddhism had to develop if it ever had in it any life to grow.

While Enlightenment and Nirvāṇa were closely related to the conception of Buddhahood itself, there was another idea of great importance to the development of Buddhism, which, however, had no direct connection apparently, though not in its ultimate signification, with the personality of the Buddha. This idea naturally proved to be most fruitful in the history of Buddhist dogmatics along with the doctrines of Enlightenment and Nirvāṇa. I mean by this the doctrine of non-Ātman which denies the existence of an ego-substance in our psychic life. When the notion of Ātman was ruling Indian minds, it was a bold announcement on the part of the Buddha to regard it as the source of ignorance and transmigration. The theory of Origination (*pratītya-samutpāda*) which seems to make up the foundation of the Buddha's teaching is thus finally resolved into the finding of a mischievous 'designer' who

works behind all our spiritual restlessness. Whatever interpretation was given to the doctrine of non-Ātman in the
early days of Buddhism, the idea came to be extended to
things inanimate as well. Not only was there no ego-substance behind our mental life, but there was no ego in the
physical world, which meant that we could not separate
in reality acting from actor, force from mass, or life from its
manifestations. So far as thinking goes, we can establish
these two pairs of conception as limiting each other, but in
the actuality of things they must all be one, as we cannot
impose our logical way of thinking upon reality in its concreteness. When we transfer this separation from thought
into reality we encounter many difficulties not only intellectual but moral and spiritual, from which we suffer un-
speakable anguish later. This was felt by the Buddha, and
he called this mixing up Ignorance (*avidyā*). The Mahāyāna doctrine of Śūnyatā was a natural conclusion. But I
need not make any remark here to the effect that the
Śūnyatā theory is not nihilism or acosmism, but that it has
its positive background which sustains it and gives life
to it.

It was in the natural order of thought now for Buddhists
to endeavour to find a philosophical explanation of Enlightenment and Nirvāṇa in the theory of non-Ātman or
Śūnyatā, and this to the best of their intellectual power and
in the light of their spiritual experience. They finally found
out that Enlightenment was not a thing exclusively belonging to the Buddha, but that each one of us could attain it if
he got rid of ignorance by abandoning the dualistic conception of life and of the world; they further concluded that
Nirvāṇa was not vanishing into a state of absolute non-
existence, which was an impossibility as long as we had to
reckon with the actual facts of life, and that Nirvāṇa in its
ultimate signification was an affirmation—an affirmation
beyond opposites of all kinds. This metaphysical understanding of the fundamental problem of Buddhism marks
the features of the Mahāyāna philosophy. As to its practical
side where the theory of Śūnyatā and the doctrine of

Enlightenment are harmoniously united and realized in life, or where the Buddhists aim to enter into the inner consciousness of the Buddha as was revealed to him under the Bodhi-trees, we will refer to it in the following section.

Almost all Buddhist scholars in Japan agree that all these characteristic ideas of the Mahāyāna are systematically traceable in Hīnayāna literature; and that all the reconstructions and transformations which the Mahāyānists are supposed to have put on the original form of Buddhism are really nothing but an unbroken continuation of one original Buddhist spirit and life, and further that even the so-called primitive Buddhism, as is expounded in the Pāli canons and in the Āgama texts of the Chinese Tripitaka, is also the result of an elaboration on the part of the earlier followers of the Buddha. If the Mahāyāna is not Buddhism proper, neither is the Hīnayāna, for the historical reason that neither of them represents the teaching of the Buddha as it was preached by the Master himself. Unless one limits the use of the term Buddhism very narrowly and only to a certain form of it, no one can very well refuse to include both Mahāyāna and Hīnayāna in the same denomination. And, in my opinion, considering the organic relation between system and experience and the fact that the spirit of the Buddha himself is present in all these constructions, it is proper that the term Buddhism should be used in a broad, comprehensive, and inward sense.

This is not the place to enter into the details of organic relationship existing between the Hīnayāna and the Mahāyāna; for the object of this essay is to delineate the course of development as traversed by Zen Buddhism before it reached the present form. Having outlined my position with regard to the definition of Buddhism and the Mahāyāna in general as a manifestation of Buddhist life and thought, or rather of the inner experience of the Buddha himself, the next step will be to see where lies the source of Zen and how it is one of the legitimate successors and transmitters of the Buddha's spirit.

Zen and Enlightenment

The origin of Zen, as is the case with all other forms of Buddhism, is to be sought in Supreme Perfect Enlightenment (*anuttara-samyak-sambodhi*) attained by the Buddha while he was sitting under the Bodhi-tree, near the city of Gaya. If this Enlightenment is of no value and signification to the development of Buddhism, Zen then has nothing to do with Buddhism, it was altogether another thing created by the genius of Bodhidharma, who visited China early in the sixth century. But if Enlightenment is the *raison d'être* of Buddhism—that is to say, if Buddhism is an edifice erected on the solid basis of Enlightenment, realized by the Buddha and making up his being—Zen is the central pillar which supports the entire structure, it composes the direct line of continuation drawn out from the content of the Buddha's illumined mind. Traditionally Zen is considered to have been transmitted by the Buddha to his foremost disciple, Mahākāśyapa, when the Buddha held out a bunch of flowers to his congregation, the meaning of which was at once grasped by Mahākāśyapa, who quietly smiled at him. The historicity of this incident is justly criticized, but knowing the value of Enlightenment we cannot ascribe the authority of Zen just to such an episode as this. Zen was in fact handed over not only to Mahākāśyapa but to all beings who will follow the steps of the Buddha, the Enlightened One.

Like a true Indian the Buddha's idea of ascetic meditation was to attain Vimoksha (or simply Moksha, deliverance) from the bondage of birth and death. There were several ways open to him to reach the goal. According to the Brahman philosophers of those days, the great fruit of deliverance could be matured by embracing religious truth, or by practising asceticism or chastity, or by learning, or by freeing oneself from passions. Each in its way was an excellent means, and if they were practised severally or all together, they might result in emancipation of some kind.

But the philosophers talked about methods and did not give one any trustworthy information concerning their actual spiritual experience, and what the Buddha wished was this self-realization, a personal experience, an actual insight into truth, and not mere discoursing about methods, or playing with concepts.[1] He detested all philosophical reasonings which he called *dṛishti* or *darśana*, for they would lead him nowhere, bring him no practical result in his spiritual life. He was never satisfied until he inwardly realized the Bodhi as the truth immediately presented to his transcendental consciousness and whose absolute nature was so inner, so self-convincing that he had no doubt whatever in regard to its universal validity.

The content of this Enlightenment was explained by the Buddha as the Dharma which was to be directly perceived (*sandiṭṭhika*), beyond limits of time (*akalika*), to be personally experienced (*ehipassika*), altogether persuasive (*opanayika*), and to be understood each for himself by the wise (*paccattaṁ veditabbo viññuhi*). This meant that the Dharma was to be intuited and not to be analytically reached by concepts. The reason why the Buddha so frequently refused to answer metaphysical problems was partly due to his conviction that the ultimate truth was to be realized in oneself through one's own efforts;[2] for all that could be gained through discursive understanding was the surface of things and not things themselves, conceptual knowledge never gave full satisfaction to one's religious yearning. The attainment of the Bodhi could not be the

[1] Cf. such Sūtras as the *Tevijja, Mahāli, Brahmajāla*, etc., in the Dīgha Nikāya. See also the *Sutta Nipāta*, especially the Atthakavagga, which is one of the earliest Buddhist texts in our possession at present. There we read about 'Ajjhattasanti' (inward peace), which cannot be attained by philosophy, nor by tradition, nor by good deeds.

[2] That the Buddha never neglected to impress his disciples with the idea that the ultimate truth was to be realized by and in oneself is evidenced throughout the Āgamas. Everywhere we encounter with such phrases as 'without depending upon another, he believed, or thought, or dissolved his doubts, or attained self-confidence in the Law'. From this self-determination followed the consciousness that one had all one's evil leakages (*āsrava*) stopped or drained off, culminating in the realization of Arhatship—which is the goal of Buddhist life.

accumulation of dialectical subtleties. And this is the position taken up by Zen Buddhism as regards what it considers a final reality. Zen in this respect faithfully follows the injunction of the Master.

That the Buddha had an insight of higher order into the nature of things than that which could be obtained through ordinary logical reasoning is evidenced everywhere even in the so-called Hīnayāna literature. To cite just one instance from the *Brahmajāla Sutta* in which the Buddha deals with all the heretical schools that were in existence in his days, he invariably makes reference after refuting them to the Tathāgata's deeper understanding which goes beyond their speculations 'wriggling like an eel'. What they discuss just for the sake of discussion and to show the keenness of their analytical faculty about the soul, future life, eternity, and other important spiritual subjects, is not productive of any actual benefits for our inner welfare. The Buddha knew well where these reasonings would finally lead to and how trivial and unwholesome they were after all. So we read in the *Brahmajāla Sutta*: 'Of these, Brethren, the Tathāgata knows that these speculations thus arrived at, thus insisted on, will have such and such a result, such and such an effect on the future condition of those who trust in them. That does he know, and he knows also other things far beyond (far better than those speculations): and having that knowledge he is not puffed up, and thus untarnished he has in his own heart realized the way of escape from them, has understood, as they really are, the rising up and passing away of sensations, their sweet taste, their danger, how they cannot be relied on; and not grasping after any [of those things men are eager for], he, the Tathāgata, is quite set free.'[1]

While the ideal of Arhatship was no doubt the entering into Nirvāṇa that leaves nothing behind (*anupādhisesha*), whatever this may mean, it did not ignore the significance of Enlightenment; no, it could not very well do so without

---

[1] *The Dialogues of the Buddha*, Sacred Books of the Buddhists, Vol. II, p. 29.

endangering its own reason of existence. For Nirvāṇa was nothing else in its essence than Enlightenment, the content was identical in either case. Enlightenment was Nirvāṇa reached while yet in the flesh, and no Nirvāṇa was ever possible without obtaining Enlightenment. The latter may have a more intellectual note in it than the former, which is a psychological state realized through Enlightenment. Bodhi is spoken of in the so-called primitive Buddhism just as much as Nirvāṇa. So long as passions (*kleśa*) were not subdued, and the mind still remained enshrouded in ignorance, no Buddhists could ever dream of obtaining a Moksha (deliverence) which is Nirvāṇa, and this deliverance from Ignorance and passions was the work of Enlightenment. Generally Nirvāṇa is understood in its negative aspect as the total extinction of everything, body and soul, but in the actuality of life no such negativist conception could ever prevail, and the Buddha never meant Nirvāṇa to be so interpreted. If there were nothing affirmative in Nirvāṇa, the Mahāyānists could never have evolved the positive conception of it later. Though the immediate disciples of the Buddha were not conscious of this, there was always the thought of Enlightenment implied in it. Enlightenment attained by the Buddha after a week's meditation under the Bodhi-tree could not be of no consequence to his Arhat-disciples, however negatively the latter tended to apply this principle to the attainment of their life-object.

The true significance of Enlightenment was effectively brought out by the Mahāyānists not only in its intellectual implications but in its moral and religious bearings. The result was the conception of Bodhisattvaship in contra-distinction to Arhatship, the ideal of their rival school. The Arhat and the Bodhisattva are essentially the same. But the Mahāyānists, perceiving a deeper sense in Enlightenment as the most important constituent element in the attainment of the final goal of Buddhism, which is spiritual freedom (*ceto-vimutti*), as the Nikāyas have it, did not wish to have it operated in themselves only, but wanted to see it

63

realized in every being sentient and even non-sentient. Not only was this their subjective yearning, but there was an objective basis on which the yearning could be justified and realized. It was the presence in every individual of a faculty designated by the Mahāyānists as Prajñā.[1] This was the principle that made Enlightenment possible in us as well as in the Buddha. Without Prajñā there could be no Enlightenment, which was the highest spiritual power in our possession. The intellect, or what is ordinarily known by Buddhist scholars as Vijñāna, was relative in its activity, and could not comprehend the ultimate truth which was Enlightenment. And it was due to this ultimate truth that we could lift ourselves above the dualism of matter and spirit, of ignorance and wisdom, of passion and non-attachment. Enlightenment consisted in personally realizing the truth, ultimate and absolute and capable of affirmation. Thus we are all Bodhisattvas now, beings of Enlightenment, if not in actuality, then potentially. Bodhisattvas are also Prajñā-sattvas, as we are universally endowed with Prajñā, which, when fully and truly operating, will realize in us Enlightenment, and intellectually (in its highest sense) lift us above appearances, which is a state designated by Nikāya Buddhists as 'emancipation of mind or reason' (*pañña-vimutti* or *sammad-añña vimutti*).

If by virtue of Enlightenment Gautama was transformed into the Buddha, and then if all beings are endowed with Prajñā and capable of Enlightenment—that is, if they are thus Bodhisattvas—the logical conclusion will be that Bodhisattvas are all Buddhas, or destined to be Buddhas as soon as sufficient conditions obtain. Hence the Mahayana doctrine that all beings, sentient or non-sentient,

---

[1] In fact, the term, *prajñā* or *paññā* in Pāli, is not an exclusive possession of the Mahāyānists, for it is also fully used by their rival disciples of the Buddha. The latter, however, failed to lay any special emphasis on the idea of enlightenment and its supreme significance in the body of Buddhism, and as the consequence Prajñā was comparatively neglected by the Hīnayānists. Mahāyānism on the other hand may be designated as the religion of Prajñā *par excellence*. It is even deified and most reverently worshipped.

are endowed with the Buddha-nature, and that our minds are the Buddha-mind and our bodies are the Buddha-body. The Buddha before his Enlightenment was an ordinary mortal, and we, ordinary mortals, will be Buddhas the moment our mental eyes[1] open in Enlightenment. In this do we not see plainly the most natural and most logical course of things leading up to the main teaching of Zen as it later developed in China and Japan?

How extensively and intensively the concept of Enlightenment influenced the development of Mahāyāna Buddhism may be seen in the composition of the *Saddharmapuṇḍarīka*, which is really one of the profoundest Mahāyāna protests against the Hīnayāna conception of the Buddha's Enlightenment. According to the latter, the Buddha attained it at Gayā while meditating under the Bodhi-tree, for they regarded the Buddha as a mortal being like themselves, subject to historical and psychological conditions. But the Mahāyānists could not be satisfied with such a realistic common sense interpretation of the personality of the Buddha; they saw something in it which went deep into their hearts and wanted to come in immediate touch with it. What they sought was finally given and they found that the idea of the Buddha's being a common soul was a delusion, that the Tathāgata arrived in his Supreme Perfect Enlightenment 'many hundred thousand myriads of kotis of æons ago', and that all those historical 'facts' in his life which are recorded in the Āgama or Nikāya literature are his 'skilful devices' (*upāya-kauśalya*) to lead creatures to full ripeness and go in the Buddha Way.[2] In other words, this means that Enlightenment is the absolute reason of the universe and the essence of Buddhahood, and therefore that to obtain Enlightenment is to realize in one's inner consciousness the ultimate truth of the world which for ever is.

[1] This is no other than 'the opening of the pure eye of the Dharma' (*virajaṁ vītamalaṁ dhamma-cakkhum udapādi*), frequently referred to in the Āgamas when one attains to Arhatship.

[2] Read, for instance, chapter xv, entitled 'Duration of Life of the Tathāgata'.

65

While the *Puṇḍarīka* emphasizes the Buddha-aspect of Enlightenment, Zen directs its attention mainly to the Enlightenment-aspect of Buddhahood. When this latter aspect is considered intellectually, we have the philosophy of Buddhist dogmatics, which is studied by scholars of the Tendai (*t'ien-tai*), Kegon (*avataṁsaka*), Hossō (*dharmalaksha*), and other schools. Zen approaches it from the practical side of life—that is, to work out Enlightenment in life itself.

Seeing that the idea of Enlightenment played such an important role in the development of Mahāyāna Buddhism, what is the content of it? Can we describe it in an intelligible manner so that our analytical intellect could grasp it and make it an object of thought? The Fourfold Noble Truth was not the content of Enlightenment, nor was the Twelvefold Chain of Causation, nor the Eightfold Righteous Path. The truth flashed through the Buddha's consciousness was not such a thought capable of discursive unfolding. When he exclaimed:

'Through birth and rebirth's endless round,
  Seeking in vain, I hastened on,
To find who framed this edifice,
    What misery!—birth incessantly!

'O builder! I've discovered thee!
This fabric thou shall ne'er rebuild!
The rafters are all broken now,
And pointed roof demolished lies!
This mind has demolition reached,
And seen the last of all desire!'[1]

he must have grasped something much deeper than mere dialectics. There must have been something most fundamental and ultimate which at once set all his doubts at rest, not only intellectual doubts but spiritual anguish. Indeed, forty-nine years of his active life after Enlightenment were commentaries on it, and yet they did not exhaust its con-

[1] *Dhammanadam*, 153, 154.

tent; nor did all the later speculations of Nāgārjuna, Aśvaghosha, Vasubandhu, and Asanga explain it away. In the *Laṅkāvatāra* therefore the author makes the Buddha confess that since his Enlightenment till his passing into Nirvāṇa he uttered not a word.[1]

Therefore, again with all his memory and learning, Ānanda could not sound the bottom of the Buddha's wisdom, while the latter was still alive. According to tradition, Ānanda's attainment to Arhatship took place at the time of the First Convocation in which he was not allowed to take part in spite of his twenty-five years' attendance upon the Buddha. Grieving over the fact, he spent the whole night perambulating in an open square, and when he was about to lay himself down on a couch all exhausted, he all of a sudden came to realize the truth of Buddhism, which with all his knowledge and understanding had escaped him all those years.

What does this mean? Arhatship is evidently not a matter of scholarship; it is something realized in the twinkling of an eye after a long arduous application to the matter. The preparatory course may occupy a long stretch of time, but the crisis breaks out at a point instantaneously, and one is an Arhat, or a Bodhisattva, or even a Buddha. The content of Enlightenment must be quite simple in nature, and yet tremendous in effect. That is to say, intellectually, it must transcend all the complications involved in an epistemological exposition of it; and psychologically, it must be the reconstruction of one's entire personality. Such a fundamental fact naturally evades description, and can be grasped only by an act of intuition and through personal experience. It is really the Dharma in its highest sense. If by 'the stirring of one thought' Ignorance came into our life,

[1] Ata etasmātokāraṇan mahāmate mayedam uktaṁ: yāṁ ca rātriṁ tathāgato 'bhisambuddho yāṁ ca rātriṁ parinirvāsyati atrāntara ekam api aksharaṁ tathāgatena na udāhṛitam na udāharishyati *Laṅkāvatāra*, chapter iii, p. 144. See also chapter vii, p. 240. (For this reason, O Mahāmati. I say unto you: During the time that elapsed between the night of the Tathāgata's Enlightenment and the night of his entrance into Nirvāṇa, not one word, not one statement was given out by him.)

the awakening of another thought must put a stop to Ignorance and bring about Enlightenment.[1] And in this there is no thought to be an object of logical consciousness or empirical reasoning; for in Enlightenment thinker and thinking and thought are merged in the one act of seeing into the very being of Self. No further explanation of the Dharma is possible, hence an appeal to *via negativa*. And this has reached its climax in the Śūnyatā philosophy of Nāgārjuna which is based upon the teaching of the Prajñāpāramitā literature of Buddhism.

So we see that Enlightenment is not the outcome of an intellectual process in which one idea follows another in sequence finally to terminate in conclusion or judgment. There is neither process nor judgment in Enlightenment, it is something more fundamental, something which makes a judgment possible, and without which no form of judgment can take place. In judgment there are a subject and a predicate; in Enlightenment subject is predicate, and predicate is subject; they are here merged as one, but not as one of which something can be stated, but as one from which arises judgment. We cannot go beyond this absolute oneness; all the intellectual operations stop here; when they endeavour to go further, they draw a circle in which they for ever repeat themselves. This is the wall against which all philosophies have beaten in vain. This is an intellectual *terra incognita*, in which prevails the principle, 'Credo quia absurdum est'. This region of darkness, however, gives up its secrets when attacked by the will, by the force of one's entire personality. Enlightenment is the illuminating of this dark region, when the whole thing is seen at one glance, and all intellectual inquiries find here their rationale. Hitherto one may have been intellectually convinced of the truth of a certain proposition, but somehow it has not yet

[1] According to Aśvaghosha's *Awakening of Faith*, Ignorance means the sudden awakening of a thought (*citta*) in consciousness. This may be variously interpreted, but as long as Ignorance is conceived, not as a process requiring a certain duration of time, but an event instantaneously taking place, its disappearance which is Enlightenment must also be an instantaneous happening.

entered into his life, the truth still lacks ultimate confirmation, and he cannot help feeling a vague sense of indeterminateness and uneasiness. Enlightenment now comes upon him in a mysterious way without any previous announcement, and all is settled with him, he is an Arhat or even a Buddha. The dragon has got its eyes dotted, and it is no more a lifeless image painted on a canvas, but winds and rains are its willing servants now.

It is quite evident that Enlightenment is not the consciousness of logical perspicuity or analytical completeness, it is something more than an intellectual sense of conclusiveness, there is something in it which engages the entire field of consciousness not only by throwing light on the whole series of links welded for the purpose of solving the problems of life, but by giving a feeling of finality to all the spiritual anguish that has ever been so disquieting to one's soul. The logical links, however accurately adjusted and perfectly wrought together, fail by themselves to be pacifying to the soul in the most thoroughgoing manner. We require something more fundamental or more immediate for the purpose, and I maintain that the mere reviewing of the Fourfold Noble Truth or the Twelvefold Chain of Origination does not result in the attainment of the Anuttara-samyak-sambodhi. The Buddha must have experienced something that went far deeper into his inmost consciousness than the mere intellectual grasping of empirical truths. He must have gone beyond the sphere of analytical reasoning. He must have come in touch with that which makes our intellectual operations possible, in fact that which conditions the very existence of our conscious life.

When Śāriputra saw Aśvajit he noticed how composed the latter was, with all his organs of sense well controlled and how clear and bright the colour of his skin was. Śāriputra could not help asking him who was his teacher and what doctrine he taught. To this Aśvajit replied : 'The great Śākyamuni, the Blessed One, is my teacher and his doctrine in substance is this:

'The Buddha hath the cause told
Of all things springing from a cause;
And also how things cease to be—
'Tis this the Mighty Monk proclaims.'

It is said that on hearing this exposition of the Dharma,
there arose in the mind of Śāriputra a clear and distinct
perception of the Dharma that whatever is subject to
origination is subject also to cessation. Śāriputra then
attained to the deathless, sorrowless state, lost sight of and
neglected for many myriads of kalpas.

The point to which I wish to call attention here is this:
is there anything intellectually remarkable and extraordinary and altogether original in this stanza that so
miraculously awakened Śāriputra from his habitually
cherished way of thinking? So far as the Buddha's Dharma
(Doctrine) was concerned, there was not much of anything
in these four lines. It is said that they are the substance of
the Dharma; if so, the Dharma may be said to be rather
devoid of substance, and how could Śāriputra ever find
here a truth concrete and efficient enough to turn him away
from the old rut? The stanza which is noted for having
achieved the conversion of not only Śāriputra but Maud-
galyāyana, has really nothing characteristic of Buddhistic
thought strong enough to produce such a great result. The
reason for this, therefore, must be sought somewhere else;
that is, not in the formal truth contained in the stanza, but
in the subjective condition of the one to whose ears it
chanced to fall and in whom it awakened a vision of another world. It was in the mind of Śāriputra itself that
opened up to a clear and distinct understanding of the
Dharma; in other words, the Dharma was revealed in him
as something growing out of himself and not as an external
truth poured into him. In a sense the Dharma had been in
his mind all the time, but he was not aware of its presence
there until Aśvajit's stanza was uttered. He was not a mere
passive recipient into which something not native to his
Self was poured. The hearing of the stanza gave him an

opportunity to experience the supreme moment. If Śāriputra's understanding was intellectual and discursive, his dialogue with Ānanda later on could not have taken place in the way it did. In the Saṁyutta-Nikāya, iii., 235*f*, we read:

Ānanda saw Śāriputra coming afar off, and he said to him: 'Serene and pure and radiant is your face, Brother Śāriputra! In what mood has Śāriputra been today?'

'I have been alone in Dhyāna, and to me came never the thought: *I* am attaining it! *I* have got it! *I* have emerged from it!'

Here we noticed the distinction between an intellectual and a spiritual understanding which is Enlightenment. When Śāriputra referred to the cause of his being so serene, pure and radiant, he did not explain it logically but just stated the fact as he subjectively interpreted it himself. Whether this interpretation of his own was correct or not takes the psychologist to decide. What I wish to see here is that Śāriputra's understanding of the doctrine of 'origination and cessation' was not the outcome of his intellectual analysis but an intuitive comprehension of his own inner life-process. Between the Buddha's Enlightenment which is sung in the Hymn of Victory and Śāriputra's insight into the Dharma as the doctrine of causation, there is a close connection in the way their minds worked. In the one Enlightenment came first and then its expression; in the other a definite statement was addressed first and then came an insight; the process is reversed here. But the inadequacy of relation between antecedent and consequence remains the same. The one does not sufficiently explain the other, when the logical and intellectual understanding alone is taken into consideration. The explanation must be sought not in the objective truth contained in the doctrine of causation, but in the state of consciousness itself of the enlightened subject. Otherwise, how do we account for the establishment of such a firm faith in self-realization or self-deliverance as this? 'He has destroyed all evil passions (*āsava*); he has attained to heart-emancipation (*cetovimutti*) and intellect-emancipation (*paññavimutti*), here in this visible world he has by himself understood, realized, and mastered the Dharma, he has dived deep into it, has passed beyond doubt, has put away perplexity, has gained full confidence, he has lived the life, has done what was to be done, has destroyed the fetter of rebirth, he has comprehended the Dharma as it is truly in itself.'[1]

This is why the *Laṅkāvatāra-Sūtra* tries so hard to tell us that language is altogether inadequate as the means of expressing and communicating the inner state of Enlightenment. While without language we may fare worse at least in our practical life, we must guard ourselves most deliberately against our trusting it too much beyond its legitimate office. The Sūtra gives the main reason for this, which is that language is the product of causal dependence, subject to change, unsteady, mutually conditioned, and based on false judgment as to the true nature of consciousness. For this reason language cannot reveal to us the ultimate signification of things (*paramārtha*). The noted analogy of finger and moon is most appropriate to illustrate the relation between language and sense, symbol and reality.

If the Buddha's Enlightenment really contained so much in it that he himself could not sufficiently demonstrate or illustrate it with his 'long thin tongue' (*prabhūtatanujihva*) through his long peaceful life given to meditation and discoursing, how could those less than he ever hope to grasp it and attain spiritual emancipation? This is the position taken up by Zen: to comprehend the truth of Enlightenment, therefore, we must exercise some other mental power than intellection, if we are at all in possession of such.

Discoursing fails to reach the goal, and yet we have an unsatiated aspiration after the unattainable. Are we then meant to live and die thus tormented for ever? If so, this is the most lamentable situation in which we find ourselves on earth. Buddhists have applied themselves most earnestly to the solution of the problem and have finally

[1] This is the usual formula given as the qualification of an Arhat, to be met with throughout the Nikāyas.

come to see that we have after all within ourselves what we need. This is the power of intuition possessed by spirit and able to comprehend spiritual truth which will show us all the secrets of life making up the content of the Buddha's Enlightenment. It is not an ordinary intellectual process of reasoning, but a power that will grasp something most fundamental in an instant and in the directest way. Prajñā is the name given to this power by the Buddhists, as I said, and what Zen Buddhism aims at in its relation to the doctrine of Enlightenment is to awaken Prajñā by the exercise of meditation.

We read in the *Saddharma-puṇḍarīka*: 'O Śāriputra, the true Law understood by the Tathāgata cannot be reasoned, is beyond the pale of reasoning. Why? For the Tathāgata appears in the world to carry out one great object, which is to make all beings accept, see, enter into, and comprehend the knowledge and insight gained by the Tathāgata, and also to make them enter upon the path of knowledge and insight attained by the Tathāgata. . . . Those who learn it from the Tathāgata also reach his Supreme Perfect Enlightenment.'[1] If such was the one great object of the Buddha's appearance on earth, how do we get into the path of insight and realize Supreme Perfect Enlightenment? And if this Dharma of Enlightenment is beyond the limits of the understanding, no amount of philosophizing will ever bring us nearer the goal. How do we then learn it from the Tathāgata? Decidedly not from his mouth, nor from the records of his sermons, nor fiom the ascetic practice, but from our own inner consciousness through the exercise of dhyana. And this is the doctrine of Zen.

Enlightenment and Spiritual Freedom

When the doctrine of Enlightenment makes its appeal to the inner experience of the Buddhist and its content is to be grasped immediately without any conceptual medium,

[1] Chapter ii, 'On Skilfulness'.

the sole authority in his spiritual life will have to be found within himself; traditionalism or institutionalism will naturally lose all its binding force. According to him, then, propositions will be true—that is, living—because they are in accordance with his spiritual insight; and his actions will permit no external standard of judgment; so long as they are the inevitable overflow of his inner life, they are good, even holy. The direct issue of this interpretation of Enlightenment will be the upholding of absolute spiritual freedom in every way, which will further lead to the unlimited expansion of his mental outlook going beyond the narrow bounds of monastic and scholastic Buddhism. This was not, however, from the Mahāyānistic point of view, against the spirit of the Buddha.

The constitution of the Brotherhood will now have to change. In the beginning of Buddhism, it was a congregation of homeless monks who subjected themselves to a certain set of ascetic rules of life. In this Buddhism was an exclusive possession of the *élite*, and the general public or Upasaka group who accepted the Threefold Refuge Formula was a sort of appendage to the regular or professional Brotherhood. When Buddhism was still in its first stage of development, even nuns (*bhikshuṇī*) were not allowed to come into the community; the Buddha received them only after great reluctance, prophesying that Buddhism would now live only half of its normal life. We can readily see from this fact that the teaching of the Buddha and the doctrine of Enlightenment were meant to be practised and realized only among limited classes of people. While the Buddha regarded the various elements of his congregation with perfect impartiality, cherishing no prejudices as to their social, racial, and other distinctions, the full benefit of his teaching could not extend beyond the monastic boundaries. If there was nothing in it that could benefit mankind in general, this exclusiveness was naturally to be expected. But the doctrine of Enlightenment was something that could not be kept thus imprisoned, it had many things in it that would overflow all the limitations set to it.

When the conception of Bodhisattvahood came to be emphatically asserted, a monastic and self-excluding community could no longer hold its ground, a religion of monks and nuns had to become a religion of laymen and laywomen. An ascetic discipline leading to the Anūpādhiśesha-Nirvāṇa had to give way to a system of teaching that would make anyone attain Enlightenment and demonstrate Nirvāṇa in his daily life. In all the Mahāyāna Sūtras, this general tendency in the unfoldment of Buddhism is vehemently asserted, showing how intense was the struggle between conservatism and progressivism.

This spirit of freedom, which is the power impelling Buddhism to break through its monastic shell and bringing forward the idea of Enlightenment ever vigorously before the masses, is the life-impulse of the universe—this unhampered activity of spirit, and everything that interferes with it, is destined to be defated. The history of Buddhism is thus also a history of freedom in one's spiritual, intellectual, and moral life. The moral aristocracy and disciplinary formalism of primitive Buddhism could not bind our spirit for a very long period of time. As the doctrine of Enlightenment grew to be more and more inwardly interpreted, the spirit rose above the formalism of Buddhist discipline. It was of no absolute necessity for one to leave his home life and follow the footsteps of the wandering monks in order to reach the supreme fruit of Enlightenment. Inward purity, and not external piety, was the thing needed for the Buddhist life. The Upasakas were in this respect as good as the Bhikshus. The fact is most eloquently illustrated in the *Vimalakīrti-Sūtra.* The chief character here is Vimalakīrti, a lay philosopher, outside the pale of the Brotherhood. None of the Buddha's disciples were his matches in the depth, breadth, and subtleties of thought, and when the Buddha told them to visit his sick-room they all excused themselves for some reason or other, except Mañjuśrī, who is Prajñā incarnate in Mahāyāna Buddhism.

That the lay-devotees thus asserted themselves even at

75

the expense of the Arhats may also be gleaned from other sources than the *Vimalakīrti*, but especially from such Sūtras as the *Śrīmalā, Gaṇḍhavyūha, Vajrasamādhi, Candrottara-dārikā*, etc. What is the most noteworthy in this connection is that woman plays an important rôle on various occasions. Not only is she endowed with philosophizing talents, but she stands on equal footing with man. Among the fifty-three philosophers or leaders of thought visited by Sudhana in his religious pilgrimage, he interviewed many women in various walks of life, some of whom were even courtesans. They all wisely discoursed with the insatiable seeker of truth. What a different state of affairs this was when compared with the reluctant admission of women into the Sangha in the early days of Buddhism! Later Buddhism may have lost something in austerity, aloofness, and even saintliness, which appeal strongly to our religious imagination, but it has gained in democracy, picturesqueness, and largely in humanity.

The free spirit which wanders out beyond the monastic walls of the Brotherhood now follows its natural consequence and endeavours to transcend the disciplinary rules and the ascetic formalism of the Hīnayānists. The moral rules that were given by the Buddha to his followers as they were called for by the contingencies of life, were concerned more or less with externalism. When the Buddha remained with them as the living spirit of the Brotherhood, these rules were the direct expressions of the subjective life; but with the Buddha's departure they grew rigid and failed to reach the inner spirit of their author, and the followers of Enlightenment revolted against them, upholding 'the spirit that giveth life'. They advocated perfect freedom of spirit, even after the fashions of antinomians. If the spirit were pure, no acts of the body could spoil it; it could wander about anywhere it liked with absolute immunity. It would even go down to hell if it were necessary or expedient for them to do so, for the sake of the salvation of the depraved. It would indefinitely postpone the entering into Nirvāṇa if there were still souls to save and minds to enlighten. According to 'the letter that killeth', no Buddhists were allowed to enter a liquor-shop, or to be familiar with inmates of the houses barred from respectability; in short, even for a moment to be thinking of violating any of the moral precepts. But to the Mahāyānists all kinds of 'expediency' or 'devices' were granted if they were fully enlightened and had their spirits thoroughly purified. They were living in a realm beyond good and evil, and as long as they were there, no acts of theirs could be classified and judged according to the ordinary measure of ethics; they were neither moral nor immoral. These relative terms had no application in a kingdom governed by free spirits which soared above the relative world of differences and oppositions.

This was most slippery ground for the Mahāyānists. When they were really enlightened and fathomed the depths of spirituality, every deed of theirs was a creative act of God, but in this extreme form of idealism, objectivity had no room, and consequently who could ever distinguish libertinism from spiritualism? In spite of this pitfall the Mahāyānists were in the right in consistently following up all the implications of the doctrine of Enlightenment. Their parting company with the Hīnayānists was inevitable.

The doctrine of Enlightenment leads to the inwardness of one's spiritual experience, which cannot be analysed intellectually without somehow involving logical contradictions. It thus seeks to break through every intelligent barrier that may be set against it; it longs for emancipation in every form, not only in the understanding but in life itself. The unscrupulous followers of Enlightenment are thus liable to degenerate into votaries of libertinism. If the Mahāyānists had remained here and had not seen further into the real nature of Prajñā, they would have certainly followed the fate of the Friends of the Free Spirit, but they knew how Enlightenment realizes its true signification in love for all beings and how freedom of spirit has its own principle to follow though nothing external is imposed upon it. For freedom does not mean lawlessness, which is the destruction and annihilation of itself, but creating out of its inner life-force all that is good and beautiful. This creating is called by the Mahāyānists 'skilful device' (*upāya-kauśalya*), in which Enlightenment is harmoniously wedded to love. Enlightenment when intellectually conceived is not dynamical and stops at illumining the path which love will tread. But Prajñā is more than merely intellectual, it produces Karuṇā (love or pity), and with her co-operation it achieves the great end of life, the salvation of all beings from Ignorance and passions and misery. It now knows no end in devising all kinds of means to carry out its own teleological functions.

The *Saddharma-Puṇḍarīka* regards the Buddha's appearance on earth and his life in history as the 'skilful devices' of world-salvation on the part of the Supreme Being of Eternal Enlightenment. This creation, however, ceases to be a creation in its perfect sense when the creator grows conscious of its teleological implications[1]; for here then is a split in his consciousness which will check the spontaneous flowing-out of spirit, and then freedom will be lost at its source. Such devices as have grown conscious of their purposes are no more 'skilful devices', and according

---

[1] In this connection it may not be amiss to say a word about what is known in Buddhism as the 'act of no-effort or no-purpose' (*anābhogacaryā*) or 'the original vows of no-purpose' (*anābhogapraṇidhāna*). This corresponds, if I judge rightly, to the Christian idea of not letting the right hand know what the left hand is doing. When spirit attains to the reality of enlightenment and as a result is thoroughly purified of all defilements, intellectual and affective, it grows so perfect that whatever it does is pure, unselfish, and conducive to the welfare of the world. So long as we are conscious of the efforts we make in trying to overcome our selfish impulses and passions, there is a taint of constraint and artificiality, which interferes with spiritual innocence and freedom, and love which is the native virtue of an enlightened spirit cannot work out all that is implied in it and meant to be exercised for the preservation of itself. The 'original vows' are the content of love and begin to be operative, anabhoga (unpurposely), only when enlightenment is really creative. This is where religious life differs from mere morality, this is where the mere enunciation of the Law of Origination (*pratītya-samutpāda*) does not constitute Buddhist life, and this is where Zen Buddhism maintains its reason of existence against the alleged positivism of the Hīnayāna and against the alleged nihilism of the Prajñā-pāramitā school.

to the Buddhists they do not reflect the perfect state of Enlightenment.

Thus the doctrine of Enlightenment is to be supplemented by the doctrine of Device (*upāya*), or the latter may be said to evolve by itself from the first when it is conceived dynamically and not as merely a contemplative state of consciousness. The earlier Buddhists showed the tendency to consider Enlightenment essentially reflective or a state of tranquillity. They made it something lifeless and altogether uncreative. This, however, did not bring out all that was contained in Enlightenment. The effective or will element which moved the Buddha to come out of his Sāgaramudrā-Samādhi—a samādhi in which the whole universe was reflected in his consciousness as the moon stamps her image upon the ocean—has now developed into the doctrine of Device. For the will is more fundamental than the intellect and makes up the ultimate principle of life. Without the 'devising' and self-regulating will, life will be the mad display of a mere blind force. The wantonness of 'a free spirit' is thus now regulated to operate in the great work of universal salvation. Its creative activity will devise all possible means for the sake of love for all beings animate as well as inanimate. Dhyāna is one of those devices which will keep our minds in balance and well under the control of the will. Zen is the outcome of the dhyāna discipline applied to the attainment of Enlightenment.

Zen and Dhyāna

The term 'Zen' (*ch'an* in Chinese), is an abbreviated form of *Zenna* or *Ch'anna*, which is the Chinese rendering of 'dhyāna', or 'jhāna', and from this fact alone it is evident that Zen has a great deal to do with this practice which has been carried on from the early days of the Buddha, indeed from the beginning of Indian culture. Dhyāna is usually rendered in English meditation, and, generally speaking, the idea is to meditate on a truth, religious or philosophical, so that it may be thoroughly comprehended and deeply engraved into the inner consciousness. This is practised in a quiet place away from the noise and confusion of the world. Allusion to this abounds in Indian literature; and 'to sit alone in a quiet place and to devote oneself to meditation exclusively' is the phrase one meets everywhere in the Āgamas.

The following conversation between Sandhana, a Buddhist, and Nigrodha, an ascetic, which is recorded in the *Udumbarika Sīhanada Suttanta*,[1] will throw much light on the habit of the Buddha. Says Sandhana, 'But the Exalted One haunts the lonely and remote recesses of the forest, where noise, where sound there hardly is, where the breezes from the pastures blow, yet which are hidden from the eyes of men, suitable for self-communing.' To this, the ascetic wanderer answers: 'Look you now, householder, know you with whom the Samana Gotama talks? with whom he holds conversation? By intercourse with whom does he attain the lucidity in wisdom? The Samana Gotama's insight is ruined by his habit of seclusion. He is not at home in conducting an assembly. He is not ready in conversation. So he keeps apart from others in solitary places. Even as a one-eyed cow that, walking in a circle, follows only the outskirts, so is the Samana Gotama.'

Again we read in the *Sāmañña-phala Sutta*:[2] 'Then, the master of this so excellent body of moral precepts, gifted with this so excellent self-restraint as to the senses, endowed with this so excellent mindfulness and self-possession, filled with this so excellent content, he chooses some lonely spot to rest at on his way—in the woods, at the foot of a tree, on a hill side, in a mountain glen, in a rocky cave, in a charnel place, or on a heap of straw in the open field. And returning thither after his round for alms he seats himself, when his meal is done, cross-legged, keeping his body erect, and his intelligence alert, intent.'

Further, in the days of the Buddha, miracle-working

---

[1] *Dialogues of the Buddha*, Part III, p. 35.
[2] *Ibid.*, Part I, p. 82.

and sophistical discussions seem to have been the chief business of the ascetics, wanderers, and Brahman metaphysicians. The Buddha was thus frequently urged to join in the debates on philosophical questions and also to perform wonders in order to make people embrace his teaching. Nigrodha's comment on the Buddha conclusively shows that the Buddha was a great disapprover of empty reasoning, devoting himself to things practical and productive of results, as well as that he was always earnestly engaged in meditation away from the world. When Chien-ku, son of a wealthy merchant in Nālandā, asked the Buddha to give his command to his disciples and make them perform for the benefit of his townspeople, the Buddha flatly refused, saying: 'My disciples are instructed to sit in solitude quietly and to be earnestly meditating on the Path. If they had something meritorious, let them conceal it, but if they had faults, let them confess.'[1]

An appeal to the analytical understanding is never sufficient to comprehend thoroughly the inwardness of a truth, especially when it is a religious one, nor is mere compulsion by an external force adequate for bringing about a spiritual transformation in us. We must experience in our innermost consciousness all that is implied in a doctrine, when we are able not only to understand it but to put it in practice. There will then be no discrepancy between knowledge and life. The Buddha knew this very well, and he endeavoured to produce knowledge out of meditation; that is, to make wisdom grow from personal, spiritual experience. The Buddhist way to deliverance, therefore, consisted in threefold discipline: moral rules (*śīla*) tranquillization (*samādhi*), and wisdom (*prajñā*). By Śīla one's conduct is

---

[1] The Pāli text that will correspond to this Chinese Sūtra in the Dīrgha-Āgama is the *Kevaddha Sutta*, but the passage quoted here is missing. See also the *Lohicca* (*Lou-chê*) and *Sāmañña-phala* in the Chinese Āgamas, in which the Buddha tells how essential the life of a recluse is to the realization of enlightenment and the destruction of the evil passions. Constant application, earnest concentration, and vigilant watchfulness —without these no Buddhists are ever expected to attain the end of their lives.

regulated externally, by Samādhi quietude is attained, and by Prajñā real understanding takes place. Hence the importance of meditation in Buddhism.

That this threefold discipline was one of the most characteristic features of Buddhism since its earliest days is well attested by the fact that the following formula, which is culled from the *Mahāparinibbāna-Sutta*, is repeatedly referred to in the Sūtra as if it were a subject most frequently discussed by the Buddha for the edification of his followers: 'Such and such is upright conduct (*sīla*); such and such is earnest contemplation (*samādhi*); such and such is intelligence (*prajñā*). Great becomes the fruit, great the advantage of intellect when it is set round with earnest contemplation. The mind set round with intelligence is set quite free from the intoxications (*āsrava*); that is to say, from the intoxication of sensuality (*kāma*), from the intoxication of becoming (*bhāva*), from the intoxication of delusion (*drishti*), from the intoxication of ignorance (*avidyā*).'[1]

Samādhi and dhyāna are to a great extent synonymous and interchangeable, but strictly samādhi is a psychological state realized by the exercise of dhyāna. The latter is the process and the former is the goal. The Buddhist scriptures make reference to so many samādhis, and before delivering a sermon the Buddha generally enters into a samādhi,[2] but never I think into a dhyāna. The latter is practised or exercised. But frequently in China dhyāna and samādhi are combined to make one word, *ch'an-ting*, meaning a state of quietude attained by the exercise of meditation

[1] The rendering is by Rhys Davids, who states in the footnote: 'The word I have here rendered "earnest contemplation" is Samādhi, which occupies in the Five Nikāyas very much the same position as faith does in the New Testament; and this section shows that the relative importance of Samādhi, Paññā, and Sīla played a part in early Buddhism just as the distinction between faith, reason, and works did afterwards in Western theology. It would be difficult to find a passage in which the Buddhist view of the relation of these *conflicting* ideas is stated with greater beauty of thought, or equal succinctness of form.' But why conflicting?

[2] One hundred and eight samādhis are enumerated in the *Mahāvyutpatti*. Elsewhere we read of 'innumerable samādhis'. Indians have been great adepts in this exercise, and many wonderful spiritualistic achievements are often reported.

or dhyāna. There are some other terms analogous to these two which are met with in Buddhist literature as well as in other Indian religious systems. They are *Saṁpatti* (coming together), *Samāhita* (collecting the thoughts), *Śamatha* (tranquillization), *Cittaikāgratā* (concentration), *Dṛishta-dharma-sukha-vihāra* (abiding in the bliss of the Law perceived), *Dhāraṇi or Dhāraṇa* (abstraction), etc. They are all connected with the central idea of dhyāna, which is to tranquillize the turbulence of self-assertive passions and to bring about a state of absolute identity in which the truth is realized in its inwardness; that is, a state of Enlightenment. The analytical tendency of philosophers is also evident in this when they distinguish four or eight kinds of dhyāna.[1]

The first dhyāna is an exercise in which the mind is made to concentrate on one single subject until all the coarse affective elements are vanished from consciousness except the serene feelings of joy and peace. But the intellect is still active, judgment and reflection operate upon the object of contemplation. When these intellectual operations too are quieted and the mind is simply concentrated on one point, it is said that we have attained the second dhyāna, but the feelings of joy and peace are still here. In the third stage of dhyāna, perfect serenity obtains as the concentration grows deeper, but the subtlest mental activities are not vanished and at the same time a joyous feeling remains. When the fourth and last stage is reached, even this feeling of self-enjoyment disappears, and what prevails in conscious-

[1] This series of dhyānas has also been adopted by Buddhists, especially by Hīnayanists. No doubt the Mahāyana conception of dhyāna is derived or rather has developed from them, and how much it differs from the Hīnayāna dhyānas will be seen later as we go on. The detailed description of these dhyānas is given in the Āgamas; see for instance the *Sāmañña-phala Sutta*, in which the fruits of the life of a recluse are discussed. These mental exercises were not strictly Buddhistic, they were taught and practised more or less by all Indian philosophers and mendicants. The Buddha, however, was not satisfied with them, because they would not bring out the result he was so anxious to have; that is, they were not conducive to enlightenment. This was the reason why he left his two old teachers, Arada and Udraka, under whom he first began his homeless life.

ness now is perfect serenity of contemplation. All the intellectual and the emotional factors liable to disturb spiritual tranquillity are successively controlled, and mind in absolute composure remains absorbed in contemplation. In this there takes place a fully adjusted equilibrium between Samatha and Vipasayana; that is, between tranquillization or cessation and contemplation.

In all Buddhist discipline this harmony is always sought after. For when the mind tips either way, it grows either too heavy (*styānam*) or too light (*auddhatyam*), either too torpid in mental activity or too given up to contemplation. The spiritual exercise ought to steer ahead without being hampered by either tendency, they ought to strike the middle path.

There are further four stages of dhyāna called 'Arūpa-vimoksha' which are practised by those who have passed beyond the last stage of dhyāna. The first is to contemplate the infinity of space, not disturbed by the manifoldness of matter; the second is on the infinity of consciousness as against the first; the third is meant to go still further beyond the distinction of space and thought; and the fourth is to eliminate even this consciousness of nondistinction, to be thus altogether free from any trace of analytical intellection. Besides these eight Samāpatti ('coming together') exercises, technically so called, the Buddha sometimes refers to still another form of meditation which is considered to be distinctly Buddhist. This is more or less definitely contrasted to the foregoing by not being so exclusively intellectual but partly effective, as it aims at putting a full stop to the operation of Saṁjñā (thought) and Vedita (sensation); that is, of the essential elements of consciousness. It is almost a state of death, total extinction, except that one in this dhyāna has life, warmth, and the sense-organs in perfect condition. But in point of fact it is difficult to distinguish this Nirodha-vimoksha (deliverance by cessation) from the last stage of the Aruppa (or Arūpa) meditation, in both of which consciousness ceases to function even in its simplest and most fundamental acts.

Whatever this was, it is evident that the Buddha, like the other Indian leaders of thought, endeavoured to make his disciples realize in themselves the content of Enlightenment by means of dhyāna, or concentration. They were thus made to progress gradually from a comparatively simple exercise up to the highest stage of concentration in which the dualism of the One and the Many vanished even to the extent of a total cessation of mentation. Apart from these general spiritual exercises, the Buddha at various times told his followers to meditate on such objects[1] as would make them masters of their disturbing passions and intellectual entanglements.

We can now see how Zen developed out of this system of spiritual exercises. Zen adopted the external form of dhyana as the most practical method to realize the end it had in view, but as to its content Zen had its own way of interpreting the spirit of the Buddha. The dhyāna practised by primitive Buddhists was not in full accord with the object of Buddhism, which is no other than the attaining of Enlightenment and demonstrating it in one's everyday life. To do away with consciousness so that nothing will disturb spiritual serenity was too negative a state of mind to be sought after by those who at all aspired to develop the positive content of the Buddha's own enlightened mind. Tranquillization was not the real end of dhyāna, nor was the being absorbed in a samādhi the object of Buddhist life. Enlightenment was to be found in life itself, in its fuller and freer expressions, and not in its cessation.

What was it that made the Buddha pass all his life in religious peregrination? What was it that moved him to sacrifice his own well-being, in fact his whole life, for the sake of his fellow-creatures? If dhyāna had no positive object except in pacifying passions and enjoying absorption

---

[1] For example, the ten subjects for meditation are: Buddha, Dharma, Sangha, Morality, Charity, Heaven, Serenity, Breathing, Impermanence, and Death. The five subjects of tranquillization are: Impurity, Compassion, Breathing, Origination, and Buddha. The four subjects of recollection are: Impurity of the Body, Evils of the Senses, Constant Change of Thought, and Transitoriness of Existence.

in the unconscious, why did the Buddha leave his seat under the Bodhi-tree and come out into the world? If Enlightenment was merely a negative state of cessation, the Buddha could not find any impulse in him that would urge him to exertion in behalf of others. Critics sometimes forget this fact when they try to understand Buddhism simply as a system of teaching as recorded in the Āgamas and in Pāli Buddhist literature. As I said before, Buddhism is also a system built by his disciples upon the personality of the Buddha himself, in which the spirit of the Master is more definitely affirmed. And this is what Zen has in its own way been attempting to do—to develop the idea of Enlightenment more deeply, positively, and comprehensively by the practice of dhyāna and in conformity with the spirit of general Buddhism, in which life, purged of its blind impulses and sanctified by an insight into its real values, will be asserted.

Zen and the Laṅkāvatāra

Of the many Sūtras that were introduced into China since the first century A.D., the one in which the principles of Zen are more expressly and directly expounded than any others, at least those that were in existence at the time of Bodhidharma, is the *Laṅkāvatāra Sūtra.* Zen, as its followers justly claim, does not base its authority on any written documents, but directly appeals to the enlightened mind of the Buddha. It refuses to do anything with externalism in all its variegated modes; even the Sūtras or all those literary remains ordinarily regarded as sacred and coming directly from the mouth of the Buddha are looked down upon, as we have already seen, as not touching the inward facts of Zen. Hence its reference to the mystic dialogue between the Enlightened One and Mahākāśyapa on a bouquet of flowers. But Bodhidharma, the founder of Zen in China, handed the *Laṅkāvatāra* over to his first Chinese disciple

Hui-k'ê as the only literature in existence at the time in China in which the principles of Zen are taught.

When Zen unconditionally emphasizes one's immediate experience as the final fact on which it is established it may well ignore all the scriptural sources as altogether unessential to its truth; and on this principle its followers have quite neglected the study of the *Laṅkāvatāra*. But to justify the position of Zen for those who have not yet grasped it and yet who are desirous of learning something about it, an external authority may be quoted and conceptual arguments resorted to in perfect harmony with its truth. This was why Dharma selected this Sūtra out of the many that had been in existence in China in his day. We must approach the *Laṅkāvatāra* with this frame of mind.

There are three Chinese translations of the Sūtra still in existence. There was a fourth one, but it was lost. The first in four volumes was produced during the Lu-Sung dynasty (A.D. 443) by Gunabhadra, the second in ten volumes comes from the pen of Bodhiruci, of the Yüan-Wei dynasty (A.D. 513), and the third in seven volumes is by Śikshānanda, of the T'ang dynasty (A.D. 700). The last-mentioned is the easiest to understand and the first the most difficult, and it was this, the most difficult one, that was delivered by Dharma to his disciple Hui-k'ê as containing the 'essence of mind'. In form and in content this translation reflects the earliest text of the Sūtra, and on it are written all the commentaries we have at present in Japan.

The special features of this Sūtra, which distinguish it from the other Mahāyāna writings, are, to give the most noteworthy ones: first, that the subject-matter is not systematically developed as in most other Sūtras, but the whole book is a series of notes of various lengths; secondly, that the Sūtra is devoid of all supernatural phenomena, but filled with deep philosophical and religious ideas concerning the central teaching of the Sūtra, which are very difficult to comprehend, due to tersity of expression and to the abstruse nature of the subject matter; thirdly, that it is in the form of dialogues exclusively between the Buddha and the Bodhisattva Mahāmati, while in the other Mahā-yāna Sūtras the principal figures are generally more than one besides the Buddha himself, who addresses them in turn; and lastly, that it contains no Dhāraṇīs or Mantrams— those mystical signs and formulas supposed to have a miraculous power. These singularities are enough to make the *Laṅkāvatāra* occupy a unique position in the whole lore of the Mahayana school.

In this characterization of the *Laṅkāvatāra Sūtra* I am referring to the first Chinese text of Guṇabhadra. The two later ones have three new chapters in addition: one of which forming the first chapter is a sort of introduction to the whole Sutra, giving the main idea of what is discussed in the body of the text itself; the remaining two are attached to the end. Of these, the one is a short collection of Dhāraṇīs, and the other which is the conclusion is known as the Gāthā chapter written throughout in verse and sum-marizes the contents of the whole Sūtra. It has, however, no paragraph making up the 'regular ending' in which the whole congregation unites in the praise of the Buddha and in its assurance of observing his instructions. There is no doubt that these three new chapters are later growth.

The main thesis of the *Laṅkāvatāra Sūtra* is the content of Enlightenment; that is, the Buddha's own inner experience (*pratyātmagati*) concerning the great religious truth of Mahāyāna Buddhism. Most of the readers of the Sūtra have singularly failed to see this, and contend that it prin-cipally explains the Five Dharmas, the Three Character-istics of Reality (*svabhāva*), the Eight Kinds of Consciousness (*vijñāna*) and the Two Forms of Non-Ego (*nairātmya*).

It is true that the Sūtra reflects the psychological school of Buddhism advocated by Asaṅga and Vasubandhu, when for instance it refers to the Ālayavijñāna as the storage of all karmic seeds; but such and other references in fact do not constitute the central thought of the Sūtra, they are merely made use of in explaining the 'noble understanding of the Buddha's inner experience' (*pratyātmāryajñāna*). Therefore

when Mahāmati finishes praising the Buddha's virtues
before the whole assembly at the summit of Mount Laṅkā,
the Buddha is quite definite in his declaration of the main
theme of his discourse in this Sūtra. Let us, however, first
quote the song of the Bodhisattva Mahāmati, since it sums
up in a concise and definite manner all the essentials of
Mahāyāna Buddhism and since at the same time it illustrates my statement concerning the union of Enlightenment and Love.

The hymn runs as follows:

'When thou reviewest the world with thy wisdom and
compassion, it is to thee like the ethereal flower, and of
which we cannot say whether it is created or vanishing,
as the categories of being and non-being are inapplicable
to it.

'When thou reviewest all things with thy wisdom and
compassion, they are like visions, they are beyond the reach
of mind and consciousness, as the categories of being and
non-being are inapplicable to them.

'When thou reviewest the world with thy wisdom and
compassion, it is eternally like a dream, of which we cannot
say whether it is permanent or it is subject to destruction,
as the categories of being and non-being are inapplicable to
it.

'In the Dharmakāya whose self-nature is a vision and a
dream, what is there to praise? Real existence is where rises
no thought of nature and no-nature.

'He whose appearance is beyond the senses and sense-
objects and is not to be seen by them or in them—how
could praise or blame be predicated of him, O Muni?

'With thy wisdom and compassion, which really defy all
qualifications, thou comprehendest the ego-less nature of
things and persons and art eternally clean of the evil
passions and of the hindrance of knowledge.

'Thou dost not vanish in Nirvāṇa, nor does Nirvāṇa abide
in thee; for it transcends the dualism of the enlightened
and enlightenment as well as the alternatives of being and
non-being.

'Those who see the Muni so serene and beyond birth, are detached from cravings and remain stainless in this life and after.'

After this says the Buddha: 'O you, sons of the Jina, question me anything you feel like asking. I am going to tell you about the state of my inner attainment (*pratyāt-magatigocaram*).' This is conclusive, nothing is left to discussion concerning the theme of the *Laṅkāvatāra*. The five Dharmas, the three Characteristics, etc., are referred to only in the course of the Buddha's exposition of the principal matter.

The two later translations, which, as aforementioned, contain some extra chapters, are divided regularly in the one into ten and in the other into eighteen chapters, while the earliest one of Guṇabhadra has just one chapter title for the whole book, 'The Gist of all the Buddhawords'. The first extra chapter which is not found in Guṇabhadra's text is remarkable in that it gives the outlines of the whole Sūtra in the form of a dialogue between the Buddha and Rāvana, Lord of the Yakshas, in the Isle of Laṅkā. When the Buddha, coming out of the Nāga's palace, views the castle of Laṅkā, he smiles and remarks that this was the place where all the Buddhas of the past preached regarding the excellent understanding of Enlightenment realized in their inner consciousness, which is beyond the analysis of logic and is not the state of mind attainable by the Tīrthya, Śrāvaka, or Pratyekabuddha. The Buddha then adds that for this reason the same Dharma will be propounded for Rāvana, Lord of the Yakshas. In response to this, the latter, making all kinds of costly offerings to the Buddha, sings in the praise of his insight and virtues: 'O Lord, instruct me in thy system of doctrine which is based on the self-nature of mind, instruct me in the doctrine of non-ego, free from prejudices and defilements, the doctrine that is revealed in thy inmost consciousness.'

In the conclusion of this chapter the Buddha reaffirms his doctrine of inner realization which is Enlightenment: 'It is like seeing one's own image in a mirror or in water, it is like seeing one's own shadow in moonlight or lamp-light, again it is like hearing one's voice echoed in the valley: as a man clings to his own false assumptions, he erroneously discriminates between truth and falsehood, and on account of this false discrimination he fails to go beyond the dualism of opposites, indeed he cherishes falsity and cannot attain tranquillity. By tranquillity is meant singleness of purpose (or oneness of things), and by singleness of purpose is meant the entrance into the most excellent samādhi, whereby is produced the state of noble understanding of self-reali-zation, which is the receptacle of Tathāgatahood (*tathā-gatagarbha*).'

From these quotations we can easily see why Bodhi-Dharma recommended this Sūtra for the special perusal of his Zen disciples. But in order to impress the reader further with the great importance of the *Laṅkāvatāra Sūtra* in the historical study of Zen in India and China, I quote a few more passages showing how the teaching of self-realization is developed in the Sūtra.

According to the author, the anuttara-samyak-sambodhi attained by the Muni of the Śākyas, whereby he became the Buddha, is realizable by transcending the ideas of being and non-being (*nāsy-asti-vikalpa*). This being the funda-mental error—this cherishing of dualism—must he got rid of as the first necessary step to reach the state of self-realization. The error comes from not perceiving the truth that all things are empty (*śūnya*), uncreated (*anutpāda*), non-dualistic (*advaya*), and have no immutably individualistic characters (*niḥsvabhāvalakshaṇa*). By the emptiness of things is meant principally that, their existence being so thoroughly mutually conditioning, nowhere obtains the false notion of distinctive individuality, and that when analysis is carried to its logical consequence there exists nothing that will separate one object from another in a final way; therefore says the Sūtra, 'Sva-para-ubhaya-abhāvāt' (there exists neither one nor another nor both). Secondly, things are uncreated, because they are not self-created, nor are they created by an outside agency. Thirdly, as their existence is reciprocally conditioning, a dualistic conception of the world is not the ultimate one, and thus it is a mistake, due to this wrong discrimination (*vikalpa*), to seek Nirvāṇa outside of Saṁsāra (birth-and-death) and Saṁsāra outside of Nirvāṇa. Fourthly, this principle of mutuality means the denial of individuality as absolute reality, for there is nothing in existence that will absolutely maintain its individuality standing above all conditions of relativity or mutual becoming—in fact, being is becoming.

For these reasons we can realize the truth of Enlightenment only by transcending the first condition of intellection, which is, according to the *Laṅkāvatāra*, Parikalpa, or Vikalpa (discrimination). The warning against this Vikalpa which is the analysing tendency of mind, or, we may say, the fundamentally dualistic disposition of consciousness, is the constant refrain of the Sūtra, while on the other hand it never forgets to emphasize the importance of self-realization which is attained by overcoming this fundamental tendency.

By thus transcending the intellectual condition, Paramārthasatya is realized, which is the ultimate truth, and which subjectively constitutes Pratyātmajñāna; it is also the eternally abiding law of the universe (*paurāṇasthiti-dharmatā*). This inwardly realized truth has many names as it is viewed in various relations in which it stands to human activities, moral, spiritual, intellectual, practical, and psychological. 'Bodhi' is enlightenment and used most generally, in Mahāyāna as well as in Hīnayāna literature, to designate the mind in which Ignorance is completely wiped out; Tathatā (thatness) or Bhūtatā (reality) is metaphysical. Nirvāṇa is conceived as a spiritual state in which all passional turmoil is quieted; Tathāgatagarbha is more psychological than ontological; Citta is used as belonging to the series of mental terms such as Manas, Manovijñāna, and other Vijñānas, and is not always synonymous with Bodhi or Pratyātmajñāna unless it is qualified with adjectives of purity; Śūnyatā is a negative term and distinctively epistemological, and Buddhist scholars, especially of the Prajñāpāramitā school, have been quite fond of this term, and we see that the *Laṅkāvatāra* too has indulged in the use of it. It goes without saying, however, that these synonyms are helpful only as sign-posts indicating the way to the content of self-realization.

Besides these, we have two or three most frequently repeated phrases to characterize the central idea of the Mahāyāna text. In fact, when the meaning of these phrases is grasped together with psychological discourse on the Citta and Vijñāna, the whole philosophy of Zen as it is expounded in the Sūtra grows transparent, and also with it the general tendency of Mahāyāna thought. The phrases are: '*Vāg-vikalpa-ahita*', or '*vāg-akshara-prativikalpanaṁ vinihata*', or *śāśvata-uccheda-sad-asad-dṛishṭi-vivarjita*'. With these the reader is most frequently greeted in the Sūtra. The first and the second phrases mean that the inner content of the noble understanding is beyond the reach of words and analytical reasoning, and the third phrase says that the ultimate truth is not to be found in eternalism, or nihilism, or realism, or non-realism.

The Sūtra sometimes goes so far as this: 'O Mahāmati, it is because the Sūtras are preached to all beings in accordance with their modes of thinking, and do not hit the mark as far as the true sense is concerned; words cannot reinstate the truth as it is. It is like mirage, deceived by which the animals make an erroneous judgment as to presence of water where there is really none; even so, all the doctrines in the Sūtras are intended to satisfy the imagination of the masses they do not reveal the truth which is the object of the noble understanding. Therefore O Mahāmati, conform yourself to the sense, and do not be engrossed in words and doctrines.'[1]

The purport of these adjectives and phrases is that no conceptual interpretation is possible of Enlightenment or self-realization and that the realization must issue from one's own inner consciousness, independent of scriptural teaching or of another's help. For all that is needed to lead one to the attainment of Pratyātmāryajñāna is within one-

[1] *Laṅkāvatāra*, Nanjō Edition, p. 77.

self, only that it is in a state of confusion owing to wrong judgments (*vikalpa*) cherished and infused (*vāsanā*) in the mind since beginningless time. It requires a direct, personal confirmation or transmission from the Buddhas, but even these latter are unable to awaken us to the exalted state of Enlightenment unless we ourselves concentrate our spiritual efforts in the work of self-emancipation. Therefore, meditation (*dhyāna*) is recommended in the Sūtra as the means of attaining to the truth of the inmost consciousness.

The idea of dhyāna as explained in the *Laṅkāvatāra*, however, is different from what we generally know in Hīnayāna literature[1]—that is, from those kinds of dhyāna mentioned in the previous part of this essay. The Sūtra distinguishes four dhyānas: the first is practised by the unlearned (*bālopacārika*), such as the Śrāvakas, Pratyekabuddhas, and devotees of the Yoga. They have been instructed in the doctrine of nonātman, and regarding the world as impermanent, impure, and pain-producing, they persistently follow these thoughts until they realize the samādhi of thought-extinction. The second dhyāna is designated 'statement-reviewing' (*artha-pravicaya*), by which is meant an intellectual examination of statements or propositions, Buddhist or non-Buddhist, such as 'Each object has its individual marks', 'There is no personal

---

[1] There is however a Sūtra in the Saṁyukta Āgama, fas. XXXIII, p. 93b (Anguttara-Nikāya, XI, 10), dealing with true dhyāna (*ājānīya-jhāna*) which is to be distinguished from untrained dhyāna (*khaḷuṅka-jhāna*). The latter is compared to an ill-disciplined horse (*khaḷuṅka*) kept in the stable that thinks nothing of his duties but only of the fodder he is to enjoy. In a similar way dhyāna can never be practised successfully by those who undertake the exercise merely for the satisfaction of their selfish objects; for such will never come to understand the truth as it is. If emancipation and true knowledge are desired, anger, sleepiness, worrying, and doubt ought to be got rid of, and then the dhyāna can be attained that does not depend upon any of the elements, or space, or consciousness, or nothingness, or unthinkability—the dhyāna that is not dependent upon this world or that world or the heavenly bodies, or upon hearing or seeing or recollecting or recognizing—the dhyāna that is not dependent upon the ideas of attachment or seeking—the dhyāna that is not in conformity with knowledge or contemplation. This 'true dhyāna' then, as is described in this Sūtra in the Nikāyas, is more of the Mahāyāna than of the Hīnayāna so called.

94

Ātman', 'Things are created by an external agency', or 'things are mutually determined'; and after the examination of these themes the practiser of this dhyāna turns his thought on the non-ātman-ness of things (*dharmanairātmya*) and on the characteristic features of the various stages (*bhūmi*) of Bodhisattvaship, and finally in accordance with the sense involved therein he goes on with his contemplative examination. The third dhyāna is called 'Attaching oneself to Thatness' (*tathatālambana*), whereby one realizes that to discriminate the two forms of non-atman-ness is still due to an analytical speculation and that when things are truthfully (*yathābhūtam*) perceived, no such analysis is possible, for then there obtains absolute oneness only. The fourth and last is 'Tathāgata-dhyāna'. In this one enters into the stage of Buddhahood where he enjoys a threefold beatitude belonging to the noble understanding of self-realization and performs wonderful deeds for the sake of all sentient beings.

In these dhyānas we observe a gradual perfection of Buddhist life culminating in the utmost spiritual freedom of Buddhahood, which is above all intellectual conditions and beyond the reach of relative consciousness. Those wonderful, unthinkable (*acintya*) deeds issuing from spiritual freedom are technically called 'deeds performed with no sense of utility' (*anābhogacaryā*), or the 'deeds of no purpose' as referred to elsewhere, and mean the perfection of Buddhist life.

The *Laṅkāvatāra* was thus handed over by Bodhidharma to his first disciple Hui-k'ê as the most illuminating document on the doctrine of Zen. But the development of Zen in China naturally did not follow the line as was indicated in the Sūtra—that is, after the Indian fashion; the soil where the dhyāna of the *Laṅkāvatāra* was transplanted did not favour its growth in the same manner as it did in the original climate. Zen was inspired with the life and spirit of the dhyāna of the Tathāgata, but it created its own mode of manifestation. Indeed this was where it showed its wonderful power of vitality and adaptation.

The Doctrine of Enlightenment as Zen in China

To understand how the doctrine of Enlightenment or self-realization came to be translated in China as Zen Buddhism, we must first see where the Chinese mind varies from the Indian generally. When this is done, Zen will appear as a most natural product of the Chinese soil, where Buddhism has been successfully transplanted in spite of many adverse conditions. Roughly, then, the Chinese are above all a most practical people, while the Indians are visionary and highly speculative. We cannot perhaps judge the Chinese as unimaginative and lacking in the dramatic sense, but when they are compared with the inhabitants of the Buddha's native land they look so grey, so sombre.

The geographical features of each country are singularly reflected in the people. The tropical luxuriance of imagination so strikingly contrasts with the wintry dreariness of common practicalness. The Indians are subtle in analysis and dazzling in poetic flight; the Chinese are children of earthly life, they plod, they never soar away in the air. Their daily life consists in tilling the soil, gathering dry leaves, drawing water, buying and selling, being filial, observing social duties, and developing the most elaborate system of etiquette. Being practical means in a sense being historical, observing the progress of time and recording its traces as they are left behind. The Chinese can very well boast of their being great recorders—such a contrast to the Indian lack of sense of time. Not satisfied with books printed on paper and with ink, the Chinese would engrave their deeds deep in stone, and have developed a special art of stone-cutting. This habit of recording events has developed their literature, and they are quite literary and not at all warlike; they love a peaceful life of culture. Their weakness is that they are willing to sacrifice facts for literary effects, for they are not very exact and scientific. Love of fine rhetoric and beautiful expressions has frequently drowned their practical sense, but here is also their art. Well restrained even in this, their soberness never reaches that form of fantasy which we encounter in most of the Mahā-yāna texts.

The Chinese are in many ways great, their architecture is great indeed, their literary achievements deserve the world's thanks, but logic is not one of their strong points; nor are their philosophy and imagination. When Buddhism with all its characteristically Indian dialectics and imageries was first introduced into China, it must have staggered the Chinese mind. Look at its gods with many heads and arms —something that has never entered into their heads, in fact into no other nation's than the Indian's. Think of the wealth of symbolism with which every being in Buddhist literature seems to be endowed. The mathematical con-ception of infinities, the Bodhisattvas' plan of world-salvation, the wonderful stage-setting before the Buddha begins his sermons, not only in their general outlines but in their details—bold, yet accurate, soaring in flight, yet sure of every step—these and many other features must have been things of wonderment to the practical and earth-plodding people of China.

One quotation from a Mahāyāna Sūtra will convince readers of the difference between Indian and Chinese minds, in regard to their imaginative powers. In the *Saddharma-puṇḍarīka* the Buddha wishes to impress his disciples as to the length of time passed since his attainment of Supreme Enlightenment; he does not merely state that it is a mistake to think that his Enlightenment took place some countable number of years ago under the Bodhi-tree near the town of Gayā; nor does he say in a general way that it happened ages ago, which is very likely the way with the Chinese, but he describes in a most analytical way in how remote an age it was that he came to Enlightenment.

'But, young men of good family, the truth is that many hundred thousand myriads of kotis of æons ago I have arrived at Supreme, Perfect Enlightenment. By way of example, young men of good family, let there be the atoms of earth of fifty hundred thousand myriads of kotis of worlds; let there exist some man who takes one of these atoms of dust and then goes in an eastern direction fifty hundred thousand myriads of kotis of worlds further on, there to deposit that atom of dust; let the man in this manner carry away from all those worlds the whole mass of earth, and in the same manner, and by the same act as supposed, deposit all those atoms in an eastern direction. Now would you think, young men of good family, that anyone should be able to weigh, imagine, count, or determine the number of these worlds? The Lord having thus spoken, the Bodhisattva Mahāsattva Maitreya and the entire host of Bodhisattvas replied: They are incalculable, O Lord, those worlds, countless, beyond the range of thought. Not even all the Śrāvakas and Pratyekabuddhas, O Lord, with their Ārya-knowledge, will be able to imagine, count, or determine them. For us also, O Lord, who are Bodhisattvas standing on the place from whence there is no turning back, this point lies beyond the sphere of our comprehension; so innumerable, O Lord, are those worlds.

'This said, the Buddha spoke to those Bodhisattvas Mahāsattvas as follows: I announce to you, young men of good family, I declare to you: However numerous be those worlds where that man deposits those atoms of dust and where he does not, there are not, young men of good family, in all those hundred thousands of myriads of kotis of worlds, so many dust atoms as there are hundred thousands of myriads of kotis of æons since I have arrived at Supreme, Perfect Enlightenment.[1]

Such a conception of number and such a method of description would never have entered the Chinese mind. They are, of course, capable of conceiving long duration, and great achievements, in which they are not behind any nation; but to express their idea of vastness in the manner of the Indian philosophers would be beyond their understanding.

.   .   .   .   .

[1] Kern's translation, *Sacred Books of the East*, Vol. XXI, pp. 299–300.

When things are not within the reach of conceptual description and yet when they are to be communicated to others, the ways open to most people will be either to remain silent, or to declare them simply to be beyond words, or to resort to negation saying, 'not this', 'not that', or if one were a philosopher, to write a book explaining how logically impossible it was to discourse on such subjects; but the Indians found quite a novel way of illustrating philosophical truths that cannot be applied to analytical reasoning. They resorted to miracles or supernatural phenomena for their illustration. Thus they made the Buddha a great magician; not only the Buddha but almost all the chief characters appearing in the Mahāyāna scriptures became magicians. And in my view this is one of the most charming features of the Mahāyāna texts—this description of supernatural phenomena in connection with the teaching of abstruse doctrine. Some may think it altogether childish and injuring the dignity of the Buddha as teacher of solemn religious truths. But this is a superficial interpretation of the matter. The Indian idealists knew far better; they had a more penetrating imagination which was always effectively employed by them whenever the intellect was put to a task beyond its power.

We must understand that the motive of the Mahāyānists who made the Buddha perform all these magical feats was to illustrate through imageries what in the very nature of things could not be done in an ordinary method open to human intellect. When the intellect failed to analyse the essence of Buddhahood, their rich imagination came in to help them out by visualizing it. When we try to explain Enlightenment logically we always find ourselves involved in contradictions. But when an appeal is made to our symbolical imagination—especially if one is liberally endowed with this faculty—the matter is more readily comprehended. At least this seems to have been the Indian way of conceiving the signification of supernaturalism.

When Vimalakīrti was asked by Śāriputra how such a small room as his with just one seat for himself could accommodate all the hosts of Bodhisattvas and Arhats and Devas numbering many thousands, who were coming there with Mañjuśrī to visit the sick philosopher, replied Vimalakīrti, 'Are you here to seek chairs or the Dharma? . . . One who seeks the Dharma finds it in seeking it in nothing.' Then learning from Mañjuśrī where to obtain seats, he asks a Buddha called Sumerudīparāja to supply him with 32,000 lion-seats, majestically decorated and as high as 84,000 yojanas. When they were brought in, his room, formerly large enough for one seat, now miraculously accommodated all the retinue of Mañjuśrī, each one of whom was comfortably seated in a celestial chair, and yet the whole town of Vaiśāli and the rest of the world did not appear on this account crammed to overflowing. Śāriputra was surprised beyond measure to witness this supernatural event, but Vimalakīrti explained that for those who understand the doctrine of spiritual emancipation, even the Mount of Sumeru could be sealed up in a seed of mustard, and the waves of the four great oceans could be made to flow into one pore of the skin (romakūpa), without even giving any sense of inconvenience to any of the fishes, crocodiles, tortoises, and other living beings in them; the spiritual kingdom was not bound in space and time.

To quote another instance from the first chapter of the Laṅkāvatāra sūtra, which does not appear in the oldest Chinese translation. When King Rāvaṇa was requesting the Buddha through the Bodhisattva Mahāmati to disclose the content of his inner experience, the king unexpectedly noticed his mountain-residence turned into numberless mountains of precious stones and most ornately decorated with celestial grandeur, and on each of these mountains he saw the Buddha manifested. And before each Buddha there stood King Rāvaṇa himself with all his assemblage as well as all the countries in the ten quarters of the world, and in each of those countries there appeared the Tathāgata, before whom again there were King Rāvaṇa, his families, his palaces, his gardens, all decorated exactly in the same style as his own. There was also the Bodhisattva Mahāmati in each of these innumerable assemblies asking the Buddha to declare the content of his inner spiritual experience; and when the Buddha finished his discourse on the subject with hundreds of thousands of exquisite voices, the whole scene suddenly vanished, and the Buddha with all his Bodhisattvas and his followers were no more; then King Rāvaṇa found himself all alone in his old palace. He now reflected: 'Who was he that asked the question? Who was he that listened? What were those objects that appeared before me? Was it a dream? or a magical phenomenon?' He again reflected: 'Things are all like this, they are all creations of one's own mind. When mind discriminates there is manifoldness of things; but when it does not it looks into the true state of things.' When he thus reflected he heard voices in the air and in his own palace, saying: 'Well you have reflected, O King! You should conduct yourself according to this view.'

The Mahāyāna literature is not the only recorder of the miraculous power of the Buddha, which transcends all the relative conditions of space and time as well as of human activities, mental and physical. The Pāli scriptures are by no means behind the Mahāyāna in this respect. Not to speak of the Buddha's threefold knowledge, which consists in the knowledge of the past, the future, and of his own emancipation, he can also practise what is known as the three wonders, which are the mystic wonder, the wonder of education, and the wonder of manifestation. But when we carefully examine the miracles described in the Nikāyas, we see that they have no other objects in view than the magnification and deification of the personality of the Buddha.

The recorders of these miracles must have thought that they could thus make their master greater and far above ordinary mortals in the estimate of their rivals. From our modern point of view it was quite childish for them to imagine that any unusual deeds performed by their master would attract, as we read in the *Kevaddha Sutta*, people's attention to Buddhism and recognize its superior value on that very account; but in those ancient days in India, the masses, nay even learned scholars, thought a great deal of supernaturalism, and naturally the Buddhists made the best possible use of this belief. But when we come to the Mahāyāna Sūtras we at once perceive that the miracles described here on a much grander scale have nothing to do with supernaturalism as such or with any ulterior motives such as propagandism or self-aggrandizement, but that they are essentially and intimately connected with the doctrine itself which is expounded in the texts. For instance, in the *Prajñā-pāramitā Sūtra* every part of the body of the Buddha simultaneously emits innumerable rays illuminating at once the furthest ends of the worlds, whereas in the *Avataṁsaka Sutra* the different parts of his body shoot out beams of light on different occasions. In the *Saddharma-puṇḍarīka Sūtra* a ray of light issues from within the circle of hair between the eyebrows of the Buddha which illuminates over eighteen hundred thousand Buddha-countries in the eastern quarter, revealing every being in them, even the inhabitants of the deepest hell called Avici. It is evident that the Mahāyāna writers of these Sūtras had in their minds something much different from the Hīnayāna compilers of the Nikāyas in their narratives of the miraculous power of the Buddha. What that something was I have here pointed out in a most general way. A systematic study in detail of the Mahāyāna supernaturalism will no doubt be an interesting one.

At all events the above references will suffice, I believe, to establish my thesis that the reason for the introduction of supernaturalism into the Mahāyāna literature of Buddhism was to demonstrate the intellectual impossibility of comprehending spiritual facts. While philosophy exhausted its resources logically to explain them, Vimalakīrti like Bāhva, a Vedic mystic, remained silent; not satisfied with this, the Indian Mahāyāna writers further introduced supernaturalistic symbolism, but it remained with the Chinese Zen Buddhists to invent their own methods to cope, according to their own needs and insight, with the difficulties of communicating one's highest and deepest spiritual experience known as Enlightenment in Buddhism.

The Chinese have no aptitude like the Indians to hide themselves in the clouds of mystery and super-naturalism. Chwang-tzŭ and Lieh-tzŭ were the nearest to the Indian type of mind in ancient China, but their mysticism does not begin to approach that of the Indian Mahāyānists in grandeur, in elaborateness, and in the height of soaring imagination. Chwang-tzŭ did his best when he rode up in the air on the back of the Tai-p'eng, whose wings soared like overhanging clouds; and Lieh-tzŭ when he could command winds and clouds as his charioteers. The later Taoists dreamed of ascending to the heavens after so many years of ascetic discipline and by taking an elixir of life concocted from various rare herbs. Thus in China we have so many Taoist hermits living in the mountains far away from human habitations. No Chinese saints or philosophers are, however, recorded in history who have been capable of equalling Vimalakīrti or Mañjuśrī or even any of the Arhats. The Confucian verdict that superior man never talks about miracles, wonders, and supernaturalism, is the true expression of Chinese psychology. The Chinese are thoroughly practical. They must have their own way of interpreting the doctrine of Enlightenment as applied to their daily life, and they could not help creating Zen as an expression of their inmost spiritual experience.

If the imagery of supernaturalism did not appeal to sober Chinese character, how did the Chinese followers of Enlightenment contrive to express themselves? Did they adopt the intellectual method of the Śūnyatā philosophy? No; this, too, was not after their taste, nor was it quite within the reach of their mental calibre. The *Prajñā-pāramitā* was an Indian creation and not the Chinese. They could have produced a Chwang-tzŭ or those Taoist dreamers of the Six Dynasties, but not a Nāgārjuna or a Śankāra.

The Chinese genius was to demonstrate itself in some other way. When they began inwardly to assimilate Buddhism as the doctrine of Enlightenment, the only course that opened to their concrete practical minds was to produce Zen. When we come to Zen after seeing all the wonderful miracles displayed by the Indian Mahāyāna writers, and after the highly abstracted speculations of the Mādhyamika thinkers, what a change of scenery do we have here? No rays are issuing from the Buddha's forehead, no retinues of Boddhisattvas reveal themselves before you, there is indeed nothing that would particularly strike your senses as odd or extraordinary, or as beyond intelligence, beyond the ken of logical reasoning. The people you associate with are all ordinary mortals like yourselves, no abstract ideas, no dialectical subtleties confront you. Mountains tower high towards the sky, rivers all pour into the ocean. Plants sprout in the spring and flowers bloom in red. When the moon shines serenely, poets grow mildly drunk and sing a song of eternal peace. How prosaic, how ordinary, we may say! but here was the Chinese soul, and Buddhism came to grow in it.

When a monk asks who is the Buddha, the master points at his image in the Buddha Hall; no explanations are given, no arguments are suggested. When the mind is the subject of discourse, asks a monk, 'What is mind, anyway?' 'Mind,' says the master. 'I do not understand, Sir.' 'Neither do I,' quickly comes from the master. On another occasion, a monk is worried over the question of immortality. 'How can I escape the bondage of birth and death?' Answers the master, 'Where are you?' The Zen adepts as a rule never waste time in responding to questions, nor are they at all argumentative. Their answers are always curt and final, which follow the questions with the rapidity of lightning. Someone asked, 'What is the fundamental teaching of the Buddha?' Said the master, 'There is enough breeze in this fan to keep me cool.' What a most matter-of-fact answer this! That inevitable formula of Buddhism, the Fourfold Noble Truth, apparently has no place in the scheme of Zen teaching, nor does that persistently enigmatic statement in the *Prajñā-pāramitā*, 'taccittam yaccittam acittam', threaten us here.

Ummon (Yün-mên) once appeared in the pulpit, and said, 'In this school of Zen no words are needed; what, then, is the ultimate essence of Zen teaching?' Thus himself proposing the question, he extended both his arms, and without further remarks came down from the pulpit. This was the way the Chinese Buddhists interpreted the doctrine of Enlightenment, this was the way they expounded the *Pratyātmajñānagocara* of the *Laṅkāvatāra*. And for the Chinese Buddhists this was the only way, if the inner experience of the Buddha were to be demonstrated, not intellectually or analytically, nor in supernatural manners, but directly in our practical life. For life, as far as it is lived *in concreto*, is above concepts as well as images. To understand it we have to dive into it and to come in touch with it personally; to pick up or cut out a piece of it for inspection murders it; when you think you have got into the essence of it, it is no more, for it has ceased to live but lies immobile and all dried up. For this reason Chinese minds, ever since the coming of Bodhidharma, worked on the problem how best to present the doctrine of Enlightenment in their native garment cut to suit their modes of feeling and thinking, and it was not until after Hui-nêng (Yenō) that they satisfactorily solved the problem and the great task of building up a school to be known thenceforward as Zen was accomplished.

That Zen was the thing Chinese minds wanted to have when they thoroughly comprehended the teaching of Buddhism is proved by the two incontestable historical facts; first, after the establishment of Zen, it was this teaching that ruled China while all the other schools of Buddhism, except the Pure Land sect, failed to survive; and secondly, before Buddhism was translated into Zen it never came into an intimate relation with the native thought of China, by which I mean Confucianism.

Let us see first how Zen came to rule the spiritual life of China. The inner sense of Enlightenment was not understood in China, except intellectually, in the earlier days of Buddhism. This was natural, seeing that it was in this respect that the Chinese mind was excelled by the Indian. As I said before, the boldness and subtlety of Mahāyāna philosophy must have fairly stunned the Chinese, who had, before the introduction of Buddhism, practically no system of thought worthy of the name, except moral science. In this latter they were conscious of their own strength; even such devout Buddhists as I-ching (Gijō) and Hs'üan-chuang (Genjō) acknowledged it, with all their ardour for the Yogācāra psychology and the Avataṁsaka metaphysics; they thought that their country, as far as moral culture was concerned, was ahead of the land of their faith or at least had nothing to learn from the latter.

As the Mahāyāna Sūtras and Shastras were translated in rapid succession by able, learned, devout scholars, both native and Indian, the Chinese mind was led to explore a region where they had not ventured very far before. In the early Chinese biographical histories of Buddhism, we notice commentators, expounders, and philosophers far outnumbering translators and adepts in dhyāna so called. The Buddhist scholars were at first quite busily engaged in assimilating intellectually the various doctrines propounded in Mahāyāna literature. Not only were these doctrines deep and complicated but they were also contradicting one another, at least on the surface. If the scholars were to enter into the depths of Buddhist thought, they had to dispose of these entanglements somehow. But if they were sufficiently critical, they could do that with comparative ease, which was, however, something we could never expect of those earlier Buddhists; for even in these modern days critical Buddhist scholars will, in some quarters, be regarded as not quite devout and orthodox. They all had not a shadow of doubt as to the genuineness of the Mahā-yānist texts as faithfully and literally recording the very words of the Buddha, and therefore they had to plan out some systems of reconciliation between diverse doctrines taught in the Scriptures. They had to find out what was the primary object of the Buddha's appearance in the world ignorant, corrupted, and given up to the karma of eternal transmigration. Such efforts on the part of Buddhist philosophers developed what is to be distinctly designated as Chinese Buddhism.

While this intellectual assimilation was going on on the one hand, the practical side of Buddhism was also assiduously studied. Some were followers of the Vinaya texts, and others devoted themselves to the mastery of dhyāna. But what was here known as dhyāna was not the dhyāna of Zen Buddhism; it was a meditation, concentrating one's thought on some ideas such as impermanence, egolessness of things, chain of causation, or the attributes of the Buddha. Even Bodhidharma, the founder of Zen Buddhism, was regarded by historians as belonging to this class of dhyāna-adepts, his peculiar merits as teacher of an entirely novel school of Buddhism were not fully appreciated. This was inevitable; the people of China were not yet quite ready to accept the new form, for they had only inadequately grasped the doctrine of Enlightenment in all its bearings.

The importance of Enlightenment in its practical aspects, however, was not altogether overlooked in the maze of doctrinal intricacies. Chih-i (Chigi, 531–597), one of the founders of the T'ien Tai school and the greatest Buddhist philosopher in China, was fully awake to the significance of dhyāna as the means of attaining Enlightenment. With all his analytical powers, his speculation had room enough for the practice of dhyāna. His work on 'Tranquillization and Contemplation' is explicit on this point. His idea was to carry out intellectual and spiritual exercises in perfect harmony, and not partially to emphasize either one of the two, Samādhi or Prajñā, at the expense of the other. Unfortunately, his followers grew more and more onesided until they neglected the dhyāna practice for the sake of intellection. Hence their antagonistic attitude

later towards advocates of Zen Buddhism, for which, however, the latter were to a certain extent to be responsible
too.

It was due to Bodhidharma (died 528)[1] that Zen came
to be the Buddhism of China. It was he that started this
movement which proved so fruitful among a people given
up to the practical affairs of life. When he declared his
message, it was still tinged with Indian colours, he could not
be entirely independent of the traditional Buddhist metaphysics of the times. His allusion to the *Vajra-samādhi* and
the *Laṅkāvatāra* was natural, but the seeds of Zen were
sown by his hands. It now remained with his native disciples to see to it that these seeds grew up in harmony with
the soil and climate. It took about two hundred years for
the Zen seeds to bear fruit, rich and vigorous in life, and
fully naturalized while retaining intact the essence of what
makes up Buddhism.

Hui-nêng (637–713), who was the sixth patriarch after
Bodhidharma, was the real Chinese founder of Zen; for
it was through him and his direct followers that Zen could
cast off the garment borrowed from India and began to
put on one cut and sewn by the native hands. The spirit
of Zen was of course the same as the one that came to
China transmitted without interruption from the Buddha,
but the form of expression was thoroughly Chinese, for it
was their own creation. The rise of Zen after this was
phenomenal. The latent energy that had been stored up
during the time of naturalization suddenly broke out in
active work, and Zen had almost a triumphal march
through the whole land of Cathay. During the T'ang
dynasty (618–906), when Chinese culture reached its consummation, great Zen masters succeeded one after another
in building up monasteries and educating monks as well as
lay-disciples who were learned not only in the Confucian
classics but in the Mahayana lore of Buddhism. The
emperors too were not behind them in paying respects to

[1] For this and the following, see the Essay entitled, 'History of Zen
Buddhism from Bodhidharma to Hui-nêng', p. 151*ff.*

these Zen seers, who were invited to come to the court in order to give sermons to these august personages. When for political reasons Buddhism was persecuted, which caused the loss of many valuable documents, works of art, and the decline of some schools, Zen was always the first to recover itself and to renew its activities with redoubled energy and enthusiasm. Throughout the Five Dynasties, in the first half of the tenth century, when China was torn up into minor kingdoms again, and general political situations seemed to be unfavourable to the thriving of religious sentiments, Zen prospered as before and the masters kept up their monastic centres undisturbed.

With the rise of the Sung dynasty (960–1279) Zen reached the height of its development and influence, while the other sects of Buddhism showed signs of rapid decline. When history opens on the pages of the Yüan (1280–1367) and the Ming (1368–1661) dynasties, Buddhism is found identified with Zen. The Kegon (Avataṁsaka), Tendai (T'ien-tai), Sanron (San-lun), Kusha (Abhidharma-kośa), Hossō (Yogācāra) and Shingon (Mantra), if they were not completely wiped out through persecution, suffered tremendously from the lack of fresh blood. Perhaps they were to die out anyway on account of their not having been completely assimilated by Chinese thought and feeling; there was too much of an Indian element which prevented them from being fully acclimatized. In any event Zen as the essence of the Buddha's mind continued to flourish so that any Chinese minds at all inclined towards Buddhism came to study Zen and neglected the rest of the Buddhist schools still in existence though at the last stage of their productive activity. The only form of Buddhism that retains its vitality to a certain extent even to this day is Zen, more or less modified to accommodate the (Pure Land) tendency that had been growing soon after the introduction of Buddhism into China.

There was reason for this state of things in the religious history of China, and it was thus that Zen dispensed with the images and concepts and modes of thinking that were imported from India along with Buddhist thought; and out of its own consciousness Zen created an original literature best adapted to the exposition of the truth of Enlightenment. This literature was unique in many senses, but it was in perfect accordance with the Chinese mental *modus operandi* and naturally powerfully moved them to the core. Bodhidharma taught his disciples to look directly into the essence of the teaching of the Buddha, discarding the outward manners of presentation; he told them not to follow the conceptual and analytical interpretation of the doctrine of Enlightenment. Literary adherents of the Sūtras objected to this and did all they could to prevent the growth of the teaching of Dharma. But it grew on in spite of oppositions.

The disciples mastered the art of grasping the central fact of Buddhism. When this was accomplished, they proceeded to demonstrate it according to their own methods, using their own terminology, regardless of the traditional or rather imported way of expression. They did not entirely abandon the old manner of speaking; for they refer to Buddha, Tathāgata, Nirvāṇa, Bodhi, Trikāya, Karma, transmigration, emancipation, and many other ideas making up the body of Buddhism; but they make no mention of the Twelvefold Chain of Origination, the Fourfold Noble Truth, or the Eightfold Righteous Path. When we read Zen literature without being told of its relation to Buddhism, we may almost fail to recognize in it such things as are generally regarded as specifically Buddhist. When Yakusan (Yüeh-shan, 751–834) saw a monk, he asked, 'Where do you come from?' 'I come from south of the Lake.' 'Is the Lake overflowing with water?' 'No, sir, it is not yet overflowing.' 'Strange,' said the master, 'after so much rain why does it not overflow?' To this last query the monk failed to give a satisfactory answer, whereupon Ungan (Yün-yen), one of Yakusan's disciples, said, 'Overflowing, indeed!' while Dōsan (Tung-shan), another of his disciples, exclaimed, 'In what kalpa did it ever fail to over-flow?' In these dialogues do we detect any trace of Buddhism?

Do they not look as if they were talking about an affair of most ordinary occurrence? But, according to the masters, their talks are brim-full of Zen, and Zen literature is indeed abounding in such apparent trivialities. In fact, so far as its phraseology and manner of demonstration are concerned, Zen looks as if it had nothing to do with Buddhism, and some critics are almost justified in designating Zen as a Chinese anomaly of Buddhism as was referred to at the beginning of this Essay.

In the history of Chinese literature, Zen writings known as *Yü-lu* (Goroku) form a class by themselves, and it is due to them that the Chinese colloquialism of the T'ang and the early Sung dynasties has been preserved. Men of letters in China despised to write except in classical style, deliberately choosing such words, phrases, and expressions as enhanced the grace of the composition. All the literature we have of those early days of Chinese culture therefore is the model of such a cultivated style. The Zen masters were not necessarily despisers of classicism, they took to fine literature as much as their contemporaries, they were well educated and learned too; but they found colloquialism a better and more powerful medium for the utterance of their inner experiences. This is generally the case with spiritual reformers, who want to express themselves through the medium most intimate to their feelings and best suited for their original ways of viewing things. They avoid wherever possible such nomenclature as has been in use and filled with old associations which are apt to lack in living purposes and therefore in vivifying effects. Living experiences ought to be told in a living language and not in worn-out images and concepts. The Zen masters therefore did what they could not help doing and made free use of the living words and phrases of the day. Does this not prove that in China Buddhism through Zen ceased to be a foreign importation and was transformed into an original creation of the native mind? And just because Zen could turn itself into a native product, it survived all the other schools of Buddhism. In other words, Zen was the only form in which the Chinese mind could accommodate, appreciate, and assimilate the Buddhist doctrine of Enlightenment.

I hope I have shown how Buddhism—that is, the doctrine of Enlightenment—had to be transformed into Zen in China, and through this transformation Zen survived the other schools of Buddhism. Let us now take up the second point, as referred to before, in which we will see how Zen came to create the Sung philosophy. When I say that Buddhism did not really affect Chinese thought until it was converted into Zen, through which the creative genius of China began to formulate its philosophy along a much deeper and more idealistic line of thought than that of the Ante-Ch'in period, there will be many who will object to this view. It is true that Buddhism began to make its influence felt among Chinese thinkers even during the latter Han dynasty, as we see, for instance, in Mou-tzŭ's 'Essay on Reason and Error' written between A.D. 190–220. After this there were many writers who discussed the Buddhist doctrines of Karma and Causation and Immortality; for these were some of the ideas introduced from India through Buddhism.

It was with the Taoists, however, the Buddhists had much heated controversy from the sixth century on. The way Buddhism exerted its influence over Taoism was not only in form of controversy but in actually moulding their thought and literature. There were so many points of contact between Taoism and Buddhism: and naturally the first object against which Buddhism worked, as it grew in importance and power not only as a religious system but as philosophy and the possessor of an inexhaustible wealth of knowledge, was Taoism; while it was admitted that Buddhism in its turn borrowed many things from Taoism in order to make itself more easily acceptable to the native minds. On the whole, Taoism owes more to Buddhism so far as its organization, rituals, literature and philosophy are concerned. Taoism systematized after the Buddhist model all the popular superstitions native to China and built up a religious medley in which the Indian elements are found more or less incongruously blended with Laotzuanism and the popular desire for immortality, worldy welfare, and what they call 'purity'.

But Taoism as it is believed popularly is so full of superstitions that it is not in vital contact with the main current of orthodox Chinese thought which is represented, maintained, and cherished by the literati including the government officials. To a greater extent Taoism is the popular and superstitious Chinese rendering of Buddhism, but there will be many critics, the present writer for one, who rather hesitate to consider the essence of Buddhism sufficiently transcribed in terms of the Taoists. Unless the Confucians were not moved to assimilate Buddhist thought in their system, so naturally that they attempted to reconstruct the whole frame of Confucian ideas, not merely for the sake of reconciliation, but for the sake of deepening, enriching, and resuscitating it, we cannot say that Buddhism entered into the life of Chinese thought and became the real possession of the Chinese mind. But this was done during the Sung dynasty when the Confucian philosophers took in Buddhist ideas into their teaching and reconstructed the whole system on a new basis, which, however, was considered by them to be the necessary course of growth for Confucianism. Whatever this was, there is no doubt that the Sung philosophy was enriched and deepened by absorbing Buddhist views. In this, all the historians of Chinese intellectual development agree.

There is a question, however, one may ask concerning this general reconstruction of Confucianism on the idealistic Buddhist scheme. If Zen did not grow up in China as the native interpretation of the Doctrine of Enlightenment and prepare the way for the rise of such great Confucian writers as Chou Tun-I (1017–1073), the Ch'êng brothers, Ch'êng Hao (1032–1085) and Ch'êng I (1035–1107), and Chu Hsi (1130–1200), would there have been a Sung revival of the orthodox Chinese teaching? To my view, without Zen the Sung dynasty would not have seen the phenomenal uprising of what the Chinese historians call the 'Science of Reason'. As we already said, Zen was the only form in which Buddhism could enter into the Chinese mind. This being the case, whatever they later produced in the realm of thought could not but be tinged with Zen. See how the psychological school of Yogācāra was received by the native thinkers. It was first advocated, propounded, and commented by Hsüan-chuang and his great disciples, but this profound study of the human mind was too analytical even for the best minds of China, and did not thrive very long after Hsüan-chuang.

Then how did the Prajñā-pāramitā philosophy fare? It was brought into China in the first century soon after the introduction of Buddhism itself and later most ably supported and interpreted by Kumārajīva and his Chinese pupils. It had a better prospect than the Yogācāra because its Chinese counterpart was found in the teaching of Lao-tzŭ and his followers. Those two groups of philosophers, Buddhist and Laotzŭan, may be classed as belonging to the same type of thought; but even in this case the Chinese did not show any great disposition to embrace this Śūnyatā system. Why was this? The reason was obvious, seeing that in spite of a certain agreement between the two schools on a very broad basis, the Śūnyatā mode of thinking was altogether too metaphysical, too high-flown, or, from the Chinese point of view, too much *in nubibus*, and the practical tendency of the native minds naturally failed to grow on it; even in the disciples of Lao-tzŭ and Chwang-tzŭ there was the taint or virtue of utilitarianism which is deeply ingrained in all the Chinese modes of feeling.

Besides the Mādhyamika school of Nāgārjuna and the Yogācāra school of Asanga, both of which developed in the country of the Buddha itself, there were chih-i's Tendai philosophy and Hsien-shou's (643–712) Avataṁsaka system of Buddhism. These latter were in a sense the creations of the native Buddhist thinkers, and if they were at all assimilable by their compatriots, they would not have been neglected, and their study, instead of being confined within a narrow circle of Buddhist specialists, would have over-flowed into the Confucian as well as the Taoist boundaries. That they did not do so proves the fact that they were still foreign and a kind of translation, not literary indeed, but more or less conceptional. Therefore, there was no other way left for Buddhism but to be transformed into Zen before it could be thoroughly acclimatized and grow as a native plant. When this was achieved because it was in the in-herent nature of Buddhism that this achievement was to take place, Zen became the flesh and bones of Chinese thought and inspired the Confucians of the Sung dynasty to reconstruct the foundation of their philosophy on the idealistic plans of Buddhism.

We may conclude now that Zen, in spite of the uncouth-ness and extraordinariness of its outward features, belongs to the general system of Buddhism. And by Buddhism we mean not only the teaching of the Buddha himself as recorded in the earliest Āgamas, but the later speculations, philosophical and religious, concerning the person and life of the Buddha. His personal greatness was such as occasion-ally made his disciples advance theories somewhat contrary to the advice supposed to have been given by their Master. This was inevitable. The world with all its contents, in-dividually as well as a whole, is subject to our subjective interpretation, not a capricious interpretation indeed, but growing out of our inner necessity, our religious yearnings. Even the Buddha as an object of one's religious experience could not escape this, his personality was so constituted as to awaken in us every feeling and thought that goes under the name of Buddhism now. The most significant and fruitful ideas that were provoked by him were concerned with his Enlightenment and Nirvāṇa. These two facts stood out most prominently in his long peaceful life of seventy-nine years, and all the theories and beliefs that are bound up with the Buddha are attempts to understand these facts in terms of our own religious experience. Thus Buddhism has grown to have a much wider meaning than is understood by most scholars.

The Buddha's Enlightenment and Nirvāṇa were two separate ideas in his life as it unfolded in history so many centuries ago, but from the religious point of view they are to be regarded as one idea. That is to say, to understand the content and the value of Enlightenment is the same as realizing the signification of Nirvāṇa. Taking a stand on this, the Mahāyānists developed two currents of thought: the one was to rely on our intellectual efforts to the furthest extent they could reach, and the other, pursuing the practical method adopted by the Buddha himself, indeed by all Indian truth-seekers, endeavoured to find in the practice of dhyāna something directly leading to Enlightenment. It goes without saying that in both of these efforts the original impulse lies in the inmost religious consciousness of pious Buddhists.

The Mahāyāna texts compiled during a few centuries after the Buddha testify to the view here presented. Of these, the one expressly composed to propagate the teaching of the Zen school is the *Laṅkāvatāra*, in which the content of Enlightenment is, so far as words admit, presented from a psychological, philosophical, and practical point of view. When this was introduced into China and thoroughly assimilated according to the Chinese methods of thinking and feeling, the main thesis of the Sūtra came to be demonstrated in such a way as is now considered characteristically Zen. The truth has many avenues of approach through which it makes itself known to the human mind. But the choice it makes depends on certain limitations under which it works. The superabundance of Indian imagination issued in supernaturalism and wonderful symbolism, and the Chinese sense of practicalness and its love for the solid everyday facts of life, resulted in Zen Buddhism. We may now be able to understand, though only tentatively by most readers at present, the following definitions of Zen offered by its masters:

When Jōshu was asked what Zen was, he answered, 'It is cloudy today and I won't answer.'

To the same question, Ummon's reply was, 'That's it.' On another occasion the master was not at all affirmative, for he said, 'Not a word to be predicated.'

These being some of the definitions given to Zen by the masters, in what relationship did they conceive of Zen as standing to the doctrine of Enlightenment taught in the Sūtras? Did they conceive it after the manner of the *Laṅkāvatāra* or after that of the *Prajñā-pāramitā*? No, Zen had to have its own way; the Chinese mind refused blindly to follow the Indian models. If this is still to be contested, read the following:

A monk asked Kan (Chien), who lived in Haryo (Pa-ling), 'Is there any difference between the teaching of the Patriarch and that of the Sūtras, or not?' Said the master, 'When the cold weather comes, the fowl flies up in the trees, while the wild duck goes down into water.' Ho-yen (Fa-yen) of Gosozan (Wu-tsu-shan) commented on this, saying: 'The great teacher of Pa-ling has expressed only a half of the truth. I would not have it so. Mine is: When water is scooped in hands, the moon is reflected in them; when the flowers are handled, the scent soaks into the robe.'

ENLIGHTENMENT AND IGNORANCE

I

STRANGE though it may seem, the fact is that Buddhist scholars are engrossed too much in the study of what they regard as the Buddha's teaching and his disciples' exposition of the Dharma, so called, while they neglect altogether the study of the Buddha's spiritual experience itself. According to my view, however, the first thing we have to do in the elucidation of Buddhist thought is to inquire into the nature of this personal experience of the Buddha, which is recorded to have presented itself to his inmost consciousness at the time of Enlightenment (*sambodhi*). What the Buddha taught his disciples was the conscious outcome of his intellectual elaboration to make them see and realize what he himself had seen and realized. This intellectual outcome, however philosophically presented, does not necessarily enter into the inner essence of Enlightenment experienced by the Buddha. When we want, therefore, to grasp the spirit of Buddhism, which essentially develops from the content of Enlightenment, we have to get acquainted with the signification of the experience of the founder—experience by virtue of which he is indeed the Buddha and the founder of the religious system which goes under his name. Let us see what record we have of this experience, and what were its antecedents and consequences.[1]

[1] The story of Enlightenment is told in the Dīgha-Nikāya, XIV, and also in the Introduction to the Jātaka Tales, in the Mahāvastu, and the Majjhima-Nikāya, XXVI and XXXVI, and again in the Samyutta-Nikāya, XII. In detail they vary more or less, but not materially. The Chinese translation of the *Sūtra on the Cause and Effect in the Past and Present*, which seems to be a later version than the Pali *Mahāpadāna*, gives a somewhat different story, but as far as my point of argument is concerned, the main issue remains practically the same. Aśvaghosha's *Buddhacarita* is highly poetical. The *Lalita-vistara* belongs to the Mahāyāna. In this

There is a Sūtra in the Dīgha-Nikāya known as the *Mahāpadāna Suttanta*, in which the Buddha is represented as enlightening his disciples concerning the six Buddhas anterior to him. The facts relating to their lives as Bodhisattvas and Buddhas are almost identical in each case except some incidental details: for the Buddhas are all supposed to have had one and the same career. When therefore Gautama, the Buddha of the present Kalpa, talks about his predecessors in this wise, including the story of Enlightenment, he is simply recapitulating his own earthly life, and everything he states here as having occurred to his predecessors, except such matters as parentage, social rank, birthplace, length of life, etc., must be regarded as also having happened to himself. This is especially true with his spiritual experience known as Enlightenment.[1]

When the Bodhisattva, as the Buddha is so designated prior to his attainment of Buddhahood, was meditating in seclusion, the following consideration came upon him: 'Verily this world has fallen upon trouble (*kiccha*); one is born, and grows old, and dies, and falls from one state, and springs up in another. And from this suffering, moreover, no one knows of any way of escape, even from decay and death. O when shall a way of escape from this suffering be made known, from decay and death?' Thus thinking, the

Essay I have tried to take my material chiefly from *The Dialogues of the Buddha*, translated by Rhys Davids, *The Kindred Sayings*, translated by Mrs. Rhys Davids, Majjhima-Nikāya, translated by Sīlacāra, and the same by Neumann, the Chinese Āgamas and others.

[1] The idea that there were some more Buddhas in the past seems to have originated very early in the history of Buddhism as we may notice here, and its further development, combined with the idea of the Jātaka, finally culminated in the conception of a Bodhisattva, which is one of the characteristic features of Mahāyāna Buddhism.

The six Buddhas of the past later increased into twenty-three or twenty-four in the *Buddha-vamsa* and *Prajñā-pāramitā* and even into forty-two in the *Lalita-vistara*. This idea of having predecessors or forerunners seems to have been general among ancient peoples. In China, Confucius claimed to have transmitted his doctrine from Yao and Shun, and Lao-tzŭ from the Emperor Huang. In India, Jainism, which has, not only in the teaching but in the personality of the founder, many similarities to Buddhism, mentions twenty-three predecessors, naturally more or less corresponding so closely to those of Buddhism.

Bodhisattva reasoned out that decay and death arose, from birth, birth from becoming, becoming from grasping, grasping from craving, until he came to the mutual conditioning of name-and-form (*nāmarūpa*) and cognition (*viññāna*).[1] Then he reasoned back and forth from the coming-to-be of this entire body of evil to its final ceasing-to-be—and at this thought there arose to the Bodhisattva an insight (*cakkhu*)[2] into things not heard of before, and knowledge arose, and reason arose, wisdom arose, light arose. (*Bodhisattassa pubbe ananussutesu dhammesu cakkhum udapādi, ñāṇam udapādi, paññā udapādi, vijjā udapādi, āloka udapādi.*)

He then exclaimed: 'I have penetrated this Dharma, deep, hard to perceive, hard to understand, calm, sublime, no mere dialectic, subtle, intelligible, only to the wise. (*Dhammo gambhīro duddaso duranubodho santo panito atakkāvacaro nipuṇo pandito vedanīyo.*) But this is a race devoting itself to the things to which it clings, devoted thereto, delighting therein. And for a race devoting itself to the things to which it clings, devoted thereto, delighting therein, this

---

[1] It is highly doubtful that the Buddha had a very distinct and definite scheme for the theory of Causation or Dependence or Origination, as the Paticca-samuppāda is variously translated. In the present Sūtra he does not go beyond Viññāna (consciousness or cognition), while in its accepted form now the Chain starts with Ignorance (*avijjā*). We have, however, no reason to consider this Tenfold Chain of Causation the earliest and most authoritative of the doctrine of Paticca-samuppāda. In many respects the Sūtra itself shows evidence of a later compilation. The point I wish to discuss here mainly concerns itself with the Buddha's intellectual efforts to explain the realities of life by the theory of causation. That the Buddha regarded Ignorance as the principle of birth-and-death, and therefore of misery in this world, is a well-established fact in the history of Buddhism.

[2] Cakkhu literally means an eye. It is often found in combination with such terms as paññā (wisdom or reason), buddha, or samanta (all-round), when it means a faculty beyond ordinary relative understanding. As was elsewhere noticed, it is significant that in Buddhism, both Mahāyāna and Hīnayāna, seeing (*passato*) is so emphasized, and especially in this case the mention of an 'eye' which sees directly into things never before presented to one's mind is quite noteworthy. It is this cakkhu or paññā-cakkhu in fact that, transcending the conditionality of the Fourfold Noble Truth or the Chain of Origination, penetrates (*sacchikato*) into the very ground of consciousness, from which springs the opposition of subject and object.

were a matter hard to perceive, to wit, that this is conditioned by that, and all that happens is by way of cause. This,
too, were a matter hard to discern: the tranquillization of
all the activities of life, the renunciation of all substrata
of rebirth, the destruction of craving, the death of passion,
quietude of heart, Nirvāṇa.'

The Buddha then uttered the following verse in which
he expressed his reluctance to preach the Dharma to the
world at large—the Dharma which was realized in him by
nana—which he saw visibly, face to face, without any
traditional instruction:

> 'This that through many toils I've won—
> Enough! why should I make it known
> By folk with lust and hate consumed
> Not this the Truth[1] that can be grasped!
> Against the stream of common thought,
> Deep, subtle, difficult, delicate,
> Unseen 'twill be by passion's slaves
> Cloaked in the murk of Ignorance.'[2]

According to this report, transmitted by the compilers
of the Nikāyas, which is also confirmed by the other
literature we have of the Buddha's Enlightenment, what
flashed through his mind must have been an experience
most unusual and not taking place in our everyday consciousness, even in the consciousness of a wise, learned,
and thoughtful man. Thus, he naturally wished to pass
away into Nirvāṇa without attempting to propagate the
Dharma, but this idea was abandoned when Great Brahma
spoke to the Buddha in verse thus:

[1] Here, as well as in the next verse, 'the truth' stands for Dharma.
[2] We have, besides this, another verse supposed to have been uttered
by the Buddha at the moment of Supreme Enlightenment; it is known as
the Hymn of Victory. It was quoted in my previous Essay on Zen
Buddhism and the Doctrine of Enlightenment. The Hymn is unknown
in the Mahāyāna literature. The *Lalita-vistara* has only this:
'Chinna vartmopasanta rajāḥ sushkā āsravā na punaḥ sravānti;
Chinne vartmani vartata duḥkhasyaisho 'nta ucyate.'

'As on a crag, on crest of mountain standing,
    A man might watch the people far below,
E'en so do thou, O Wisdom fair, ascending,
    O Seer of all, the terraced heights of Truth,
Look down, from grief released, upon the nations
    Sunken in grief, oppressed with birth and age.

Arise, thou Hero! Conqueror in the battle!
    Thou freed from debt! Lord of the pilgrim band!
Walk the world o'er, and sublime and blessed Teacher!
    Teach us the Truth; there are who'll understand.'

There is no doubt that it was this spiritual experience that converted the Bodhisattva into the Buddha, the Perfectly Wise, the Bhagavat, the Arhat, the King of the Dharma, the Tathagata, the All-knowing One, and the Conqueror. In this, all the records we have, Hīnayāna and Mahāyāna agree.

Here, then, arises the most significant question in the history of Buddhism. What was it in this experience that made the Buddha conquer Ignorance (*avijjā, avidyā*) and freed him from the Defilements (*āsava, āśrava*)? What was the insight or vision he had into things, which had never before been presented to his mind? Was it his doctrine of universal suffering due to Thirst (*taṇhā, triṣhṇā*) and Grasping (*upādāna*)? Was it his causation theory by which he traced the source of pain and suffering to Ignorance?

It is quite evident that his intellectual activity was not the efficient cause of Enlightenment. 'Not to be grasped by mere logic' (*atakkāvacara*) is the phrase we constantly encounter in Buddhist literature, Pāli and Sanskrit. The satisfaction the Buddha experienced in this case was altogether too deep, too penetrating, and too far-reaching in result to be a matter of mere logic. The intellectual solution of a problem is satisfying enough as far as the blockage has been removed, but it is not sufficiently fundamental to enter into the depths of our soul-life. All scholars are not saints and all saints are by no means scholarly. The Buddha's intellectual survey of the Law of Origination (*paticca-samuppāda*), however perfect and thoroughgoing, could not make him so completely sure of his conquest over Ignorance, Pain, Birth, and Defilements. Tracing things to their origin or subjecting them to a scheme of concatenation is one thing, but to subdue them, to bring them to subjection in the actuality of life, is quite another thing. In the one the intellect alone is active, but in the other there is the operation of the will—and the will is the man. The Buddha was not the mere discoverer of the Twelvefold Chain of Causation, he took hold of the chain itself in his hands and broke it into pieces so that it would never again bind him to slavery.

His insight reached the bottom of his being and saw it really as it was, and the seeing was like the seeing of your own hand with your own eyes—there was no reflection, no inference, no judgment, no comparison, no moving either backward or forward step by step, the thing was seen and that was the end of it, there was nothing to talk about, nothing to argue, or to explain. The seeing was something complete in itself—it did not lead on to anything inside or outside, within or beyond. And it was this completeness, this finality, that was so entirely satisfying to the Buddha, who now knew that the chain was found broken and that he was a liberated man. The Buddha's experience of Enlightenment therefore could not be understood by referring it to the intellect which tantalizes but fails to fulfil and satisfy.

The Buddha's psychological experience of life as pain and suffering was intensely real and moved him to the very depths of his being, and in consequence the emotional reaction he experienced at the time of Enlightenment was in proportion to this intensity of feeling. All the more evident, therefore, it is that he could not rest satisfied with an intellectual glancing or surveying of the facts of life. In order to bring a perfect state of tranquillity over the waves of turmoil surging in his heart, he had to have recourse to something more deeply and vitally concerned with his inmost being. For all we can say of it, the intellect is after all a spectator, and when it does some work it is as a hireling for better or for worse. Alone it cannot bring about the state of mind designated as enlightenment. The feeling of perfect freedom, the feeling that 'aham hi araha loke, aham sattha anuttaro', could not issue from the consciousness of an intellectual superiority alone. There must have been in the mind of the Buddha a consciousness far more fundamental which could only accompany one's deepest spiritual experience.

To account for this spiritual experience the Buddhist writers exhaust their knowledge of words relating to the understanding, logical or otherwise. 'Knowledge' (*vijjā*), 'understanding' (*pajānanā*), 'reason' (*ñāṇa*), 'wisdom' (*paññā*), 'penetration' (*abhisameta*), 'realization' (*abhisambuddha*), 'perception' (*sañjānanam*), and 'insight' (*dassana*),[1] are some of the terms they use. In truth, so long as we confine ourselves to intellection, however deep, subtle, sublime, and enlightening, we fail to see into the gist of the matter. This is the reason why even the so-called primitive Buddhists who are by some considered positivists, rationalists, and agnostics, were obliged to assume some faculty dealing with things far above relative knowledge, things that do not appeal to our empirical ego.

The Mahāyāna account of Enlightenment as is found in the *Lalita-vistara* (chapter on 'Abhisambodhana') is more explicit as to the kind of mental activity or wisdom which converted the Bodhisattva into the Buddha. For it was through '*ekacittekshaṇa-samyukta-prajñā*' that supreme perfect knowledge was realized (*abhisambodha*) by the Buddha. What is this Prajñā? It is the understanding of a higher order than that which is habitually exercised in acquiring relative knowledge. It is a faculty both intellectual and spiritual, through the operation of which the soul is enabled to break the fetters of intellection. The latter is always

[1] *The Mahāvyutpatti*, CXLII, gives a list of thirteen terms denoting the act of comprehending with more or less definite shades of meaning: buddhi, mati, gati, mataṁ, dṛishtaṁ, abhisamitāvī, samyagavabodha, supratividdha, abhilakshita, gātiṁgata, avabodha, pratyabhijñā, and menire.

dualistic inasmuch as it is cognizant of subject and object, but in the Prajñā which is exercised 'in unison with one-thought-viewing' there is no separation between knower and known, these are all viewed (*ikshana*) in one thought (*ekacitta*), and enlightenment is the outcome of this. By thus specifying the operation of Prajñā, the Mahāyānists have achieved an advance in making clearer the nature of sambodhi: for when the mind reverses its usual course of working and, instead of dividing itself externally, goes back to its original inner abode of oneness, it begins to realize the state of 'one-thought-viewing' where Ignorance ceases to scheme and the Defilements do not obtain.

Enlightenment we can thus see is an absolute state of mind in which no 'discrimination' (*parikalpana* or *vikalpa*), so called, takes place, and it requires a great mental effort to realize this state of viewing all things 'in one thought'. In fact, our logical as well as practical consciousness is too given up to analysis and ideation; that is to say, we cut up realities into elements in order to understand them; but when they are put together to make the original whole, its elements stand out too conspicuously defined, and we do not view the whole 'in one thought'. And as it is only when 'one thought' is reached that we have enlightenment, an effort is to be made to go beyond our relative empirical consciousness, which attaches itself to the multitudinosity and not to the unity of things. The most important fact that lies behind the experience of Enlightenment, therefore, is that the Buddha made the most strenuous attempt to solve the problem of Ignorance and his utmost will-power was brought forth to bear upon a successful issue of the struggle.

We read in the *Katha-Upanishad*: 'As rain water that has fallen on a mountain ridge runs down on all sides, thus does he who sees a difference between qualities run after them on all sides. As pure water poured into pure water remains the same, thus, O Gautama, is the self of a thinker who knows.' This pouring pure water into pure water is, as we have it here, the 'viewing all qualities in one thought' which finally cuts off the hopelessly entangling logical mesh by merging all differences and likenesses into the absolute oneness of the knower (*jñānin*) and the known (*jñeya*). This, however, in our practical dualistic life, is a reversion, a twisting, and a readjustment.

Eckhart, the great German mystic, is singularly one with the 'one-thought-viewing' of things as done by Buddhists when he expresses his view thus: 'Das Auge darin ich Gott sehe, ist dasselbe Auge, darin Gott mich sieht. Mein Auge und Gottes Auge ist ein Auge und ein Gesicht und ein Erkennen und eine Liebe.'[1] The idea of reversion is more clearly expressed in Jacob Boehme's simile of the 'umge-wandtes Auge' with which God is recognized.

Enlightenment, therefore, must involve the will as well as the intellect. It is an act of intuition born of the will. The will wants to know itself as it is in itself, *yathābhūtam dassana*, free from all its cognitive conditions. The Buddha attained this end when a new insight came upon him at the end of his ever-circulatory reasoning from decay and death to Ignorance and from Ignorance to decay and death, through the twelve links of the Paṭicca-samuppāda. The Buddha had to go over the same ground again and again, because he was in an intellectual *impasse* through which he could not move further on. He did not repeat the process, as is originally imagined, for his own philosophical edification.

The fact was that he did not know how to escape this endless rotation of ideas; at this end there was birth, there was decay and death, and at the other end there was Ignorance. The objective facts could not be denied, they boldly and uncomfortably confronted him, while Ignorance balked the progress of his cognitive faculty moving farther onward or rather inward. He was hemmed in on both sides, he did not know how to find his way out, he went first this way and then that way, forever with the same result—the utter inutility of all his mental labour. But he had an indomitable will; he wanted, with the utmost efforts of his will, to get into the very truth of the matter; he knocked and knocked until the doors of Ignorance gave way: and

[1] Franz Pfeiffer, p. 312, Martensen, p. 29.

they burst open to a new vista never before presented to his intellectual vision. Thus he was able to exclaim to Upaka, the naked ascetic, whom he happened to meet on his way to Benares after Enlightenment:

> 'All-conqueror I, knower of all,
> From every soil and stain released,
> Renouncing all, from craving ceased,
> Self-taught; whom should I Master call?
>
> That which I know I learned of none,
> My fellow is not on the earth.
> Of human or of heavenly birth
> To equal me there is not one.
>
> I truly have attained release,
> The world's unequalled teacher I,
> Alone, enlightened perfectly,
> I dwell in everlasting peace.'[1]

When we speak of enlightenment or illumination we are apt to think of its epistemological aspect and to forget the presence of a tremendous will-power behind it—the power in fact making up the entire being of an individual. Especially as in Buddhism the intellect stands forth prominently, perhaps more than it ought to, in the realization of the ideal Buddhist life; scholars are tempted to ignore the significance of the will as the essentially determinate factor in the solution of the ultimate problem. Their attention has thus been directed too much towards the doctrine of the Paṭicca-samuppāda or the Ariyasacca, which they considered constituted the final teaching of Buddhism. But in

[1] Translated by Bhikkhu Sīlācāra. The original Pāli runs as follows:
Sabbābhibhū sabbavidū 'ham asmi,
Sabbesu dhammesu anūpalitto,
Sabbaṁjaho tanhakkhaye vimutto
Sayaṁ abhiññāya kam uddiseyyaṁ.
Na me ācariyo atthi, sadiso me na vijjati,
Sadevakasmiṁ lokasmiṁ na 'tthi me patipuggalo. .
Ahaṁ hi arahā loke, ahaṁ satthā anuttaro,
Eko 'mhi sammasambuddho, sītibhūto 'smi, nibbuto.
Dīgha-Nikāya, XXVI.

this they have been sadly at fault, nor have they been right in taking Buddhism for a sort of ethical culture, declaring that it is no more than a system of moral precepts (*śila*), without a soul, without a God, and consequently without a promise of immortality. But the true Buddhist ideas of Ignorance, Causation, and Moral Conduct had a far deeper foundation in the soul-life of man. Ignorance was not a cognitive ignorance, but meant the darkness of spiritual outlook. If Ignorance were no more than cognitive, the clearing-up of it did not and could not result in enlightenment, in freedom from the Fetters and Defilements, or Intoxicants as some Pāli scholars have them. The Buddha's insight penetrated the depths of his being as the will, and he knew what this was, yathābhūtam, or in its tathābhāva (thatness or suchness), he rose above himself as a Buddha supreme and peerless. The expression 'Anuttara-samyak-sambodhi' was thus used to designate this pre-eminently spiritual knowledge realized by him.

Ignorance, which is the antithesis of Enlightenment, therefore acquires a much deeper sense here than that which has hitherto been ascribed to it. Ignorance is not merely not knowing or not being acquainted with a theory, system or law; it is not directly grasping the ultimate facts of life as expressive of the will. In Ignorance knowing is separated from acting, and the knower from that which is to be known; in Ignorance the world is asserted as distinct from the self; that is, there are always two elements standing in opposition. This is, however, the fundamental condition of cognition, which means that as soon as cognition takes place there is Ignorance clinging to its very act. When we think we know something, there is something we do not know. The unknown is always behind the known, and we fail to get at this unknown knower, who is indeed the inevitable and necessary companion to every act of cognition. We want, however, to know this unknown knower, we cannot let this go unknown, ungrasped without actually seeing what it is; that is, Ignorance is to be enlightened. This involves a great contradiction, at least epistomologically. But until we transcend this condition there is no peace of mind, life grows unbearable.

In his search for the 'builder' (*gahākara*), the Buddha was always accosted by Ignorance, an unknown knower behind knowing. He could not for a long time lay his hands on this one in a black mask until he transcended the dualism of knower and known. This transcending was not an act of cognition, it was self-realization, it was a spiritual awakening and outside the ken of logical reasoning, and therefore not accompanied by Ignorance. The knowledge the knower has of himself, in himself—that is, as he is to himself—is unattainable by any proceedings of the intellect which is not permitted to transcend its own conditions. Ignorance is brought to subjection only by going beyond its own principle. This is an act of the will. Ignorance in itself is no evil, nor is it the source of evil, but when we are ignorant of Ignorance, of what it means in our life, then there takes place an unending concatenation of evils. Taṇhā (craving) regarded as the root of evil can be overcome only when Ignorance is understood in its deeper and proper signification.

II

Therefore, it betrays an utter ignorance on the part of Buddhist scholars when they relegate Ignorance to the past in trying to explain the rationale of the Twelvefold Chain of Causation (*paṭicca-samuppāda*)[1] from the temporal point of view. According to them the first two factors (*angāni*) of the Paṭicca-samuppāda belong to the past, while the following eight belong to the present and the last two to the future.

---

[1] Ordinarily, the Chain runs as follows: 1. Ignorance (*avijjā, avidyā*); 2. Disposition (*sankhāra, saṁskāra*); 3. Consciousness (*viññāna, vijñāna*); 4. Name and Form (*nāmarūpa*); 5. Six Sense-organs (*salāyatana, saḍāyatana*); 6. Touch (*phassa, sparśa*); 7. Feeling (*vedana*); 8. Desire (*taṇhā, tṛshṇā*); 9. Clinging (*upādāna*); 10. Becoming (*bhāva*); 11. Birth (*jāti*); and 12. Old Age and Death (*jarāmaranaṁ*).

Ignorance, from which starts the series of the Nidānas, has no time-limits, for it is not of time but of the will, as is enlightenment. When time-conception enters, enlightenment, which is negatively the dispelling of Ignorance, loses all its character of finality, and we begin to look around for something going beyond it. The Fetters would ever be tightening around us, and the Defilements would be our eternal condition. No gods would sing of the Awakened One as 'a lotus unsoiled by the dust of passion, sprung from the lake of knowledge; a sun that destroys the darkness of delusion; a moon that takes away the scorching heat of the inherent sins of existence.'[1]

If Enlightenment made the whole universe tremble in six different ways as is recorded in the Sūtras, Ignorance over which it finally prevailed must have as much power, though diametrically opposed to it in value and virtue, as Enlightenment. To take Ignorance for an intellectual term and then to interpret it in terms of time-relation, altogether destroys its fundamental character as the first in the series of the Twelve Nidānas. The extraordinary power wielded by the Buddha over his contemporaries as well as posterity was not entirely due to his wonderful analytical acumen, though we have to admit this in him; it was essentially due to his spiritual greatness and profound personality, which came from his will-power penetrating down into the very basis of creation. The vanquishing of Ignorance was an exhibition of this power which therefore was invincible and against which Māra with all his hosts was utterly powerless either to overwhelm or to entice. The failure to see into the true meaning of Ignorance in the system of the Paṭicca-samuppāda or in the Ariyasacca will end unavoidably in misconstruing the essential nature of Enlightenment and consequently of Buddhism.

In the beginning, which is really no beginning and which has no spiritual meaning except in our finite life, the will wants to know itself, and consciousness is awakened, and with the awakening of consciousness the will is split in two.

[1] *The Buddhacarita*, Book XIV.

The one will, whole and complete in itself, is now at once actor and observer. Conflict is inevitable; for the actor now wants to be free from the limitations under which he has been obliged to put himself in his desire for consciousness. He has in one sense been enabled to see, but at the same time there is something which he, as observer, cannot see. In the trail of knowledge, Ignorance follows with the inevitability of fate, the one accompanies the other as shadow accompanies object, no separation can be effected between the two companions. But the will as actor is bent on going back to his own original abode where there was yet no dualism, and therefore peace prevailed. This longing for the home, however, cannot be satisfied without a long, hard, trying experience. For the thing once divided in two cannot be restored to its former unity until some struggle is gone through with. And the restoration is more than a mere going back, the original content is enriched by the division, struggle, and resettlement.

When first the division takes place in the will, consciousness is so enamoured of its novelty and its apparent efficiency in solving the practical problems of life that it forgets its own mission, which is to enlighten the will. Instead of turning its illuminating rays within itself—that is, towards the will from which it has its principle of existence—consciousness is kept busy with the objective world of realities and ideas; and when it tries to look into itself, there is a world of absolute unity where the object of which it wishes to know is the subject itself. The sword cannot cut itself. The darkness of Ignorance cannot be dispelled because it is its own self. At this point the will has to make a heroic effort to enlighten itself, to redeem itself, without destroying the once-awakened consciousness or rather by working out the principle lying at the basis of consciousness. This was accomplished as we see in the case of the Buddha, and he became more than mere Gautama, he was the Awakened One and the Exalted and supremely Enlightened. In willing there is really something more than mere willing, there is thinking and seeing. By this seeing, the will sees itself and is thereby made free and its own master. This is knowing in the most fundamental sense of the term and herein consists the Buddhist redemption.

Ignorance prevails as long as the will remains cheated by its own offspring or its own image, consciousness, in which the knower always stands distinguished from the known. The cheating, however, cannot last, the will wishes to be enlightened, to be free, to be by itself. Ignorance always presupposes the existence of something outside and unknown. This unknown outsider is generally termed ego or soul, which is in reality the will itself in the state of Ignorance. Therefore, when the Buddha experienced Enlightenment, he at once realized that there was no Ātman, no soulentity as an unknown and unknowable quantity. Enlightenment dispelled Ignorance and with it all the bogies conjured up from the dark cave of ego disappeared. Ignorance in its general use is opposed to knowledge, but from the Buddhist point of view, in which it stands contrasted to Enlightenment, it means the ego (*ātman*), which is so emphatically denied by the Buddha. This is not to be wondered at, seeing that the Buddha's teaching centred in the doctrine of Enlightenment, the dispelling of Ignorance.

Those who see only the doctrine of non-ātman in Buddhism, and fail to inquire into the meaning of Enlightenment are incapable of appreciating the full significance of the Buddha's message to the world. If he simply denied the existence of an ego-entity from the psychological point of view after reducing it into its component factors, scientifically he may be called great as his analytical faculties stood far above those of his contemporaries in this respect; but his influence as a spiritual leader would not have reached so far and endured so long. His theory of non-ātman was not only established by a modern scientific method, but essentially was the outcome of his inner experience. When Ignorance is understood in the deeper sense, its dispelling unavoidably results in the negation of an ego-entity as the basis of all our life-activities. Enlightenment is a positive conception, and for ordinary minds it is quite hard to comprehend it in its true bearings. But when we know what it means in the general system of Buddhism, and concentrate our efforts in the realization of it, all the rest will take care of themselves, such as the notion of Ego, attachment to it, Ignorance, Fetters, Defilements, etc. Moral Conduct, Contemplation, and Higher Understanding—all these are meant to bring about the desired end of Buddhism; that is, Enlightenment. The Buddha's constant reiteration of the theory of causation, telling his disciples how, when this is cause, that is effect, and how, when cause disappears, effect also disappears, is not primarily to get them acquainted with a kind of formal logic, but to let them see how Enlightenment is casually related to all human happiness and spiritual freedom and tranquillity.

So long as Ignorance is understood as logical inability to know, its disappearance can never bring out the spiritual freedom to which even the earliest known literature of Buddhism makes so frequent and so emphatic allusions. See how the Arhat's declaration of spiritual independence reads in the Nikāyas: 'There arose in me insight, the emancipation of my heart became unshakeable, this is my last birth, there is now no rebirth for me.'[1] This is quite a strong statement showing how intensely and convincingly one has seized the central facts of life. The passage is indeed one of the characterizations of Arhatship, and when a fuller delineation of it is made, we have something like the following: 'To him, thus knowing, thus seeing,[2] the heart is set free from the defilement of lust, is set free from the

---

[1] Nānañ ca pana me dassanaṁ udapādi akuppa me ceto-vimutti ayaṁ antima jāti natthi dāni dāni punabbhavo.

[2] 'Thus knowing, thus seeing' (*evam jānato evam passato*) is one of the set phrases we encounter throughout Buddhist literature, Hīnayāna and Mahāyāna. Whether or not its compilers were aware of the distinction between knowing and seeing in the sense we make now in the theory of knowledge, the coupling is of great signification. They must have been conscious of the inefficiency and insufficiency of the word 'to know' in the description of the kind of knowledge one has at the moment of enlightenment. 'To see' or 'to see face to face' signifies the immediateness and utmost perspicuity and certainty of such knowledge. As was mentioned elsewhere, Buddhism is rich in terminology of this order of cognition.

defilement of becoming, is set free from the defilement of Ignorance. In him, thus set free, there arises the knowledge of his emancipation, and he knows that rebirth has been destroyed, that the Higher Life has been fulfilled, that what had to be done has been accomplished, and after this present life there will be no beyond.'[1] In essence the Arhat is the Buddha and even the Tathāgata, and in the beginning of the history of Buddhism the distinction between these terms did not seem quite sharply marked. Thus to a great extent they may be qualified in the same terms.

When the Buddha was talking with his disciples concerning various speculations prevalent in his days, he made the following remarks about the knowledge of things in command by the Tathāgata:

'That does he know, and he knows also other things far beyond, far better than those speculations; and having that knowledge he is not puffed up; and thus untarnished he has, in his own heart, realized the way of escape from them, has understood, as really they are, the rising up and passing away of sensations, their sweet taste, their danger, how they cannot be relied on, and not grasping after any of those things men are eager for, he the Tathāgata is quite set free. These are those other things, profound, difficult to realize, and hard to understand, tranquillizing, sweet, not to be grasped by logic, subtle, comprehensible only by the wise, which the Tathāgata, having himself realized and seen face to face, hath set forth; and it is concerning these that they who would rightly praise the Tathāgata in accordance with the truth, should speak.'[2]

These virtues for which the Tathagata was to be praised were manifestly not derived from speculation and analytical reasoning. His intellectual sight was just as keen and far-reaching as any of his contemporaries, but he was

---

[1] Tassa evam jānato evam passato kāmāsavāpi cittaṁ vimuccati bhavāsavāpi cittaṁ vimuccati avijjasavapi cittaṁ vimuccati, vimuttasmiṁ vimuttamit ñānam hoti. Khina jāti vusitaṁ brahmacariyaṁ kataṁ karaṇīyam naparaṁ itthattāyāti pajānāti.

[2] *The Brahmajāla Sutta*, p. 43. Translation by Rhys Davids.

endowed with a higher faculty, will-power, which was exercised to its fullest capacity in order to bring about all these
virtues which belonged to the entire being of Tathāgatahood. And naturally there was no need for him to face these
metaphysical problems that agitated the philosophers of his
days; they were solved in him, when he attained his spiritual
freedom and serenity, in their entirety, in their synthetic
aspect, and not partially or fragmentarily—which should
be the case if they were presented to the Buddha's cognition
as philosophical problems. In this light is to be read the
Mahāli Sutta. Some scholars wonder why two entirely disconnected ideas are treated together in one body of the
Sūtra, which, however, shows scholarly ignorance in regard to matters spiritual, as they fail to notice the true
import of Enlightenment in the system of Buddhist faith.
To understand this we need imaginative intuition directly
penetrating the centre of life, and not always do mere
literary and philological talents succeed in unravelling its
secrets.

The *Mahāli Sutta* is a Pāli Sūtra in the Dīgha-Nikāya,
in which Mahāli asks the Buddha as to the object of the
religious life practised by his disciples, and the following is
the gist of his answer: The Buddhists do not practise self-
concentration in order to acquire any miraculous power
such as hearing heavenly sounds or seeing heavenly sights.[1]

[1] The idea of performing miracles systematically through the power
acquired by self-concentration seems to have been greatly in vogue in
India even from the earliest days of her civilization, and the Buddha was
frequently approached by his followers to exhibit his powers to work
wonders. In fact, his biographers later turned him into a regular miracle-
performer, at least as far as we may judge by the ordinary standard of
logic and science. But from the Prajñā-pāramitā point of view, according
to which 'because what was preached by the Tathāgata as the possession
of qualities, that was preached as no-possession of qualities by the
Tathāgata, and therefore it is called the possession of qualities' (yaishā
bhagavan lakshaṇasampat tathāgatena bhāshitā alakshaṇasampad
eshā tathāgatena bhāshita; tenocyate lakshaṇasampad iti), the idea of
performing wonders acquires quite a new signification spiritually. In the
Kevaddha Sutta three wonders are mentioned as having been understood
and realized by the Buddha: the mystic wonder, the wonder of education, and the wonder of manifestation. The possessor of the mystic
wonder can work the following logical and physical impossibilities:

There are things higher and sweeter than that, one of which is the complete destruction of the Three Bonds (delusion of self, doubt, and trust in the efficacy of good works and ceremonies) and the attainment of such a state of mind as to lead to the insight of the higher things in one's spiritual life. When this insight is gained the heart grows serene, is released from the taint of Ignorance, and there arises the knowledge of emancipation. Such questions as are asked by you, O Mahāli, regarding the identity of body and soul, are idle ones; for when you attain to the supreme insight and see things as they really are in themselves—that is, emancipated from the Bonds, Taints, and Deadly Flows—those questions that are bothering you at the moment will completely lose their value and no more be asked in the way you do. Hence no need of my answering your questions.

This dialogue between the Buddha and Mahāli well illustrates the relation between Enlightenment and the problem of the soul. There is no need of wondering why the Buddha did not definitely solve the ever-recurring question instead of ignoring it in the manner as he did and talking about something apparently in no connection with the point at issue. This is one of the instances by which we must try to see into the meaning of Ignorance.

III

One of the reasons, however, why the Buddha left some metaphysical questions unanswered or indeterminate

'From being one he becomes multiform, from being multiform he becomes one; from being visible he becomes invisible; he passes without hindrance to the further side of a wall or a battlement or a mountain, as if through air; he penetrates up and down through solid ground as if through water; he walks on water without dividing it, as if on solid ground; he travels cross-legged through the sky like the birds on wing; he touches and feels with the hand even the moon and sun, beings of mystic power and potency though they be; he reaches even in the body up to the heaven of Brahma.' Shall we understand this literally and intellectually? Cannot we interpret it in the spirit of the Prajñā-pāramitā idealism? Why? Taccittam yacittam acittam. (Thought is called thought because it is no-thought.)

(*avyākata*) was due to the fact that Buddhism is a practical system of spiritual discipline and not a metaphysical discourse. The Buddha naturally had his theory of cognition, but this was secondary inasmuch as the chief aim of Buddhist life was to attain Enlightenment from which spiritual freedom ensues. Enlightenment vanquishes Ignorance lying at the root of birth and death and laying fetters of every description, intellectual as well as effective. And this vanquishing of Ignorance cannot be achieved except by the exercise of one's will-power; all the other attempts, especially merely intellectual, are utterly futile. Hence the Buddha's conclusion: 'These questions[1] are not calculated to profit, they are not concerned with the Dharma, they do not redound to the elements of right conduct, nor to detachment, nor to purification from lusts, nor to quietude, nor to tranquillization of heart, nor to real knowledge, nor to the insight of the higher stages of the Path, nor to Nirvāṇa. Therefore is it that I express no opinion upon them.' What the Buddha on the other hand expounded was: 'What pain is, what the origin of pain is, what the cessation of pain is, and the method by which one may reach the cessation of pain.' For these are all practical matters to be not only fully understood and realized, but actively mastered by any one who really desires to accomplish the great deed of emancipation.

That the Buddha was very much against mere knowledge and most emphatically insisted on actually seeing and personally experiencing the Dharma, face to face, is in evidence everywhere in the Nikāyas as well as in the Mahāyāna texts. This has been indeed the strongest point in the teaching of Buddhism. When a Brahman philosopher was referring to his knowledge of the Three Vedas and a union with that which he has not seen, the Buddha ridiculed him in one of his strong phrases: 'So you say that the Brahmans are not able to point the way to union with that which they have seen, and you further say that neither any one of them,

---

[1] The questions are: Is the world eternal? Is the world not eternal? Is the world finite? Is the world infinite? *Potthapāda-Sutta.*

nor of their pupils, nor of their predecessors even to the seventh generation, has ever seen Brahma. And you further say that even the Rishis of old, whose words they hold in such deep respect, did not pretend to know, or to have seen where, or whence, or whither Brahma is. Yet these Brahmans versed in the Three Vedas say, forsooth, that they can point out the way to union with that which they know not, neither have seen. . . . They are like a string of blind men clinging one to the other, neither can the foremost see, nor can the middle one see, nor can the hindmost see. The talk of those Brahmans versed in the Three Vedas is but blind talk: the first sees not, the middle one sees not, nor can the last see.'

Enlightenment or the dispelling of Ignorance, which is the ideal of the Buddhist life, we can see now most clearly, is not an act of the intellect, but the transforming or re-modelling of one's whole being through the exercise of the most fundamental faculty innate in every one of us. Mere understanding has something foreign in it and does not seem to come so intimately into life. If Enlightenment had really such a tremendous effect on our spiritual outlook as we read in the Sūtras, it could not be the outcome of just getting acquainted with the doctrine of Causation. Enlightenment is the work of Paññā, which is born of the will which wants to see itself and to be in itself. Hence the Buddha's emphasis on the importance of personal experience; hence his insistence on meditation in solitude as the means of leading to the experience. Meditation, through which the will endeavours to transcend the condition it has put on itself in the awakening of consciousness, is therefore by no means the simple act of cogitating on the theory of Origination or Causation, which for ever moves in a circle, starting from Ignorance and ending in Ignorance. This is the one thing that is most needed in Buddhism. All the other metaphysical problems involve us in a tangled skein, in a matted mass of thread.

Ignorance is thus not to be got rid of by metaphysical means but by the struggle of the will. When this is done, we are also freed from the notion of an ego-entity which is the product or rather the basis of Ignorance, on which it depends and thrives. The ego is the dark spot where the rays of the intellect fail to penetrate, it is the last hiding-lair of Ignorance, where the latter serenely keeps itself from the light. When this lair is laid bare and turned inside out, Ignorance vanishes like frost in the sun. In fact, these two are one and the same thing, Ignorance and the idea of ego. We are apt to think that when Ignorance is driven out and the ego loses its hold on us, we have nothing to lean against and are left to the fate of a dead leaf blown away hither and thither as the wind listeth. But this is not so; for Enlightenment is not a negative idea meaning simply the absence of Ignorance. Indeed, Ignorance is the negation of Enlightenment and not the reverse. Enlightenment is affirmation in the truest sense of the word, and therefore it was stated by the Buddha that he who sees the Dharma sees the Buddha, and he who sees the Buddha sees the Dharma, and again that he who wants to see the Buddha ought not to seek him in form, nor in voice, etc. When Ignorance ruled supreme, the ego was conceived to be a positive idea, and its denial was nihilistic. It was quite natural for Ignorance to uphold the ego where it found its original home. But with the realization of Enlightenment, the whole affair changes its aspect, and the order instituted by Ignorance is reversed from top to bottom. What was negative is now positive, and what was positive now negative. Buddhist scholars ought not to forget this revaluation of ideas that comes along with Enlightenment. Since Buddhism asserts Enlightenment to be the ultimate fact of Buddhist life, there is in it nothing negativistic, nothing pessimistic.

IV

As philosophy tends to emphasize unduly the importance of abstract ideas and logical inferences and forgets to keep itself constantly in touch with the actual world of experience, the Buddha, as I have repeatedly stated, flatly refused to subscribe to theorization (*takka* or *vitakka*) at the expense of practical discipline. Enlightenment was the fruit of such discipline, and the dispelling of Ignorance could not be effected by any other means. If the Buddha could be said to have had any system of thought governing the whole trend of his teaching, it was what we may call radical empiricism. By this I mean that he took life and the world as they were and did not try to read them according to his own interpretation. Theorists may say this is impossible, for we put our subjectivity into every act of perception, and what we call an objective world is really a reconstruction of our innate ideas. Epistemologically this may be so, but spiritually a state of perfect freedom is obtained only when all our egoistic thoughts are not read into life and the world is accepted as it is as a mirror reflects a flower as flower and the moon as moon. When therefore I say Buddhism is radical empiricism, this is not to be understood epistemologically but spiritually. This is really the meaning of 'yathābhūtam', or 'yathātatham'—the term quite frequently used in the Buddhist canon and in fact forming a most important refrain of Buddhist thought.

In the *Sāmañña-phala Sutta*, in the Dīgha-Nikāya, we are told in an ascending scale what the ultimate fruits of Buddhist life are, and the scale terminates in the 'yathābhūtam' acceptance of the world:

'With his heart thus serene, made pure, translucent, cultured, devoid of evil, supple, ready to act, firm, and imperturbable, he directs and bends down to the knowledge of the destruction of the Defilements (*āsavā*). He knows as it really is: "This is pain." He knows as it really is: "This is the origin of pain." He knows as it really is: "This is the cessation of pain." He knows as it really is: "This is the path that leads to the cessation of pain." He knows as they really are: "These are the Defilements." He knows as it really is: "This is the origin of the Defilements." He knows as it really is: "This is the cessation of the Defilements." He knows as it really is: "This is the path that leads to the cessation of the Defilements." To him, thus knowing, thus seeing, the heart is set free from the Defilement of Lusts (*kāma*), is set free from the Defilement of Existence (*bhāva*), is set free from the Defilement of Ignorance (*avijjā*). In him, thus set free, there arises the knowledge of his emancipation, and he knows: "Rebirth has been destroyed. The higher life has been fulfilled. What had to be done has been accomplished. After this present life there will be no beyond!" '

How shall we understand this? As in the case of the Twelve Nidānas, the Fourfold Noble Truth will surely fail to yield up its deepest signification when we approach it intellectually. For it is no more than a restatement of the dogma of dependent origination, however different in form, the same principle is asserted both in the Paṭicca-samuppāda and in the Ariya-sacca. The latter points out the practical method of escape from the fetters of karma while the former draws out in view the plans of its *modus operandi*. As concepts, both formulas remain just what they are—that is, effectless and inefficient to produce a spiritual revolution. The Buddha's idea of formulating the Fourfold Truth was to see it practically applied to the realization of an ideal. The elaborate mental discipline which is explained in the previous parts of the *Sāmaññaphala* is but preparatory to this final catastrophe. Without a serene, pure, and firm heart, the truth can never be grasped as it really is. A keen, penetrating intellect may know of the truth and discourse about it, but as to its realization in life a disciplined mind is required.

The passages above quoted are intelligible only when they are seen in the light of spiritual life. Buddhism may be logical, but if we fail to perceive anything further than that we sorely distort it. The logicality of Buddhist teaching is just one aspect of it and not a very important one. We may even regard this logicalness as incidental to Buddhism, and those who are entranced by it remain quite ignorant of the true import of Buddhism. 'He knows as it really is,' ti yathābhūtam pajānāti—we must come to this; for Yathā-bhūta-ñāṇa-dassana is the insight that destroys the Defilements (*āsavānaṁ khaya-ñāṇa*) and produces the consciousness of spiritual emancipation (*cetovimutti*). Without this Ñāṇa or Ñāṇa-dassana (insight or intuition), no detachment, no freedom would be possible to a Buddhist, nor would he ever be assured of his ultimate deliverance from the bondage of existence as well as of the attainment of the higher life (*brahmacarya*). The 'knowing thus, seeing thus' does not mean an intellectual comprehension of facts or truths which fall outside the pale of one's own experience, but it is the perception of events that have actually taken place within oneself. Even an intellectual comprehension will be impossible when there is no experience that goes to support its validity. For those who have no spiritual training along the line of the Hindu dhyāna exercises, the mental state culminating in the yathābhūtam contemplation of the world will be a very difficult subject to be in sympathy with. But in this light only the Buddha's discourse on the fruits of the Sāmañña life is to be understood.

The Defilements (*āsavā*), or Oozings (*lou*), as the Chinese translators have them, are three, sometimes four, in number. They are the Defilements of Desire (*kāma*), Existence (*bhāva*), Ignorance (*avijjā*), and Intellection (*diṭṭhi*). What kind of insight is it that destroys all these Defilements? And what is it that will be left in us after such a destruction? The answers may be anticipated to be thoroughly nihilistic, because nothing but absolute void will be seemingly the result of such destruction. Especially when we read a verse like the following (*Sutta-nipāta*, vv. 949 and 1099) we may reasonably be tempted to regard the teaching of the Buddha as absolutely negativistic:

> 'What is before thee, lay it aside;
> Let there be nothing behind thee;
> If thou wilt not grasp after what is in the middle,
> Thou wilt wander calm.'[1]

[1] Cf. *Dhammapāda*, v. 385. 'He for whom there is neither this nor that side, nor both, him, the fearless and unshackled, I call indeed a Brahman.'

But the fact is, from the spiritual point of view, that it is only after the destruction of the Defilements and a release from every form of attachment that one's inmost being gets purified and sees itself as it really is, not indeed as an ego standing in contrast to the not-ego, but as something transcending opposites and yet synthesizing them in itself. What is destroyed is the dualism of things and not their oneness. And the release means going back to one's original abode. The insight therefore is to see unity in multiplicity and to understand the opposition of the two ideas as not conditioning each other but as both issuing from a higher principle; and this is where perfect freedom abides. When the mind is trained enough, it sees that neither negation (*niratta*) nor affirmation (*atta*) applies to reality, but that the truth lies in knowing things as they are, or rather as they become. A mind really sincere and thoroughly purified is the necessary preliminary to the understanding of reality in its suchness. As the result we have 'ti yathābhūtam pajānāti', and this came later to be formulated by the Mahāyānists into the doctrine of Thatness or Suchness (*bhūtatathatā*). The trained mind that has gone through the four dhyāna exercises as prescribed in the Nikāyas further develops into what is known among the Mahāyānists as the Ādarśa-jñānam (mirror-insight), which corresponds to the Bhūta-ñāṇa in the Anguttara Nikāya. The last simile in the Buddha's discourse on the fruits of the Sāmañña life, which sums up the spiritual attainment of the Buddhists, becomes now quite intelligible. It runs thus:

'Just, O king, as if in a mountain fastness there were a pool of water, clear, translucent, and serene; and a man, standing on the bank and with eyes to see, should perceive the oysters and the shells, the gravel and the pebbles and the shoals of fish, as they move about or lie within it: he would know: This pool is clear, transparent, and serene, and there within it are the oysters and the shells, and the sand and gravel, and the shoals of fish are moving about or lying still.'

The radical empiricism of the 'Yathābhūtam' teaching

of the Buddha is here graphically presented, which reminds us of the Buddha in the *Itivuttaka*, v. 109, describing
himself as the spectator standing on the shore (*cakkhumā
puriso tīre ṭhito*). To understand this simile intellectually will
be sheer nonsense. The writer describes his mental attitude
from a higher plane of thought which has been realized
by him after a long training. Sambodhi or Enlightenment is
the Buddhist term given to this realization. The destruction
of the four Defilements is the negative phase of the experience which is the insight to which the Buddha's serene and
translucent mind was directed and bent down. When the
destructive activity alone is considered, Enlightenment is
annihilating and negativistic; but when the insight opens
to the suchness of truth, it is most emphatically affirmative.
This is where lies that 'matchless island possessing nothing
and grasping after nothing, called Nirvāṇa, the destruction
of decay and death'. (*Sutta-nipāta*, v. 1094.) Remember that
what is here destroyed is decay and death and not life; for it
is through Enlightenment that life is for the first time
restored to its native freedom and creativeness.

The simile of mirror (*ādarśā*) may, however, suggest that
the Buddhist attitude towards the world is merely passive
and lacking in energizing inspirations. This, however,
betrays the ignorance on the part of the critic of the
Buddha's own life, which was so unselfishly devoted for
forty-nine long and peaceful years to the promotion of the
general spiritual welfare of his people; not only this, but
the critic has also forgotten to notice the extraordinary
missionary enterprises of the Buddha's disciples as well as
their intellectual activities which developed into the
Mahāyānist school of Buddhism. Whatever this be, the
charge of passivity against Buddhist *weltanschauung* is wrong
even when it is considered apart from the historical facts
of Buddhism. Passivity, we notice in Enlightenment, is
merely apparent. As a general statement, a thing absolutely passive is unthinkable, unless it is a state of absolute
nothingness without any kind of content in it. So long as
Enlightenment is the outcome of a most strenuous spiritual

effort, it is a positive state of mind in which lies hidden an inexhaustible reservoir of possibilities; it is a unity in which a world of multitudinosity is lodged. 'Noisy go the small waters, silent goes the vast ocean.'[1] In the vast ocean of Enlightenment there is the silence of unity. The Avataṁsaka philosophers too compare it to the immense expanse of an ocean, calm and translucent, which reflects all the shining bodies of heaven, but where at the same time possibilities of roaring and all-devouring waves lie innocently embosomed.

So asks the Buddha in the *Mahāli Sutta*: 'When a monk knows thus and sees thus, would that make him ready to take up the question, Is the soul the same as the body, or is the soul one thing and the body another?' It is thus evident that the Buddha's teaching always centred in the practical realization of Enlightenment as 'asavem khata-nana', insight that destroys the Defilements and releases one from every attachment (*upādāna*). He did not shun the discussion of the metaphysical problems merely because they were metaphysical, but because they were not conducive to the attainment of the ultimate end of Buddhist life, which is the purification of spirit and not the display of epistemological subtlety. Ignorance was to be dispelled in our inner experience, and not by intellectually understanding the principle of dependent origination whether expressed as the Paṭicca-samuppāda or as the Ariya-sacca.

Further, that Enlightenment consists in seeing into things 'yathābhūtam' or 'yathātatham', free from doubt, not disturbed by intellection or theorization, may be gleaned from the last gāthā in the *Itivuttaka*, where the Buddha is praised for his various virtues. I quote the first three stanzas:

'Having insight into all the world,
In all the world as it really is,
He is detached from all the world
And without compare in all the world.

[1] *Sutta-nipāta*, v. 720. Sanantā yanti kussobbhā, tunḥi yāti mahodadhi.

All surpassing in everything, steadfast,
Freed from all ties,
The highest repose belongs to him
Who has attained Nirvāṇa, with no fear from any side.

This Enlightened One, with Defilements destroyed,
Undisturbed, and free from doubt,
Has attained destruction of all karma,
And is released in the destruction of the substratum.'

V

Viewing things 'yathābhūtam' is, so to speak, the intellectual or noetic aspect of Enlightenment, though not in the sense of discursive understanding; there is another aspect of Enlightenment which will be the subject of consideration here. I mean its relation to samādhi or dhyāna. This is preliminary, as I said before, to the realization, but it also shows that the realization thus attained is something more than merely seeing into truth. If Enlightenment were just this seeing or having insight, it would not be so spiritually enlightening as to bring about a complete riddance of evil passions and the sense of perfect freedom. Intuitions could not go so penetratingly into the source of life and set all doubts at rest and sever all bonds of attachment unless one's consciousness were thoroughly prepared to take in the All in its wholeness as well as its suchness. Our senses and ordinary consciousness are only too apt to be disturbed and to turn away from the realization of truth. Mental discipline thus becomes indispensable.

We must remember that the Buddha had this discipline under his two Samkhya teachers and that even after his Enlightenment he made it a rule for his disciples to train themselves in the dhyāna exercises. He himself retired into solitude whenever he had opportunities for it. This was not of course merely indulging in contemplation or in making the world reflect in the mirror of consciousness. It was a kind of spiritual training even for himself and even after Enlightenment. In this respect the Buddha was simply following the practice of all other Indian sages and philosophers. This, however, was not all with him; he saw some deeper meaning in the discipline which was to awaken the highest spiritual sense for comprehending the Dharma. Indeed, without this ultimate awakening, dhyāna, however exalting, was of no import to the perfection of Buddhist life. So we have in the *Dhammapāda*, v. 372: 'Without knowledge (*paññā, prajñā*) there is no meditation (*jhāna, dhyāna*), without meditation there is no knowledge: he who has knowledge and meditation is near unto Nirvāṇa.' This mutual dependence of jhāna and paññā is what distinguished Buddhism from the rest of the Indian teachings at the time. Jhāna or dhyāna must issue in paññā, must develop into seeing the world as it really is (*yathābhūtam*); for there is no Buddhism in meditation merely as such. And this was the reason why the Buddha got dissatisfied with the teaching of his teachers; it, to use his own words, did 'not lead to perfect insight, to supreme awakening, to Nirvāṇa' (*na abhiññāya na sambhodāya na nibbānāya samvattati*). To be abiding in the serenity of nothingness was enjoyable enough, but it was falling into a deep slumber, and the Buddha had no desire to sleep away his earthly life in a daydream. There must be a seeing into the life and soul of things. To him paññā or prajñā was the most essential part of his doctrine, and it had to grow out of dhyāna, and the dhyāna that did not terminate in paññā was not at all Buddhistic. The boat was to be emptied indeed, but staying in an 'empty house' (*suññāgāram*) and doing nothing is blankness and annihilation; an eye must open and see the truth fully and clearly, the truth (*paramam ariyasaccam*) that liberates life from its many bondages, and encumbrances. (Majjhima Nikāya, 140.) Sings the *Dhammapāda* again (v. 373):

'A monk who has entered his empty house, and whose mind is tranquil,

Feels a more than human delight when he sees the truth
clearly.'

As thus the aim of the dhyāna exercises is to prepare
the mind for the realization of the paramasacca which
destroys and liberates, and as the truth is realizable only
by the awakening of the parama-paññā which is the
knowledge (ñāṇa) that puts an end to all misery (sabba-
dukkha), the Buddha never fails duly to impress the importance of paññā on the minds of his disciples; for instance, in his general disciplinary scheme given to them
under the three headings: śīla (morality), jhāna (meditation), and paññā (intuitive knowledge). Whatever super-
sensual pleasures one may experience in the jhāna exercises, the Buddha considered them to be far short of the
ultimate goal of Buddhist life; every one of such pleasures
had to be abandoned as it would entangle the mind and
interrupt its ascending course to the awakening of paññā.
It was through this awakening alone that the consciousness
of emancipation or going back to one's original spiritual
abode could be attained. And by emancipation the Buddha
meant to be free from all forms of attachment, both sensual
(rūpam) and intellectual (viññānaṁ). So says he in the
Majjhima Nikāya, 138: Let not thy mind be disturbed by
external objects, nor let it go astray among thy own ideas.
Be free from attachments, and fear not. This is the way to
overcome the sufferings of birth and death.

As long as there is the slightest trace of attachment anywhere, outwardly or inwardly, there remains the substratum of selfhood, and this is sure to create a new force of
karma and involve us in the eternal cycle of birth-and-
death. This attachment is a form of obsession or illusion or
imagination. Nine of such self-conceited illusions are
mentioned in the Nikāyas, all of which come out of the
wrong speculations of selfhood and naturally lead to
attachment in one way or another. They are the ideas that
'I am', 'I am that', 'I shall be', 'I shall not be', 'I shall have
form', 'I shall be without form', 'I shall have thought', 'I

shall be without thought', 'I shall neither have thought nor be without thought'.[1] We have to get rid of all these *maññitaṁs*, arrogant, self-asserting conceptions, in order to reach the final goal of Buddhist life. For when they are eliminated, we cease to worry, to harbour hatred, to be belabouring, and to be seized with fears—which is tranquillization (*santi*), and Nirvāṇa, and the seeing into the reality and truth of things. When paññā is awakened in us, morality is abandoned, meditation left behind, and there remains only an enlightened state of consciousness in which spirit moveth as it listeth.

The well-known simile of the raft (*kullūpamaṁ*)[2] which may seem somewhat unintelligible to some of the Buddhist critics who are used to an altogether different 'intellectual landscape', is a good illustration of the Buddhist teaching of non-attachment. The teaching, 'Kullūpamaṁ vo bhikkhave ājānantehi dhammā pi vo pahātabbā, pageva adhammā' (Like unto a raft, all dharmas indeed must be abandoned, much more un-dharmas!), is really the most fundamental keynote running through the whole course of the history of Buddhist dogmatics. The philosophy of Prajñā-pāramitā, which is considered by some quite deviating from the spirit of primitive Buddhism, is in no way behind in upholding this doctrine of non-attachment— for instance, as we see in the *Vajracchedikā Sūtra*. In fact, the theory of Śūnyatā as expounded in all the Prajñāsūtras is no more than philosophizing on the doctrine of non-attachment.[3] The *Vajracchedikā* has:

'Tasmād iyaṁ thathāgatena sandhāya vāg bhāshi

---

[1] The Majjhima-Nikāya, 140, *Dhātuvibhangasuttam*. Asmīti bhikkhu maññitaṁ etaṁ; Ayam aham asmīti maññitaṁ etaṁ; Bhavissan ti maññitaṁ etaṁ; Na bhavissan ti maññitaṁ etaṁ; Rūpi bhavissan ti maññitaṁ etaṁ; Arūpī bhavissan ti maññitaṁ etaṁ; Saññī bhavissan ti maññitaṁ etaṁ: Asaññi bhavissan ti maññitaṁ etaṁ; Nevasaññi-nasaññi bhavissan ti maññitaṁ etaṁ.

[2] Majjhima Nikāya, 22.

[3] Cf. *Sutta-Nipāta*, v. 21. 'By me is made a well-constructed raft, so said Bhagavat, I have passed over to Nirvana, I have reached the further bank, having overcome the torrent of passions; there is no further use for a raft; therefore, if thou like, rain, O sky!'

kolopamaṁ dharmaparyāyam ājānadbhir dharmā eva tā prahātavyāḥ prāgeva adharmā.'

The simile itself runs as follows (Majjhima Nikāya, 22):

'In the simile of a raft do I teach my doctrine to you, O monks, which is designed for escape, not for retention. Listen attentively and remember well what I am going to say. Suppose that a man coming upon a long journey finds in his way a great broad water, the hither side beset with fears and dangers, but the further side secure and free from fears, and no boat wherewith to cross the flood nor any bridge leading from this to the other shore. And suppose this man to say to himself: Verily this is a great and wide water, and the hither side is full of fears and dangers, but the further side secure and free from fears; and there is neither boat nor bridge to take me from this to that further shore. How if I gather some reeds and twigs and leaves and bind them together into a raft; and then, supported on that raft, and labouring with hands and feet, cross in safety to that other shore? Accordingly, O monks, suppose this man to gather together reeds and twigs and leaves and branches and bind them all together into a raft, and launching forth upon it and labouring with hands and feet, attain in safety the other shore. And now, the flood crossed, the further shore attained, suppose the man should say: Very serviceable indeed has this my raft been to me. Supported by this raft and working with hands and feet, I am safely crossed to this other shore; how now if I lift the raft up on my head or lay it upon my shoulder, and so proceed withersoever I wish? What think ye, O monks? So doing, would this man be acting rightly as regards his raft?

'Nay, verily, O Lord!

'And what then ought this man to do if he would act rightly as regards the raft? Thus, O monks, ought the man to consider: Truly this raft has been serviceable to me! Supported by this raft and exerting hands and feet, I am crossed in safety to this further shore. How now if I lay this raft up on the bank or leave it to sink in the water and so proceed upon my journey? So doing, O monks, the man would be acting rightly as regards his raft.

'In like manner also do I teach my doctrine to you in the simile of a raft, which is meant, O monks, for escape and not for retention. Understanding the simile of the raft, O monks, you must leave dharmas behind, how much more un-dharmas!'[1]

The teaching of the Buddha may now be summed up as follows: Seeing things thus or 'yathābhūtam' is the same as the attainment of perfect spiritual freedom; or we may say that when we are detached from evil passions based upon the wrong idea of selfhood and when the heart grows conscious of its own emancipation, we are then for the first time fully awakened to the truth as it really is. These two events, seeing and being freed, are mutually dependent, so intimately that the one without the other is unthinkable, is impossible; in fact they are two aspects of one identical experience, separated only in our limited cognition. Paññā

---

[1] I left here 'dharmas' untranslated. For this untranslatable term, some have 'righteousness', some 'morality', and some 'qualities'. This is, as is well known, a difficult term to translate. The Chinese translators have rendered it by *fa*, everywhere, regardless of the context. In the present case, 'dharma' may mean 'good conduct', 'prescribed rules of morality', or even 'any religious teaching considered productive of good results'. In the *Laṅkāvatāra-sūtra*, chapter i, reference is also made to the transcending of both 'adharma' and 'dharma', saying: 'Dharmā eva prahātavyāḥ prāgevādharmāḥ.' And it is explained that this distinction comes from falsely asserting (*vikalpagrahaṇam*) the dualism of what is and what is not, while the one is the self-reflection of the other. You look into the mirror and finding an image thereon you take it for a reality, while the image is yourself and nobody else. The one who views the world thus has the rightful view of it, 'ya evam pasyati sa samyakpasyati.' Indeed, when he takes hold of *ekāgra* (one-pointedness or oneness of things) he realizes the state of mind in which his inner wisdom reveals itself (*svapratyātmaryajñānagocara*) and which is called the Tathāgatagarbha. In this illustration 'dharma' and 'adharma' are synonyms of being (*sat*) and non-being (*asat*) or affirmation (*asti*) and negation (*nāsti*). Therefore, the abandoning of dharma and adharma (*dharmādharmayoh prahāṇam*) means the getting rid of dualism in all its complexities and implications. Philosophically, this abandoning is to get identified with the Absolute, and morally to go beyond good and evil, right and wrong. Also compare *Sutta-Nipāta*, verse 886, where dualism is considered to be the outcome of false philosophical reasoning 'Takkañ ca diṭṭhisu pakappayitvā, saccaṁ musā ti dvayadhammam āhu.'

without jhāna is no paññā, and jhāna without paññā is no jhāna. Enlightenment is the term designating the identification-experience of paññā and jhāna, of seeing 'yathā-bhūtam' and abandoning the dharma-raft of every denomination. In this light should the following be understood:

'Therefore, O monks, whatever of matter (or body, *rūpam*) there is, whether of the past, of the future, or of the present time, whether internal or external, whether coarse or fine, mean or exalted, far or near, all matter (or body) is to be regarded as it really is, in the light of perfect knowledge (*sammāpaññā*), thus: "This is not of me," "This am I not," "This is not my Self." So with the rest of the five aggregates (*khaṇḍa*): *vedanā* (sensations), *saññā* (concepts), *sankhāra* (formative principle), and *viññānaṁ* (consciousness). One who thus seeing the world turns away from the world is truly freed from evil passions and has the consciousness of freedom. Such is called one who has the obstacles removed, trenches filled, one who has destroyed, is free, one whose fight is over, who has laid down his burden, and is detached.'[1]

In short, he has every quality of the Enlightened, in whom the will and the intellect are harmoniously blended.

VI

Ignorance is departure from home and Enlightenment is returning. While wandering, we lead a life full of pain and suffering, and the world wherein we find ourselves is not a very desirable habitat. This is, however, put a stop to by Enlightenment, as thus we are enabled once more to get settled at home where reign freedom and peace. The will negates itself in its attempt to get an insight into

[1] Abridged from the Majjhima Nikāya, 22, p. 139. Cf. also the Samyutta Nikāya, XII, 70, p. 125.

its own life, and dualism follows. Consciousness cannot transcend its own principle. The will struggles and grows despondent over its work. 'Why?' the intellect asks, but it is the question no human intellect can ever hope to solve; for it is a mystery deeply inherent in the will. Why did the Heavenly Father have to send his only child to redeem the creation which was his own handiwork and yet went further astray from its home? Why had Christ to be so dejected over the destiny of the erring children of God? This is an eternal mystery, and no relative understanding is made to grapple with these questions. But the very fact that such questions are raised and constantly threaten one's spiritual peace shows that they are not idle metaphysical problems to be solved by professional philosophers, but that they are addressed directly to one's inmost soul, which must struggle and make effort to subdue them by a higher and deeper power native to itself—far higher and deeper than mere dialectic of cognition.

The story of the prodigal son[1] is such a favourite theme, both for Buddhists and Christians, and in this do we not discover something eternally true, though tragic and unfathomable, which lies so deep in every human heart? Whatever this may be, the will finally succeeds in recognizing itself, in getting back to its original abode. The sense of peace one finds in Enlightenment is indeed that of a wanderer getting safely home. The wandering seems to have altogether been unnecessary from the logical point of view. What is the use of losing oneself if one has to find oneself again? What boots it after all—this going over from one to ten and from ten to one? Mathematically, all this is nonsensical. But the spiritual mystery is that returning is not merely counting backwards so many figures that were counted before in a reverse way. There is an immense difference here between physics and psychology. After returning one is no longer the same person as before. The

---

[1] For the Buddhist version of the story, see the *Saddharma-pundarīka Sūtra*, chapter iv, and the *Vajrasamādhi Sūtra*, chapter iv (Chinese translation).

will, back from his excursion through time-consciousness, is God himself.

In the *Vajrasamādhi Sūtra* the Bodhisattva Apratisthita asks the Buddha why the father was so unkind as not to recall his wandering son before fifty years expired, to which the Buddha answers, 'Fifty years is not to be understood as indicating time-relation here; it means the awakening of a thought.' As I would interpret, this means the awakening of consciousness—a split in the will, which now, besides being actor, is knower. The knower, however, gradually grows to be the spectator and critic, and even aspires to be the director and ruler. With this arises the tragedy of life, which the Buddha makes the basis of the Fourfold Noble Truth. That pain (*duḥka*) is life itself as it is lived by most of us, is the plain, undisguised statement of facts. This all comes from Ignorance, from our consciousness not being fully enlightened as to its nature, mission, and function in relation to the will. Consciousness must first be reduced to the will when it begins to work out its 'original vows' (*pūrvapraṇidhāna*) in obedience to its true master. 'The awakening of a thought marks the beginning of Ignorance and is its condition. When this is vanquished, 'a thought' is reduced to the will, which is Enlightenment. Enlightenment is therefore returning.

In this respect Christianity is more symbolic than Buddhism. The story of Creation, the Fall from the Garden of Eden, God's sending Christ to compensate for the ancestral sins, his Crucifixion, and Resurrection—they are all symbolic. To be more explicit, Creation is the awakening of consciousness, or the 'awakening of a thought'; the Fall is consciousness going astray from the original path; God's idea of sending his own son among us is the desire of the will to see itself through its own offspring, consciousness; Crucifixion is transcending the dualism of acting and knowing, which comes from the awakening of the intellect; and finally Resurrection means the will's triumph over the intellect—in other words, the will seeing itself in and through consciousness. After Resurrection the will is no more blind striving, nor is the intellect mere observing the dancer dance. In real Buddhist life these two are not separated; seeing and acting, they are synthesized in one whole spiritual life, and this synthesis is called by Buddhists Enlightenment, the dispelling of Ignorance, the loosening of the Fetters, the wiping-off of the Defilements, etc. Buddhism is thus free from the historical symbolism of Christianity; transcending the category of time, Buddhism attempts to achieve salvation in one act of the will; for returning effaces all the traces of time.

The Buddha himself gave utterance to the feeling of return when his eye first opened to the Dharma unheard of before at the realization of Enlightenment. He said, 'I am like a wanderer who, after going astray in a desolate wilderness, finally discovers an old highway, an old track beaten by his predecessors, and who finds, as he goes along the road, the villages, palaces, gardens, woods, lotus-ponds, walls, and many other things where his predecessors used to have their dwellings.[1] Superficially, this feeling of

[1] Samyutta XII, 65, Nagara; cf. also one of the *Prajñā-pāramitā sūtras* which is known as one preached by Mañjuśrī (Nanjō Catalogue, No. 21). In the Sūtra we find that the Buddha, after mentioning the simile of a gem-digger, makes reference to a man who feels overwhelmed with delight when people talk pleasantly about the old towns and villages once visited by himself. The same sort of a delightful feeling is expressed by one who will listen to the discourse on Prajñā-pāramitā and understand it; for he was in his past lives present at the assembly which was gathered about the Buddha delivering sermons on the same subject. That the understanding of the doctrine of Prajñā-pāramitā is a form of memory is highly illuminating when considered in relation to the theory of Enlightenment as advanced here.

That the ushering of Enlightenment is accompanied by the feeling of return or remembrance is also unmistakably noted by the writer of the *Kena-Upanishad* (VI, 50):
'Now in respect to the Ātman:
It is as though something forces its way into consciousness
And consciousness suddenly remembers—
Such a state of mind illustrates the awakening of knowledge of the Ātman.'
Sonadanda the Brahman had the following to say when he grasped the meaning of the Buddha's discourse on the characteristics of the true Brahman (Rhys Davids' translation): 'Most excellent, O Gotama, most excellent! Just as if a man were to set up that which has been thrown

returning to an old familiar abode seems to contradict the statement made concerning 'an insight to things never before presented to one's mind'; but the contradiction is logical and not spiritual. So long as the Buddha was going over the Chain of Origination from the epistemological point of view—that is, as long as he attempted to get back to his native will through the channel of empirical consciousness—he could not accomplish his end. It was only when he broke through the wall of Ignorance by the sheer force of his will that he could tread the ancient path. The path was altogether unrecognizable by his intelligent eye, which was one of the best of the kind; even the Buddha could not ignore the law governing its usage; the Chain was not to be cut asunder by merely reckoning its links of cause and effect backward and forward. Knowledge—that is, Ignorance—drove Adam from the Garden of Eden to the world of pain and patience (*sahaloka*), but it was not knowledge that would reconcile him to his Father, it was the Will dispelling Ignorance and ushering Enlightenment.

The sense of return or that of recognizing old acquaintances one experiences at the time of Enlightenment is a familiar fact to students of Zen Buddhism. To cite one instance, Chi-i (531–597), who is generally known by his honorary title as Chih-chê Tai-shih, was the founder of the T'ien-tai school of Buddhist philosophy in China. He was also trained in meditation by his teacher Hui-szŭ (513–577), and though not belonging to the orthodox lineage of the Zen masters, he is reckoned as one. When he came to the master, he was set to exercise himself in a Samādhi known as 'Fa-hua San-mei' (*saddharmapuṇḍarīkasamādhi*). While exercising himself in it, he came across a certain passage in the Sūtra, and his mind was opened, and he at once realized the statement referred to by his master, which was this— that he with the master personally attended the Buddha's

down, or were to reveal that which had been hidden away, or were to point out the right road to him who has gone astray, or were to bring a light into the darkness so that those who had eyes could see external forms—just even so has the truth been made known to me, in many a figure, by the venerable Gotama.'

congregation at the Vulture Peak where the Buddha discoursed on the Sūtra. Then said the master, 'If not for you no one could see the truth: and if not for me no one could testify it.' It is often remarked by Zen masters that the holy congregation at the Vulture Peak is still in session. This, however, ought not to be confounded with the remembering of the past, which is one of the miraculous gifts of the Buddhist saints. It has nothing to do with such memory, for in Enlightenment there are more things than are implied in mere time-relations. Even when the *Prajñā-pāramitā-sūtras* expressly refer to one's previous presence at the discourse on the subject, this is not a form of mere recollection; the understanding is not a psychological phenomenon, the prajñā goes much more penetratingly into the depths of one's personality. The sense of return to something familiar, to the one thoroughly acquainted with it, really means the will getting settled once more in its old abode, after many a venturesome wandering, with an immense treasure of experience now and full of wisdom that will light up its unending career.

VII

It may not be altogether out of place here to make a few remarks concerning the popular view which identifies the philosophy of Schopenhauer with Buddhism. According to this view, the Buddha is supposed to have taught the negation of the will to live, which was insisted upon by the German pessimist, but nothing is further from the correct understanding of Buddhism than this negativism. The Buddha does not consider the will blind, irrational, and therefore to be denied; what he really denies is the notion of ego-entity due to Ignorance, from which notion come craving, attachment to things impermanent, and the giving way to egoistic impulses. The object the Buddha always has in view and never forgets to set forth whenever he thinks opportune is the Enlightenment of the will and not its negation. His teaching is based upon affirmative propositions. The reason why he does not countenance life as it is lived by most of us is because it is the product of Ignorance and egoism, which never fail to throw us into the abyss of pain and misery. The Buddha pointed the way to escape this by Enlightenment and not by annihilation.

The will as it is in itself is pure act, and no taint of egoism is there; this is awakened only when the intellect through its own error grows blind as to the true working of the will and falsely recognizes here the principle of individuation. The Buddha thus wants an illumined will and not the negation of it. When the will is illumined, and thereby when the intellect is properly directed to follow its original course, we are liberated from the fetters which are put upon us by wrong understanding, and purified of all the defilements which ooze from the will not being correctly interpreted. Enlightenment and emancipation are the two central ideas of Buddhism.

The argument Aśvaghosha puts into the mouth of the Buddha against Arada (or Ālāra Kālāma), the Samkhya philosopher, is illuminating in this respect. When Arada told the Buddha to liberate the soul from the body as when the bird flies from the cage or the reed's stalk is loosened from its sheath, which will result in the abandonment of egoism, the Buddha reasons in the following way: 'As long as the soul continues there is no abandonment of egoism. The soul does not become free from qualities as long as it is not released from number and the rest; therefore, so long as there is no freedom from qualities, there is no liberation declared for it. There is no real separation of the qualities and their subject; for fire cannot be conceived apart from its form and heat. Before the body there will be nothing embodied, so before the qualities there will be no subject; how, if it was originally free, could the soul ever become bound? The body-knower (the soul), which is unembodied, must be either knowing or unknowing; if it is knowing there must be some object to be known, and if there is this object

it is not liberated. Or if the soul be declared to be unknowing, then what use to you is this imagined soul? Even
without such a soul, the existence of the absence of knowledge is notorious, as, for instance, in a log of wood or a wall.
And since each successive abandonment is held to be still
accompanied by qualities, I maintain that the absolute
attainment of our end can only be found in the abandonment of everything.'[1]

As long as the dualistic conception is maintained in
regard to the liberation of the soul, there will be no real
freedom as is truly declared by the Buddha. 'The abandonment of everything' means the transcending of the
dualism of soul and body, of subject and object, of that
which knows and that which is known, of 'it is' and 'it
is not', of soul and soul-lessness; and this transcending is
not attained by merely negating the soul or the will, but
by throwing light upon its nature, by realizing it as it is in
itself. This is the act of the will. An intellectual contemplation which is advocated by the Samkhya philosophers
does not lead one to spiritual freedom, but to the realm of
passivity which is their 'realm of nothingness'. Buddhism
teaches freedom and not annihilation, it advocates spiritual
discipline and not mental torpor or emptiness. There must
be a certain turning away in one's ordinary course of life,
there must be a certain opening up of a new vista in one's
spiritual outlook if one wants to be the true follower of the
Buddha. His aversion to asceticism and nihilism as well as
to hedonism becomes intelligible when seen in this light.

The Majjhima-Nikāya's account of the Buddha's interview with the Samkhya thinkers somewhat differs from the
Mahāyāna poet's, but in a way gives a better support to my
argument as regards the Buddha's Enlightenment. The
reason why he was not satisfied with the teaching and
discipline of Ālāra Kālāma and Uddaka is stated to be
this: 'This doctrine does not lead to turning away, to dis-
passion, to cessation, to quietude, to perfect penetration, to

[1] *Buddhacarita*, translated by E. B. Cowell, pp. 131–132.

supreme awakening, to Nirvāṇa, but only to attainment
to the Realm of Nothingness.' What did then the Buddha
understand by Nirvāṇa which literally means annihilation
or cessation, but which is grouped here with such terms as
awakening, turning away (that is, revaluation), and penetration, and contrasted to nothingness? There is no doubt,
as far as we can judge from these qualifications, that
Nirvāṇa is a positive conception pointing to a certain deter-
minable experience. When he came up to the bank of the
Nairanjana and took his seat of soft grass on a shady, peaceful spot, he made up his mind not to leave the place until
he realized in himself what he had been after ever since his
wandering away from home. According to the *Lalitavistara*,
he at that moment made this vow (*praṇidhana*):

'Let my body be dried up on this seat,
Let my skin and bones and flesh be destroyed:
So long as Bodhi is not attained, so hard to attain for many a
    kalpa,
My body and thought will not be removed from this seat.'[1]

Thus resolved, the Buddha finally came to realize Supreme
Enlightenment for which he had belaboured for ever so
many lives. How does this vary from his former attainments under Uddaka and Ālāra Kālāma? Let him express
himself:

'Then, disciples, myself subject to birth, but perceiving
the wretchedness of things subject to birth and seeking after
the incomparable security of Nirvāṇa which is birthless, to
that incomparable security I attained, even to Nirvāṇa
which is birthless.

'Myself subject to growth and decay, but perceiving
the wretchedness of things subject to growth and decay
and seeking after the incomparable security of Nirvāṇa
which is free from growth and decay, to that incomparable
security I attained, even to Nirvāṇa which is free from
growth and decay.

[1] Lefmann's edition, p. 289.

'Myself subject to disease, but perceiving the wretchedness of things subject to disease and seeking after the incomparable security of Nirvāṇa which is free from disease, to that incomparable security I attained, even to Nirvāṇa which is free from disease.

'Myself subject to death, but perceiving the wretchedness of things subject to death and seeking after the incomparable security of Nirvāṇa which is deathless, to that incomparable security I attained, even to Nirvāṇa which is deathless.

'Myself subject to sorrow, but perceiving the wretchedness of things subject to sorrow and seeking after the incomparable security of Nirvāṇa which is sorrowless, to that incomparable security I attained, even to Nirvāṇa which is sorrowless.

'Myself subject to stain, but perceiving the wretchedness of things subject to stain and seeking the incomparable security of Nirvāṇa which is stainless, to that incomparable security I attained, even to Nirvāṇa which is stainless.

'Then I saw and knew: "Assured am I of deliverance; this is my final birth; never more shall I return to this life!" '[1]

When Nirvāṇa is qualified as birthless, deathless, stainless, sorrowless, and free from growth and decay and disease, it looks negativistic enough. But if there were nothing affirmed even in these negations, the Buddha could not rest in 'the incomparable security' (*anuttaram yogakkhemam*) of Nirvāṇa and been assured of final emancipation. What thus the Buddha denied, we can see, was Ignorance as to the true cause of birth and death, and this Ignorance was dispelled by the supreme effort of the will and not by mere dialectic reasoning and contemplation. The will was asserted and the intellect was awakened to its true significance. All the desires, feelings, thoughts, and strivings thus illuminated cease to be egoistic and are no more the cause of defilements and fetters and many other hindrances, of which so many are referred to in all Buddhist

[1] *Ariyapapariyesana-sutta*, Majjhima-Nikāya, XXVI, p. 167.

literature. Mahāyāna and Hīnayāna. In this sense the Buddha is the Jina, Conqueror, not an empty conqueror over nothingness, but the conqueror of confusion, darkness, and Ignorance.

HISTORY OF ZEN BUDDHISM FROM BODHIDHARMA TO HUI-NÊNG (YENŌ)

(A.D. 520—A.D. 713)

My intention here is not to make a thoroughly critical and scientific study of the history of Zen Buddhism; for this presupposes some knowledge of the development of Buddhism in China, and there are, as far as my knowledge extends, no text-books on the subject, which are accessible to readers of this book. The main object of the present Essay will therefore be to acquaint them first with the traditional history of Zen as it is told by its followers both in Japan and China. Its critical investigation will follow when readers are in a degree prepared for the task.

The traditional origin of Zen in India before its introduction into China, which is recorded in Zen literature, is so mixed with legends that no reliable facts can be gathered from it. In the days when there was yet no critical study of anything and when things, especially relating to religion, were believed in a wholesale manner, we could not expect anything else. It may now be too late to try to unravel the mysteries enveloping the origin of Zen in India except in a general and logical way from the historical facts already known concerning the development of Mahāyāna Buddhism. In fact, Zen Buddhism, as was already discussed, is the product of the Chinese mind, or rather the Chinese elaboration of the Doctrine of Enlightenment. Therefore, when we want to narrate the history of Zen, it may be better in some respects not to go to India but to stay in China and study the psychology and philosophy of her people and the surrounding conditions that made it possible for Zen to achieve a successful growth in the land of the celestials, always remembering that it is a practical interpretation of the Doctrine of Enlightenment.

Some scholars may, however, object to this kind of treatment of the subject, on the ground that if Zen is at all a form of Buddhism, or even the essence of it as is claimed by its followers, it cannot be separated from the general history of Buddhism in India. This is quite true, but as far as facts are concerned, Zen as such did not exist in India—that is, in the form as we have it today; and therefore when we try to go beyond China to trace its origin and development, the only way open to us will be the one I have followed in my previous Essays collected here. That is to say, we must consider Zen the Chinese interpretation of the Doctrine of Enlightenment, which is expounded in all Buddhist literature, most intensively in the Mahāyāna and more or less provisionally in the Hīnayāna. As time went on this doctrine steadily grew to occupy the minds of the Buddha's followers and to control the course of development of Buddhist thought generally; for was it not through Enlightenment that Gautama became the Buddha, the Enlightened One? and is it not the object of Buddhism to follow the footsteps of its founder in the attainment of final emancipation? But the Chinese adherents of Bodhism[1] or the upholders of Enlightenment did not wish to swallow Indian Buddhism undigested. The practical imagination of the Chinese people came thus to create Zen, and developed it to the best of their abilities to suit their own religious requirements.

When we compare Zen as a finished product with the Doctrine of Enlightenment, as the latter began to unfold itself in primitive Buddhism, we find a wide and seemingly impassable gap between the two. This was, however, naturally to be expected. Let us consider the following facts. In the beginning the Buddha was somewhat timid to disclose the entire secrets of the reason of Buddhahood, thinking that his disciples were not quite capable of following every step he had taken himself. The feeling he first had after Enlightenment governed him almost throughout the entire

[1] Used to designate the school which upholds the Doctrine of Enlightenment (*sambodhi*).

course of his earthly life. It was this: that the Perfect
Supreme Enlightenment attained by him was too exalted
an object for sentient beings to strive after, and that even
when it were disclosed to them they would not fully comprehend it but might defile it to their own demerit. Did he
not even think of passing into Nirvāṇa right after Enlightenment? His whole life, in spite of the advice of the Brah-
madeva, seems to have been controlled by this feeling—the
reluctance to reveal the entirety of his inmost self-realization (*pratyātmajñāna*, according to the terminology of the
Laṅkāvatāra). In point of fact, the Buddha himself might
have communicated what he realized to all his disciples
unreservedly, but the impression we get from the Āgama
or Nikāya literature is that he was actually reluctant to do
so. At least this was the way the earlier writers of the canonical books attempted to represent their master whatever
their motives might be. This being the case, the idea of
Enlightenment was not brought forward so fully and conspicuously in Hīnayāna literature as at once to command
our attention. But as I pointed out, this idea lies only
superficially buried among the other and less-important
ideas, and can easily be made manifest by logically and
psychologically following up the course of events related in
the canonical writings concerning the Enlightenment of the
Buddha.

The earlier writers conceived the Fourfold Noble Truth
or the Twelvefold Chain of Causation, or the Eightfold Path
of Righteousness to be the central teaching of Buddhism,
which also included on the psychological side the theory of
non-ego (*anātman*). But when we reflect, both philosophically and from the Zen point of view, on the life of the
Buddha and on the ultimate principle of Buddhahood,we
cannot help thinking of his Enlightenment as the most
significant and most essential and most fruitful part of
Buddhism. Therefore, what the Buddha really wished to
impart to his disciples must be said to have been the
Doctrine of Enlightenment in spite of the Hīnayānistic interpretation or understanding of what is known as primitive

Buddhism. But so long as Buddhism flourished in India, this its central idea remained what it was; that is, such as is developed in most of the Mahāyāna Sūtras. It was only after Bodhidharma, who brought it to China, that the idea took root there and grew up to what we designate now specifically as the Zen school of Buddhism. The history of Zen, therefore, properly speaking or in its narrower sense, may best be regarded as beginning in China. The Indian soil was too metaphysical, too rich in romantic imagination, for Zen to grow as such in its pure form.

While the attainment of Buddhahood or Arhatship was the ultimate goal of his teaching, the Buddha was practical and always close to the facts of life and insisted in his ordinary sermons on a life regulated by moral rules. Nor had he any desire to disclose intellectually or metaphysically the content of Enlightenment which must be experienced but cannot be explained. He never neglected to emphasize the significance of self-realization, for Nirvāṇa or Enlightenment was to be attained personally through one's own efforts in one's own inner consciousness. The Fourfold Noble Truth or the Twelvefold Chain of Causation or the Theory of Non-ego was an intellectual guide to the realization of the Buddhist life. Such teaching could not have any practical meaning except as finally leading to Enlightenment.

The Buddha never thought that his followers would come to lay the entire stress of his teaching on these intellectual structures which could not stand by themselves without being supported by an inner spirit. The Eightfold Path of Righteousness was an ethical guide to Enlightenment, and as such it was regarded by the Buddha. Those who have no higher insight into his teaching than reading a moral signification in it take it for a kind of ethical culture and no more. They think that Buddhism is a positivism as philosophy and its Brotherhood (saṁgha) a body of moral ascetics. They praise the Buddha as the originator of a scientific religious system free from spiritualistic superstitions which so frequently and abundantly grow around religion. But we know better because these comments are not in full accord with the teaching of the Buddha, for they only reflect one side of it and fail to take an inner and comprehensive view of the whole field. If these critics took up the practice of dhyana as constituting the essence of Buddhism along with the above considerations, they may be said to have come nearer to the goal; but even this dhyana is a form of spiritual exercise which will prepare the way to the final realization of Nirvāna. Dhyāna in itself does not distinguish Buddhism from the other philosophico-religious systems which existed in India in the day of the Buddha. Therefore, to understand Zen as expressing the Doctrine of Enlightenment, which is the reason of Buddhism, we must wait for the rise of the Mahāyāna movements. And when this was introduced into China by Bodhidharma, it grew up to what we now know by the name of Zen Buddhism.

I

The legendary story of the origin of Zen in India runs as follows: Śākyamuni was once engaged at the Mount of the Holy Vulture in preaching to a congregation of his disciples. He did not resort to any lengthy verbal discourse to explain his point, but simply lifted a bouquet of flowers before the assemblage, which was presented to him by one of his lay-disciples. Not a word came out of his mouth. Nobody understood the meaning of this except the old venerable Mahākāśyapa, who quietly smiled at the master, as if he fully comprehended the purport of this silent but eloquent teaching on the part of the Enlightened One. The latter perceiving this opened his gold-tongued mouth and proclaimed solemnly, 'I have the most precious treasure, spiritual and transcendental, which this moment I hand over to you, O venerable Mahākāśyapa!'

Orthodox Zen followers generally blindly take this

incident to be the origin of their doctrine, in which, according to them, is disclosed the inmost mind of the Buddha as well as the secret of the religion. As Zen claims to be the inmost essence of Buddhism and to have been directly transmitted by the Buddha to his greatest disciple, Mahākāśyapa, its followers naturally look for the particular occasion when this transmission took place between the master and the disciple. We know in a general way that Mahākāśyapa succeeded the Buddha as the leader of the Faith, but as to his special transmission of Zen, we have no historical records in the Indian Buddhist writings at present in our possession. This fact is, however, specially mentioned for the first time, as far as we know, in a Chinese Zen history called *The Records of the Spread of the Lamp*, compiled by Li Tsun-hsü, in 1029, and also in *The Accounts of the Orthodox Transmission of the Dharma*, compiled by Ch'i-sung in 1064, where this incident is only referred to as not quite an authentic one historically. In *The Records of the Transmission of the Lamp*, written in 1004, which is the earliest Zen history now extant, the author does not record any particular event in the life of the Buddha regarding the Zen transmission. As all the earlier histories of Zen are lost, we have at present no means to ascertain how early the Zen tradition started in China. Probably it began to be talked about among the Zen followers when their religion had been well established in China late in the eighth century.

In those days there must have been some necessity to invent such a legend for the authorization of Zen Buddhism; for as Zen grew in strength the other schools of Buddhism already in existence grew jealous of its popular influence and attacked it as having no authorized records of its direct transmission from the founder of Buddhism, which was claimed by the devotees of Zen. This was the case especially when the latter made so light of the doctrinal teaching discussed in the Sūtras and Śastras, as they thought that the ultimate authority of Zen issued out of their own direct personal experience. In this latter they were quite insistent; but they were not, nor could they be, so critical and independent as to ignore altogether the authority of historical Buddhism, and they wanted somehow to find the record that the Buddha handed Zen over to Mahākāśyapa and from Mahākāśyapa on to the twenty-eighth patriarch, Bodhidharma, who became the first patriarch of Zen in China. A line of twenty-eight Indian patriarchs thus came to be established by Zen historians, while, according to other schools, there were only twenty-three or twenty-four patriarchs after the founder. When the historians had the need for the special transmission of Zen from the Buddha to Mahākāśyapa, they felt it necessary to fill up the gap between the twenty-third or twenty-fourth patriarch and Bodhidharma himself, who according to them was the twenty-eighth.

From the modern critical point of view it did not matter very much whether Zen originated with Bodhidharma in China or with the Buddha in India, inasmuch as Zen is true, and has an enduring value. And again from the historian's point of view, which tries scientifically to ascertain the source of development resulting in Zen Buddhism, it is only important to find a logical connection between the Mahāyāna Doctrine of Enlightenment in India and its practical application by the Chinese to the actualities of life; and as to any special line of transmission in India before Bodhidharma as was established by the Zen devotees, it is not a matter of much concern nor of great importance. But as soon as Zen is formulated into an independent system, not only with its characteristic features but with its historically ascertainable facts, it will be necessary for the historians to trace its line of transmission complete and not interrupted; for in Zen, as we shall see later, it is of the utmost importance for its followers to be duly certified or approved (*abbhanumodana*) by the master as to the genuineness or orthodox character of their realization. Therefore, as long as Zen is the product of the Chinese soil from the Indian seed of Enlightenment as I take it, no special line of transmission need be established in India unless it is in a general logical manner such as was attempted in my previous Essays.

The twenty-eight patriarchs of Zen regarded by its followers as the orthodox line of transmission are as follows:

1. Śākyamuni.	15. Kāṇadeva.
2. Mahākāśyapa.	16. Ārya Rāhulata.
3. Ānanda.	17. Saṁghanandi.
4. Śaṇavāsa.	18. Saṁghayaśas.
5. Upagupta.	19. Kumārata.
6. Dhṛitaka.	20. Jayata.
7. Micchaka.	21. Vasubandhu.
8. Buddhanandi.	22. Manura.
9. Buddhamitra.	23. Haklenayaśas.
10. Bhikshu Parśva.	24. Bhikshu Siṁha.
11. Puṇyayaśas.	25. Vāśasita.
12. Aśvaghosha.	26. Puṇyamitra.
13. Bhikshu Kapimala.	27. Prajñātara.
14. Nāgārjuna.	28. Bodhidharma.

To be consistent with the view that Zen was a 'special transmission from the Buddha outside of his doctrinal teaching', Zen historians have extended this transmission even beyond Śākyamuni; for, according to tradition prevalent already among primitive Buddhists, there were at last six Buddhas prior to the Buddha of the present kalpa who was the Muni of the Śākyas; and these several Buddhas had each to leave a gāthā of 'Dharma transmission' which is systematically preserved in Zen history. Now if the six Buddhas of the past had their gāthās, why not those patriarchs between Śākyamuni and Bodhidharma, all inclusively? Or, if any one of them had at all any kind of gāthā, why not the rest of them too? So, they have all bequeathed their gāthās of transmission regularly prefaced with the words, 'I now hand over to you the eye-treasure of the Great Law, which you will guard and ever be mindful of.' No doubt they are fictitious productions of the historical imagination which was so highly exercised by the early writers of Zen history, evidently inspired by an extraordinary zeal for their orthodox faith.

The translators of these patriarchal verses are, according to the author of the *Records of the Right Transmission*, Chih-chaing-liang-lou, of the First Wei dynasty, and Na-lien-ya-shê, of the Eastern Wei; the former came from Middle India and the latter from Kabul. Their book, known as the *Account of Succession in the Law*, disappeared after the repeated persecutions carried out by the reigning dynasties, but the stories of these patriarchs were quoted at least in the two books, the *Pao-lin Ch'uan* and the *Shêng-chou Chi*, both compiled prior to the *Transmission of the Lamp*, in which they are referred to. But they too were lost some time after Kaisu (Ch'i-sung) in the Sung dynasty. Therefore at present the *Transmission of the Lamp* is the earliest history of Zen, where the twenty-eight patriarchs and their verses of law-transmission are recorded in detail.

To quote as samples two of the six Buddhas' gāthās, the first Buddha Vipaśyi declares:

'This body from within the Formless is born,
It is like through magic that all forms and images appear:
Phantom beings with mentality and consciousness have no reality from the very beginning;
Both evil and happiness are void, have no abodes.'

The gāthā of the sixth Buddha, Kāśyapa, who just preceded the Muni of the Śākyas, runs thus:

'Pure and immaculate is the nature of all sentient beings;
From the very beginning there is no birth, no death;
This body, this mind—a phantom creation it is;
And in phantom transformation there are neither sins nor merits.'

When the Buddha belonging to the present age ordered Mahākāśyapa to be the orthodox transmitter of the Good Law, he uttered the following verse:

'The Dharma is ultimately a dharma which is no-dharma;
A dharma which is no-dharma is also a dharma;
As I now hand this no-dharma over to thee;
What we call the Dharma, the Dharma—where after all is the
    Dharma?'[1]

The sixth patriarch, Dhṛitaka, has:

'Penetrate into the ultimate truth of mind,
And we have neither things nor no-things;
Enlightened and not-enlightened—they are the same;
Neither mind nor thing there is.'

The twenty-second patriarch, Manura, gave his view
thus:

'The mind moveth with the ten thousand things:
Even when moving, it is serene.
Perceive its essence as it moveth on,
And neither joy nor sorrow there is.'

In these gāthās we notice the teaching generally
characteristic of Mahāyāna Buddhism as it prevailed in
India. As I said before, as far as the doctrinal side of
Buddhism was concerned, Zen had nothing particularly to
offer as its own; for its *raison d'être* consists in its being a
spiritual experience and not in its being a special system of
philosophy or of certain dogmas conceptually synthesized.
We have Zen only when the Mahāyāna Buddhist speculation is reduced to the actual things of life and becomes the
direct expression of one's inner life. And this did not come
to pass until Buddhism was transplanted into China and
made there to grow nourished by a people whose practical
turn of mentality refused to swallow the Indian tradition
undigested. The form of thought as adopted in the so-called
patriarchal verses did not appeal to the Chinese mind. When
they got into the thought itself, they wished to express it in
their own way, they wished to live the thought as was

[1] This translation is not at all satisfactory.

natural to them, and not to hoard it as something imported from abroad and not inherently belonging to their psychology.

When Bodhidharma gave his full sanction to his disciples, he is supposed to have composed the following gāthā:

'The original reason of my coming to this country
Was to transmit the Law in order to save the confused;
One flower with five petals is unfolded,
And the bearing of fruit will by itself come.'

By this 'bearing of fruit' did Dharma prophesy the full development of Zen later in China? The 'five petals' are supposed to mean the five Zen Fathers in China after Dharma when Zen came to be recognized as a branch of Buddhism with a message of its own. Whether this gāthā was really a prophetic one by Dharma himself, or whether it was composed by some Zen historian after the sixth patriarch Hui-nêng (Yenō), we have no means to decide. The one thing is certain historically that Dharma's teaching began to be naturalized in China about two hundred years after him and assimilated by her people in a manner best suited to their mental idiosyncrasies. Zen in the form we have it today could not mature anywhere outside China. India was too metaphysical, or too given up to mystic imagination. It was the home for the Yuishiki (Yogācāra), the Shingon (Mantra school), the Kegon (Avataṁsaka), or the Sanron (Śūnyatā or Mādhyamika). As for Zen, it needed a mind which had already been deeply steeped in the Laotzŭan ideas and feelings and yet could not detach itself from the details of daily life. Aloofness, romanticism, a certain practical temperament, and yet an even, steady, well-balanced character—these were needed to develop Zen to its present form. That is to say, if Mahāyāna Buddhism, as was expounded by Nāgārjuna and Aśvaghosha, and in the *Vimalakīrti*, *Prajñāpāramitā*, and other Sutras, especially in the *Laṅkāvatāra*, were not worked upon by

Chinese genius, Zen as such could not at all have come into existence.

It may not altogether be out of place here to show by concrete examples how much the Indian method diverges from the typically Chinese one in demonstrating the truth of Zen Buddhism. As I have repeatedly illustrated, Buddhism, whether primitive or developed, is a religion of freedom and emancipation, and the ultimate aim of its discipline is to release the spirit from its possible bondage so that it can act freely in accordance with its own principles. This is what is meant by non-attachment (*apratishṭita-cittam*). The idea is negative inasmuch as it is concerned with untying the knots of the intellect and passion, but the feeling implied is positive, and the final object is attained only when the spirit is restored to its original activity. The spirit knows its own way, and what we can do is to rid it of all the obstacles our ignorance has piled before it. 'Throw them down' is therefore the recurring note in the Buddhist teaching.

The Indian Buddhist way of impressing the idea is this: a Brahman named Black-nails came to the Buddha and offered him two huge flowering trees which he carried each in one of his hands through his magical power. The Buddha called out, and when the Brahman responded the Buddha said, 'Throw them down!' The Brahman let down the flowering tree in his left hand before the Buddha. The latter called out again to let them go, whereupon Black-nails dropped the other flowering tree in the right hand. The Buddha still kept up his command. Said the Brahman: 'I have nothing now to let go. What do you want me to do?' 'I never told you to abandon your flowering plants,' said the Buddha, 'what I want you to do is to abandon your six objects of sense, your six organs of sense, and your six consciousnesses. When these are all at once abandoned and there remains nothing further to be abandoned, it is then that you are released from the bondage of birth-and-death.'

In contrast to this plain, though somewhat roundabout,

talk of the Buddha, the following case of Jōshu (Chao-chou)[1] is direct and concise and disposes of the matter in a most unequivocal manner. A monk came and asked the master, 'How is it when a man brings nothing with him?' 'Throw it away!' was Jōshu's immediate response. 'What shall he throw down when he is not burdened at all?' 'If so, carry it along!' The Zen masters delight in paradoxes, and Jōshu's remark here is a typical one.

The problem of emancipation is important, but the still more important one is, 'Who or what is the Buddha?' When this is mastered, Buddhism has rendered its full service. What did the Indian philosophers think of the Buddha? There was an old lady who lived at the time of the Buddha. She was born at the same time as the Buddha himself and lived in the eastern part of the city. She had a singular aversion against the Buddha and never wished to see him. Whenever he passed by she would run away. But whichever way she turned she would encounter him, east or west. She covered her face with her hands, and lo! she saw the Buddha between her fingers. This is beautiful and illuminating. What follows is the Zen way of treating the subject: A monk came to Ch'i-an, who was one of the disciples of Ma-tsu, and asked, 'What is the original body of Vairochana?' Said the master, 'Would you mind passing that water-pitcher over to me?' The monk handed it to the master as asked. Then the master requested him to put it back where he got it. The monk did so. But not getting any answer as he thought to his first question, he asked again, 'What is the original body of Vairochana Buddha?' The master expressed his regret, saying, 'Long it is since the departure of the old Buddha!' These two instances will suffice to illustrate where the Chinese Zen mind deviates from the Indian.

---

[1] Jōshu (778–897) was one of the early masters of Zen in the T'ang dynasty when it began to flourish with its vigorous freshness. He attained to a high age of one hundred and twenty. His sermons were always short and to the point, and his answers are noted for their being so natural and yet so slippery, so hard to catch.

II

The history of Zen dates with the coming of Bodhidharma (Bodai-Daruma) from the west, A.D. 520. He
came to China with a special message which is summed
up in the following lines:

'A special transmission outside the scriptures;
No dependence upon words and letters;
Direct pointing at the soul of man;
Seeing into one's nature and the attainment of Buddhahood.'

These four lines as describing the principles of Zen
teaching as distinguished from other schools of Buddhism
already in existence in China were formulated later and not
by Dharma himself. We cannot exactly tell who was the
real author, as we have no definite information on this
subject. One historian, Tsung-chien, who compiled from
the T'ien-tai point of view a Buddhist history entitled *The
Rightful Lineage of the Śākya Doctrine in 1257*, ascribes it to
Nansen Fu-gwan; probably the formula originated in those
days when Baso (Ma-tsu), Hyakjo (Pai-chang), Ōbaku
(Huang-po), Sekitō (Shih-tou), and Yakusan (Yüeh-shan)
were flourishing in the 'West of the River' and in the 'South
of the Lake'. Since then they have been regarded as
characteristically Zen, and it was Dharma that breathed
this spirit into the minds of the Chinese Buddhists. The
latter had more or less been given up, on the one hand, to
philosophizing, and, on the other hand, to practising
contemplation. They were not acquainted with the direct
method of Zen which was to see straightway into the
truth of Enlightenment and attain Buddhahood without
going through so many stages of preparation prescribed by
the scholars.

Our knowledge of the life of Bodhidharma comes from
two sources. One, which is the earliest record we have of

him is by Tao-hsüan in his *Biographies of the High Priests* which was compiled early in the T'ang dynasty, A.D. 645. The author was the founder of a Vinaya sect in China and a learned scholar, who, however, was living before the movement of the new school to be known as Zen came into maturity under Hui-nêng, the sixth patriarch, who was nine years old when Tao-hsüan wrote his *Biographies*. The other source is the *Records of the Transmission of the Lamp*, A.D. 1004, compiled by Tao-yüan early in the Sung dynasty. This was written by a Zen monk after Zen had received full recognition as a special branch of Buddhism, and contains sayings and doings of its masters. The author often refers to some earlier Zen histories as his authorities, which are, however, lost now, being known by the titles only.

It is quite natural that these two accounts of the life of Bodhi-Dharma should vary at several points. The first was written when Zen was not yet fully established as a school, and the second by one of the Zen masters. In the first, Dharma, the founder of Zen, is treated as one of the many other Buddhist priests eminent in various fields as trans-lators, commentators, scholars, Vinaya-followers, masters of meditation, possessors of miraculous virtues, etc., and Dharma could not naturally occupy in such a history any very prominent position distinguishing himself from the other 'high priests'. He is described merely as one of those 'masters of meditation' whose conception of dhyana did not differ from the old traditional one as was practised by the Hinayana followers.

Tao-hsüan did not understand the message of Dharma in its full signification, though he could read in it some-thing not quite of the so-called 'practice of meditation'. And therefore it is sometimes argued by scholars that there is not much of Zen in Tao-hsüan's account of Dharma worthy of its first Chinese promulgator and that therefore Dharma could not be so regarded as is claimed by the followers of the Zen school of Buddhism. But this is not doing justice to Zen, nor to Tao-hsüan, who never thought of writing a Zen history before Zen came to be known as such. Tao-hsüan could not be a prophetic historian. While the biographical history of Tao-yüan contains much that is to be discredited as regards the life of Bodhidharma, especially that part of his life before he came to China, we have reason to believe that the greater part of Tao-yüan's account of Dharma's doings after his arrival in China is historical. In this latter respect Tao-hsüan must be taken as complementing Tao-yüan. It is not quite in accord with the spirit of fair critical judgment to be partial to one authority at the expense of the other without duly weighing all the historically known circumstances that contributed to the making of these histories.

According to Tao-hsüan, Bodhidharma left many writings or sayings which were apparently still in circulation at the time of the author of the *Biographies of the High Priests*, but the only authentic writing of the Zen founder's at present in our possession is a very short one, which is preserved in Tao-hsüan's *Biographies*, as well as in Tao-yüan's *Records*. There are some other essays ascribed to Dharma,[1] but most of which, though deeply imbibing the spirit of Zen, are spurious except one which I am inclined to think to be genuinely his. It is entitled 'On the Pacification of the Soul'. Together with the first one, which is generally known under the title 'Meditation on Four Acts', we have just two pieces of writings handed down as Dharma's. Though I do not think that the 'Meditation on Four Acts' could be the best possible specimen of writing to be bequeathed by the founder of Zen, which will admit us straightway into the very essence of Zen, I will give here an English translation of it as the most reliable essay of Bodhidharma, the first patriarch of Zen in China.

There are two versions, as I said before, of this writing, the one in the *Biographies* and the other in the *Records*, and they do not quite agree with each other in some points. The main drift is the same, but in detail they vary.

[1] *Six Essays by Bodhidharma* is the book in which the so-called writings of Bodhidharma are collected. See also the Essay 'On Satori' which follows.

The question now is: which is the more original one?
Chronologically the *Biographies* were compiled earlier than
the *Records*, but the latter presupposes some earlier writings
which were utilized for its compilation. We have no means
to ascertain the reliability of the documents thus made use
of, and then the authority of the *Biographies* is not absolute.
Therefore the only profitable method of judging the
respective merit of the two versions is to compare them
from the literary point of view and see what light such
comparison will shed on the nature of each. The result I
have reached is that the author of the *Biographies* used the
one preserved in the *Records*, which is more faithful to the
original if there were any such besides this very version. The
reason for this conclusion is that Dharma's writing appears
much improved after the editing of Tao-hsüan, the author
of the *Biographies*; for he had to edit it for his own purposes.
Thus edited, Dharma's writing is now in a better style;
that is, more concise, more to the point, and more refined.
For this reason the following translation is made from Tao-
yüan's *Records* in which the author had every reason to
reproduce the original as it stood.

'[Bodhidharma], the Teacher of the Law, was the third
son of a great Brahman king in South India, of the Western
Lands. He was a man of wonderful intelligence, bright and
far-reaching; he thoroughly understood everything that he
ever learned. As his ambition was to master the doctrine
of the Mahāyāna, he abandoned the white dress of a layman and put on the black robe of monkhood, wishing to
cultivate the seeds of holiness. He practised contemplation
and tranquillization, he knew well what was the true
significance of worldly affairs. Inside and outside he was
transpicuous; his virtues were more than a model to the
world. He was grieved very much over the decline of the
orthodox teaching of the Buddha in the remoter parts of
the earth. He finally made up his mind to cross over land
and sea and come to China and preach his doctrine in the
kingdom of Wei. Those that were spiritually inclined
gathered about him full of devotion, while those that could

not rise above their own one-sided views talked about him slanderingly.

'At the time there were only two monks called Tao-yih and Hui-k'ê, who while yet young had a strong will and desire to learn higher things. Thinking it a great opportunity of their lives to have such a teacher of the Law in their own land, they put themselves under his instruction for several years. Most reverently they followed him, asked questions to be enlightened, and observed his directions well. The Teacher of the Law was moved by their spirit of sincerity and disciplined them in the true path, telling them, "This is the way to obtain peace of mind," and "This is the way to behave in the world," "This is the way to live harmoniously with your surroundings," and "This is the upāya (means)." These being the Mahāyāna ways to keep the mind tranquil, one has to be on guard against their wrongful applications. By this mental pacification *Pi-kuan*[1] is meant; by this behaviour, the Four Acts; by this harmony with things, the protection from slander and ill-disposition; and by this Upāya, detachment.

'Thus I[2] have briefly stated the story of what follows.

'There are many ways to enter the Path, but briefly speaking they are of two sorts only. The one is "Entrance by Reason" and the other "Entrance by Conduct". By "Entrance by Reason" we mean the realization of the spirit of Buddhism by the aid of the scriptural teaching. We then come to have a deep faith in the True Nature which is one and the same in all sentient beings. The reason why it does not manifest itself is due to the overwrapping of

---

[1] This is the most significant phrase in Dharma's writing. I have left it untranslated, for later this will be explained fully.

[2] The author of this story or prefatory note is T'an-lin (Donrin), who, according to Dr. Tokiwa, of the Tokyo Imperial University, was a learned scholar partaking in the translation of several Sanskrit works. He is also mentioned in connection with Yeka (Hui-k'ê) in the biography of the latter by Tao-hsüan. If Donrin were more of a scholar as we can see by this identification than a genuine Zen master, it was quite natural for him to write down this 'Meditation on Four Acts', which mainly appeals as it stands to the scholarly interpretation of Zen. While the doctrine of *Pi-kuan* is emphatically Zen, there is much in the 'Meditation' that lends itself to the philosophizing of Zen.

external objects and false thoughts. When one, abandoning the false and embracing the true, and in simpleness of thought abides in *Pi-kuan*, one finds that there is neither selfhood nor otherness, that the masses and the worthies are of one essence, and firmly holds on to this belief and never moves away therefrom. He will not then be guided by any literary instructions, for he is in silent communion with the principle itself, free from conceptual discrimination, for he is serene and not-acting. This is called "Entrance by Reason".

'By "Entrance by Conduct" is meant the Four Acts in which all other acts are included. What are the four? 1. How to requite hatred; 2. To be obedient to karma; 3. Not to seek after anything; and 4. To be in accord with the Dharma.

'1. What is meant by "How to requite hatred"? Those who discipline themselves in the Path should think thus when they have to struggle with adverse conditions: During the innumerable past ages I have wandered through multiplicity of existences, all the while giving myself to unimportant details of life at the expense of essentials, and thus creating infinite occasions for hate, ill-will, and wrong-doing. While no violations have been committed in this life, the fruits of evil deeds in the past are to be gathered now. Neither gods nor men can foretell what is coming upon me. I will submit myself willingly and patiently to all the ills that befall me, and I will never bemoan or complain. In the Sūtra it is said not to worry over ills that may happen to you. Why? Because through intelligence one can survey [the whole chain of causation]. When this thought arises, one is in concord with the principle because he makes the best use of hatred and turns it into the service in his advance towards the Path. This is called the "way to requite hatred".

'2. By "being obedient to karma" is meant this: There is no self (ātman) in whatever beings that are produced by the interplay of karmaic conditions; pain and pleasure we suffer are also the results of our previous action. If I am rewarded with fortune, honour, etc., this is the outcome of my past deeds which, by reason of causation, affect my present life. When the force of karma is exhausted, the result I am enjoying now will disappear; what is then the use of being joyful over it? Gain or loss, let us accept karma as it brings us the one or the other; the spirit itself knows neither increase nor decrease. The wind of gladness does not move it, as it is silently in harmony with the Path. Therefore this is called "being obedient to karma".

'3. By "not seeking after anything" is meant this: Men of the world, in eternal confusion, are attached everywhere to one thing or another, which is called seeking. The wise, however, understand the truth and are not like the vulgar. Their minds abide serenely in the uncreated while the body turns about in accordance with the laws of causation. All things are empty and there is nothing desirable and to be sought after. Wherever there is the merit of brightness there follows the demerit of darkness. This triple world where one stays too long is like a house on fire; all that has a body suffers, and who would ever know what is rest? Because the wise are thoroughly acquainted with this truth, they get never attached to anything that becomes, their thoughts are quieted, they never seek. Says the Sūtra: Wherever there is seeking, there you have sufferings; when seeking ceases you are blessed. Thus we know that not to seek is verily the way to the truth. Therefore I preach to you not "to seek after anything".

'4. By "being in accord with the Dharma" is meant that the reason in its essence is pure which we call the Dharma, and that this reason is the principle of emptiness in all that is manifested, as it is above defilements and attachments, and as there is no Self or Other in it. Says the Sūtra: in the Dharma there are no sentient beings, because it is free from the stains of being; in the Dharma there is no Self because it is free from the stain of selfhood. When the wise understand this truth and believe in it, their conduct will be "in accordance with the Dharma".

'As the Dharma in essence has no desire to possess, the wise are ever ready to practise charity with their body, life, property, and they never begrudge, they never know what an ill grace means. As they have a perfect understanding of the threefold nature of emptiness they are above partiality and attachment. Only because of their will to cleanse all beings of their stains, they come among them as of them, but they are not attached to the form. This is known as the inner aspect of their life. They, however, know also how to benefit others, and again how to glorify the path of enlightenment. As with the virtue of charity, so with the other five virtues [in the Prajñāpāramitā]. That the wise practise the six virtues of perfection is to get rid of confused thoughts, and yet they are not conscious of their doings. This is called "being in accord with the Dharma".'

The doctrine of the Two Entrances is evidently taken from the *Vajrasamādhi-sūtra*;[1] and that of the Four Acts is an amplification of the second form of Entrance as is expounded in the Sūtra. A comparison with the passage from it will make this point clear at once:

'Said the Buddha: The two entrances are "Entrance by Reason" and "Entrance by Conduct". "Entrance by Reason" means to have a deep faith in that all sentient beings are identical in essence with the true nature which is neither unity nor multiplicity; only it is beclouded by external objects. The nature in itself neither departs nor comes. When a man in singleness of thought abides in *chüeh-kuan*, he will clearly see into the Buddha-nature, of which we cannot say whether it exists or exists not, and in which there is neither selfhood nor otherness. He will also find that the nature is the same both in the masses and in the worthies. He thus firmly holds the ground of the diamond-heart and never moves away therefrom; he is serene and not-doing, and free from conceptual discrimination. This is called "Entrance by Reason".

' "Entrance by Conduct" means not to be unsteady and

---

[1] Translated into Chinese during the Northern Liang dynasty, which lasted from A.D. 397–439. The translator's name is lost.

reclining in mind and not to be in its shadows changing like a stream. Wherever you are, let your thought be serene and not to be seeking after anything. Let it be like unto the great earth unmoved even in a raging storm. Giving up all thoughts of egoism in your heart, save all beings and let them cross over to the other shore. There are no births, no signs, no clinging, no abandoning; in the mind of a Bodhisattva there is no going-out, no coming-in. When this mind which neither goes out nor comes in enters into that which is never entered into, it is called entering. This is the way the Bodhisattva enters into the Dharma. The Dharma is not empty in form, and the Dharma of non-emptiness is not to be put aside as non-entity. Why? The Dharma that is not non-entity is filled with virtues. It is neither mind nor shadows, it is pure in its suchness.'

In comparing these two texts the reader will be impressed with the most important and most striking change Bodhi-Dharma made in his quotation, which is the substituting of *pi-kuan* for *chüeh-kuan*. *Pi* ordinarily means 'wall' or 'precipice', and is often found in combination with *li*, 'standing', in such phrases as *pi li wan jên*, to describe an unscalable wall, or figuratively to represent the attitude, for instance, of Acala-Vidyārāja standing straight up. What was the reason of Dharma's changing *chüeh*, 'to awaken', or 'to be enlightened' into a word which apparently has no organi crelation to the following *kuan*, 'to perceive' or 'to contemplate'? The novel combination is a very important one, for it alters the sense of the whole context in which it occurs.

Tao-hsüan, the author of the *Biographies*, refers to Dharma's *tai ch'êng pi kuan* (Mahāyānistic wall-contemplation) in his commentary notes to Zen, as the most meritorious work Dharma achieved in China. For this reason he is often spoken of as the *pi-kuan* Brahman—that is, wall-contemplating Brahman—and in Japan the monks belonging to the Sōtō school of Zen are supposed to follow the example of the founder of their religion when they keep up the practice of sitting facing the wall while meditating. But this is evidently a superficial interpretation of the phrase *pi-kuan*; for how could mere wall-gazing start a revolutionary movement in the Buddhist world as is implied in Tao-hsüan's life of Dharma?[1] How could such an innocent practice provoke a terrible opposition among scholars of those days? To my view, *pi-kuan* has a far deeper meaning, and must be understood in the light of the following passage in the *Records*, which is quoted from a work known as the *Pieh-chi*, meaning some special document of prior existence:

'The master first stayed in the Shōrinji (Shao-lin-szŭ) monastery for nine years, and when he taught the second patriarch, it was only in the following way: "Exterally keep yourself away from all relationships, and, internally, have no pantings (or hankerings, *ch'uan*) in your heart;[2] when your mind is like unto a straight-standing wall you may enter into the Path.' Hui-k'ê tried variously to explain [or to discourse on] the reason of mind, but failed to realize the truth itself. The master simply said, "No! No!" and never proposed to explain to his disciple what was the mind-essence in its thought-less state [that is, in its pure being]. [Later] said Hui-k'ê, "I know now how to keep myself away from all relationships." "You make it a total annihilation, do you not?" queried the master. "No, master," replied Hui-k'ê, "I do not make it a total annihilation."

[1] We read in Tao-hsüan's *Biographies* that wherever Bodhidharma stayed he taught people in his Zen doctrine, but as the whole country at the time was deeply plunged into scholastic discussions, there was a great deal of slanderous talk against meditation when they learned of Bodhidharma's message.

[2] Is it possible that this passage has some reference to the *Vajrasamādhi* where Bodhisattva Mahābala speaks of a 'flaccid mind' and a 'strong mind'? The former which is possessed by most common people 'pants' (or gasps or hankers) very much, and prevents them from successfully attaining to the Tathāgata-dhyāna, while the 'strong mind' is characteristic of one who can enter upon the realm of reality (*bhūtakoṭi*). So long as there are 'pantings' (or gaspings) in the mind, it is not free, it is not liberated, and cannot identify itself with the suchness of reason. The mind must be 'strong' or firm and steady, self-possessed and concentrating, before it is ready for the realization of Tathāgata-dhyāna—a dhyāna going far beyond the reach of the so-called four dhyānas and eight samādhis.

"How do you testify your statement?" "For I know it always in a most intelligible manner, but to express it in words—that is impossible." Thereupon, said the master, "That is the mind-essence itself transmitted by all the Buddhas. Harbour no doubts about it." '

In fact, this passage sums up the special message contained in Dharma's teaching, and in it we may get an adequate answer as to the exact meaning of *pi-kuan*. The term must have been a novel one in his day, and the originality of his views really lay in the creative sense of the one word '*pi*'. It was so concrete, so graphic, and there was nothing abstract and conceptual about it. Hence Tao-hsüan's special reference to Dharma's teaching as the *Tai-chêng pi-kuan* (Mahāyānistic wall-contemplation). While there was nothing specifically Zen in his doctrine of 'Two Entrances and Four Acts', the teaching of *pi-kuan*, wall-contemplation, was what made Bodhidharma the first patriarch of Zen Buddhism in China.

The author of the *Rightful Transmission of the Śākya Doctrine* interprets *pi-kuan* as meaning the state of mind where no 'external dusts get in'. This may be all right, but we are not told where he finds the authority for this way of understanding. Had he in mind Dharma's remark to Hui-k'ê as recorded in the document known as *Pieh-chi*? In any event the underlying meaning of the 'wall-contemplation' must be found in the subjective condition of a Zen master, which is highly concentrated and rigidly exclusive of all ideas and sensuous images. To understand the phrase '*pi-kuan*' as simply meaning 'wall-gazing' will be sheer absurdity. If the specific message of Dharma as the founder of Zen in China is to be sought anywhere in the writings of his, which are still in existence, it must be in this 'Mahāyānistic wall-contemplation'.

Besides this writing, which is the only one left by Dharma in our possession at present, we have the *Laṅkā-vatāra-sūtra*, *Vajrasamādhi-sūtra*, and *Vajracchedikā-sūtra*, through which we can also have a glimpse into the central teaching of Bodhidharma. Zen, unlike other schools of

Buddhism, has no particular Sūtras to be called the 'foundation canon' on which its followers would base the principal tenets of their school; but Dharma recommended the *Laṅkāvatarā* to his first disciple Hui-k'ê (Yeka), as containing the teaching most intimately related to Zen, and after him this scriptural writing came to be studied chiefly by Zen scholars.[1] As to the importance of the *Vajrasamādhi* as expounding the philosophy of Zen, we can easily understand it from Dharma's own reference to the Sūtra in his writing as was already pointed out.

With regard to the *Vajracchedikā-sūtra*, most people think of it as having nothing to do with Zen prior to the fifth patriarch, Hungjên (Gunin); for it was he who, for the first time, introduced it among his own disciples, while Dharma himself made no allusion whatever to this, one of the most popular Buddhist texts in China. But according to Hui-nêng's Preface to the *Vajracchedikā*, which is still preserved, 'ever since the coming-west of Dharma he wanted to propagate the meaning of this Sūtra and lead people to understand the Reason and to see into the Nature.' If this were actually the case, Dharma, to say the least, must have had some knowledge of this Sūtra from the very beginning of his career in China, and the connection in a way between this and Zen must have been more fundamental than that between the *Laṅkāvatāra* and Zen. The prevalent notion then that the *Vajracchedikā* came only in vogue after Hungjên and Hui-nêng must be revised. Whatever this may be, the *Laṅkāvatāra* is too difficult a material for popular consumption, and it was natural that this Sūtra came to be gradually superseded by the *Vajracchedikā* as Zen gained more and more in power and influence. As one of the Sūtras belonging to the Prajñāpāramitā class of Buddhist literature, the teaching of the *Vajracchedikā* was comparatively simple and had something much akin to the Laotzŭan ideas of emptiness and non-doing. It was not hard for the average Chinese to follow its philosophy of Śūnyatā; in

[1] This subject was treated in another place, though rather sketchily, and will be further elaborated later in an independent Essay.

fact this agreed well with a certain aspect of Chinese thought.[1]

However, with Zen followers all literature was like a finger pointing at the moon, and there was not much in itself that will actually lead one to the seeing of one's own inner nature; for this seeing was a realization which must be attained by one's own personal efforts apart from the mere understanding of letters. All Buddhist Sūtras including the *Laṅkāvatāra*, *Vajrasamādhi*, and *Vajracchedikā* could not be of much help to the real earnest seekers of the truth, so long as his idea is to grasp the naked facts with his own ungloved hands. This was possible only when his own inner consciousness opened by itself, from within, through his whole-souled efforts. Literature is helpful only when it indicates the way, it is not the thing itself.

The earlier part of Bodhidharma's life while in India as narrated in the *Records* may be discredited as containing a large dose of fiction, but the latter part of it cannot so easily be disposed of. This is where it supplements the story in Tao-hsüan's *Biographies*, which was written by a good historian however, who did not know anything about the future development of Zen. According to the *Records* then, the first great personage Dharma had an interview with when he came to China was the king of Liang, the greatest Buddhist patron of the time. And the interview took place in the following manner:

The Emperor Wu of Liang asked Dharma:

[1] In this connection I wish to make some remarks against certain scholars who consider the philosophy of Śūnyatā to be really the foundation of Zen. Such scholars fail utterly to grasp the true purport of Zen, which is first of all an experience and not at all a philosophy or dogma. Zen can never be built upon any set of metaphysical or psychological views; the latter may be advanced after the Zen experience has taken place, but never before. The philosophy of the Prajñāpāramitā can never precede Zen, but must always follow it. Buddhist scholars like those at the time of Dharma are too apt to identify teaching and life, theory and experience, description and fact. When this confusion is allowed to grow, Zen Buddhism will cease to yield an intelligent and satisfactory interpretation. Without the fact of Enlightenment under the Bodhi-tree near the Nairañjanā, no Nāgārjunas could ever hope to write a single book on the Prajñā philosophy.

'Ever since the beginning of my reign I have built so many temples, copied so many sacred books, and supported so many monks and nuns; what do you think my merit might be?'

'No merit whatever, sire!' Dharma bluntly replied.

'Why?' demanded the Emperor astonished.

'All these are inferior deeds,' thus began Dharma's significant reply, 'which would cause their author to be born in the heavens or on this earth again. They still show the traces of worldliness, they are like shadows following objects. Though they appear actually existing, they are no more than mere non-entities. As to a true meritorious deed, it is full of pure wisdom and is perfect and mysterious, and its real nature is beyond the grasp of human intelligence. Such as this is not to be sought after by any worldly achievement.'

The Emperor Wu thereupon asked Bodhidharma again, 'What is the first principle of the holy doctrine?'

'Vast emptiness, and there is nothing in it to be called holy, sire!' answered Dharma.

'Who is it then that is now confronting me?'

'I know not, sire!'

The answer was simple enough, and clear enough too, but the pious and learned Buddhist Emperor failed to grasp the spirit pervading the whole attitude of Dharma.

Seeing that there was no further help to be given to the Emperor, Dharma left his dominion and retired into a monastery in the state of Wei, where he sat quietly practising the 'wall-contemplation', it is said, for nine long years, until he came to be known as the *Pi-kuan* Brahman.[1]

One day a monk Shên-kuang visited him and most earnestly implored him to be enlightened in the truth of Zen, but Dharma paid no attention. Shên-kuang was not to be disappointed, for he knew that all the great spiritual

---

[1] As I stated before, there is a confusion between Dharma's *mien-pi* habit of sitting and his doctrine of the *pi-kuan* meditation. The confusion dates quite early, and even at the time of the author of the *Records* the original meaning of *pi-kuan*, wall-contemplation, must have been lost.

leaders of the past had gone through with many a heart-rending trial in order to attain the final object of their aspiration. One evening he stood in the midst of the snow waiting for Dharma to notice him when at last the fast-falling snow buried him almost to his knees.

Finally, the master turned back and said, 'What do you wish me to do for you?' Said Kuang, 'I am come to receive your invaluable instructions; pray open your gate of mercy, and extend your hand of salvation to this poor suffering mortal.' 'The incomparable doctrine of Budd-hism,' replied Dharma, 'can be comprehended only after a long hard discipline and by enduring what is most difficult to endure, and by practising what is most difficult to practise. Men of inferior virtue and wisdom are not allowed to understand anything about it. All the labours of such ones will come to naught.'

Kuang at last cut off his left arm with the sword[1] he was carrying, and presented it before the teacher as a token of his sincerity in the desire to be instructed in the doctrine of all the Buddhas. Said Dharma, 'This is not to be sought through another.'

'My soul is not yet pacified. Pray, master, pacify it.'

'Bring your soul here, and I will have it pacified.'

Kuang hesitated for a moment but finally said, 'I have sought it these many years and am still unable to get hold of it!'

'There! it is pacified once for all.' This was Dharma's sentence.[2]

---

[1] Sometimes this man is said to be a civilian and sometimes a soldier embracing Confucianism.

[2] As one can readily see, this story is more or less fictitious. I mean Kuang's standing in the snow and cutting off his arm in order to demonstrate his earnestness and sincerity. Some think that the snow story and that of self-mutilation do not belong to that of Kuang, but are borrowed from some other sources, as Tao-hsüan makes no reference to them in his book. The loss of the arm was due to a party of robbers who attacked Kuang after his interview with Dharma. We have no way to verify these stories either way. The whole setting, however, is highly dramatic, and there must have been once in the history of Zen some necessity to interweave imagination largely with facts, whatever they may be.

Dharma then told him to change his name into Hui-k'ê.

Nine years passed, and Dharma wished to return to his native country. He called in all his disciples before him, and said, 'The time is come for me to depart, and I want to see what your attainments are.'

'According to my view,' said Tao-fu, 'the truth is above affirmation and negation, for this is the way it moveth.'

Dharma said, 'You have got my skin.'

Next came in the nun, Tsung-ch'ih, and said, 'As I understand it, it is like Ānanda's viewing the Buddhaland of Akshobhya: it is seen once and never again.'

Dharma said, 'You have got my flesh.'

Tao-yü was another disciple who presented his view, saying: 'Empty are the four elements and non-existent the five skandhas. According to my view, there is not a thing to be grasped as real.'

Dharma said, 'You have got my bone.'

Finally, Hui-k'ê—that is, Shên-kuang—reverently bowing to the master, kept standing in his seat and said nothing.

Dharma then announced, 'You have my marrow.'[1]

Mystery envelops the end of Bodhidharma's life in China; we do not know how, when, and where he passed away from this earth. Some say that he was poisoned by his rivals, others say that he went back to India, crossing the desert, and still others report that he came over to Japan. In one thing they all agree, which is this: he was quite old, being, according to Tao-hsüan, over one hundred and fifty years at his death.

---

[1] According to Hsieh-sung, the author of the *Right Transmission of the Law*, Bodhidharma has here followed Nāgārjuna in the anatomy of Zen-understanding. For Nāgārjuna says in his famous commentary on the *Prajñāpāramitā-sūtra*, 'Moral conduct is the skin, meditation is the flesh, the higher understanding is the bone, and the mind subtle and good is the marrow.' 'This subtle mind,' says Hsieh-sung, 'is what is secretly transmitted from the Buddha to his successors in the faith. He then refers to Chih-I of the Sui dynasty, who regards this mind as the abode of all the Buddhas and as the middle way in which there is neither unity nor multiplicity and which can never be adequately expressed in words.

III

After Bodhidharma, Hui-k'ê (486–593) was the chief exponent of Zen Buddhism. He was already a learned scholar before he came to his teacher for instruction, not only in the Chinese classics but in Buddhist lore. No amount of learning, however, satisfied him; indeed he seems to have had a sort of enlightenment in his way, which he wanted to be testified to by Dharma. After he left the master he did not at once begin his preaching, hiding himself among the lower strata of society. He evidently shunned being looked up to as a high priest of great wisdom and understanding. However, he did not neglect quietly preaching the Law whenever he had an occasion. He was simply quiet and unassuming, refusing to show himself off. But one day when he was discoursing about the Law before a temple gate, there was another sermon going on inside the temple by a resident priest, learned and honoured. The audience, however, left the reverend lecturer inside and gathered around the street-monk, probably clad in rags and with no outward signs of ecclesiastical dignity. The high priest got angry over the situation. He accused the beggar-monk to the authorities as promulgating a false doctrine, whereupon Hui-k'ê was arrested and put to death. He did not specially plead innocent but composedly submitted, saying that he had according to the law of karma an old debt to pay up. This took place in A.D. 593, and he was one hundred and seven years old when he was killed.

According to Tao-hsüan, Hui-k'ê's eloquence flew directly from his heart, not encrusted with learning or scholarly discourse. While he was preaching in an important city on the meaning of Zen, those who could not rise above 'the letter that killeth' took his teaching for heresy, as the words of a devil devoid of sense. Especially among them a master of meditation called Tao-hüan, who had about one thousand followers about him, at once

PLATE I. LOOKING FOR THE COW

PLATE II. SEEING THE TRACES OF THE COW

PLATE III. SEEING THE COW

PLATE IV. CATCHING THE COW

PLATE V. HERDING THE COW

PLATE VI. COMING HOME ON THE COW'S BACK

PLATE VII. THE COW FORGOTTEN, LEAVING THE
MAN ALONE

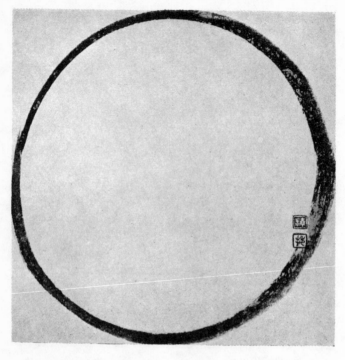

PLATE VIII. THE COW AND THE MAN BOTH GONE
OUT OF SIGHT

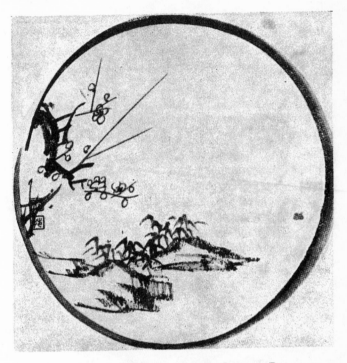

PLATE IX. RETURNING TO THE ORIGIN, BACK TO
THE SOURCE

PLATE X. ENTERING THE CITY WITH BLISS-
BESTOWING HANDS

assumed an offensive attitude towards Hui-k'ê. He sent one of his disciples to the Zen exponent, perhaps to find out what kind of man he really was. As soon as the disciple learned what was the teaching of the so-called heretic, he was so deeply impressed by this man that he was converted into a Zen advocate. Tao-hüan despatched another of his followers to call the first one back, but he followed the example of the predecessor. Several other messengers were sent one after another, but the result was altogether discouraging. Later when Tao-hüan happened to meet his first messenger, he asked: 'How was it that I had to send for you so many times? Did I not open your eye after taking pains so much on my part?' The former disciple, however, mystically answered: 'My eye has been right from the first, and it was through you that it came to squint.' This stirred the master's ire, and it was through his machination, writes Tao-hsüan, that Hui-k'ê had to suffer official persecution.

This story taken from Tao-hsüan's *Biographies* varies from that in the Tao-yüan's *Records*, but they both agree in making Hui-k'ê a martyr at the hands of his enemy. There is no doubt that in the Zen teaching of Bodhidharma and his first Chinese disciple, Hui-k'ê, there was something that was unintelligible to most of the Buddhists of the time who had been trained either in the abstract metaphysics or in the tranquillizing exercises, or in the mere morality, of Buddhism. The exponents of Zen then must have emphasized the truth to be awakened in one's inner consciousness, even at the expense of the canonical teaching as is variously elucidated in the Sūtras and Śastras, many of which in translations had already been in circulation. This must have excited the conservatists and literalists.

Like Bodhidharma, Hui-k'ê did not leave any literary writing, though we know from their biographies that both had their sermons collected and in the case of Hui-k'ê 'classified',[1] whatever this may mean. The following pre-

[1] According to this, there must have been a special volume of sermons, and letters by Hui-k'ê, which were compiled evidently by his disciples

served extracts, however, may throw light on the teaching of Hui-k'ê. A lay-disciple called Hsiang wrote a letter to Hui-k'ê; 'Shadow follows a body and echo rises from a sound. He who in pursuit of the shadow tires out the body, does not know that the body produces the shadow; and he who attempts to stop an echo by raising his voice, does not understand that the voice is the cause of the echo. [In a similar way] he who seeks Nirvāṇa by cutting desires and passions is to be likened to one who seeks a shadow apart from its original body; and he who aspires to Buddhahood thinking it to be independent of the nature of sentient beings is to be likened to one who tries to listen to an echo by deadening its original sound. Therefore, the ignorant and the enlightened are walking in one passageway; the vulgar and the wise are not to be differentiated from each other. Where there are no names, we create names, and because of these names judgments are formed. Where there is no theorizing, we theorize, and because of this theorizing, disputes arise. They are all phantom creations and not realities, and who knows who is right and who is wrong? They are all empty, no substantialities have they, and who knows what is and what is not? So we realize that our gain is not real gain and our loss not real loss. This is my view and may I be enlightened if I am at fault?'

To this Hui-k'ê answered: 'You have truly comprehended the Dharma as it is; the deepest truth lies in the principle of identity. It is due to one's ignorance that the maṇi-jewel is taken for a piece of brick, but lo! when one is suddenly awakened to self-enlightenment it is realized that one is in possession of the real jewel. The ignorant and the enlightened are of one essence, they are not really to be separated. We should know that all things are such as they are. Those who entertain a dualistic view of the world are to be pitied, and I write this letter for them. When we

and admirers before they were put down in writing and thoroughly revised by the author himself. In the case of Bodhidharma too, according to Tao-hsüan, his sayings were apparently in circulation in the day of Tao-hsüan, that is, early in the T'ang dynasty.

know that between this body and the Buddha there is nothing to separate one from the other, what is the use of seeking after Nirvana [as something external to ourselves]?'

Next to Hui-k'ê came Sêng-ts'an, who succeeded as the third patriarch. The interview between master and disciple took place in this manner: A layman of forty troubled with *fêng-yang*[1] according to the *Records*, came to Hui-k'ê and asked:

'I am suffering from *fêng-yang*; pray cleanse me of my sins.'

'Bring your sins here,' said Hui-k'ê, 'and I will cleanse you of them.'

The lay-disciple was silent for a while but finally said, 'As I seek my sins, I find them unattainable.'

'I have then finished cleansing you altogether. You should thenceforth take refuge in the Buddha, Dharma, and Saṁgha (Brotherhood), and abide therein.'

'As I stand before you, O master,' asked Sêng-ts'an, 'I know that you belong to the Brotherhood, but pray tell me what are the Buddha and the Dharma?'

Replied the master: 'Mind is the Buddha, Mind is the Dharma; and the Buddha and the Dharma are not two. The same is to be said of the Brotherhood (*saṁgha*).'

This satisfied the disciple, who now said, 'Today for the first time I realize that sins are neither within nor without nor in the middle; just as Mind is, so is the Buddha, so is the Dharma; they are not two.'[2]

He was then ordained by Hui-k'ê as a Buddhist monk, and after this he fled from the world altogether, and nothing much of his life is known. This was partly due to the persecution of Buddhism carried on by the Emperor of the Chou dynasty. It was in the twelfth year of K'ai-huan, of

[1] Understood by some to be leprosy.

[2] In the *Vimalakīrti*, chapter iii, 'The Disciples', we have the following: 'Do not worry about the sins you have committed, O monks,' said Vimalakīrti. 'Why? Because sins are in their essence neither within nor without nor in the middle. As the Buddha taught us, all things are defiled when Mind is defiled; all things are pure when Mind is pure; and Mind is neither within nor without nor in the middle. As is Mind, so are sins and defilements, so are all things—they never transcend the suchness of truth.'

the Sui dynasty (A.D. 592), that he found a disciple worthy to be his successor. His name was Tao-hsin. He asked the master:

'Pray show me the way to deliverance.'

'Who has ever put you in bondage?'

'Nobody.'

'If so,' said the master, 'why should you ask for deliverance?'

This put the young novice on the way to final enlightenment, which he attained after many years' study under the master. When Sêng-ts'an thought that the time was ripe to consecrate him as his successor in the faith, he handed him, as the token of the rightful transmission of the Law, the robe which had come down from Bodhidharma, the first patriarch of Zen in China. He died in A.D. 606. While much of his life is obscure, his thought is gleaned from a metrical composition known as *Hsin-hsin-ming*, or 'Inscribed on the Believing Mind', which is one of the most valuable contributions by the masters to the interpretation of Zen teaching. Here follows a somewhat liberal translation of the poem:

INSCRIBED ON THE BELIEVING MIND[1]

The Perfect Way knows no difficulties
Except that it refuses to make preference:

[1] *Hsin* is one of those Chinese words which defy translation. When the Indian scholars were trying to translate the Buddhist Sanskrit works into Chinese they discovered that there were five classes of Sanskrit terms which could not be satisfactorily rendered into Chinese. We thus find in the Chinese Tripitaka such words as *prajñā*, *bodhi*, *buddha*, *nirvāṇa*, *dhyāna*, *bodhisattva*, etc., almost always untranslated; and they now appear in their original form among the technical Buddhist terminology. If we could leave *hsin* with all its nuance of meaning in this translation, it would save us from the many difficulties that face us in its English rendering. For *hsin* means mind, heart, soul, spirit—each singly as well as all inclusively. In the present composition by the third patriarch of Zen it has sometimes an intellectual connotation, but at other times it can properly be done by 'heart'. But as the predominant note of Zen Buddhism is more intellectual than anything else, though not in the sense of being logical or philosophical, I decided here to translate *hsin* by 'mind' rather than by 'heart'.

Only when freed from hate and love,
It reveals itself fully and without disguise.

A tenth of an inch's difference,
And heaven and earth are set apart:
If you want to see it manifest,
Take no thought either for or against it.

To set up what you like against what you dislike—
This is the disease of the mind:
When the deep meaning [of the Way] is not understood
Peace of mind is disturbed and nothing is gained.

[The Way is] perfect like unto vast space,
With nothing wanting, nothing superfluous:
It is indeed due to making choice
That its suchness is lost sight of.

Pursue not the outer entanglements,
Dwell not in the inner void;
When the mind rests serene in the oneness of things,
The dualism vanishes by itself.

And when oneness is not thoroughly understood,
In two ways loss is sustained—
The denial of reality may lead to its absolute negation,
While the upholding of the void may result in contradicting itself.
Wordiness and intellection—
The more with them the further astray we go;
Away therefore with wordiness and intellection,
And there is no place where we cannot pass freely.[1]

[1] This means: When the absolute oneness of things is not properly understood, negation as well as affirmation will tend to be a one-sided view of reality. When Buddhists deny the reality of an objective world, they do not mean that they believe in the unconditioned emptiness of things; they know that there is something real which cannot be done away with. When they uphold the doctrine of void, this does not mean that all is nothing but an empty hollow, which leads to a self-contradiction. The philosophy of Zen avoids the error of one-sidedness involved in realism as well as in idealism.

When we return to the root, we gain the meaning;
When we pursue the external objects, we lose the
    reason.
The moment we are enlightened within,
We go beyond the voidness of a world confrontıng us.

Transformations going on in an empty world which
    confronts us,
Appear real all because of Ignorance:
Try not to seek after the true,
Only cease to cherish opinions.

Tarry not with dualism,
Carefully avoid pursuing it;
As soon as you have right and wrong,
Confusion ensues, the mind is lost.

The two exist because of the one,
But hold not even to this one;
When the one mind is not disturbed,
The ten thousand things offer no offence.

When no offence is offered by them, they are as if not
    existing;
When the mind is not disturbed, it is as if there is no
    mind.
The subject is quieted as the object ceases,
The object ceases as the subject is quieted.

The object is an object for the subject,
The subject is a subject for an object:
Know that the relativity of the two
Rests ultimately on the oneness of the void.

In the oneness of the void the two are one,
And each of the two contains in itself all the ten thou-
    sand things:
When no discrimination is made between this and that,
How can a one-sided and prejudiced view arise?

The Great Way is calm and large-minded,
Nothing is easy, nothing is hard:
Small views are irresolute,
The more in haste the tardier they go.

Clinging never keeps itself within bounds,
It is sure to go in the wrong way:
Let go loose, and things are as they may be,
While the essence neither departs nor abides.

Obey the nature of things, and you are in concord with
 the Way,
Calm and easy and free from annoyance;
But when your thoughts are tied, you turn away from
 the truth,
They grow heavier and duller and are not at all sound.

When they are not sound, the soul is troubled;
What is the use of being partial and one-sided then?
If you want to walk the course of the One Vehicle,
Be not prejudiced against the six-sense-objects.

When you are not prejudiced against the six sense-
 objects,
You in turn identify yourself with Enlightenment;
The wise are non-active,
While the ignorant bind themselves up;
While in the Dharma itself there is no individuation,
They ignorantly attach themselves to particular objects.
It is their own minds that create illusions—
Is it not the greatest of self-contradictions?

Ignorance begets the dualism of rest and unrest,
The enlightened have no likes and dislikes:
All forms of dualism
Are ignorantly contrived by the mind itself.
They are like unto visions and flowers in the air:
Why should we trouble ourselves to take hold of them?

Gain and loss, right and wrong—
Away with them once for all!

If an eye never falls asleep,
All dreams will by themselves cease:
If the mind retains its oneness,
The ten thousand things are of one suchness.
When the deep mystery of one suchness is fathomed,
All of a sudden we forget the external entanglements:
When the ten thousand things are viewed in their one-
    ness,
We return to the origin and remain what we are.

Forget the wherefore of things,
And we attain to a state beyond analogy:
Movement stopped is no movement,
And rest set in motion is no rest.
When dualism does no more obtain,
Even oneness itself remains not as such.

The ultimate end of things where they cannot go any
    further,
Is not bound by rules and measures:
The mind in harmony [with the Way] is the principle
    of identity
In which we find all doings in a quiescent state;
Irresolutions are completely done away with,
And the right faith is restored to its native straightness;

Nothing is retained now,
Nothing is to be memorized,
All is void, lucid, and self-illuminating,
There is no stain, no exertion, no wasting of energy—
This is where thinking never attains,
This is where the imagination fails to measure.

In the higher realm of True Suchness
There is neither 'other' nor 'self':

When a direct identification is asked for,
We can only say, 'Not two.'[1]

In being not two all is the same,
All that is is comprehended in it:
The wise in the ten quarters,
They all enter into this absolute faith.

This absolute faith is beyond quickening [time] and
     extension [space].
One instant is ten thousand years;
No matter how things are conditioned, whether with
    'to be' or 'not to be',
It is manifest everywhere before you

The infinitely small is as large as large can be,
When external conditions are forgotten;
The infinitely large is as small as small can be,
When objective limits are put out of sight.

What is is the same with what is not,
What is not is the same with what is:
Where this state of things fails to obtain,
Be sure not to tarry.

One in all,
All in one—
If only this is realized,
No more worry about your not being perfect!

The believing mind is not divided,
And undivided is the believing mind—
This is where words fail,
For it is not of the past, future, or present.

Under Tao-hsin (580–651), the fourth patriarch, Zen
was divided into two branches. The one known as

[1] I.e. Tat tvam asi.

Gozusan (Niu-t'ou Shan), did not live long after the passing
of its founder, Fa-jung, who lived at Mount Niu-t'ou, and is
considered not belonging to the orthodox line of Zen. The
other branch was headed by Hung-jên, who is regarded by
historians as the fifth patriarch, and it is his school that has
survived. He came to the master when he was still a mere
boy, and what pleased his master at their interview was
the way he answered. When Tao-hsin asked what was his
family name (*hsing*), he said:

'I have a nature (*hsing*), and it is not an ordinary
one.'

'What is that?'

'It is the Buddha-nature (*fo-hsing*).'

'Then you have no name?'

'No, master,' said the boy, 'for it is empty in its nature.'
Here is a play of words; the characters denoting 'family
name' and that for 'nature' are both pronounced *hsing*.
When Tao-hsin was referring to the 'family name' the
young follower took it for 'nature' purposely, whereby to
express his view by a figure of speech.

Tao-hsin's interview with Fa-jung, the founder of the
Niu-t'ou school of Zen, was significant, showing where
their views differed and how the one came to be converted
into the orthodox understanding of Zen. It was during the
Chên-kuan era of the T'ang dynasty that Tao-hsin, learning of the presence of an extraordinary saintly man in
Niu-t'ou mountains, decided to see who he could be. When
Tao-hsin came to a Buddhist temple in the mountains he
inquired after the man and was informed of a lonely
anchorite who would never rise from his seat nor salute
people even when they were approaching him. When
Tao-hsin proceeded further into the mountains he saw
him as he was told, sitting quietly and paying no attention
to the presence of a stranger. He then asked the hermit what
he was doing here. 'I am contemplating on Mind,' was the
reply. Tao-hsin then demanded: 'What is he that is contemplating? What is Mind that is contemplated?' Fa-jung
was not prepared to answer such questions. Thinking that

the visitor was a man of deep understanding, he rose from the seat and saluting him asked who he was. When he found that the visitor was no other personage than Tao-hsin himself, whose reputation he was not ignorant of, he thanked him for the visit. They were now about to enter a little hut nearby where they might talk about religion, when Tao-hsin saw some wild animals such as tigers and wolves wandering about the place, and he threw up his hands as if he were greatly frightened. Fa-jung remarked, 'I see this is still with you.' The fourth patriarch responded at once, 'What do you see yet?' No answer came from the hermit. After a while the patriarch traced the character 'Buddha' (*fo*) on the stone on which Fa-jung was in the habit of sitting in meditation. Seeing it, the latter looked as if shocked. Said the patriarch, 'I see this is still with you.' But Fa-jung failed to see the meaning of this remark and earnestly implored to be instructed in the ultimate teaching of Buddhism. This was done, and Fa-jung became the founder of the Niu-t'ou school of Zen Buddhism.

Tao-hsin died at the age of seventy-two, A.D. 651.

Hung-jên, 601–674, the fifth patriarch, came from the same province as his predecessor, Ch'i-chou, now in the district of Fu-pei. His temple was situated in Wang-mei Shan (Yellow Plum Mountain), where he preached and gave lessons in Zen to his five hundred pupils. He is claimed by some to have been the first Zen master who attempted to interpret the message of Zen according to the doctrine of the *Vajracchedikā-sūtra*. Though I cannot quite agree with this view, for the reason already referred to elsewhere, we can consider the fifth patriarch the beginning of a turning in the history of Zen, which opened up to a full view under the sixth patriarch, Hui-nêng. Until now the Zen followers had kept quiet, though working steadily, without arresting public attention; the masters had retired either into the mountains or in the hurly-burly of the world where nobody could tell anything about their doings. But the time had at last come for a full proclamation of Zen, and Hung-jên was the first who appeared in the field preparing the way for his successor, Hui-nêng.

Besides this orthodox line of patriarchs, there were some sporadic expositors of Zen throughout the sixth and the seventh centuries. Several of them are mentioned, but there must have been many more such who were either altogether forgotten or not at all known to the world. The two best known are Pao-chih (died 514) and Fu-hsi (died 569); and their lives are recorded in the *Records* as 'adepts in Zen but not appearing in the world, though well-known at the time'. This is a strange phrasing, and it is hard to know definitely what 'not appearing in the world' means. Usually it applies to one who does not occupy any recognized position in an officially registered monastery. But of those that are classed under this heading there is one at least to whom the designation does not properly apply; for Chi-i was a great high priest occupying an influential ecclesiastical post in the Sui dynasty. Whatever this was, those recorded here did not belong to the orthodox Zen school. The Tendai (T'ien-tai) followers object to see two of their Fathers Hui-szŭ and Chi-i mentioned as 'adepts in Zen but not appearing in the world, though well-known at the time'. They think that these two are great names in the history of their school and ought not to be so indifferently referred to in the records of the Zen masters. But from the Zen point of view this classification is justifiable for the reason that the Tendai, except its metaphysics, is another current of Zen started independently of the line of Bodhidharma, and if this were allowed to take a more practical course of development it should surely have resulted in Zen as we have it now. But its metaphysical side came to be emphasized at the expense of the practical, and for this reason the Tendai philosophers were ever at war with the Zen, especially with the ultra-left wing, which was inflexible in denouncing an appeal to ratiocination and literary discoursing and Sūtra-learning. In my view the Tendai is a variation of Zen and its first promulgators may justly be classed as Zen masters, though not of the pedigree to which belong Shih-t'ou, Yüeh-shan, Ma-tsu, Lin-chi, etc.

While there were thus in the sixth and seventh centuries some other lines of Zen about to develop, the one started by Bodhidharma was uninterruptedly carried on by Hui-k'ê, Shêng-t'san, Tao-hsin, and Hung-jên, who proved to be the most fruitful and successful. The differentiation of two schools under the fifth patriarch, by Hui-nêng and Shên-hsiu, helped the further progress of pure Zen by eliminating unessential or rather undigested elements. That the school of Hui-nêng survived the other proves that his Zen was in perfect accord with Chinese psychology and modes of thinking. The Indian elements which had been found attached to the Zen of Bodhidharma and his successors down to Hui-nêng, were something grafted and not native to Chinese genius. And therefore when Zen came to be fully established under Hui-nêng and his followers, it had nothing further to obstruct its free development until it became almost the only ruling power in the Chinese world of Buddhism. We must carefully watch how Hui-nêng came to be Hung-jên's successor and where he differed from his rival school under Shên-hsiu.

IV

Hui-nêng (638–713) came from Hsin-chou in the southern parts of China. His father died when he was yet young. He supported his mother by selling wood in town. When one day he came out of a house where he sold some fuel, he heard a man reciting a Buddhist Sūtra. The words deeply touched his heart. Finding what Sūtra it was and where it was possible to get it, a longing came over him to study it with the master. The Sūtra was the *Diamond Sūtra (Vajracchedikā-sūtra)* and the master was the fifth patriarch residing at Yellow Plum in Chin-chou. Hui-nêng somehow managed to get money enough for the support of his aged mother while he was gone.

It took him about a month to reach Yellow Plum, where he at once proceeded to see Hung-jên at the head of five hundred monks (sometimes said to be seven or even ten hundred). At the first interview asked the patriarch:

'Where do you come from? and what do you want here?'

'I am a farmer from Hsin-chou and wish to become a Buddha.'

'So you are a Southerner,' said the patriarch, 'but the Southerners have no Buddha-nature; how could you expect to attain Buddhahood?'

This, however, did not discourage the bold seeker after the truth, for he at once responded, 'There may be Southerners and Northerners, but as far as Buddha-nature goes, how could you make such a distinction in it?'

This pleased the master very much. Hui-nêng was given an office as rice-pounder for the Brotherhood. More than eight months, it is said, he was employed in this menial labour, when the fifth patriarch wished to select his spiritual successor from among his many disciples. One day he made an announcement that any one who could prove his thorough comprehension of the religion would be given the patriarchal mantle and proclaimed as his legitimate heir. Shên-hsiu (died 706), who was the most learned of all the disciples and thoroughly versed in the lore of his religion, and who was therefore considered by his brethren in the faith to be in possession of an unqualified right to the honour, composed a stanza expressing his view, and posted it on the outside wall of the meditation hall, which read:

'This body is the Bodhi-tree,
The soul is like a mirror bright;
Take heed to keep it always clean,
And let not dust collect on it.'

All those who read these lines were greatly impressed, and secretly cherished the idea that the author of this gāthā would surely be awarded the prize. But when they awoke the next morning they were surprised to see another written alongside of it, which ran as follows:

'The Bodhi is not like the tree,
The mirror bright is nowhere shining;
As there is nothing from the first,
Where can the dust itself collect?'

The writer of these lines was an insignificant layman in the service of the monastery, who spent most of his time in pounding rice and splitting wood for the Brotherhood. He had such an unassuming air that nobody ever thought much of him, and therefore the entire community was now set astir to see this challenge made upon its recognized authority. But the fifth patriarch saw in this unpretentious monk a future leader of mankind, and decided to transfer to him the robe of his office. He had, however, some misgivings concerning the matter; for the majority of his disciples were not enlightened enough to see anything of deep religious intuition in the lines by the rice-pounder, Hui-nêng: and if he were publicly awarded the honour they might do him harm. So the fifth patriarch gave a secret sign to Hui-nêng to come to his room at midnight, when the rest of the Brotherhood was fast asleep. Then he gave him the robe as insignia of his authority and in acknowledgment of his unsurpassed spiritual attainment, and with the assurance that the future of their faith would be brighter than ever. The patriarch then advised him that it would be wise for him to hide his own light under a bushel until the proper time arrived for his public appearance and active propaganda, and also that the robe which was handed down from Bodhidharma as the sign of faith should no more be given up to Hui-nêng's successors, because Zen was now fully recognized by the outside world in general and there was no more necessity to symbolize the faith by the transference of the robe. That night Hui-nêng left the monastery.

This narrative is taken from the literature left by the followers of the sixth patriarch and is naturally partial in his favour. If we had another record left by Shên-hsiu and his school, the account here reproduced may materially differ. In fact, we have at least one document telling Shên-hsiu's relation to Hung-jên. It is the memorial inscription on his gravestone written by Chang-shuo, one of his lay-disciples. In this inscription Shên-hsiu is referred to as the one to whom the Dharma has been transmitted from his master, Hung-jên. Judging from this, the patriarchal authority of Hui-nêng was not an undisputed one at the time, or the orthodox order of succession was not settled until some time later, when the school of Hui-nêng had been well established in authority over all the other schools of Zen that might have been existing then. Unfortunately, this memorial inscription does not give any further information concerning Hui-nêng's relation to Hung-jên, but even from the above narrative we can gather certain facts of importance which will shed light on the history of Zen.

First, what necessity was there to make Hui-nêng an unlearned rustic in contrast with the erudition and wide information ascribed to Shên-hsiu? Or was Hui-nêng really such an ignoramus as could not read anything written? But the *Fa-pao-t'an-ching*, a collection of his sermons, contains passages quoted from such Sūtras as the *Nirvāṇa*, *Vajracchedikā*, *Laṅkāvatāra*, *Saddharma-puṇḍarīka*, *Vimalakīrti*, *Amitābha*, and *Bodhisattva-śīla-sūtra*. Does this not evince the fact that the author was not altogether unacquainted with Mahāyāna literature? Probably he was not a learned scholar as compared with Shên-hsiu, but in the narratives of his life we can trace some systematic effort to make him more unlettered than he actually was. What, let me ask, do we read in this attempt at the hand of the editors? In my opinion this emphasizing of the contrast between the two most eminent disciples of the fifth patriarch was at the same time the emphasizing of the real character of Zen as independent of learning and intellectuality. If Zen is, as its followers claim, a 'special transmission outside the scriptural teaching', the understanding of it must be possible even for the unlettered and unphilosophizing. The greatness of Hui-nêng as Zen master is all the more enhanced. This was in all likelihood the reason why the sixth patriarch was unreasonably and sometimes even dramatically made unlettered.

Secondly, why was not the patriarchal robe transferred beyond Hui-nêng? If Hung-jên advised him to keep it with him, what does the advice really imply? That the life of the possessor of the robe would be threatened points to the fact that there was a dispute among the disciples of Hung-jên. Did they regard the robe as the symbol of patriarchal authority? But what advantages, material or spiritual, accrued from the ownership of it? Did the teaching of Bodhidharma come now to be believed as the genuine transmission of the Buddha? And for that reason did the robe really cease to signify anything relative to the truth of Zen? If so, when Bodhidharma first declared his special mission as teacher of Zen, was he looked upon as a heretic and persecuted accordingly? The legend that he was poisoned by his rival teachers from India seems to corroborate this. At all events, the question of the robe is deeply connected with the status of Zen teaching among the various schools of Buddhism at the time, and also with its firmer hold on the popular minds than ever before.

Thirdly, the secrecy observed in all the transactions between Hung-jên and Hui-nêng concerning the transmission of the Dharma naturally arrests our attention. To raise the rice-pounder, who is not even an ordained monk, to the rank of a patriarch, though only in name, to succeed a great master who stands at the head of several hundred disciples, seems to be a real cause for envy and jealousy and even for hatred. But if one were really enlightened enough to take charge of the important position of spiritual leadership, could not a combined effort of master and pupil withstand all the opposition? Perhaps even enlightenment could not stand against human passions so irrational and elemental. I cannot, however, help imagining an attempt

on the part of the biographers of Hui-nêng at the dramati-
zation of the whole scene. I am very likely mistaken, and
there might have been some historical conditions of which
we are now ignorant due to the lack of documents.

Three days after the flight of Hui-nêng from the Yellow
Plum Mountain, the news of what had happened in secret
became noised abroad throughout the monastery, and a
party of indignant monks, headed by one named Ming,
pursued the fugitive, Hui-nêng, who, in accordance with
his master's instructions, was silently leaving the Brotherhood. When he was overtaken by the pursuers while crossing a mountain-pass far from the monastery, he laid down
his robe on a rock near by and said to the monk, Ming:
'This robe symbolizes our patriarchal faith and is not to
be carried away by force. Take this along with thee, however, if thou so desirest.'

Ming tried to lift it, but it was as heavy as a mountain.
He halted, hesitated, and trembled with awe. At last he
said: 'I come here to obtain the faith and not the robe.
O my brother monk, pray dispel my ignorance.'

Said the sixth patriarch: 'If thou comest for the faith,
stop all thy hankerings. Think not of good, think not of
evil, but see what at this moment thy own original face
doth look like, which thou hadst even prior to thy own
birth.'

Being thus demanded, Ming at once perceived the fundamental truth of things, which hitherto he had sought in
things without. He now understood everything, as if he had
taken a cupful of cold water and tasted it to his own satisfaction. Out of the immensity of his feeling he was literally
bathed in tears and perspiration, and most reverently
approaching the patriarch he saluted him and asked, 'Besides this hidden sense as is embodied in these significant
words, is there anything which is secret?'

The patriarch answered: 'In what I have shown to thee
there is nothing hidden. If thou reflectest within thyself
and recognizest thy own face, which was before the world,
secrecy is in thyself.'

Whatever historical circumstances surrounded Hui-nêng in those remote days, it is certain that in this statement, 'to see one's own face even before one was born,' we find the first proclamation of the new message, which was destined to unroll a long history of Zen and to make Hui-nêng really worthy of the patriarchal robe. We can see here what a new outlook Hui-nêng has succeeded in opening to the traditional Indian Zen. In him we do not recognize anything of Buddhism as far as phraseology goes, which means that he opened up his own way of presenting the truth of Zen after his original and creative experience. Prior to him the Zen experience had some borrowings, either in wording or in method, to express itself. To say 'You are the Buddha', or 'You and the Buddha are one', or 'The Buddha is living in you', is too stale, too flat, because too abstract and too conceptual. They contain deep truth but are not concrete nor vivifying enough to rouse our dormant souls from insensibility. They are filled up too much with abstractions and learned phraseology. Hui-nêng's simple-mindedness, not spoiled by learning and philosophizing, could grasp the truth at first hand. Hence his unusual freshness in the way he handled the problem. We may come to this again later.

V

Hung-jên died, A.D. 675, four years[1] after the Dharma was transmitted to Hui-nêng. He was seventy-four years old. But Hui-nêng never started his mission work until some years later, for in accordance with the advice of his master he lived a secluded life in the mountains. One day he thought that it was time for him to go out in the world. He was now thirty-nine years old, and it was in the first year of I-fêng (A.D. 676) during the T'ang dynasty. He came to Fa-hsing temple in the province of Kuang, where a

[1] There is, however, a variation from five years to fifteen years according to different authorities.

learned priest, Yin-tsung, was discoursing on the *Nirvāṇa Sūtra*. He saw some monks arguing on the fluttering pennant; one of them said, 'The pennant is an inanimate object and it is the wind that makes it flap.' Against this it was remarked by another monk that 'Both wind and pennant are inanimate things, and the flapping is an impossibility.' A third one protested, 'The flapping is due to a certain combination of cause and condition'; while a fourth one proposed a theory, saying, 'After all there is no flapping pennant, but it is the wind that is moving by itself.' The discussion grew quite animated when Hui-nêng interrupted with the remark, 'It is neither wind nor pennant but your own mind that flaps.' This at once put a stop to the heated argument. The priest-scholar, Yin-tsung, was greatly struck by the statement of Hui-nêng, so conclusive and authoritative. Finding out very soon who this Hui-nêng was, Yin-tsung asked him to enlighten him on the teaching of the master of Yellow Plum Mountain. The gist of Hui-nêng's reply was as follows:

'My master had no special instruction to give; he simply insisted upon the need of our seeing into our own Nature through our own efforts; he had nothing to do with meditation, or with deliverance. For whatever can be named leads to dualism, and Buddhism is not dualistic. To take hold of this non-duality of truth is the aim of Zen. The Buddha-Nature of which we are all in possession, and the seeing into which constitutes Zen, is indivisible into such oppositions as good and evil, eternal and temporal, material and spiritual. To see dualism in life is due to confusion of thought; the wise, the enlightened, see into the reality of things unhampered by erroneous ideas.'

This was the beginning of Hui-nêng's career as Zen master. His influence seems to have been immediate and far-reaching. He had many disciples numbering thousands. He did not, however, go around preaching and proselytizing. His activities were confined in his own province in the south, and the Pao-lin monastery at T'sao-ch'i was his headquarters. When the Emperor Kao-tsung learned that

Hui-nêng succeeded Hung-jên as one of Dharma's spiritual descendants in the faith of Zen, he sent him one of his Court officials with an imperial message, but Hui-nêng refused to come up to the capital, preferring his stay in the mountains. The messenger, however, wished to be instructed in the doctrine of Zen, that he might convey it to his august master at Court. Said Hui-nêng in the main as follows:

'It is a mistake to think that sitting quietly in contemplation is essential to deliverance. The truth of Zen opens by itself from within and it has nothing to do with the practice of dhyāna. For we read in the *Vajracchedikā* that those who try to see the Tathāgata in one of his special attitudes, as sitting or lying, do not understand his spirit, and that the Tathāgata is designated as Tathāgata because he comes from nowhere and departs nowhere, and for that reason he is the Tathāgata. His appearance has no whence, and his disappearance no whither, and this is Zen. In Zen, therefore, there is nothing to gain, nothing to understand; what shall we then do with sitting cross-legged and practising dhyāna? Some may think that understanding is needed to enlighten the darkness of ignorance, but the truth of Zen is absolute in which there is no dualism, no conditionality. To speak of ignorance and enlightenment, or of Bodhi and Kleśa (wisdom and passions), as if they were two separate objects which cannot be merged in one, is not Mahāyānistic. In the Mahāyāna every possible form of dualism is condemned as not expressing the ultimate truth. Everything is a manifestation of the Buddha-Nature, which is not defiled in passions, nor purified in enlightenment. It is above all categories. If you want to see what is the nature of your being, free your mind from thought of relativity and you will see by yourself how serene it is and yet how full of life it is.'

While Hui-nêng was working for the cause of Zen in the South, Shên-hsiu, representing another school, was active in the North. Before he was converted into Buddhism he was a learned Confucian and thus destined from the start to cut a different figure, compared with his brother-disciple, Hui-nêng. The Emperor Wu of the T'ang dynasty was one of the devoted followers of Shên-hsiu, and naturally around him were gathered a large number of courtiers and government officers. When the Emperor Chung-tsung came to the throne, A.D. 685, he was all the more treated with reverence, and it was Chang-shuo, one of the state ministers, who inscribed a biographical sketch and eulogy on the memorial stone erected over his grave when he died. One of his sermons recorded reads:

> 'The teaching of all the Buddhas
> In one's own Mind originally exists:
> To seek the Mind without one's Self,
> Is like running away from the father.'

He died in A.D. 706, seven years prior to Hui-nêng. His school, known as the Northern in contrast to Hui-nêng's Southern school, prospered in the North far better than the latter did in the South. But when Ma-tsu (died 788) and Shih-t'ou (700–790) began their active propaganda in the South and finally established the foundations of Zen teaching, Shên-hsiu's school failed to find able successors and finally disappeared altogether, so that all the records we have of their movements come from the rival school. It thus came to pass that Hui-nêng, and not Shên-hsiu, was recognized as the sixth patriarch of Zen Buddhism in China.

The difference between the Southern and the Northern school of Zen is one inherent in human mind; if we call the one intellectual or intuitional, the other would be regarded as pragmatical. The reason why the Southern school is known as 'abrupt' or 'instant' (*yugapad*) against the 'gradual' *kramavrittya* school of the North is because it upholds that the coming of enlightenment is instantaneous, and does not allow any gradation as there are no stages of progress in it; whereas the Northern school emphasizes the process of arriving at enlightenment which is naturally gradual, requiring much time and concentration. Hui-nêng was a great advocate of absolute idealism, while Shên-hsiu was a realist and refused to ignore a world of particulars where Time rules over all our doings. An idealist does not necessarily ignore the objective aspect of reality, but his eyes are always fixed at one point which stands by itself, and his surveyings are done from this absolute point. The doctrine of abruptness is thus the result of looking at the multitudinousness of things in absolute unity. All true mystics are followers of the 'abrupt' school. The flight from the alone to the alone is not, and cannot be, a gradual process. The teaching of Shên-hsiu is to be heeded as the practical advice to those who are actually engaged in the study of Zen, but it fails to describe the character of the experience known as 'the seeing into one's own Nature', which was the special message of Hui-nêng as distinguished from those of the other Buddhist schools. That the school of Shên-hsiu could not survive as a branch of Zen was natural enough, for Zen could not be anything else but an instantaneous act of intuition. As it opens up all of a sudden a world hitherto undreamed of, it is an abrupt and discrete leaping from one plane of thought to another. Hsiu missed the ultimate object of Zen when he emphasized the process to reach the end. As a practical adviser he was excellent and full of merit.

The ideas of instantaneity and graduation in the realization of the truth of Zen originally comes from the *Laṅkāvatāra* (Nanjō's edition, p. 55), where this distinction is made in regard to cleansing one's mind of its stream of ideas and images. According to the Sūtra, this cleansing is in one sense gradual but in another abrupt or instantaneous. When it is regarded as like the ripening of a fruit, the modelling of a vessel, the growing of a plant, or the mastering of an art, which takes place gradually and in time, it is an act of gradual process; but when it is comparable to a mirror reflecting objects, or to the Ālaya reproducing all mental images, the cleansing of mind takes place instantaneously. Thus the Sūtra recognizes the two types of minds: with some the cleansing to a state of enlightenment can be obtained gradually after a long practice of meditation, perhaps through many a successive life; but to others it may come all of a sudden, even without previously conscious efforts. The division of the two schools as regards the abrupt realization of enlightenment is based not only on the statements in the Sūtra but ultimately on facts of psychology. The point at issue, however, was not a question of time; whether enlightenment took place as an act of one moment or not ceased to concern them; for the difference now developed into that of their general philosophical attitude and outlook towards the fact of enlightenment itself. The question of physical time has thus turned into that of psychology in its more profound aspect.

When process is emphasized, the end is forgotten, and process itself comes to be identified with end. When a disciple of Shên-hsiu came to Hui-nêng to be instructed in Zen, he asked what was the teaching of Shên-hsiu, and the disciple informed him thus: 'My master usually teaches us to stop the working of our minds and to sit quietly in meditation for a long time at a stretch, without lying down.' To this Hui-nêng responded, 'To stop the working of mind and to sit quietly in meditation is a disease and not Zen, and there is no profit whatever to be gained from a long sitting.' Then he gave him the following gāthā:

> 'While living, one sits up and lies not,
> When dead, one lies and sits not;
> A set of ill-smelling skeleton!
> What is the use of toiling and moiling so?'

This shows exactly where Hui-nêng stands in relation to his rival Shên-hsiu, who is so taken up with the practical details of the process of Zen. Those two gāthās inscribed on the monastery wall at Yellow Plum Mountain while they were yet under the tutorship of Hung-jên, are eloquent enough to bring out the characteristic features of the two schools.[1]

When Hui-nêng further asked the monk from the north as to the teaching of his teacher in regard to morality (*śīla*), meditation (*dhyāna*), and wisdom (*prajñā*), the monk said, 'According to my master Hsiu, morality consists in not doing anything that is bad; wisdom in reverently practising all that is good; and meditation in purifying the heart.' Replied Hui-nêng: 'My view is quite different. All my teaching issues from the conception of Self-nature, and those who assert the existence of anything outside it betray their ignorance of its nature. Morality, Meditation, and Wisdom—all these are forms of Self-Nature. When there is nothing wrong in it, we have morality; when it is free from ignorance, it is wisdom; and when it is not disturbed, it is meditation. Have a thorough understanding once for all as to the being of Self-Nature, and you know that nothing dualistic obtains in it; for here you have nothing to be particularly distinguished as enlightenment, or ignorance, or deliverance, or knowledge, and yet from this nothingness there issues a world of particulars as objects of thought. For him who has once had an insight into his own Nature, no special posture as a form of meditation is to be recommended; everything and anything is good to him, sitting, or lying, or standing. He enjoys perfect freedom of spirit, he moves along as he feels, and yet he does nothing wrong, he is always acting in accord with his Self-Nature, his work is play. This is what I call "the seeing into one's own Nature"; and this seeing is instantaneous as much as the working is, for there is no graduating process from one stage to another.'

---

[1] These accounts, whether truly historical or not, concerning the controversy between the two leaders of Zen early in the T'ang dynasty prove how heated was the rivalry between the North and the South. The *Sermons of the Sixth Patriarch* (*Fa-pao-t'an-ching*) themselves appear as if written with the sole object of refuting the opponents of the 'abrupt' school.

VI

Some of the sermons of the sixth patriarch are preserved in the book known as the *Platform Sūtra on the Treasure of the Law* (*Fa-pao-t'an-ching*). The title 'Sūtra' has generally been given to writings ascribed to the Buddha or those somehow personally connected with him, and that a collection of the sermons of Hui-nêng has been so honoured shows what a significant position he occupies in the history of Chinese Buddhism. 'The Platform Sūtra' has a reference to the famous ordination platform erected by Gunabhadra, the first translator of the *Lankāvatāra*, of the Liu-sung dynasty, A.D. 420–479. At the time of the erection during the Liang dynasty, as well as later, it was prophesied by Chih-yüeh (according to another authority by Paramārtha) that some years later a Bodhisattva in the flesh would be ordained on this platform and deliver sermons on the Buddha's 'spiritual seal'. Thus the 'Platform Sūtra' means orthodox teaching of the Zen given from this platform.

The sermons here preserved are mere fragments of those delivered during the thirty-seven years of Hui-nêng's active missionary life. Even of these fragments how much is to be regarded as genuine and authoritative is a question to which we cannot at present give a definite answer, as the book seems to have suffered the vicissitudes of fate, partly showing the fact that the Zen message of the sixth patriarch was extraordinary in many respects so as to arouse antagonism and misunderstanding among Buddhists. When this antagonism later reached its climax, it is reported that the book was burned up as against the genuine teaching of Buddhism. Except a few sentences and passages, however, which can at once be rejected as spurious, we may take the *Platform Sūtra* on the whole as expressing the spirit and teaching of the sixth patriarch of Zen.

The principal ideas of Hui-nêng, which make him the

real Chinese founder of Zen Buddhism, may be summed up as follows:

1. We can say that Zen has come to its own consciousness by Hui-nêng. While Bodhidharma brought it from India and successfully transplanted it in China, it did not fully realize its special message at the time. More than two centuries were needed before it grew aware of itself and knew how to express itself in the way native to the Chinese mind; the Indian mode in which its original teaching had been expressed, as was the case with Bodhidharma and his immediate disciples, had to give way as it were to become truly Chinese. As soon as this transformation or transplantation was accomplished in the hands of Hui-nêng his disciples proceeded at once to work out all its implications. The result was what we have as the Zen school of Buddhism. How then did Hui-nêng understand Zen?

According to him Zen was the 'seeing into one's own Nature'. This is the most significant phrase ever coined in the development of Zen Buddhism. Around this Zen is now crystallized, and we know where to direct our efforts and how to represent it in our consciousness. After this the progress of Zen Buddhism was rapid. It is true that this phrase occurs in the life of Bodhidharma in the *Records of the Transmission of the Lamp*, but it is in the part of his life on which we cannot put much reliance. Even when the phrase was actually used by Dharma it was not necessarily considered by him the essence of Zen as distinguishing itself from other schools of Buddhism. Hui-nêng, however, was fully aware of its signification, and impressed the idea unequivocally upon the minds of his audience. When he made his first declaration of Zen for the benefit of Yin-tsung, the statement was quite unmistakable: 'We talk of seeing into our own Nature, and not of practising dhyāna or obtaining liberation.' Here we have the gist of Zen, and all his later sermons are amplifications of this idea.

By 'Nature' he understood Buddha-Nature, or, more particularly from the intellectual point of view, Prajñā. He says that this Prajñā is possessed by every one of us, but owing to the confusion of thought we fail to realize it in ourselves. Therefore, we must be instructed and properly guided by an adept in Zen Buddhism, when we shall open a spiritual eye and by ourselves see into the Nature. This Nature knows no multiplicity, it is absolute oneness, being the same in the ignorant as well as in the wise. The difference comes from confusion and ignorance. People talk so much, think so much of Prajñā, but fail altogether to realize it in their own minds. It is like talking about food all day; however much we may talk we forever remain hungry. You may explain the philosophy of Śūnyatā for ten thousand years, but so long as you have not yet seen into your Nature it is absolutely of no avail. There are again some people who regard Zen as consisting in sitting quietly with an empty mind devoid of thoughts and feelings. Such know not what Prajñā is, what Mind is. It fills the universe, and never rests from work. It is free, creative, and at the same time it knows itself. It knows all in one and one in all. This mysterious working of Prajñā issues from your own Nature. Do not depend upon letters but let your own Prajñā illumine within yourself.

2. The inevitable result of it was the 'abrupt' teaching of the Southern school. The seeing is an instant act as far as the mental eye takes in the whole truth at one glance —the truth which transcends dualism in all form; it is abrupt as far as it knows no gradations, no continuous unfolding. Read the following passage from the *Platform Sūtra*, in which the essentials of the abrupt doctrine are given:

'When the abrupt doctrine is understood there is no need of disciplining oneself in things external. Only let a man always have a right view within his own mind, no desires, no external objects will ever defile him. This is the seeing into his Nature. O my friends, have no fixed abode inside or outside[1], and your conduct will be perfectly free

[1] This is a constant refrain in the teaching of the *Prajñāpāramitā Sūtras*—to awaken one's thought where there is no abode whatever (no kvacit pratishṭitaṁ cittaṁ utpādayitavyam). When Jōshu called on

and unfettered. Take away your attachment and your walk will know no obstructions whatever. . . . The ignorant will grow wise if they abruptly get an understanding and open their hearts to the truth. O my friends, even the Buddhas will be like us common mortals when they have no enlightenment, and even we mortals will be Buddhas when we are enlightened. Therefore we know that all things are in our own minds. Why do we not then instantly see into our own minds and find there the truth of Suchness? In the *Sūtra on the Moral Conduct of the Bodhisattva* we read that we are all pure in our Self-Nature, and that when we know our own minds we see into this Nature and all attain to Buddhahood. Says the *Vimalakīrti Sūtra*, "An instant opening leads us into the Original Mind." O my good friends, while under my master Jên I realized the truth the moment I heard him speak and had an instant [i.e. abrupt] glimpse into the true essence of Suchness. This is the reason why I now endeavour by means of this doctrine to lead truthseekers to an instant [i.e. abrupt] realization of Bodhi. When you by yourselves look into your minds, you perceive at once what the Original Nature is. . . .

'Those who know by themselves do not look for anything external. If they adhere to the view that liberation comes through external aid, through the office of a good, wise friend, they are entirely at fault. Why? There is a knower in your own mind, and it is this that makes you realize the truth by yourselves. When confusion reigns in you and false views are entertained, no amount of teaching by others, good, wise friends of yours, will be of use for your salvation. When, on the other hand, your genuine Prajñā shines forth, all your confused thoughts will vanish in an instant.

Ungo, the latter asked, 'O you, old wanderer! how is it that you not do seek an abiding place for yourself?' 'Where is my abiding place?' 'There is an old temple ruin at the foot of this mountain.' 'That is a fitting place for your old self,' responded Jōshu. Later, he came to Shūyūsan, who asked him the same question, saying, 'O you, old wanderer! why don't you get settled?' 'Where is the place for me to get settled?' 'Why, this old wanderer doesn't know even where to get settled for himself.' Said Jōshu, 'I have been engaged these thirty years in training horses, and today I have been kicked around by a donkey!'

Knowing thus what your Self-Nature is, you reach Buddha-hood by this single understanding, one knowledge.'

3. When the seeing into Self-Nature is emphasized and intuitive understanding is upheld against learning and philosophizing, we know that as one of its logical conclusions the old view of meditation begins to be looked down on as merely a discipline in mental tranquillization. And this was exactly the case with the sixth patriarch. Since the beginning of Buddhism there have been two currents of thought concerning the meaning of meditation: the one was, like Ārada and Udraka, who were the two teachers of the Buddha, to take it for suspending all psychic activities or for wiping consciousness clean of all its modes; and the other was to regard meditation simply as the most efficacious means for coming in touch with the ultimate reality. This fundamental difference of views with regard to meditation was a cause of the unpopularity at first of Bodhidharma among the Chinese Buddhists, scholars, and dhyāna-masters of the time. It was also a factor of divergence between the Niu-t'ou school of Zen and the orthodox teaching of the fourth patriarch, as well as between the Northern and the Southern schools of Zen Buddhism after the fifth patriarch. Hui-nêng, the sixth patriarch, came out as a strong advocate of intuitionalism and refused to interpret the meaning of dhyāna statically, as it were. For the Mind, according to him, at the highest stage of meditation was not a mere being, mere abstraction devoid of content and work. He wanted to grasp something which lay at the foundation of all his activities mental and physical, and this something could not be a mere geometrical point, it must be the source of energy and knowledge. Hui-nêng did not forget that the will was after all the ultimate reality and that enlightenment was to be understood as more than intellection, more than quietly contemplating the truth. The Mind or Self-Nature was to be apprehended in the midst of its working or functioning. The object of dhyāna was thus not to stop the working of Self-Nature but to make us plunge right into its stream and seize it in the very act. His

intuitionalism was dynamic. In the following dialogues both Hui-nêng and his disciples are still using the older terminology, but the import of this parley is illustrative of the point I want to specify.

Hsüan-chiao first studied T'ien-tai philosophy and later while reading the *Vimalakīrti* he discovered his Self-Nature. Being advised to see the sixth patriarch in order to have his experience certified or testified, he came to Tsao-ch'i. He walked round the master three times, and erecting his staff straight stood before him. Said the master, 'Monks are supposed to observe three hundred rules of conduct and eighty thousand minor ones; whence comest thou, so full of pride?'

'Birth-and-death is a matter of grave concern, and time waits for nobody!' said the T'ien-tai philosopher.

'Why dost thou not grasp that which is birthless and see into that which is timeless?' the master demanded.

'Birthless is that which grasps, and timeless is that which sees into.'

'That is so, that is so,' agreed the master.

When this was over, Hsüan-chiao came to Hui-nêng again in the full attire of the Buddhisk monk, and reverently bowing to the master wished to take leave of him.

Said the master, 'Why departest thou so soon?'

'There is from the very beginning no such thing as movement, and then why talkest thou of being soon?'

'Who knows that there is no movement?' retorted the master.

'There,' exclaimed Hsüan-chiao, 'thou makest a judgment thyself!'

'Thou truly comprehendest the intent of that which is birthless.'

'How could the birthless ever have an intent?' Hsüan-chiao asked.

'If there were no intent, who could ever judge?'

'Judgments are made with no intent whatever.' This was the conclusion of Chiao.

The master then expressed his deep appreciation of

Hsüan-chiao's view on the subject, saying, 'Well thou hast said!'

Chih-huang was an adept in meditation, which he studied under the fifth patriarch. After twenty years' discipline he thought he well understood the purport of meditation or samādhi. Hsüan-t'sê, learning his attainment, visited him, and said, 'What are you doing there?' 'I am entering into a samādhi.' 'You speak of entering, but how do you enter into samādhi—with a thought-ful mind or with a thought-less mind? If you say with a thought-less mind, all non-sentient beings such as plants or bricks could attain samādhi. If you say with a thought-ful mind, all sentient beings could attain it.' 'When I enter into samādhi,' said Chih-huang, 'I am not conscious of either being thought-ful or being thought-less.' 'If you are conscious of neither, you are right in samādhi all the while; why do you then talk at all of entering into it or coming out of it? If, however, there is really entering or coming out, it is not Great Samādhi.' Chih-huang did not know how to answer. After a while he asked who was Hsüan-t'sê's teacher and what was his understanding of samādhi. Said Hsüan-t'sê, 'Hui-nêng is my teacher, and according to him [the ultimate truth] lies mystically serene and perfectly quiet; substance and function are not to be separated, they are of one Suchness. The five skandhas are empty in their nature, and the six sense-objects have no reality. [The truth knows of] neither entering nor going out, neither being tranquil nor disturbed. Dhyāna in essence has no fixed abode. Without attaching yourself to an abode, be serene in dhyāna. Dhyāna in essence is birthless; without attaching yourself to the thought of birth [-and-death], think in dhyāna. Have your mind like unto space and yet have no thought of space.' Thus learning of the sixth patriarch's view on samādhi or dhyāna, Chih-huang came to the master himself and asked to be further enlightened. Said the patriarch: 'What Hsüan-t'sê told you is true. Have your mind like unto space and yet entertain in it no thought of emptiness. Then the truth will have its full activity unimpeded. Every movement of yours will come out of an innocent heart, and the ignorant and the wise will have an equal treatment in your hands. Subject and object will lose their distinction, and essence and appearance will be of one suchness. [When a world of absolute oneness is thus realized,] you have attained to eternal samādhi.'

To make the position of the sixth patriarch on the subject of meditation still clearer and more definite, let me quote another incident from his *Platform Sūtra*. A monk once made reference to a gāthā composed by Wo-luan which read as follows:

'I, Wo-luan, know a device
Whereby to blot out all my thoughts:
The objective world no more stirs the mind,
And daily matures my Enlightenment!'

Hearing this, the sixth patriarch remarked: 'That is no enlightenment but leads one into a state of bondage. Listen to my gāthā:

'I, Hui-nêng, know no device,
My thoughts are not suppressed:
The objective world ever stirs the mind,
And what is the use of maturing Enlightenment?'

These will be sufficient to show that Hui-nêng, the sixth patriarch, was on the one hand no quietist, nor nihilist advocating the doctrine of absolute emptiness, while on the other hand he was no idealist either, in the sense of denying an objective world. His dhyāna was full of action, yet above a world of particulars, so long as it was not carried away by it and in it.

4. Hui-nêng's method of demonstrating the truth of Zen was purely Chinese and not Indian. He did not resort to abstract terminology nor to romantic mysticism. The method was direct, plain, concrete, and highly practical. When the monk Ming came to him and asked for instruction, he said, 'Show me your original face before you

were born.' Is not the statement quite to the point? No philosophic discourse, no elaborate reasoning, no mystic imagery, but a direct unequivocal dictum. In this the sixth patriarch cut the first turf and his disciples quickly and efficiently followed in his steps. Notice how brilliantly Lin-chi made use of this method in his sermon on a 'true man of no title'. (See the Introduction.)

To give another instance. When Hui-nêng saw Huai-jang, of Nan-yüeh, he said, 'Whence comest thou?' which was followed by 'What is it that so cometh?' It took Huai-jang eight long years to answer the question satisfactorily. Afterwards this way of questioning became almost an established form of greeting with Zen masters. Nan-yüan asked a newly arrived monk, 'Whence comest thou?' 'I am from Han-shang.' Said the master, 'You are at fault as much as I am.' Hsiang-yên asked San-shêng, 'Whence comest thou?' 'From Lin-chi.' 'Bringest thou his sword?' San-shêng took up his seat-cloth (*tso-chu*) and struck Hsiang-yên across his mouth and went away. The Venerable Ch'en asked a monk, 'Whence comest thou?' 'From Yang-shan.' 'You art a liar!' was the verdict of the master. Another time he asked another monk, 'Whence comest thou?' 'From West of the River, sir.' 'How many sandals hast thou worn out?' This monk had evidently a gentler treatment.

This difference of method between the Indian and the Chinese often raised the question as to the difference, if there be, between the 'Tathāgata Dhyāna' and the 'Patriarchal Dhyāna'. For instance, when Hsiang-yên showed his song of poverty to Yang-shan, the latter said, 'You understand the Tathāgata Dhyāna but not yet the Patriarchal Dhyāna.' When asked about the difference, Mu-chou replied, 'The green mountains are green mountains, and the white clouds are white clouds.'

Hui-nêng died at the age of seventy-six in A.D. 713, while the T'ang dynasty was enjoying its halcyon days and Chinese culture reached the highest point in its history. A little over one hundred years after the passing of the sixth patriarch, Liu Tsung-yüan, one of the most brilliant literati in the history of Chinese literature, wrote a memorial inscription on his tombstone when he was honoured by the Emperor Hsien-tsung with the posthumous title, Great Mirror (*tai-chien*), and in this we read: 'In a sixth transmission after Dharma there was Tai-chien. He was first engaged in menial labour and servile work. Just a few words from the master were enough and he at once understood the deepest meaning conveyed in them. The master was greatly impressed, and finally conferred on him an insignia of faith. After that he hid himself in the Southern district; nobody heard of him again for sixteen years, when he thought the time was ripe for him to come out of the seclusion. He was settled at T'sao-ch'i[1] and began to teach. The number of disciples is said once to have reached several thousands.

'According to his doctrine, non-doing is reality, emptiness is the truth, and the ultimate meaning of things is vast and immovable. He taught that human nature in its beginning as well as in the end is thoroughly good and does not require any artificial weeding-out, for it has its root in that which is serene. The Emperor Chung-tsung heard of him and sent his courtier twice asking him to appear at Court, but failed to get him out. So the Emperor had his words instead which he took for his spiritual guidance. The teaching [of the sixth patriarch] in detail is generally accessible today; all those who talk at all about Zen find their source of information in T'sao-ch'i.'

[1] This is the name of the place where Hui-nêng had his Zen headquarters.

After Hui-nêng Zen was split up into several schools, two of which have survived even down to this day, in China as well as in Japan. The one represented by Hsing-szŭ, of Ch'ing-yüan (died 740), continues now as the Sōtō (T'sao-tung) school of Zen, and the other, coming down the line of Huai-jang, of Nan-yüeh (677–744), is now represented by the Rinzai (Lin-chi) school. Though much modified in various aspects, the principle and spirit of Zen Buddhism is still alive as it was in the days of the sixth patriarch, and as one of the great spiritual heritages of the East it is still wielding its unique influence, especially among the cultured people in Japan.

ON SATORI—THE REVELATION OF A
NEW TRUTH IN ZEN BUDDHISM

I

THE essence of Zen Buddhism consists in acquiring a new viewpoint of looking at life and things generally. By this I mean that if we want to get into the inmost life of Zen, we must forgo all our ordinary habits of thinking which control our everyday life, we must try to see if there is any other way of judging things, or rather if our ordinary way is always sufficient to give us the ultimate satisfaction of our spiritual needs. If we feel dissatisfied somehow with this life, if there is something in our ordinary way of living that deprives us of freedom in its most sanctified sense, we must endeavour to find a way somewhere which gives us a sense of finality and contentment. Zen proposes to do this for us and assures us of the acquirement of a new point of view in which life assumes a fresher, deeper, and more satisfying aspect. This acquirement, however, is really and naturally the greatest mental cataclysm one can go through with in life. It is no easy task, it is a kind of fiery baptism, and one has to go through the storm, the earthquake, the over-throwing of the mountains, and the breaking in pieces of the rocks.

This acquiring of a new point of view in our dealings with life and the world is popularly called by Japanese Zen students 'satori' (*wu* in Chinese). It is really another name for Enlightenment (*annuttara-samyak-sambodhi*), which is the word used by the Buddha and his Indian followers ever since his realization under the Bodhi-tree by the River Nairañjanā. There are several other phrases in Chinese designating this spiritual experience, each of which has a special connotation, showing tentatively how this pheno-menon is interpreted. At all events there is no Zen without

229

satori, which is indeed the Alpha and Omega of Zen Buddhism. Zen devoid of satori is like a sun without its light and
heat. Zen may lose all its literature, all its monasteries,
and all its paraphernalia; but as long as there is satori in
it it will survive to eternity. I want to emphasize this most
fundamental fact concerning the very life of Zen; for there
are some even among the students of Zen themselves who
are blind to this central fact and are apt to think when Zen
has been explained away logically or psychologically, or as
one of the Buddhist philosophies which can be summed
up by using highly technical and conceptual Buddhist
phrases, Zen is exhausted, and there remains nothing
in it that makes it what it is. But my contention is, the
life of Zen begins with the opening of satori (*kai wu* in
Chinese).

Satori may be defined as an intuitive looking into the
nature of things in contradistinction to the analytical or
logical understanding of it. Practically, it means the unfolding of a new world hitherto unperceived in the confusion of a dualistically-trained mind. Or we may say that
with satori our entire surroundings are viewed from quite
an unexpected angle of perception. Whatever this is, the
world for those who have gained a satori is no more the old
world as it used to be; even with all its flowing streams and
burning fires, it is never the same one again. Logically
stated, all its opposites and contradictions are united and
harmonized into a consistent organic whole. This is a
mystery and a miracle, but according to the Zen masters
such is being performed every day. Satori can thus be had
only through our once personally experiencing it.

Its semblance or analogy in a more or less feeble and
fragmentary way is gained when a difficult mathematical
problem is solved, or when a great discovery is made, or
when a sudden means of escape is realized in the midst of
most desperate complications; in short, when one exclaims
'Eureka! Eureka!' But this refers only to the intellectual
aspect of satori, which is therefore necessarily partial and
incomplete and does not touch the very foundations of life

considered one indivisible whole. Satori as the Zen experience must be concerned with the entirety of life. For what Zen proposes to do is the revolution, and the revaluation as well, of oneself as a spiritual unity. The solving of a mathematical problem ends with the solution, it does not affect one's whole life. So with all other particular questions, practical or scientific, they do not enter the basic life-tone of the individual concerned. But the opening of satori is the remaking of life itself. When it is genuine—for there are many simulacra of it—its effects on one's moral and spiritual life are revolutionary, and they are so enhancing, purifying, as well as exacting. When a master was asked what constituted Buddhahood, he answered, 'The bottom of a pail is broken through.' From this we can see what a complete revolution is produced by this spiritual experience. The birth of a new man is really cataclysmic.

In the psychology of religion this spiritual enhancement of one's whole life is called 'conversion'. But as the term is generally used by Christian converts, it cannot be applied in its strict sense to the Buddhist experience, especially to that of the Zen followers; the term has too affective or emotional a shade to take the place of satori, which is above all noetic. The general tendency of Buddhism is, as we know, more intellectual than emotional, and its doctrine of Enlightenment distinguishes it sharply from the Christian view of salvation; Zen as one of the Mahāyāna schools naturally shares a large amount of what we may call transcendental intellectualism, which does not issue in logical dualism. When poetically or figuratively expressed, satori is 'the opening of the mind-flower', or 'the removing of the bar', or 'the brightening up of the mind-works'.

All these tend to mean the clearing up of a passage which has been somehow blocked, preventing the free, unobstructed operation of a machine or a full display of the inner works. With the removal of the obstruction, a new vista opens before one, boundless in expanse and reaching the end of time. As life thus feels quite free in its activity, which was not the case before the awakening, it now enjoys itself to the fullest extent of its possibilities, to attain which is the object of Zen discipline. This is often taken to be equivalent to 'vacuity of interest and poverty of purpose'. But according to the Zen masters the doctrine of non-achievement concerns itself with the subjective attitude of mind which goes beyond the limitations of thought. It does not deny ethical ideals, nor does it transcend them; it is simply an inner state of consciousness without reference to its objective consequences.

II

The coming of Bodhi-dharma (Bodai-daruma in Japanese, P'u-ti Ta-mo in Chinese) to China early in the sixth century was simply to introduce this satori element into the body of Buddhism, whose advocates were then so engrossed in subtleties of philosophical discussion or in the mere literary observance of rituals and disciplinary rules. By the 'absolute transmission of the spiritual seal', which was claimed by the first patriarch, is meant the opening of satori, obtaining an eye to see into the spirit of the Buddhist teaching.

The sixth patriarch, Yenō (Hui-nêng), was distinguished because of his upholding the satori aspect of dhyāna against the mere mental tranquillization of the Northern school of Zen under the leadership of Jinshu (Shên-hsiu). Baso (Ma-tsu), Ōbaku (Huang-po), Rinzai (Lin-chi), and all the other stars illuminating the early days of Zen in the T'ang dynasty were advocates of satori. Their life-activities were unceasingly directed towards the advancement of this; and as one can readily recognize, they so differed from those merely absorbed in contemplation or the practising of dhyana so called. They were strongly against quietism, declaring its adherents to be purblind and living in the cave of darkness. Before we go on it is advisable, therefore, to have this point clearly understood so that we leave no doubt as to the ultimate purport of Zen, which is by no means wasting one's life away in a trance-inducing practice, but consists in seeing into the life of one's being or opening an eye of satori.

There is in Japan a book going under the title of *Six Essays by Shoshitsu* (that is, by Bodhidharma, the first patriarch of Zen); the book contains no doubt some of the sayings of Dharma, but most of the Essays are not his; they were probably composed during the T'ang dynasty when Zen Buddhism began to make its influence more generally felt among the Chinese Buddhists. The spirit, however, pervading the book is in perfect accord with the principle of Zen. One of the Essays entitled 'Kechimyakuron', or 'Treatise on the Lineage of Faith', discusses the question of *Chien-hsing*,[1] or satori, which, according to the author, constitutes the essence of Zen Buddhism. The following passages are extracts.

'If you wish to seek the Buddha, you ought to see into your own Nature (*hsing*); for this Nature is the Buddha himself. If you have not seen into your own Nature, what is the use of thinking of the Buddha, reciting the Sūtras, observing a fast, or keeping the precepts? By thinking of the Buddha, your cause [i.e. meritorious deed] may bear fruit; by reciting the Sūtras your intelligence may grow brighter; by keeping the precepts you may be born in the heavens; by

---

[1] *Hsing* means nature, character, essence, soul, or what is innate to one. 'Seeing into one's Nature' is one of the set phrases used by the Zen masters, and is in fact the avowed object of all Zen discipline. Satori is its more popular expression. When one gets into the inwardness of things, there is satori. This latter, however, being a broad term, can be used to designate any kind of a thorough understanding, and it is only in Zen that it has a restricted meaning. In this article I have used the term as the most essential thing in the study of Zen; for 'seeing into one's Nature' suggests the idea that Zen has something concrete and substantial which requires being seen into by us. This is misleading, though satori too I admit is a vague and naturally ambiguous word. For ordinary purposes, not too strictly philosophical, satori will answer, and whenever *chien-hsing* is referred to it means this: the opening of the mental eye. As to the sixth patriarch's view on 'seeing into one's Nature', see above under *History of Zen Buddhism*.

practising charity you may be rewarded abundantly; but as to seeking the Buddha, you are far away from him. If your Self is not yet clearly comprehended, you ought to see a wise teacher and get a thorough understanding as to the root of birth-and-death. One who has not seen into one's own Nature is not to be called a wise teacher.

'When this [seeing into one's own Nature] is not attained, one cannot escape from the transmigration of birth-and-death, however well one may be versed in the study of the sacred scriptures in twelve divisions. No time will ever come to one to get out of the sufferings of the triple world. Anciently there was a Bhikshu Zenshō (Shan-hsing[1]) who was capable of reciting all the twelve divisions of scriptures, yet he could not save himself from transmigration, because he had no insight into his own Nature. If this was the case even with Zenshō, how about those moderners who, being able to discourse only on a few Sūtras and Śastras, regard themselves as exponents of Buddhism? They are truly simple-minded ones. When Mind is not understood it is absolutely of no avail to recite and discourse on idle literature. If you want to seek the Buddha, you ought to see into your own Nature, which is the Buddha himself. The Buddha is a free man—a man who neither works nor achieves. If, instead of seeing into your own Nature, you turn away and seek the Buddha in external things, you will never get at him.

'The Buddha is your own Mind, make no mistake to bow (to external objects]. "Buddha" is a Western word, and in this country it means "enlightened nature"; and by "enlightened" is meant "spiritually enlightened". It is one's own spiritual Nature in enlightenment that responds to the external world, comes in contact with objects, raises the eyebrows, winks the eyelids, and moves the hands and legs. This Nature is the Mind, and the Mind is the Buddha,

---

[1] According to the *Mahāparinirvāna-sūtra*, translated into Chinese by Dharmaraksha, A.D. 423, Vol. XXXIII, he was one of the three sons of the Buddha while he was still a Bodhisattava. He was most learned in all Buddhist lore, but his views tended to be nihilistic and he finally fell into hell.

and the Buddha is the Way, and the Way is Zen. This simple word, Zen, is beyond the comprehension both of the wise and the ignorant. To see directly into one's original Nature, this is Zen. Even if you are well learned in hundreds of the Sūtras and Śastras, you still remain an ignoramus in Buddhism when you have not yet seen into your original Nature. Buddhism is not there [in mere learning]. The highest truth is unfathomably deep, is not an object of talk or discussion, and even the canonical texts have no way to bring it within our reach. Let us once see into our own original Nature and we have the truth, even when we are quite illiterate, not knowing a word. . . .

'Those who have not seen into their own Nature may reach the Sūtras, think of the Buddha, study long, work hard, practise religion throughout the six periods of the day, sit for a long time and never lie down for sleep, and may be wide in learning and well informed in all things; and they may believe that all this is Buddhism. All the Buddhas in successive ages only talk of seeing into one's Nature. All things are impermanent; until you get an insight into your Nature, do not say "I have perfect knowledge". Such is really committing a very grave crime. Ānanda, one of the ten great disciples of the Buddha, was known for his wide information, but did not have any insight into Buddhahood, because he was so bent on gaining information only. . . .'

The sixth patriarch, Hui-nêng (Yenō), insists on this in a most unmistakable way when he answers the question: 'As to your commission from the fifth patriarch of Huang-mei, how do you direct and instruct others in it?' The answer was, 'No direction, no instruction there is; we speak only of seeing into one's Nature and not of practising dhyāna and seeking deliverance thereby.' Elsewhere they are designated as the 'confused' and 'not worth consulting with'; they that are empty-minded and sit quietly, having no thoughts whatever; whereas 'even ignorant ones, if they all of a sudden realize the truth and open their mental eyes, are, after all, wise men and may attain even to Buddha-hood'. Again, when the patriarch was told of the method of instruction adopted by the masters of the Northern school of Zen, which consisted in stopping all mental activities, quietly absorbed in contemplation, and in sitting cross-legged for the longest while at a stretch, he declared such practices to be abnormal and not at all to the point, being far from the truth of Zen, and added this stanza which was quoted elsewhere:

> 'While living, one sits up and lies not,
> When dead, one lies and sits not;
> A set of ill-smelling skeleton!
> What is the use of toiling and moiling so?'

When at Demboin, Baso used to sit cross-legged all day and meditating. His master, Nangaku Yejo (Nan-yüeh Huai-jang, 677–744), saw him and asked:

'What seekest thou here thus sitting cross-legged?'

'My desire is to become a Buddha.'

Thereupon the master took up a piece of brick and began to polish it hard on a stone near by.

'What workest thou on so, my master?' asked Baso.

'I am trying to turn this into a mirror.'

'No amount of polishing will make a mirror of the brick, sir.'

'If so, no amount of sitting cross-legged as thou doest will make of thee a Buddha,' said the master.

'What shall I have to do then?'

'It is like driving a cart; when it moveth not, wilt thou whip the cart or the ox?'

Baso made no answer.

The master continued: 'Wilt thou practise this sitting cross-legged in order to attain dhyāna or to attain Buddha-hood? If it is dhyāna, dhyāna does not consist in sitting or lying; if it is Buddhahood, the Buddha has no fixed forms. As he has no abiding place anywhere, no one can take hold of him, nor can he be let go. If thou seekest Buddhahood by thus sitting cross-legged, thou murderest him. So long as thou freest thyself not from sitting so,[1] thou never comest to the truth.'

These are all plain statements, and no doubts are left as to the ultimate end of Zen, which is not sinking oneself into a state of torpidity by sitting quietly after the fashion of a Hindu saint and trying to exclude all the mental ripplings that seem to come up from nowhere, and after a while pass away—where nobody knows. These preliminary remarks will help the reader carefully to consider the following 'Questions and Answers' (known as *Mondō* in Japanese); for they will illustrate my thesis that Zen aims at the opening of satori, or at acquiring a new point of view as regards life and the universe. The Zen masters, as we see below, are always found trying to avail themselves of every apparently trivial incident of life in order to make the disciples' minds flow into a channel hitherto altogether unperceived. It is like picking a hidden lock, the flood of new experiences gushes forth from the opening. It is again like the clock's striking the hours; when the appointed time comes it clicks, and the whole percussion of sounds is released. The mind seems to have something of this mechanism; when a certain moment is reached, a hitherto closed screen is lifted, an entirely new vista opens up, and the tone of one's whole life thereafter changes. This mental clicking or opening is called satori by the Zen masters and is insisted upon as the main object of their discipline.

In this connection the reader will find the following words of Meister Eckhart quite illuminative: 'Upon this matter a heathen sage hath a fine saying in speech with another sage: "I become aware of something in me which flashes upon my reason. I perceive of it that it is something,

---

[1] That is, from the idea that this sitting cross-legged leads to Buddhahood. From the earliest periods of Zen in China, the quietest tendency has been running along the whole history with the intellectual tendency which emphasizes the satori element. Even today these currents are represented to a certain extent by the Sōtō on the one hand and the Rinzai on the other, while each has its characteristic features of excellence. My own standpoint is that of the intuitionalist and not that of the quietest; for the essence of Zen lies in the attainment of satori.

but what it is I cannot perceive. Only meseems that, could I conceive it, I should comprehend all truth".'[1]

III

The records quoted below do not always give the whole history of the mental development leading up to a satori; that is, from the first moment when the disciple came to the master until the last moment of realization, with all the intermittent psychological vicissitudes which he had to go through. The examples are just to show that the whole Zen discipline gains meaning when there takes place this turning of the mental hinge to a wider and deeper world. For when this wise and deeper world opens, everyday life, even the most trivial thing of it, grows loaded with the truths of Zen. On the one hand, therefore, satori is a most prosaic and matter-of-fact thing, but on the other hand, when it is not understood it is something of a mystery. But after all, is not life itself filled with wonders, mysteries, and unfathomabilities, far beyond our discursive understanding?

A monk asked Jōshu (Chao-chou Tsung-shên, 778–897) to be instructed in Zen. Said the master, 'Have you had your breakfast or not?' 'Yes, master, I have,' answered the monk. 'If so, have your dishes washed,' was an immediate response, which, it is said, at once opened the monk's mind to the truth of Zen.

This is enough to show what a commonplace thing satori is; but to see what an important role this most trivial incident of life plays in Zen, it will be necessary to add some remarks which were made by the masters, and through these the reader may have a glimpse into the content of satori. Ummon (Yün-mên Wên-yen, died 949), who lived a little later than Jōshu, commented on him:

---

[1] W. Lehmann, *Meister Eckhart*. Göttingen, 1917, p. 243. Quoted by Professor Rudolf Otto in his *The Idea of the Holy*, p. 201.

'Was there any special instruction in the remark of Jōshu, or not? If there was, what was it? If there was not, what satori was it that the monk attained?' Later, Umpō Monyetsu (Yün-feng Wên-yüeh, 997–1062) made a retort, saying: 'The great master Ummon does not know what is what, hence this comment of his. It was altogether unnecessary, it was like painting legs to the snake and growing a beard to the eunuch. My view differs from his: that monk who seems to have attained a satori goes to hell as straight as an arrow!'

Now, what does this all mean—Jōshu's remark about washing the dishes, the monk's attainment of satori, Ummon's alternatives, and Monyetsu's assurance? Are they speaking against each other? Is this much ado about nothing? This is where Zen is difficult to grasp and at the same time difficult to explain. Let me add a few more queries. How did Jōshu make the monk's eye open by such a prosaic remark? Did the remark have any hidden meaning, however, which happened to coincide with the mental tone of the monk? How was the monk so mentally prepared for the final stroke of the master, whose service was just pressing the button, as it were? Nothing of satori is so far gleaned from washing the dishes; we have to look somewhere else for the truth of Zen. At any rate, we could not say that Jōshu had nothing to do with the monk's realization. Hence Ummon's remark, which is somewhat enigmatic, yet to the point. As to Monyetsu's comment, it is what is technically known as *Nenro*, 'handling and playing', or 'playful criticism'. He appears to be making a disparaging remark about Ummon, but in truth he is joining hands with his predecessors.

Tokusan (Teh-shan Hsüan-chien, 779–865) was a great scholar of the *Diamond Sūtra* (*Vajracchedikā*). Learning that there was such a thing as Zen ignoring all the written scriptures and directly laying hands on one's soul, he came to Ryutan (Lung-t'an) to be instructed in the doctrine. One day Tokusan was sitting outside trying to see into the mystery of Zen. Ryutan said, 'Why don't you come in?'

Replied Tokusan, 'It is pitch dark.' A candle was lighted and handed over to Tokusan. When the latter was at the point of taking it, Ryutan suddenly blew the light out, whereupon the mind of Tokusan was opened.[1]

Hyakujo (Pai-chang Huai-hai, 724–814) one day went out attending his master Baso (Ma-tsu). A flock of wild geese was seen flying and Baso asked:

'What are they?'

'They are wild geese, sir.'

'Whither are they flying?'

'They have flown away, sir.'

Baso, abruptly taking hold of Hyakujo's nose, gave it a twist. Overcome with pain, Hyakujo cried aloud: 'Oh! Oh!'

'You say they have flown away,' Baso said, 'but all the same they have been here from the very beginning.'

This made Hyakujo's back wet with cold perspiration. He had satori.

Is there any connection in any possible way between the washing of the dishes and the blowing out of a candle and the twisting of the nose? We must say with Ummon: If there is none, how could they all come to the realization of the truth of Zen? If there is, what inner relationship is there? What is this satori? What new point of viewing things is this? So long as our observation is limited to those conditions which preceded the opening of a disciple's eye we cannot perhaps fully comprehend where lies the ultimate issue. They are matters of everyday occurrence, and if Zen lies objectively among them, every one of us is a master before we are told of it. This is partly true inasmuch as there is nothing artificially constructed in Zen, but if the nose is to be really twisted or the candle blown out in order

[1] In Claud Field's *Mystics and Saints of Islam*, p. 25, we read under Hasan Basri: 'Another time I saw a child coming toward me holding a lighted torch in his hand, "Where have you brought the light from?" I asked him. He immediately blew it out, and said to me, "O Hasan, tell me where it is gone, and I will tell you whence I fetched it".' Of course the parallel is here only apparent, for Tokusan got his enlightenment from quite a different source than the mere blowing out of the candle. Still, the parallel in itself is interesting enough to be quoted here.

to take the scale off the eye, our attention must be directed inwardly to the working of our minds, and it will be there where we are to take hold of the hidden relation existing between the flying geese and the washed dishes and the blown-out candle and any other happenings that weave out infinitely variegated patterns of human life.

Under Daiye (Tai-hui, 1089–1163), the great Zen teacher of the Sung dynasty, there was a monk named Dōken (Tao-ch'ien) who had spent many years in the study of Zen, but who had not yet delved into its secrets, if there were any. He was discouraged when he was sent on an errand to a distant city. A trip requiring half a year to finish would surely be a hindrance rather than a help to his study. Sogen (Tsung-yüan), one of his fellow-monks, took pity on him and said: 'I will accompany you on this trip and do all that I can for you. There is no reason why you cannot go on with your meditation even while travelling.' They started together.

One evening Dōken despairingly implored his friend to assist him in the solution of the mystery of life. The friend said: 'I am willing to help you in every way, but there are five things in which I cannot be of any help to you. These you must look after yourself.' Dōken expressed the desire to know what they were. 'For instance,' said the friend, 'when you are hungry or thirsty, my eating of food or drinking does not fill your stomach. You must drink and eat yourself. When you want to respond to the calls of nature, you must take care of them yourself, for I cannot be of any use to you. And then it will be nobody else but yourself that will carry this corpse of yours [i.e. the body] along this highway.' This remark at once opened the mind of the truth-seeking monk, who, transported with his discovery, did not know how to express his joy. Sogen now told him that his work was done and that his further companionship would have no meaning after this. So they parted company and Dōken was left alone to continue the trip. After the half-year, Dōken came back to his own monastery. Daiye, his teacher, happened to meet him on his way down the mountain, and made the following remark, 'This time he knows it all.' What was it, one may remark, that flashed through Dōken's mind when his friend gave him such matter-of-fact advice?

Kyōgen (Hsian-yen) was a disciple of Hyakujo. After the master's death he went to Yisan (Wei-shan, 771–853) who was a senior disciple of Hyakujo. Yisan asked him: 'I am told that you have been under my late master Hyakujo, and also that you have remarkable intelligence; but the understanding of Zen through this medium necessarily ends in intellectual and analytical comprehension, which is not of much use. Yet you may have had an insight into the truth of Zen. Let me have your view as to the reason of birth-and-death; that is, as to your own being before your parents gave birth to you.'

Thus asked, Kyōgen did not know how to reply. He retired into his own room and assiduously made research among his notes which he had taken of the sermons given by his late master. He failed to come across a suitable passage he might present as his own view. He returned to Yisan and implored him to teach in the faith of Zen. But Yisan said: 'I really have nothing to impart to you, and if I tried to do so you may have occasion to make me an object of ridicule later on. Besides, whatever I can instruct you is my own and will never be yours.' Kyōgen was disappointed and considered his senior disciple unkind. Finally he came to the decision to burn up all his notes and memorandums which were of no help to his spiritual welfare, and, retiring altogether from the world, to spend the rest of his life in solitude and simplicity in accordance with the Buddhist rules. He reasoned: 'What is the use of studying Buddhism, so difficult to comprehend and too subtle to receive instructions from another? I shall be a plain homeless monk, troubled with no desire to master things too deep for thought.' He left Yisan and built a hut near the tomb of Chu (Hui-chung), the National Master, at Nan-yang. One day he was weeding and sweeping the ground, and when a piece of rock brushed away struck a bamboo, the sound produced by the percussion unexpectedly elevated his mind to a state of satori. The question proposed by Yisan became transparent; his joy was boundless, he felt as if meeting again his lost parent. Besides, he came to realize the kindness of his abandoned senior brother monk who refused him instruction. For he now knew that this would not have happened to him if Yisan had been unkind enough to explain things for him.

Below is the verse he composed soon after his achievement, from which we may get an idea of his satori:

'One stroke has made me forget all my previous knowledge,
No artificial discipline is at all needed;
In every movement I uphold the ancient way,
And never fall into the rut of mere quietism;
Wherever I walk no traces are left,
And my senses are not fettered by rules of conduct;
Everywhere those who have attained to the truth,
All declare this to be of the highest order.'

IV

There is something, we must admit, in Zen that defies explanation, and to which no master however ingenious can lead his disciples through intellectual analysis. Kyōgen or Tokusan had enough knowledge of the canonical teachings or of the master's expository discourses; but when the real thing was demanded of them they significantly failed to produce it either to their inner satisfaction or for the master's approval. The satori, after all, is not a thing to be gained through the understanding. But once the key is within one's grasp, everything seems to be laid bare before him; the entire world assumes then a different aspect. By those who know, this inner change is recognized. The Dōken before he started on his mission and the Dōken after the realization were apparently the same person; but as soon as Daiye saw him he knew what had taken place in him, even when he uttered not a word. Baso twisted Hyakujo's nose, and the latter turned into such a wild soul as to have the audacity to roll up the matting before his master's discourse had hardly begun (see below). The experience they have gone through within themselves is not a very elaborate, complicated, and intellectually demonstrable thing; for none of them ever try to expound it by a series of learned discourses; they do just this thing or that, or utter a single phrase unintelligible to outsiders, and the whole affair proves most satisfactory both to the master and to the disciple. The satori cannot be a phantasm, empty and contentless, and lacking in real value, while it must be the simplest possible experience perhaps because it is the very foundation of all experiences.

As to the opening of satori, all that Zen can do is to indicate the way and leave the rest all to one's own experience; that is to say, following up the indication and arriving at the goal—this is to be done by oneself and without another's help. With all that the master can do, he is helpless to make the disciple take hold of the thing unless the latter is inwardly fully prepared for it. Just as we cannot make a horse drink against his will, the taking hold of the ultimate reality is to be done by oneself. Just as the flower blooms out of its inner necessity, the looking into one's own nature must be the outcome of one's own inner overflowing. This is where Zen is so personal and subjective, in the sense of being inner and creative. In the Āgama or Nikāya literature we encounter so frequently such phrases as 'Atta-dīpā viharatha attā saraṇā ananña-saraṇā', or 'sayaṁ abhiññā', or 'Diṭṭha-dhammo patta-dhammo vidita-dhammo pariyogālha-dhammo aparappaccayo satthu sāsane'; they show that Enlightenment is the awakening, within oneself and not depending on others, of an inner sense in one's consciousness, enabling one to create a world of eternal harmony and beauty—the home of Nirvāṇa.

I said that Zen does not give us any intellectual assistance, nor does it waste time in arguing the point with us; but it merely suggests or indicates, not because it wants to be indefinite, but because that is really the only thing it can do for us. If it could, it would do anything to help us come to an understanding. In fact Zen is exhausting every possible means to do that, as we can see in all the great masters' attitudes towards their disciples.[1] When they are actually knocking them down, their kindheartedness is never to be doubted. They are just waiting for the time when their pupils' minds get all ripened for the final moment. When this is come, the opportunity of opening an eye to the truth of Zen lies everywhere. One can pick it up in the hearing of an inarticulate sound, or listening to an unintelligible remark, or in the observation of a flower blooming, or in the encountering of any trivial everyday incident such as stumbling, rolling up a screen, using a fan, etc. These are all sufficient conditions that will awaken one's inner sense. Evidently a most insignificant happening, and yet its effect on the mind infinitely surpasses all that one could expect of it. A light touch of an ignited wire, and an explosion shaking the very foundations of the earth. In fact, all the causes of satori are in the mind. That is why when the clock clicks, all that has been lying there bursts up like a volcanic eruption or flashes out like a bolt of lightning.[2] Zen calls this 'returning to one's own home'; for its followers will declare: 'You have now found yourself; from the very beginning nothing has been kept away from you. It was yourself that closed the eye to the fact. In Zen there is nothing to explain, nothing to teach, that will add to your knowledge. Unless it grows out of yourself, no knowledge is really of value to you, a borrowed plumage never grows.'

Kōzankoku (Huang San-ku), a Confucian poet and statesman, came to Kwaido (Hui-t'ang, 1024–1100) to be initiated into Zen. Said the Zen master: 'There is a passage in the text you are so thoroughly familiar with

[1] See the Essay entitled 'Practical Methods of Zen Instruction'.

[2] The lightning simile in the *Kena-Upanishad* (IV, 30), as is supposed by some scholars, is not to depict the feeling of inexpressive awe as regards the nature of Brahman, but it illustrates the bursting out of enlightenment upon consciousness. 'A—a—ah' is most significant here.

which fitly describes the teaching of Zen. Did not Confucius declare: "Do you think I am holding back something from you, O my disciples? Indeed, I have held nothing back from you"?' Sankoku tried to answer, but Kwaido immediately made him keep silence by saying, 'No, no!' The Confucian disciple felt troubled in mind, and did not know how to express himself. Some time later they were having a walk in the mountains. The wild laurel was in full bloom and the air was redolent. Asked the Zen master, 'Do you smell it?' When the Confucian answered affirmatively, Kwaido said, 'There, I have kept nothing back from you!' This suggestion from the teacher at once led to the opening of Kōzankoku's mind. Is it not evident now that satori is not a thing to be imposed upon another, but that it is self-growing from within? Though nothing is kept away from us, it is through a satori that we become cognizant of the fact, being convinced that we are all sufficient unto ourselves. All that therefore Zen contrives is to assert that there is such a thing as self-revelation, or the opening of satori.

V

As satori strikes at the primary fact of existence, its attainment marks a turning-point in one's life. The attainment, however, must be thorough-going and clear-cut in order to produce a satisfactory result. To deserve the name 'satori' the mental revolution must be so complete as to make one really and sincerely feel that there took place a fiery baptism of the spirit. The intensity of this feeling is proportional to the amount of effort the opener of satori has put into the achievement. For there is a gradation in satori as to its intensity, as in all our mental activity. The possessor of a lukewarm satori may suffer no such spiritual revolution as Rinzai, or Bukkō (Fo-kuang), whose case is quoted below. Zen is a matter of character and not of the intellect, which means that Zen grows out of the will as the first principle of life. A brilliant intellect may fail to unravel all the mysteries of Zen, but a strong soul will drink deep of the inexhaustible fountain. I do not know if the intellect is superficial and touches only the fringe of one's personality, but the fact is that the will is the man himself, and Zen appeals to it. When one becomes penetratingly conscious of the working of this agency, there is the opening of satori and the understanding of Zen. As they say, the snake has now grown into the dragon; or, more graphically, a common cur—a most miserable creature wagging its tail for food and sympathy, and kicked about by the street boys so mercilessly—has now turned into a golden-haired lion whose roar frightens to death all the feeble-minded.

Therefore, when Rinzai was meekly submitting to the 'thirty blows' of Ōbaku, he was a pitiable sight; as soon as he attained satori he was quite a different personage, and his first exclamation was, 'There is not much after all in the Buddhism of Ōbaku.' And when he saw the reproachful Ōbaku again, he returned his favour by giving him a slap on the face. 'What an arrogance, what an impudence!' Ōbaku exclaimed; but there was reason in Rinzai's rudeness, and the old master could not but be pleased with this treatment from his former tearful Rinzai.

When Tokusan gained an insight into the truth of Zen he immediately took up all his commentaries on the *Diamond Sūtra*, once so valued and considered indispensable that he had to carry them wherever he went; he now set fire to them, reducing all the manuscripts to nothingness. He exclaimed, 'However deep your knowledge of abstruse philosophy, it is like a piece of hair placed in the vastness of space; and however important your experience in things worldly, it is like a drop of water thrown into an unfathomable abyss.'

On the day following the incident of the flying geese, to which reference is made elsewhere, Baso appeared in the preaching-hall, and was about to speak before a congregation, when Hyakujo came forward and began to roll up the matting.[1] Baso without protesting came down from his seat and returned to his own room. He then called Hyakujo and asked him why he rolled up the matting before he had uttered a word.

'Yesterday you twisted my nose,' replied Hyakujo, 'and it was quite painful'

'Where,' said Baso, 'was your thought wandering then?'

'It is not painful any more today, master.'

How differently he behaves now! When his nose was pinched, he was quite an ignoramus in the secrets of Zen. He is now a golden-haired lion, he is master of himself, and acts as freely as if he owned the world, pushing away even his own master far into the background.

There is no doubt that Satori goes deep into the very root of individuality. The change achieved thereby is quite remarkable, as we see in the examples above cited.

VI

Some masters have left in the form of verse known as 'Ge' (*gāthā*) what they perceived or felt at the time when their mental eye was opened. The verse has the special name of 'Tōki-no-ge'[2], and from the following translations the reader may draw his own conclusions as to the nature and content of a satori so highly prized by the Zen followers. But there is one thing to which I would like to call his attention, which is that the contents of these gāthās are so varied and dissimilar as far as their literary and intelligible sense is concerned that one may be at a loss how to make a comparison of these divers exclamations. Being sometimes merely descriptive verses of the feelings of the author at the

[1] This is spread before the Buddha and on it the master performs his bowing ceremony, and its rolling up naturally means the end of a sermon.

[2] *Tou chi chia*, meaning 'the verse of mutual understanding' which takes place when the master's mind and the disciple's are merged in each other's.

moment of satori, analysis is impossible unless the critic himself has once experienced them in his own inner life. Nevertheless these verses will be of interest to the psychological students of Buddhist mysticism even as merely emotional utterances of the supreme moment.

The following is by Chōkei (Chang-ching, died 932), whose eye was opened when he was rolling up the screen:

> 'How deluded I was! How deluded indeed!
> Lift up the screen and come see the world!
> "What religion believest thou?" you ask.
> I raise my hossu[1] and hit your mouth.'

Hōyen (Fa-yen) of Gosozan (Wu-tso-shan), who died in 1104, succeeded Shutan (Shou-tuan), of Haku-un (Pai-yün), and was the teacher of Yengo (Yüan-wu), composed the following when his mental eye was first opened:

> 'A patch of farm land quietly lies by the hill.
> Crossing my hands over the chest I ask the old farmer kindly:
> "How often have you sold it and bought it back by yourself?"
> I like the pines and bamboos that invite a refreshing breeze.'

Yengo (Yüan-wu, 1063–1135) was one of the greatest teachers in the Sung dynasty and the author of a Zen text book known as the *Hekiganshu*. His verse stands in such contrast to that of his teacher, Hōyen, and the reader will find it hard to unearth anything of Zen from the following romanticism:

> 'The golden duck no more issues odorous smoke behind the
>   brocade screens,
> Amidst flute-playing and singing, he retreats, thoroughly in
>   liquor and supported by others:
> A happy event in the life of a romantic youth,
> It is his sweetheart alone that is allowed to know.'

[1] It was originally a mosquito driver, but now it is a symbol of religious authority. It has a short handle, a little over a foot long, and a longer tuft of hair, usually a horse's tail or a yak's.

Yenju, of Yōmeiji (Yung-ming Yen-shou, 904–975), who belonged to the Hōgen school of Zen Buddhism, was the author of a book called *Shukyōroku* ('Record of Truth-Mirror') in one hundred fasciculi, and flourished in the early Sung. His realization took place when he heard a bundle of fuel dropping on the ground.

> 'Something dropped! It is no other thing;
> Right and left, there is nothing earthy:
> Rivers and mountains and the great earth,—
> In them all revealed is the Body of the Dharmarāja.

The first of the following two verses is by Yōdainen (Yang Tai-nien, 973–1020), a statesman of the Sung dynasty, and the second by Iku, of Toryō (Tu-ling Yü), who was a disciple of Yōgi (Yang-ch'i, 1024–1072), the founder of the Yōgi Branch of the Rinzai school:

> 'An octagonal millstone rushes through the air;
> A golden-coloured lion has turned into a cur:
> If you want to hide yourself in the North Star,
> Turn round and fold your hands behind the South Star.'

> 'I have one jewel shining bright,
> Long buried it was underneath worldly worries;
> This morning the dusty veil is off, and restored is its lustre,
> Illumining rivers and mountains and ten thousand things.'

A sufficient variety of the verses has been given here to show how they vary from one another and how it is impossible to suggest any intelligible explanation of the content of satori by merely comparing them or by analysing them. Some of them are easily understood, I suppose, as expressive of the feeling of a new revelation; but as to what that revelation itself is, it will require a certain amount of personal knowledge to be able to describe it more intelligently. In any event, all these masters testify to the fact that there is such a thing in Zen as satori through which one is admitted into a new world of value. The old way of viewing things is abandoned and the world acquires a new signification. Some of them would declare that they were 'deluded' or that their 'previous knowledge' was thrown into oblivion, while others would confess they were hitherto unaware of a new beauty which exists in the 'refreshing breeze' and in the 'shining jewel'.

VII

When our consideration is limited to the objective side of satori as illustrated so far, it does not appear to be a very extraordinary thing—this opening an eye to the truth of Zen. The master makes some remarks, and if they happen to be opportune enough, the disciple will come at once to a realization and see into a mystery hitherto undreamed of. It seems all to depend upon what kind of mood or what state of mental preparedness one is in at the moment. Zen is after all a haphazard affair, one may be tempted to think; but when we know that it took Nangaku (Nan-yüeh) eight long years to answer the question 'Who is he that thus cometh towards me?' we shall realize the fact that there was in him a great deal of mental anguish and tribulation which he had to go through before he could come to the final solution and declare, 'Even when one asserts that it is a somewhat, one misses it altogether.' We must try to look into the psychological aspect of satori, where is revealed the inner mechanism of opening the door to the eternal secrets of the human soul. This is done best by quoting some of the masters themselves whose introspective statements are on record.

Kōhō (Kao-fêng, 1238-1285) was one of the great masters in the latter part of the Sung dynasty. When his master first let him attend to the 'Jōshu's Mu',[1] he exerted himself hard on the problem. One day his master, Set-sugan (Hsüeh-yen), suddenly asked him, 'Who is it that carries for you this lifeless corpse of yours?' The poor fellow did not know what to make of the question, for the master was merciless, and it was usually followed by a hard knocking down. Later, in the midst of his sleep one night, he recalled the fact that once when he was under another master he was told to find out the ultimate signification of the statement 'All things return to one',[2] and this kept him up the rest of that night and through the several days and nights that succeeded. While in this state of an extreme mental tension he found himself one day looking at Goso Hōyen's verse on his own portrait, which partly read:

> 'One hundred years—thirty-six thousand morns,
> This same old fellow moveth on for ever!'

This at once made him dissolve his eternal doubt as to 'Who's carrying around this lifeless body of yours?' He was baptized and became an altogether new man.

He leaves us in his *Goroku* ('Sayings Recorded') an account of those days of the mental strain in the following narrative: 'In olden days when I was at Sōkei (Shuang-ching), and before one month was over after my return to the Meditation Hall there, one night while deep in sleep I

---

[1] This is one of the most noted koans and generally given to the uninitiated as an eye-opener. When Jōshu was asked by a monk whether there was Buddha-Nature in the dog, the master answered 'Mu!' (*wu* in Chinese), which literally means 'no'. But as it is nowadays understood by the followers of Rinzai, it does not mean anything negative as the term may suggest to us ordinarily, it refers to something most assuredly positive, and the novice is told to find it out by himself, not depending upon others (*aparapaccaya*), as no explanation will be given nor is any possible. This koan is popularly known as 'Jōshu's Mu or Muji'. A koan is a theme or statement or question given to the Zen student for solution, which will lead him to a spiritual insight. The subject will be fully treated in the Second Series of the *Essays in Zen Buddhism*.

[2] Another koan for beginners. A monk once asked Jōshu, 'All things return to the One, but where does the One return?' To which the master answered, 'When I was in the province of Seiju (Ts'ing-chou) I had a monkish garment made which weighed seven kin (*chin*).

suddenly found myself fixing my attention on the question
"All things return to the One, but where does this One
return?" My attention was so rigidly fixed on this that I
neglected sleeping, forgot to eat, and did not distinguish
east from west, nor morning from night. While spreading
the napkin, producing the bowls, or attending to my
natural wants, whether I moved or rested, whether I
talked or kept silent, my whole existence was wrapped up
with the question "Where does this One return?" No other
thoughts ever disturbed my consciousness; no, even if I
wanted to stir up the least bit of thought irrelevant to
the central one, I could not do so. It was like being screwed
up or glued; however much I tried to shake myself off, it
refused to move. Though I was in the midst of a crowd or
congregation, I felt as if I were all by myself. From morning
till evening, from evening till morning, so transparent, so
tranquil, so majestically above all things were my feelings.
Absolutely pure and not a particle of dust! My one thought
covered eternity; so calm was the outside world, so obliv-
ious of the existence of other people I was. Like an idiot,
like an imbecile, six days and nights thus elapsed when I
entered the Shrine with the rest, reciting the Sūtras, and
happened to raise my head and looked at the verse by
Goso. This made me all of a sudden awake from the spell,
and the meaning of "Who carries this lifeless corpse of
yours?" burst upon me—the question once given by my old
master. I felt as if this boundless space itself were broken up
into pieces, and the great earth were altogether levelled
away. I forgot myself, I forgot the world, it was like one
mirror reflecting another. I tried several koan in my mind
and found them so transparently clear! I was no more
deceived as to the wonderful working of Prajñā (transcendental wisdom).' When Kōhō saw his old master later,
the latter lost no time in asking him, 'Who is it that carries
this lifeless corpse of yours?' 'Kōhō burst out a 'Kwatz!'
Thereupon the master took up a stick ready to give him a
blow, but the disciple held it back, saying, 'You cannot give
me a blow today.' 'Why can't I?' was the master's demand.

Instead of replying to him, however, Kōhō left the room briskly. The following day the master asked him, 'All things return to the One, and where does the One return to?' 'The dog is lapping the boiling water in the cauldron.' 'Where did you get this nonsense?' reprimanded the master. 'You had better ask yourself,' promptly came the response. The master rested well satisfied.

Hakuin (1683–1768)[1] is another of those masters who have put down their first Zen experience in writing, and we read in his book entitled *Orategama* the following account: 'When I was twenty-four years old I stayed at the Yegan Monastery of Echigo. ["Jōshu's Mu" being my theme at the time] I assiduously applied myself to it. I did not sleep days and nights, forgot both eating and lying down, when quite abruptly a great mental fixation[2] (*tai-i*) took place. I felt as if freezing in an ice-field extending thousands of miles, and within myself there was a sense of utmost transparency. There was no going forward, no slipping backward; I was like an idiot, like an imbecile, and there was nothing but "Jōshu's Mu". Though I attended the lectures by the master, they sounded like a discussion going on somewhere in a distant hall, many yards away. Sometimes my sensation was that of one flying in the air. Several days passed in this state, when one evening a temple-bell struck, which upset the whole thing. It was like smashing an ice-basin, or pulling down a house made of jade. When I suddenly awoke again I found that I myself was Gantō[3]

---

[1] He is the founder of the modern Japanese Rinzai school of Zen. All the masters belonging to this school at present in Japan trace back their line of transmission to Hakuin.

[2] Literally, 'a great doubt', but it does not mean that, as the term 'doubt' is not understood here in its ordinary sense. It means a state of concentration brought to the highest pitch.

[3] Gantō (Yen-t'ou, 828–887) was one of the great Zen teachers in the T'ang dynasty. But he was murdered by an outlaw, when his death-cry is said to have reached many miles around. When Hakuin first studied Zen, this tragic incident in the life of an eminent Zen master who is supposed to be above all human ailments, troubled him very much, and he wondered if Zen were really the gospel of salvation. Hence this allusion to Gantō. Notice also here that what Hakuin discovered was a

(Yen-t'ou) the old master, and that all through the shifting changes of time not a bit [of my personality] was lost. Whatever doubts and indecisions I had before were completely dissolved like a piece of thawing ice. I called out loudly: "How wondrous! how wondrous! There is no birth-and-death from which one has to escape, nor is there any supreme knowledge (*Bodhi*) after which one has to strive. All the complications[1] past and present, numbering one thousand seven hundred, are not worth the trouble of even describing them".'

The case of Bukkō (Fo-kuang), the National Teacher,[2] was more extraordinary than that of Kakuin, and fortunately in this case, too, we have his own recording of it in detail. 'When I was fourteen,' writes Bukkō, 'I went up to Kinzan. When seventeen I made up my mind to study Buddhism and began to unravel the mysteries of "Jōshu's Mu". I expected to finish the matter within one year, but I did not come to any understanding of it after all. Another year passed without much avail, and three more years, also

living person and not an abstract reason or anything conceptual. Zen leads us ultimately to somewhat living, working, and this is known as 'seeing into one's own Nature' (*chien-hsing*).

[1] Koans (*kung-an*) are sometimes called 'complications', (*kê-t'êng*) literally meaning 'vines and wistarias' which are entwining and entangling, for according to the masters there ought not to be any such thing as a koan in the very nature of Zen, it was an unnecessary invention making things more entangled and complicated than ever before. The truth of Zen has no need for koans. It is supposed that there are one thousand seven hundred koans which will test the genuineness of satori.

[2] Tsu-yüan (1226–1286) came to Japan when the Hōjō family was in power at Kamakura. He established the Engakuji monastery, which is one of the chief Zen monasteries in Japan. While still in China his temple was invaded by soldiers of the Yüan dynasty, who threatened to kill him, but Bukkō was immovable and quietly uttered the following verse:

'Throughout heaven and earth there is not a piece of ground where a single stick could be inserted;
I am glad that all things are void, myself and the world:
Honoured be the sword, three feet long, wielded by the great Yüan swordsmen;
For it is like cutting a spring breeze in a flash of lightning.'

finding myself with no progress. In the fifth or sixth year, while no special change came over me, the "Mu" became so inseparably attached to me that I could not get away from it even while asleep. This whole universe seemed to be nothing but the "Mu" itself. In the meantime I was told by an old monk to set it aside for a while and see how things would go with me. According to this advice, I dropped the matter altogether and sat quietly. But owing to the fact that the "Mu" had been with me so long, I could in no way shake it off however much I tried. When I was sitting, I forgot that I was sitting; nor was I conscious of my own body. Nothing but a sense of utter blankness prevailed. Half a year thus passed. Like a bird escaped from its cage, my mind, my consciousness moved about [without restraint] sometimes eastward, sometimes westward, sometimes north-ward or southward. Sitting[1] through two days in succession, or through one day and night, I did not feel any fatigue.

'At the time there were about nine hundred monks re-siding in the monastery, among whom there were many devoted students of Zen. One day while sitting, I felt as if my mind and my body were separated from each other and lost the chance of getting back together. All the monks about me thought that I was quite dead, but an old monk among them said that I was frozen to a state of immov-ability while absorbed in deep meditation, and that if I were covered up with warm clothings I should by myself come to my senses. This proved true, for I finally awoke from it; and when I asked the monks near my seat how long I had been in that condition, they told me it was one day and night.

'After this, I still kept up my practice of sitting. I could now sleep a little. When I closed my eyes a broad expanse of emptiness presented itself before them, which then assumed the form of a farmyard. Through this piece of land I walked and walked until I got thoroughly familiar with the ground. But as soon as my eyes were opened the vision altogether disappeared. One night, sitting far into the

[1] That is, sitting cross-legged in meditation.

night, I kept my eyes open and was aware of my sitting up in my seat. All of a sudden the sound of striking the board in front of the head monk's room reached my ear, which at once revealed me the "original man" in full. There was then no more of that vision which appeared at the closing of my eyes. Hastily I came down from the seat and ran out into the moonlit night and went up to the garden house called Ganki, where looking up to the sky I laughed loudly, "Oh, how great is the Dharmakāya! Oh, how great and immense for evermore!"

'Thence my joy knew no bounds. I could not quietly sit in the Meditation Hall; I went about with no special purpose in the mountains, walking this way and that. I thought of the sun and the moon traversing in a day through a space 4,000,000,000 miles wide. "My present abode is in China", I reflected then, "and they say the district of Yang is the centre of the earth. If so, this place must be 2,000,000,000 miles away from where the sun rises; and how is it that as soon as it comes up its rays lose no time in striking my face?" I reflected again, "The rays of my own eye must ravel just as instantaneously as those of the sun as it reaches the latter; my eyes, my mind, are they not the Dharmakāya itself?" Thinking thus, I felt all the bounds snapped and broken to pieces that had been tying me for so many ages. How many numberless years had I been sitting in the hole of ants! Today even in every pore of my skin there lie all the Buddha-lands in the ten quarters! I thought within myself, "Even if I have no greater satori, I am now all-sufficient unto myself".'

Here is the stanza composed by Bukkō at the moment of satori, describing his inner feelings:

'With one stroke I have completely smashed the cave of the ghosts;
Behold, there rushes out the iron face of the monster Nata!
Both my ears are as deaf and my tongue is tied;
If thou touchest it idly, the fiery star shoots out!'[1]

[1] This lively utterance reminds one of a lightning simile in the *Kena-Upanishad* (IV, 30):

VIII

These cases will be sufficient to show what mental process one has to to through before the opening of satori takes place. Of course these are prominent examples and highly accentuated, and every satori is not preceded by such an extraordinary degree of concentration. But an experience more or less like these must be the necessary antecedent to all satori, especially to that which is to be gone through at the outset of the study. The mirror of mind or the field of consciousness then seems to be so thoroughly swept clean as not to leave a particle of dust on it.

When thus all mentation is temporarily suspended, even the consciousness of an effort to keep an idea focused at the centre of attention is gone—that is, when, as the Zen followers say, the mind is so completely possessed or identified with its object of thought that even the consciousness of identity is lost as when one mirror reflects another, the subject feels as if living in a crystal palace, all transparent, refreshing, buoyant, and royal. But the end has not yet been reached, this being merely the preliminary condition leading to the consummation called satori. If the mind remains in this state of fixation, there will be no occasion for its being awakened to the truth of Zen. The state of 'Great Doubt' (*tai-gi*), as it is technically known, is the antecedent. It must be broken up and exploded into the next stage,

'This is the way It [that is, Brahman] is to be illustrated:
When lightnings have been loosened,—
a—a—ah!
When that has made the eyes to be closed,—
a—a—ah!
So far concerning Deity [devata].'
Lightning flash is a favourite analogue with the Zen masters too; the unexpected onrush of satori into the ordinary field of consciousness has something of the nature of lightning. It comes so suddenly and when it comes the world is at once illumined and revealed in its entirety and in its harmonious oneness; but when it vanishes everything falls back into its old darkness and confusion.

which is looking into one's nature or the opening of satori.

The explosion, as it is nothing else, generally takes place when this finely balanced equilibrium tilts for one reason or another. A stone is thrown into a sheet of water in perfect stillness, and the disturbance at once spreads all over the surface. It is somewhat like this. A sound knocks at the gate of consciousness so tightly closed, and it at once reverberates through the entire being of the individual. He is awakened in the most vivid sense of the word. He comes out baptized in the fire of creation. He has seen the work of God in his very workshop. The occasion may not necessarily be the hearing of a temple bell, it may be reading a stanza, or seeing something moving, or the sense of touch irritated, when a most highly accentuated state of concentration bursts out into a satori.

The concentration, however, may not be kept up to such an almost abnormal degree as in the case of Bukkō. It may last just a second or two, and if it is the right kind of concentration, and rightly handled by the master, the inevitable opening of the mind will follow. When the monk Jō (Ting) asked Rinzai 'What is the ultimate principle of Buddhism?' the master came right down from his seat, took hold of the monk, slapped him with his hand, and pushed him away from him. The monk stood stupefied. A bystander suggested, 'Why don't you make a bow?' Obeying the order, Jō was about to bow, when he abruptly awoke to the truth of Zen.

In this case Jō's self-absorption or concentration did not seemingly last very long; the bowing was the turning point, it broke up the spell and restored him to sense, not to an ordinary sense of awareness, but to the inward consciousness of his own being. Generally we have no records of the inner working prior to a satori, and may pass lightly over the event as a merely happy incident or some intellectual trick having no deeper background. When we read such records, we have to supply from our own experience, whatever this is, all the necessary antecedent conditions for breaking up into a satori.

IX

So far the phenomenon called satori in Zen Buddhism has been treated as constituting the essence of Zen, as the turning point in one's life which opens the mind to a wider and deeper world, as something to be gleaned even from a most trivial incident of everyday life; and then it was explained how satori is to come out of one's inner life, and not by any outside help except as merely indicating the way to it. Next I proceeded to describe what a change satori brings in one's idea of things—that is, how it all upsets the former valuation of things generally, making one stand now entirely on a different footing. For illustrations, some verses were quoted which were composed by the masters at the moment of their attainment of satori. They are mostly descriptive of the feelings they experienced, such as those by Bukkō and Yōdainen and Yengo and others are typical of this class, as they have almost no intellectual elements in them. If one tries to pick up something from these verses by a mere analytical process, one will be greatly disappointed. The psychological side of satori, which is minutely narrated by Hakuin and others, will be of great interest to those who are desirous of making a psychological inquiry into Zen. Of course these narratives alone will not do, for there are many other things one has to consider in order to study it thoroughly, among which I may mention the general Buddhist attitude towards life and the world and the historical atmosphere in which the students of Zen find themselves.

I wish to close this Essay by making a few general remarks in the way of recapitulation on the Buddhist experience known as satori.

1. People often imagine that the discipline of Zen is to induce a state of self-suggestion through meditation. This is not quite right. As we can see from the various instances above cited, satori does not consist in producing a certain

premeditated condition by intensely thinking of it. It is the growing conscious of a new power in the mind, which enabled it to judge things from a new point of view. Ever since the unfoldment of consciousness we have been led to respond to the inner and outer conditions in a certain conceptual and analytical manner. The discipline of Zen consists in upsetting this artificially constructed framework once for all and in remodelling it on an entirely new basis. The older frame is called 'Ignorance' (*avidyā*) and the new one 'Enlightenment' (*sambodhi*). It is evident therefore that meditating on a metaphysical or symbolical statement which is a product of our relative consciousness plays no part in Zen, as I have touched on this in the Introduction.

2. Without the attainment of satori no one can enter into the mystery of Zen. It is the sudden flashing of a new truth hitherto altogether undreamed of. It is a sort of mental catastrophe taking place all at once after so much piling of matters intellectual and demonstrative. The piling has reached its limit and the whole edifice has now come to the ground, when behold a new heaven is opened to your full survey. Water freezes suddenly when it reaches a certain point, the liquid has turned into a solidity, and it no more flows. Satori comes upon you unawares when you feel you have exhausted your whole being. Religiously this is a new birth, and, morally, the revaluation of one's relationship to the world. The latter now appears to be dressed in a different garment which covers up all the ugliness of dualism, which is called in Buddhist phraseology delusion (*māyā*) born of reasoning (*tarka*) and error (*vikalpa*).

3. Satori is the *raison d'être* of Zen, and without which Zen is no Zen. Therefore every contrivance (*upāya*), disciplinary or doctrinal, is directed toward the attainment of satori. Zen masters could not remain patient for satori to come by itself; that is, to come sporadically and at its own pleasure. They earnestly seek out some way to make people deliberately or systematically realize the truth of Zen. Their manifestly enigmatical presentations of it were mostly to create a state of mind in their disciples, which

would pave the way to the enlightenment of Zen. All the intellectual demonstrations and exhortatory persuasions so far carried out by most religious and philosophical leaders failed to produce the desired effect. The disciples were led further and further astray. Especially when Buddhism was introduced into China with all its Indian equipments, with its highly metaphysical abstractions, and in a most complicated system of moral discipline, the Chinese were at a loss how to grasp the central point of the doctrine of Buddhism. Daruma, Yenō, Baso, and other masters noticed the fact. The natural outcome was the proclamation of Zen; satori was placed above Sūtra-reading and scholarly discussion of the Sastras, and it came to be identified with Zen. Zen therefore without satori is like pepper without its pungency. But at the same time we must not forget that there is such a thing as too much satori, which is indeed to be detested.

4. This emphasizing in Zen of satori above everything else makes the fact quite significant that Zen is not a system of dhyāna as practised in India and by other schools of Buddhism than the Zen. By dhyāna is understood popularly a kind of meditation or contemplation; that is the fixing of thought, especially in Mahāyāna Buddhism, on the doctrine of emptiness (*śūnyatā*). When the mind is so trained as to be able to realize the state of perfect void in which there is not a trace of consciousness left, even the sense of being unconscious having departed—in other words, when all forms of mental activity are swept clean from the field of consciousness, which is now like a sky devoid of every speck of cloud, a mere broad expanse of blue—dhyāna is said to have reached its perfection. This may be called ecstasy or trance, but it is not Zen. In Zen there must be a satori; there must be a general mental upheaval which destroys the old accumulations of intellectuality and lays down a foundation for a new faith; there must be the awakening of a new sense which will review the old things from an angle of perception entirely and most refreshingly new. In dhyāna there are none of these things, for it is merely a quieting exercise

of the mind. As such it has doubtless its own merits, but Zen ought not to be identified with such dhyānas. The Buddha therefore got dissatisfied with his two Sankhya teachers, in whose teaching the meditations were so many stages of self-abstraction or thought-annihilation.

5. Satori is not seeing God as he is, as may be contended by some Christian mystics. Zen has from the very beginning made clear its principal thesis, which is to see into the work of creation and not interview the creator himself. The latter may be found then busy moulding his universe, but Zen can go along with its own work even when he is not found there. It is not depending on his support. When it grasps the reason of living a life, it is satisfied. Hōyen, of Gosozan, used to produce his own hand and asked his disciples why it is called a hand. When one knows the reason, there is satori and one has Zen. Whereas with the God of mysticism there is the grasping of a definite object, and when you have God, what is not God is excluded. This is self-limiting. Zen wants absolute freedom, even from God. 'No abiding place' means that; 'Cleanse your mouth even when you utter the word "Buddha"' amounts to the same thing. It is not that Zen wants to be morbidly unholy and godless, but that it knows the incompleteness of a name. Therefore when Yakusan (Yüeh-shan) was asked to give a lecture, he did not say a word, but instead came down from the pulpit and went off to his own room. Hyakujo (Pai-chang) merely walked forward a few steps, stood still, and opened his arms—which was his exposition of a great principle of Buddhism.

6. Satori is the most intimate individual experience and therefore cannot be expressed in words or described in any manner. All that one can do in the way of communicating the experience to others is to suggest or indicate, and this only tentatively. The one who has had it understands readily when such indications are given, but when we try to have a glimpse of it through the indices given we utterly fail. We are then like the man who says that he loves the most beautiful woman in the world and yet who knows

nothing of her pedigree or social position, of her personal name or famiIy name, knows nothing of her individuality, physical as well as moral. We are again like the man who puts up a staircase in a place where four crossroads meet, to mount up thereby into the upper story of a mansion, and yet who knows not just where that mansion is, in the East or West, in the North or South. The Buddha was quite to the point when he thus derided all those philosophers and vain talkers of his day, who merely dealt in abstractions, empty hearsays, and fruitless indications. Zen therefore wants us to build the staircase right at the front of the very palace into whose upper story we are to mount up. When we can say 'This is the very personality, this is the very house,' we have the satori interviewed face to face and realized by oneself. (*Diṭṭhe va dhamme sayaṁ abhiññā sacchikatvā.*)

7. Satori is not a morbid state of mind, a fit subject for abnormal psychology. If anything it is a perfectly normal state of mind. When I speak of a mental upheaval, one may be led to consider Zen something to be shunned by ordinary people. This is a mistaken view of Zen, unfortunately often held by prejudiced critics. As Nansen (Nan-ch'üan) declared, it is your 'everyday thought'. When later a monk asked a master[1] what was meant by 'everyday thought', he said,

'Drinking tea, eating rice,
I pass my time as it comes;
Looking down at the stream, looking up at the mountains,
How serene and relaxed I feel indeed!'

It all depends upon the adjustment of the hinge whether the door opens in or out. Even in the twinkling of an eye, the whole affair is changed, and you have Zen, and you are as perfect and normal as ever. More than that, you have in the meantime acquired something altogether new. All your mental activities are now working to a different key,

[1] Pao-tz'u Wên-ch'in, a disciple of Pao-fu Ts'ung-chan, who died A.D. 928.

which is more satisfying, more peaceful, and fuller of joy than anything you ever had. The tone of your life is altered. There is something rejuvenating in it. The spring flowers look prettier, and the mountain stream runs cooler and more transparent. The subjective revolution that brings out this state of things cannot be called abnormal. When life becomes more enjoyable and its expanse is as broad as the universe itself, there must be something in satori quite healthy and worth one's striving after its attainment.

8. We are supposedly living in the same world, but who can tell the thing we popularly call a stone lying before this window is the same thing to all of us? According to the way we look at it, to some the stone ceases to be a stone, while to others it forever remains a worthless specimen of geological product. And this initial divergence of views calls forth an endless series of divergencies later in our moral and spiritual lives. Just a little twisting, as it were, in our modes of thinking, and yet what a world of difference will grow up eventually between one another! So with Zen, satori is this twisting, or rather screwing, not in the wrong way, but in a deeper and full sense, and the result is the revelation of a world of entirely new values.

Again, you and I sip a cup of tea. The act is apparently alike, but who can tell what a wide gap there is subjectively between you and me? In your drinking there may be no Zen, while mine is brim full of it. The reason is, the one moves in the logical circle and the other is out of it; that is to say, in one case rigid rules of intellection so called are asserting themselves, and the actor even when acting is unable to unfetter himself from these intellectual bonds; while in the other case the subject has struck a new path and is not at all conscious of the duality of his act; in him life is not split into object and subject or into acting and acted. The drinking at the moment to him means the whole fact, the whole world. Zen lives and is therefore free, whereas our 'ordinary' life is in bondage; satori is the first step to freedom.

9. Satori is Enlightenment (*sambodhi*). So long as Buddhism is the doctrine of Enlightenment, as we know it to be, from its earliest as well as from its later literature, and so long as Zen asserts satori to be its culmination, satori must be said to represent the very spirit of the Buddhist teaching. When it announces itself to be the transmission of the Buddha-citta (*fo-hsin*) not dependent upon the logical and discursive exposition in the canonical writings, either Hīnayāna or Mahāyāna, it is by no means exaggerating its fundamental characteristic as distinguished from the other schools of Buddhism that have grown up in Japan and China. Whatever this may be, there is no doubt that Zen is one of the most precious and in many respects the most remarkable spiritual possessions bequeathed to Eastern people. Even when it is considered the Buddhist form of speculative mysticism not unknown to the West in the philosophy of Plotinus, Eckhart, and their followers, its complete literature alone since the sixth patriarch, Yenō (Hui-nêng, 638–713), so well preserved, is worth the serious study of scholars and truth-seekers. And then the whole body of the koans systematically grading the progress of the spiritual awakening is the wonderful treasure in the hands of the Zen monks in Japan at present.

PRACTICAL METHODS OF
ZEN INSTRUCTION

'WHAT is Zen?' This is one of the most difficult questions to answer—I mean to the satisfaction of the inquirer; for Zen refuses even tentatively to be defined or described in any manner. The best way to understand it will be, of course, to study and practice it at least some years in the Meditation Hall. Therefore, even after the reader has carefully gone over this Essay, he will still be at sea as to the real signification of Zen. It is, in fact, in the very nature of Zen that it evades all definition and explanation; that is to say, Zen cannot be converted into ideas, it can never be described in logical terms. For this reason the Zen masters declare that it is 'independent of letter', being 'a special transmission outside the orthodox teachings'. But the purpose of this Essay is not just to demonstrate that Zen is an unintelligible thing and that there is no use of attempting to discourse about it. My object, on the contrary, will be to make it clear to the fullest extent of my ability, however imperfect and inadequate that may be. And there are several ways to do this. Zen may be treated psychologically, ontologically, or epistemologically, or historically as I did in the first part of this book to a certain extent. These are all extremely interesting each in its way, but they are a great undertaking requiring years of preparation. What here I propose to do, therefore, will be a practical exposition of the subject-matter by giving some aspects of the *modus operandi* of Zen instruction as carried out by the masters for the enlightenment of the pupils. The perusal of these accounts will help us to get into the spirit of Zen to the limits of its intelligibility.

I

As I conceive it, Zen is the ultimate fact of all philosophy and religion. Every intellectual effort must culminate in it, or rather must start from it, if it is to bear any practical fruits. Every religious faith must spring from it if it has to prove at all efficiently and livingly workable in our active life. Therefore Zen is not necessarily the fountain of Buddhist thought and life alone; it is very much alive also in Christianity, Mahommedanism, in Taoism, and even in positivistic Confucianism. What makes all these religions and philosophies vital and inspiring, keeping up their usefulness and efficiency, is due to the presence in them of what I may designate as the Zen element. Mere scholasticism or mere sacerdotalism will never create a living faith. Religion requires something inwardly propelling, energizing, and capable of doing work. The intellect is useful in its place, but when it tries to cover the whole field of religion it dries up the source of life. Feeling or mere faith is so blind and will grasp anything that may come across and hold to it as the final reality. Fanaticism is vital enough as far as its explosiveness is concerned, but this is not a true religion, and its practical sequence is the destruction of the whole system, not to speak of the fate of its own being. Zen is what makes the religious feeling run through its legitimate channel and what gives life to the intellect.

Zen does this by giving one a new point of view of looking at things, a new way of appreciating the truth and beauty of life and the world, by discovering a new source of energy in the inmost recesses of consciousness, and by bestowing on one a feeling of completeness and sufficiency. That is to say, Zen works miracles by overhauling the whole system of one's inner life and opening up a world hitherto entirely undreamt of. This may be called a resurrection. And Zen tends to emphasize the speculative element, though confessedly it opposes this more than anything else in the whole process of the spiritual revolution, and in this respect Zen is truly Buddhistic. Or it may be better to say that Zen makes use of the phraseology belonging to the sciences of speculative philosophy. Evidently, the feeling element is not so prominently visible in Zen as in the Pure Land sects where 'bhakti' (faith) is all in all; Zen on the other hand emphasizes the faculty of seeing (*darśana*) or knowing (*vidyā*) though not in the sense of reasoning out, but in that of intuitively grasping.

According to the philosophy of Zen, we are too much of a slave to the conventional way of thinking, which is dualistic through and through. No 'interpenetration' is allowed, there takes place no fusing of opposites in our everyday logic. What belongs to God is not of this world, and what is of this world is incompatible with the divine. Black is not white, and white is not black. Tiger is tiger, and cat is cat, and they will never be one. Water flows, a mountain towers. This is the way things or ideas go in this universe of the senses and syllogisms. Zen, however, upsets this scheme of thought and substitutes a new one in which there exists no logic, no dualistic arrangement of ideas. We believe in dualism chiefly because of our traditional teaching. Whether ideas really correspond to facts is another matter requiring a special investigation. Ordinarily we do not inquire into the matter, we just accept what is instilled into our minds; for to accept is more convenient and practical, and life is to a certain extent, though not in reality, made thereby easier. We are in nature conservatives, not because we are lazy, but because we like repose and peace, even superficially. But the time comes when traditional logic holds true no more, for we begin to feel contradictions and splits and consequently spiritual anguish. We lose trustful repose which we experienced when we blindly followed the traditional ways of thinking. Eckhart says that we are all seeking repose whether consciously or not just as the stone cannot cease moving until it touches the earth. Evidently the repose we seemed to enjoy before we were awakened to the contradictions involved in our logic was not the real one, the stone has kept moving down towards the ground. Where then is the ground of non-dualism on which the soul can be really and truthfully tranquil and blessed? To quote Eckhart again, 'Simple people conceive that we are to see God as if He stood on that side and we on this. It is not so; God and I are one in the act of my perceiving Him.' In this absolute oneness of things Zen establishes the foundations of its philosophy.

The idea of absolute oneness is not the exclusive possession of Zen, there are other religions and philosophies that preach the same doctrine. If Zen, like other monisms or theisms, merely laid down this principle and did not have anything specifically to be known as Zen, it would have long ceased to exist as such. But there is in Zen something unique which makes up its life and justifies its claim to be the most precious heritage of Eastern culture. The following 'mondō' or dialogue (literally questioning and answering) will give us a glimpse into the ways of Zen. A monk asked Jōshu (Chao-chou), one of the greatest masters in China, 'What is the one ultimate word of truth?' Instead of giving him any specific answer he made a simple response saying, 'Yes.' The monk who naturally failed to see any sense in this kind of response asked for a second time, and to this the master roared back, 'I am not deaf!'[1] See how irrelevantly (shall I say) the all-important problem of absolute oneness or of the ultimate reason is treated here! But this is characteristic of Zen, this is where Zen transcends logic and overrides the tyranny and misrepresentation of ideas. As I said before, Zen mistrusts the intellect, does not rely upon

[1] Another time when Jōshu was asked about the 'first word', he coughed. The monk remarked, 'Is this not it?' 'Why, an old man is not even allowed to cough!'—this came quickly from the old master. Jōshu had still another occasion to express his view on the one word. A monk asked, 'What is the one word?' Demanded the master, 'What do you say?' 'What is the one word?'—the question was repeated when Jōshu gave his verdict, 'You make it two.'

Shuzan (Shu-shan) was once asked, 'An old master says, "There is one word which when understood wipes out the sins of innumerable kalpas": what is this one word?' Shuzan answered, 'Right under your nose!' 'What is the ultimate meaning of it?' 'This is all I can say':—this was the conclusion of the master.

traditional and dualistic methods of reasoning, and handles problems after its own original manners.

To cite another instance before going further into the subject proper. The same old Jōshu was asked another time, 'One light divides itself into hundreds of thousands of lights; may I ask where this one light originates?'[1] This question like the last mentioned is one of the deepest and most baffling problems of philosophy. But the old master did not waste much time in answering the question, nor did he resort to any wordy discussion. He simply threw off one of his shoes without a remark. What did he mean by it? To understand all this, it is necessary that we should acquire a 'third eye', as they say, and learn to look at things from a new point of view.

How is this new way of looking at things demonstrated by the Zen masters? Their methods are naturally very uncommon, unconventional, illogical, and consequently incomprehensible to the uninitiated. The object of the present Essay will be to describe those methods classified under the following general headings: I. Verbal Method, and II. Direct Method. The first method may be further divided into: 1. Paradox; 2. Going Beyond Opposites; 3. Contradiction; 4. Affirmation; 5. Repetition; and 6. Exclamation. The Direct Method, so called, means a display of physical force, and may be subdivided into several groups

---

[1] There are many mondoes purporting to the same subject. The best known one by Jōshu is quoted elsewhere; of others we mention the following. A monk asked Risan (Li-shan), 'All things are reduced to emptiness, but where is emptiness reduced?' Risan answered, 'The tongue is too short to explain it to you.' 'Why is it too short?' 'Within and without, it is of one suchness,' said the master.

A monk asked Keisan (Ch'i-shan), 'When relations are dissolved, all is reduced to emptiness; but where is emptiness reduced?' The master called out to the monk, and the monk responded 'Yes', whereupon the master called his attention, saying, 'Where is emptiness?' Said the monk, 'Pray, you tell me.' Keisan replied, 'It is like the Persian tasting pepper.' While the one light is an etiological question as long as its origin is the point at issue, the questions here referred to are teleological because the ultimate reduction of emptiness is the subject for solution. But as Zen transcends time and history, it recognizes only one beginningless and endless course of becoming. When we know the origin of the one light, we also know where emptiness ends.

such as gesture, striking, performance of a definite set of acts, directing others to move about, etc. But as I do not mean to offer here any scientific and thorough-going classification of the Zen masters' ways of dealing with their pupils in order to initiate them into the mysteries of Zen, I will not attempt to be exhaustive in this article. Later I will write fully about the Direct Method. If I make the reader acquire here a kind of understanding as to the general tendencies and peculiarities of Zen Buddhism, I regard my task as a success.

II

It is well known that all mystics are fond of paradoxes to expound their views. For instance, a Christian mystic may say: 'God is real, yet he is nothing, infinite emptiness; he is at once all-being and no-being. The divine kingdom is real and objective; and at the same time it is within myself —I myself am heaven and hell.' Eckhart's 'divine darkness' or 'immovable mover' is another example. I believe we can casually pick up any such statements in mystic literature and compile a book of mystic irrationalities. Zen is no exception in this respect, but in its way of thus expressing the truth there is something we may designate characteristically Zen. It principally consists in the concreteness and vividness of expression. It generally refuses to lend an ear to abstractions. A few examples will be given. According to Fudaishi (Fu-ta-shih):

'Empty-handed I go and yet the spade is in my hands;
 I walk on foot, and yet on the back of an ox I am riding:
 When I pass over the bridge,
 Lo, the water floweth not, but the bridge doth flow.'

This sounds altogether out of reason, but in fact Zen abounds with such graphic irrationalities. 'The flower is not red, nor is the willow green'—is one of the best known utterances of Zen, and is regarded as the same as its affirmative: 'The flower is red and the willow is green.' To put it in logical formula, it will run like this: 'A is at once A and not-A.' If so, I am I and yet you are I. An Indian philosopher asserts that *Tat twam asi*, Thou art it. If so, heaven is hell and God is Devil. To pious orthodox Christians, what a shocking doctrine this Zen is! When Mr. Chang drinks Mr. Li grows tipsy. The silent thundering Vimalakīrti confessed that he was sick because all his fellow-beings were sick. All wise and loving souls must be said to be the embodiments of the Great Paradox of the universe. But I am digressing. What I wanted to say was that Zen is more daringly concrete in its paradoxes than other mystical teachings. The latter are more or less confined to general statements concerning life or God or the world, but Zen carries its paradoxical assertions into every detail of our daily life. It has no hesitation in flatly denying all our most familiar facts of experience. 'I am writing here and yet I have not written a word. You are perhaps reading this now and yet there is not a person in the world who reads. I am utterly blind and deaf, but every colour is recognized and every sound discerned.' The Zen masters will go on like this indefinitely. Basho (Pa-chiao), a Korean monk of the ninth century, once delivered a famous sermon which ran thus: 'If you have a staff (*shujo*, or *chu-chang* in Chinese), I will give you one; if you have not, I will take it away from you.'

When Jōshu, the great Zen master of whom mention was repeatedly made, was asked what he would give when a poverty-stricken fellow should come to him, he replied, 'What is wanting in him?'[1] When he was asked on another

[1] Another time a monk was told, 'Hold on to your poverty!' Nanyin Yegu's (Nan-yüan Hui-yung's) answer to his poverty-stricken monk was more consoling: 'You hold a handful of jewels yourself.' The subject of poverty is the all-important one in our religious experience—poverty not only in the material but also in the spiritual sense. Asceticism must have as its ground-principle a far deeper sense than to be merely curbing human desires and passions; there must be in it something positive and highly religious. 'To be poor in spirit,' whatever meaning it may have in Christianity, is rich in signification for Buddhists, especially for Zen

occasion, 'When a man comes to you with nothing, what would you say to him?' his immediate response was, 'Cast it away!' We may ask him, When a man has nothing, what will he cast? When a man is poor, can he be said to be sufficient unto himself? Is he not in need of everything? Whatever deep meaning there may be in these answers of Jōshu, the paradoxes are quite puzzling and baffle our logically trained intellect. 'Carry away the farmer's oxen, and make off with the hungry man's food' is a favourite phrase with the Zen masters, who think we can thus best cultivate our spiritual farm and fill up the soul hungry for the substance of things.

It is related that Ōkubo Shibun, famous for painting bamboo, was requested to execute a kakemono representing a bamboo forest. Consenting, he painted with all his known skill a picture in which the entire bamboo grove was in red. The patron upon its receipt marvelled at the extraordinary skill with which the painting had been executed, and, repairing to the artist's residence, he said, 'Master, I have come to thank you for the picture; but, excuse me, you have painted the bamboo red.' 'Well,' cried the master, 'in what colour would you desire it?' 'In black of course,' replied the patron. 'And who,' answered the artist, 'ever saw a black-leaved bamboo?' When one is so used to a certain way of looking at things, one finds it so full of difficulties to veer round and start on a new line of procedure. The true colour of the bamboo is perhaps neither red nor black nor green nor any other colour known to us. Perhaps it is red, perhaps it is black just as well. Who knows? The imagined paradoxes may be after all really not paradoxes.

---

followers. A monk, Sei-jei (Ch'ing-shi), came to Sozan (Ts'ao-shan), a great master of the Sōtō school in China, and said, 'I am a poor lonely monk: pray have pity on me.' 'O monk, come on forward!' Whereupon the monk approached the master, who then exclaimed, 'After enjoying three cupfuls of fine *chiu* (liquor) brewed at Ch'ing-yüan, do you still protest that your lips are not at all wet?' As to another aspect of poverty, cf. Hsiang-yen's poem of poverty.

III

The next form in which Zen expresses itself is the denial of opposites, somehow corresponding to the mystic 'via negativa'. The point is not to be 'caught', as the masters would say, in any of the four propositions (*catushkotia*): 1. 'It is A'; 2. 'It is not-A'; 3. 'It is both A and not-A'; and 4. 'It is neither A nor not-A.' When we make a negation or an assertion, we are sure to get into one of these logical formulas according to the Indian method of reasoning. So long as the intellect is to move among the ordinary dualistic groove, this is unavoidable. It is in the nature of our logic that any statement we can make is to be so expressed. But Zen thinks that the truth can be reached when it is neither asserted nor negated. This is indeed the dilemma of life, but the Zen masters are ever insistent on escaping the dilemma. Let us see if they escape free.

According to Ummon, 'In Zen there is absolute freedom; sometimes it negates and at other times it affirms; it does either way at pleasure.' A monk asked, 'How does it negate?' 'With the passing of winter there cometh spring.' 'What happens when spring cometh?' 'Carrying a staff across the shoulders, let one ramble about in the fields, East or West, North or South, and beat the old stumps to one's heart's content.' This was one way to be free as shown by one of the greatest masters in China. Another way follows.

The masters generally go about with a kind of short stick known as shippé (*chu-pi*), or at least they did so in old China. It does not matter whether it is a shippé or not; anything, in fact, will answer our purpose. Shuzan, a noted Zen master of the tenth century, held out his stick and said to a group of his disciples: 'Call it not a shippé; if you do, you assert. Nor do you deny its being a shippé; if you do, you negate. Apart from affirmation and negation, speak, speak!' The idea is to get our heads free from dualistic tangles and philosophic subtleties. A monk came out of the rank, took the shippé away from the master's hand, and threw it down on the floor. Is this the answer? Is this the way to respond to the master's request 'to speak'? Is this the way to transcend the four propositions—the logical conditions of thinking? In short, is this the way to be free? Nothing is stereotyped in Zen, and somebody else may solve the difficulty in quite a different manner. This is where Zen is original and creative.

Ummon expressed the same idea with his staff, which he held up, saying: 'What is this? If you say it is a staff, you go right to hell; but if it is not a staff, what is it?' Hima's (Pi-mo's) way somewhat deviated from this. He used to carry a forked stick and whenever a monk came up to him and made a bow, he applied the stick on the neck of the monk, and said: 'What devil taught you to be a homeless monk? What devil taught you to go round? Whether you can say something, or whether you cannot say anything, all the same you are to die under my fork: speak, speak, be quick!' Tokusan (Tê-shan) was another master who flourished a stick to the same effect; for he used to say, 'No matter what you say, or what you say not, just the same thirty blows for you!'

When the ownership of a kitten was disputed between two parties of monks, the Master Nansen (Nan-ch'üan P'u-yüan, 749–835) came out, took hold of the animal, and said to them, 'If you can say a word, this will be saved: if not, it will be slain.' By 'a word', of course, he meant one that transcended both affirmation and negation, as when Jōshu was asked for 'one word of the ultimate truth'. No one made a response, whereupon the master slew the poor creature. Nansen looks like a hard-hearted Buddhist, but his point is: To say it is involves us in a dilemma; to say it is not puts us in the same predicament. To attain to the truth, this dualism must be avoided. How do you avoid it? It may not only be the loss of the life of a kitten, but the loss of your own life and soul, if you fail to ride over this *impasse*. Hence Nansen's drastic procedure. Later, in the evening, Jōshu, who was one of his disciples, came back, when the master told him of the incident of the day. Jōshu at once took off one of his straw sandals and putting it over his head began to depart. Upon this, said the master, 'What a pity you were not today with us, for you could have saved the kitten.' This strange behaviour, however, was Jōshu's way of affirming the truth transcending the dualism of 'to be' (*sat*) and 'not to be' (*asat*).

While Kyōzan (Yang-shan, 804–899) was residing at Tōhei (Tung-ping), of Shao-chou, his master Isan (Wei-shan, 771–853), both of whom were noted Zen masters of the T'ang dynasty, sent him a mirror accompanied with a letter. Kyōzan held forth the mirror before a congregation of monks and said: 'O monks, Isan has sent here a mirror. Is this Isan's mirror or mine own? If you say it is Isan's, how is it that the mirror is in my hands? If you say it is mine own, has it not come from Isan? If you make a proper statement, it will be retained here. If you cannot, it will be smashed in pieces.' He said this for three times, but nobody even made an attempt to answer. The mirror was then smashed. This was somewhat like the case of Nansen's kitten. In both cases the monks failed to save the innocent victim or the precious treasure, simply because their minds were not yet free from intellectualism and were unable to break through the entanglements purposely set up by Nansen in one case and by Kyōzan in the other. The Zen method of training its followers thus appears so altogether out of reason and unnecessarily inhuman. But the master's eyes are always upon the truth absolute and yet attainable in this world of particulars. If this can be gained, what does it matter whether a thing known as precious be broken and an animal be sacrificed? Is not the recovering of the soul more important than the loss of a kingdom?

Kyōgen (Hsiang-yen), a disciple of Isan (Wei-shan), with whom we got acquainted just now, said in one of his sermons: 'It is like a man over a precipice one thousand feet high, he is hanging himself there with a branch of a tree between his teeth; the feet are far off the ground, and his hands are not taking hold of anything. Suppose another man coming to him to propose a question, "What is the meaning of the first patriarch coming over here from the West?" If this man should open the mouth to answer, he is sure to fall and lose his life; but if he would make no answer, he must be said to ignore the inquirer. At this critical moment what should he do?' This is putting the negation of opposites in a most graphically illustrative manner. The man over the precipice is caught in a dilemma of life and death, and there can be no logical quibblings. The cat may be sacrificed at the altar of Zen, the mirror may be smashed on the ground, but how about one's own life? The Buddha in one of his former lives is said to have thrown himself down into the maw of a man-devouring monster, in order to get the whole stanza of the truth. Zen, being practical, wants us to make the same noble determination to give up our dualistic life for the sake of enlightenment and eternal peace. For it says that its gate will open when this determination is reached.

The logical dualism of 'to be' (*asti*) and 'not to be' (*nāsti*) is frequently expressed by Zen masters by such terms of contrast as are used in our daily parlance: 'taking life' and 'giving life', 'capturing' and 'releasing', 'giving' and 'taking away', 'coming in contact' and 'turning away from', etc. Ummon once held up his staff and declared, 'The whole world, heaven and earth, altogether owes its life and death to this staff.' A monk came out and asked, 'How is it killed?' 'Writhing in agony!' 'How is it restored to life?' 'You had better be a chef.' 'When it is neither put to death nor living, what would you say?' Ummon rose from his seat and said, 'Mo-hê-pan-jê-po-lo-mi-ta!' (*Mahā-prajñā-pāramitā*). This was Ummon's synthesis—'the one word' of the ultimate truth, in which thesis and antithesis are concretely unified, and to which the four propositions are inapplicable (*rahita*).

IV

We now come to the third class I have styled 'Contradiction', by which I mean the Zen master's negation, implicitly or expressly, of what he himself has stated or what has been stated by another. To one and the same question his answer is sometimes 'No', sometimes 'Yes'. Or to a well-known and fully established fact he gives an unqualified denial. From an ordinary point of view he is altogether unreliable, yet he seems to think that the truth of Zen requires such contradictions and denials; for Zen has a standard of its own, which, to our common-sense minds, consists just in negating everything we properly hold true and real. In spite of these apparent confusions, the philosophy of Zen is guided by a thorough-going principle which, when once grasped, its topsy-turviness becomes the plainest truth.

A monk asked the sixth patriarch of the Zen sect in China, who flourished late in the seventh and early in the eighth centuries, 'Who has attained to the secrets of Wobai (Huang-mei)?' Wobai is the name of the mountain where the fifth patriarch, Hung-jên, used to reside, and it was a well-known fact that Hui-nêng, the sixth patriarch, studied Zen under him and succeeded in the orthodox line of transmission. The question was therefore really not a plain regular one, seeking an information about facts. It had quite an ulterior object. The reply of the sixth patriarch was, 'One who understands Buddhism has attained to the secrets of Wobai.'

'Have you then attained them?'

'No, I have not.'

'How is it,' asked the monk, 'that you have not?'

The answer was, 'I do not understand Buddhism.'[1]

[1] An analogous story is told of Sekito Kisen (Shih-t'ou Hsi-ch'ien), who is grandson in faith of the sixth patriarch. The story is quoted elsewhere.

Did he not really understand Buddhism? Or is it that not to understand is to understand? This is also the philosophy of the *Kena-Upanishad*.

The self-contradiction of the sixth patriarch is somewhat mild and indirect when compared with that of Dōgo (Tao-wu). He succeeded to Yakusan (Yüeh-shan Wei-yen, 751–834), but when he was asked by Gohō (Wu-fêng) whether he knew the old master of Yakusan, he flatly denied it, saying, 'No, I do not.' Gohō was, however, persistent. 'Why do you not know him?' 'I do not, I do not' was the emphatic statement of Dōgo. The latter thus singularly enough refused to give any reason except simply and forcibly denying the fact which was apparent to our common-sense knowledge.

Another emphatic and unequivocal contradiction by Tesshikaku (T'ieh-tsui Chiao) is better known to students of Zen than the case just cited. He was a disciple of Jōshu (Chao-chou). When he visited Hōgen (Fa-yen Wên-i, died 958), another great Zen master, the latter asked him what was the last place he came from. Tesshikaku replied that he came from Jōshu. Said Hōgen:

'I understand that a cypress tree once became the subject of his talk: was that really so?'

Tesshikaku was positive in his denial, saying, 'He had no such talk.'

Hōgen protested. 'All the monks coming from Jōshu lately speak of his reference to a cypress tree in answer to a monk's question, "What was the real object of the coming East of Bodhidharma?" How do you say that Jōshu made no such reference to a cypress tree?'

Whereupon Tesshikaku roared, 'My late master never made such a talk; no slighting allusion to him, if you please!'

Hōgen greatly admired this attitude on the part of the disciple of the famous Jōshu, and said, 'Truly, you are a lion's child!'

In Zen literature, Dharma's coming from the West— that is, from India—is quite frequently made the subject of the discourse. When a question is asked as to the real object of his coming over to China, it refers to the ultimate principle of Buddhism, and has nothing to do with his personal motive which made him cross the ocean, landing him at some point along the southern coast of China. The historical fact is not the issue here. And to this all-important question numerous answers are given, but so varied and so unexpectedly odd, yet according to Zen masters all expressive of the truth of their teaching.

This contradiction, negation, or paradoxical statement is the inevitable result of the Zen way of looking at life. The whole emphasis of its discipline is placed on the intuitive grasping of the inner truth deeply hidden in our consciousness. And this truth thus revealed or awakened within oneself defies intellectual manipulation, or at least cannot be imparted to others through any dialectical formulas. It must come out of oneself, grow within oneself, and become one with one's own being. What others—that is, ideas or images—can do is to indicate the way where lies the truth. This is what Zen masters do. And the indicators given by them are naturally unconventionally free and refreshingly original. As their eyes are always fixed on the ultimate truth itself, anything and everything they can command is utilized to accomplish the end, regardless of its logical conditions and consequences. This indifference to logic is sometimes asserted purposely, just to let us know the truth of Zen is independent of the intellect. Hence the statement in the *Prajñā-pāramitā-Sūtra*, that 'Not to have any Dharma to discourse about—this is discoursing about the Dharma.' (*Dharmadeśanā dharmadeśaneti subhūte nāsti sa kaścid dharmo yo dharmadeśana nāmotpalabhyate.*)

Haikyu (P'ei Hsiu), a state minister of the T'ang dynasty, was a devoted follower of Zen under Ōbaku. One day he showed him a manuscript in which his understanding of Zen was stated. The master took it, and setting it down beside him, made no movement to read it, but remained silent for some little while. He then said, 'Do you understand?' 'Not quite,' answered the minister. 'If you have an understanding here,' said the master, 'there is something of Zen. But if it is committed to paper and ink, nowhere is our religion to be found.' Something analogous to this we have already noticed in Hakuin's interview with Shōju Rōnin. Being a living fact, Zen is only where living facts are handled. Appeal to the intellect is real and living as long as it issues directly from life. Otherwise, no amount of literary accomplishment or of intellectual analysis avails in the study of Zen.

V

So far Zen appears to be nothing but a philosophy of negation and contradiction, whereas in fact it has its affirmative side, and in this consists the uniqueness of Zen. In most forms of mysticism, speculative or emotional, their assertions are general and abstract, and there is not much in them that will specifically distinguish them from some of the philosophical dictums. Sings Blake, for instance:

> 'To see a world in a grain of sand,
> And a heaven in a wild flower,
> Hold infinity in the palm of your hand
> And eternity in an hour.'

Again, listen to the exquisite feelings expressed in the lines of Wither:

> 'By the murmur of a spring,
>   Or the least bough's rustling;
> By a daisy, whose leaves spread
> Shut when Titan goes to bed;
> Or a shady bush or tree—
> She could more infuse in me
> Than all nature's beauties can
> In some other wiser men.'

It is not very difficult to understand these poetic and mystical feelings as expressed by the highly sensitive souls, though we may not all realize exactly as they felt. Even when Eckhart declares that 'the eye with which I see God is the same with which God sees me', or when Plotinus refers to 'that which mind, when it turns back, thinks before it thinks itself', we do not find it altogether beyond our understanding to get at their meaning as far as the ideas are concerned which they try to convey in these mystical utterances. But when we come to statements by the Zen masters, we are entirely at sea how to take them. Their affirmations are so irrelevant, so inappropriate, so irrational, and so nonsensical—at least superficially—that those who have not gained the Zen way of looking at things can hardly make, as we say, head or tail of them.

The truth is that even with full-fledged mystics they are unable to be quite free from the taint of intellection, and leave, as a rule, 'traces' by which their holy abode could be reached. Plotinus' 'flight from alone to alone' is a great mystical utterance proving how deeply he delved into the inner sanctuary of our consciousness. But there is still something speculative or metaphysical about it, and when it is put side by side with the Zen utterances to be cited below, it has, as the masters would say, a mystic flavour on the surface. So long as the masters are indulging in negations, denials, contradictions, or paradoxes, the stain of speculation is not quite washed off them. Naturally, Zen is not opposed to speculation as it is also one of the functions of the mind. But Zen has travelled along a different path altogether unique, I think, in the history of mysticism, whether Eastern or Western, Christian or Buddhist. A few examples will suffice to illustrate my point.

A monk asked Jōshu, 'I read in the Sūtra that all things return to the One, but where does this One return to?' Answered the master, 'When I was in the province of Tsing I had a robe made which weighed seven *chin*.' When Kōrin (Hsiang-lin Yüan) was asked what was the signification of Bodhidharma's coming from the West, his reply was, 'After a long sitting one feels fatigued.' What is the logical relation between the question and the answer? Does it refer to Dharma's nine years' sitting against the wall, as the tradition has it? If so, was his propaganda much ado for nothing except his feeling fatigued? When Kwazan (Hê-shan) was asked what the Buddha was, he said, 'I know how to play the drum, rub-a-dub, rub-a-dub!' (*chieh ta ku*). When Baso Dōichi was sick, one of his disciples came and inquired about his condition, 'How do you feel today?' 'Nichimen-butsu, Gwachimen-butsu!' was the reply, which literally means 'sun-faced Buddha, moon-faced Buddha!' A monk asked Jōshu, 'When the body crumbles all to pieces and returns to the dust, there eternally abides one thing. Of this I have been told, but where does this one thing abide?' The master replied, 'It is windy again this morning.' When Shuzan (Shou-shan) was asked what was the principal teaching of Buddhism, he quoted a verse:

> 'By the castle of the king of Ch'u,
> Eastward flows the stream of Ju.'

'Who is the teacher of all the Buddhas?' was the question put to Bokuju (Mu-chou), who in reply merely hummed a tune, 'Ting-ting, tung-tung, ku-ti, ku-tung!' To the question what Zen was, the same master gave the following answer, 'Namu-sambo!' (*namoratnatrayāya*). The monk, however, confessed that he could not understand it, where-upon the master exclaimed, 'O you miserable frog, whence is this evil karma of yours?' On another occasion the same question called forth a different answer, which was, 'Makahannyaharamii!' (*mahāprajñāpāramitā*). When the monk failed to comprehend the ultimate meaning of the phrase, the master went on:

> 'My robe is all worn out after so many years' usage,
> And parts of it in shreds loosely hanging, have been blown away to the clouds.'

To quote another case from Bokuju, he was once asked by a monk, 'What is the doctrine that goes beyond the Buddhas and Fathers?' The master, immediately holding up his staff, said to the congregation, 'I call this a staff, and what would you call it?' No answer was forthcoming, whereupon the master, again holding forth the staff, asked the monk, 'Did you not ask me about the doctrine that goes beyond the Buddhas and Fathers?'

When Nanyin Yegu (Nan-yüan Hui-yung) was once asked what the Buddha was, he said, 'What is not the Buddha?' Another time his answer was, 'I never knew him.' There was still another occasion when he said, 'Wait until there is one, for then I will tell you.' So far Nanyin does not seem to be so very incomprehensible, but what follows will challenge our keenest intellectual analysis. When the inquiring monk replied to the master's third statement, saying, 'If so, there is no Buddha in you,' the master promptly asserted, 'You are right there.' This evoked a further question, 'Where am I right, sir?' 'This is the thirtieth day of the month,' replied the master.

Kisu Chijo (Kuei-tsung Chih-ch'ang) was one of the able disciples of Baso (Ma-tsu). When he was weeding in the garden, a Buddhist scholar versed in the philosophy of Buddhism came to see the master. A snake happened to pass by them, and the master at once killed it with a spade. The philosopher-monk remarked, 'How long I have heard of the name of Kisu, and how reverently I have thought of it! But what do I see now but a rude-mannered monk?' 'O my scholar-monk,' said the master, 'you had better go back to the Hall and have a cup of tea over there.' Kisu's retort as it stands here is quite unintelligible as far as our common-sense knowledge of worldly affairs goes; but according to another informant Kisu is reported, when he was reproached by the monk, to have said, 'Who is the rude-mannered one, you or I?' Then said the monk, 'What is rude-mannered?' The master held up the spade. 'What is refined?' He now assumed the attitude as if to kill the snake. 'If so,' said the monk, 'you are behaving according to the law.' 'Enough with my lawful or unlawful behaviour,' demanded the master; 'when did you see my killing the snake, anyway?' The monk made no answer.

Perhaps this is sufficient to show how freely Zen deals with those abstruse philosophical problems which have been taxing all human ingenuity ever since the dawn of intelligence. Let me conclude this part with a sample sermon delivered by Goso Hōyen (Wu-tsu Fa-yen); for a Zen master occasionally—no, quite frequently—comes down to the dualistic level of understanding and tries to deliver a speech for the edification of his pupils. But being a Zen sermon we naturally expect something unusual in it. Goso was one of the ablest Zen masters of the twelfth century. He was the teacher of Yengo (Yüan-wu), famous as the author of the *Hekiganshu*. One of his sermons runs thus:

'Yesterday I came across one topic which I thought I might communicate to you, my pupils, today. But an old man such as I am is apt to forget, and the topic has gone off altogether from my mind. I cannot just recall it.' So saying, Goso remained quiet for some little time, but at last he exclaimed, 'I forget, I forget, I cannot remember!' He resumed, however: 'I know there is a mantram in one of the Sūtras known as *The King of Good Memory*. Those who are forgetful may recite it, and the thing forgotten will come again. Well, I must try.' He then recited the mantram, 'Oṁ o-lo-lok-kei svāha!' Clapping his hands and laughing heartily, he said: 'I remember, I remember; this it was: When you seek the Buddha, you cannot see him: when you look for the patriarch, you cannot see him. The muskmelon is sweet even to the stems, the bitter gourd is bitter even to the roots.'

He then came down from the pulpit without further remark.

VI

In one of his sermons Eckhart, referring to the mutual relationship between God and man, says: 'It is as if one stood before a high mountain and cried, "Art thou there?" The echo comes back, "Art thou there?" If one cries,

"Come out!" the echo answers, "Come out!" ' Something like this is to be observed in the Zen masters' answers now classified under 'Repetition'. It may be found hard for the uninitiated to penetrate into the inner meaning of those parrot-like repetitions which sometimes sound like mimicry on the part of the master. In this case, indeed, the words themselves are mere sounds, and the inner sense is to be read in the echoing itself if anywhere. The understanding, however, must come out of one's own inner life, and what the echoing does is to give this chance of self-awakening to the earnest seekers of truth. When the mind is so turned as to be all ready to break into a certain note, the master turns the key and it sings out its own melody, not learned from anybody else but discovered within itself. And this turning the key in the form of repetition in this case is what interests us in the following quotations.

Chōsui (Ch'ang-shui Tzu-hsüan) once asked Yekaku (Hui-chiao), of Mount Rōya (Lang-yeh), who lived in the first half of the eleventh century, 'How is it that the Originally Pure has all of a sudden come to produce mountains and rivers and the great earth?' The question is taken from the *Śūrangama-sūtra* in which Purna asks of the Buddha how the Absolute came to evolve this phenomenal world. For this is a great philosophical problem that has perplexed the greatest minds of all ages. So far all the interpretations making up the history of thought have proved unsatisfactory in one way or another. Chōsui, also being a student of philosophy in a way, has now come to his teacher to be enlightened on the subject. But the teacher's answer was no answer as we understand it, for he merely repeated the question, 'How is it that the Originally Pure has all of a sudden come to produce mountains and rivers and the great earth?' Translated into English, this dialogue loses much of its zest. Let me write it down in Japanese-Chinese: Chōsui asked, '*Shō-jō hon-nen un-ga kos-sho sen-ga dai-ji?*' and the master echoed, '*Shō-jō hon-nen un-ga kos-sho sen-ga dai-ji?*'

This was not, however, enough. Later, in the thirteenth

century, another great Zen master, Kido (Hsü-t'ang), commented on this in a still more mystifying manner. His sermon one day ran in this wise: 'When Chōsui asked Yekaku, "*Shō-jō hon-nen un-ga kos-sho sen-ga dai-ji?*" the question was echoed back to the questioner himself, and it is said that the spiritual eye of the disciple was then opened. I now want to ask you how this could have happened. Were not the question and the answer exactly the same? What reason did Chōsui find in this? Let me comment on it.' Whereupon he struck his chair with the hossu, and said, '*Shō-jō hon-nen un-ga kos-sho sen-ga dai-ji?*' His comment complicates the matter instead of simplifying it.

This has ever been a great question of philosophy—this question of unity and multiplicity, of mind and matter, of thought and reality. Zen, being neither idealism nor realism, proposes its own way of solution as is illustrated in the case of the Originally Pure. The following one solves the problem also in its own way. A monk asked Chōsa Keishin, 'How do we, transforming (*chuan*) mountains and rivers and the earth, reduce them into the Self?' Replied the master, 'How do we, transforming the Self, produce mountains and rivers and the earth?' The monk confessed ignorance, whereupon said the master:

'In this city south of the Lake, people are thriving well,—
Cheap rice and plentiful fuel and prospering neighbourhood.'

Tōsu Daido (T'ou-tzŭ Tai-t'ung), of the T'ang dynasty, who died in the year 914, answered 'The Buddha' when he was questioned, 'What is the Buddha?' He said 'Tao' when the question was, 'What is Tao?' He answered 'The Dharma' to the question 'What is the Dharma?'

When Jōshu asked Kwanchu (Tai-tz'ŭ Huan-chung) of the ninth century, 'What is the being [or substance] of Prajñā?' Kwanchu, without giving any answer, simply echoed the question, 'What is the being of Prajñā?' And this brought out a hearty laugh on the part of Jōshu. Prajñā may be translated supreme intelligence, and

Mañjuśrī is regarded by the Mahāyānists as the embodiment of Prajñā. But in this case Mañjuśrī has nothing to do with it. The question is concerned with the substantial conception of Prajñā, which, being a form of mental activity, requires something to abide in. According to Buddhist philosophy, there are three fundamental conceptions to explain the problem of existence: Substance or Being (bhāva), Appearance or Aspect (lakshana), and Function or Activity (kritya). Or, to use the terms of the Mādhyamika, the three conceptions are actor, act, and acting. Prajñā being an intellectual acting, there must be an agent or substance behind it. Hence the question, What is the being or body of Prajñā? Now, the answer or echo given out by Kwanchu does not explain anything; we are at a loss as far as its conceptual signification goes. The Zen masters do not give us any literary clue to get around what we see on the surface. When we try to understand it intellectually, it slips away from us. It must be approached therefore from another plane of unconsciousness. Unless we move on to the same plane where the masters stand, or unless we abandon our so-called common-sense way of reasoning, there is no possible bridge which will carry us over the chasm dividing our intellection from their apparently psittacine repetitions.

In this case, as in other cases, the idea of the masters is to show the way where the truth of Zen is to be experienced, but not in and through the language which they use and which we all use, as the means of communicating ideas. Language, in case they resort to words, serves as an expression of feelings or moods or inner states, but not of ideas, and therefore it becomes entirely incomprehensible when we search its meaning in the words of the masters as embodying ideas. Of course, words are not to be altogether disregarded, inasmuch as they correspond to the feelings or experiences. To know this is more important in the understanding of Zen.

Language is then with the Zen masters a kind of exclamation or ejaculation as directly coming out of their inner spiritual experience. No meaning is to be sought in the expression itself, but within ourselves, in our own minds, which are awakened to the same experience. Therefore when we understand the language of the Zen masters, it is the understanding of ourselves and not the sense of the language which reflects ideas and not the experienced feelings themselves. Thus it is impossible to make those understand Zen who have not had any Zen experience yet, just as it is impossible for the people to realize the sweetness of honey who have never tasted it before. With such people, 'sweet' honey will ever remain as an idea altogether devoid of sense; that is, the word has no life with them.

Goso Hōyen first studied the Yogācāra school of Buddhist philosophy and came across the following passage, 'When the Bodhisattva enters on the path of knowledge, he finds that the discriminating intellect is identified with Reason, and that the objective world is fused with Intelligence, and there is no distinction to be made between the knowing and the known.' The anti-Yogācārians refuted this statement, saying that if the knowing is not distinguished from the known, how is knowledge at all possible? The Yogācārians could not answer this criticism, when Hsüan-chuang, who was at the time in India, interposed and saved his brethren in faith from the quandary. His answer was, 'It is like drinking water; one knows by oneself whether it is cold or not.' When Goso read this he questioned himself, 'What is this that makes one know thus by oneself?' This was the way he started on his Zen tour, for his Yogācāra friends, being philosophers, could not enlighten him, and he finally came to a Zen master for instruction.

Before we proceed to the next subject, let me cite another case of echoing. Hōgen Mon-yeki (Fa-yen Wen-i), the founder of the Hōgen branch of Zen Buddhism, flourished early in the tenth century. He asked one of his disciples, 'What do you understand by this: "Let the difference be even a tenth of an inch, and it will grow as wide as heaven and earth"?' The disciple said, 'Let the difference be even a tenth of an inch, and it will grow as wide as heaven and earth.' Hōgen, however, told him that such an answer will never do. Said the disciple, 'I cannot do otherwise; how do you understand?' The master at once replied, 'Let the difference be even a tenth of an inch and it will grow as wide as heaven and earth.'[1]

Hōgen was a great master of repetitions, and there is another interesting instance. After trying to understand the ultimate truth of Zen under fifty-four masters, Tokushō (Tê-shao, 907–971) finally came to Hōgen; but tired of making special efforts to master Zen, he simply fell in with the rest of the monks there. One day when the master ascended the platform, a monk asked, 'What is one drop of water dripping from the source of So[2] (Ts'ao)?' Said the master, 'That is one drop of water dripping from the source of So.' The monk failed to make anything out of the repetition and stood as if lost; while Tokushō, who happened to be by him, had for the first time his spiritual eye opened to the inner meaning of Zen, and all the doubts he had been cherishing secretly down in his heart were thoroughly dissolved. He was altogether another man after that.

Such cases as this conclusively show that Zen is not to be sought in ideas or words, but at the same time they also show that without ideas or words Zen cannot convey itself to others. To grasp the exquisite meaning of Zen as expressing itself in words and yet not in them is a great art which is to be attained only after so many vain attempts. Tokushō, who after such an experience finally came to realize the mystery of Zen, did his best later to give vent to his view which he had gained under Hōgen. It was while he was residing at the Monastery of Prajñā that he had the following 'mondō' and sermon. When Tokushō came out into the Hall a monk asked him: 'I understand this was an ancient wise man's saying: When a man sees Prajñā he is

---

[1] When this is literally translated, it grows too long and loses much of its original force. The Chinese runs thus: *Hao li yu ch'a t'ien ti hsüan chüeh.* It may better be rendered, 'An inch's difference and heaven and earth are set apart.'

[2] That is, Ts'ao-ch'i, where the sixth patriarch of Zen used to reside. It is the birthplace of Chinese Zen Buddhism.

tied to it; when he sees it not he is also tied to it. Now I wish to know how it is that a man seeing Prajñā could be tied to it.' Said the master, 'You tell me what it is that is seen by Prajñā.' Asked the monk, 'When a man sees not Prajñā, how could he be tied to it?' 'You tell me,' said the master, 'if there is anything that is not seen by Prajñā.' The master then went on: 'Prajñā seen is no Prajñā, nor is Prajñā unseen Prajñā: how could one apply the predicate, seen or unseen, to Prajñā? Therefore it is said of old that when one thing is missing the Dharmakāya is not complete; when one thing is superfluous the Dharmakāya is not complete: and again that when there is one thing to be asserted the Dharmakāya is not complete; when there is nothing to be asserted the Dharmakāya is not complete. This is indeed the essence of Prajñā.'

The 'repetition' seen in this light may grow to be intelligible to a certain degree.

VII

As was explained in the preceding section, the principle underlying the various methods of instruction used by the Zen masters is to awaken a certain sense in the pupil's own consciousness, by means of which he intuitively grasps the truth of Zen. Therefore, the masters always appeal to what we may designate 'direct action' and are loth to waste any lengthy discourse on the subject. Their dialogues are always pithy and apparently not controlled by rules of logic. The 'repetitive' method as in other cases conclusively demonstrates that the so-called answering is not to explain but to point the way where Zen is to be intuited.

To conceive the truth as something external which is to be perceived by a perceiving subject is dualistic and appeals to the intellect for its understanding, but according to Zen we are living right in the truth, by the truth, from which we cannot be separated. Says Gensha (Hsüan-sha), 'We are here as if immersed in water head and shoulders under-neath the great ocean, and yet how piteously we are ex-tending our hands for water!' Therefore, when he was asked by a monk, 'What is my self?' he at once replied, 'What would you do with a self?' When this is intellectually analysed, he means that when we begin to talk about self we immediately and inevitably establish the dualism of self and not-self, thus falling into the errors of intellectualism. We are in the water—this is the fact, and let us remain so, Zen would say, for when we begin to beg for water we put ourselves in an external relation to it and what has hitherto been our own will be taken away from us.

The following case may be interpreted in the same light: A monk came to Gensha and said, 'I understand you to say that the whole universe is one transpicuous crystal; how do I get at the sense of it?' Said the master, 'The whole universe is one transpicuous crystal, and what is the use of under-standing it?' The day following the master himself asked the monk, 'The whole universe is one transpicuous crystal, and how do you understand it?' The monk replied, 'The whole universe is one transpicuous crystal, and what is the use of understanding it?' 'I know,' said the master, 'that you are living in the cave of demons.' While this looks another case of 'Repetition', there is something different in it, some-thing more of intellection, so to speak.

Whatever this is, Zen never appeals to our reasoning faculty, but points directly at the very object one wants to have. While Gensha on a certain occasion was treating an army officer called Wei to tea, the latter asked, 'What does it mean when they say that in spite of our having it every day we do not know it?' Gensha without answering the question took up a piece of cake and offered it to him. After eating the cake the officer asked the master again, who then remarked, 'Only we do not know it even when we are using it every day.' This is evidently an object lesson. Another time a monk came to him and wanted to know how to enter upon the path of truth. Gensha asked, 'Do you hear the murmuring of the stream?' 'Yes, I do,' said the monk.

'There is a way to enter,' was the master's instruction. Gensha's method was thus to make the seeker of the truth directly realize within himself what it was, and not to make him merely the possessor of a second-hand knowledge. '*Ein begriffener Gott ist kein Gott*,' declares Terstegen.

It is thus no wonder that the Zen masters frequently make an exclamatory utterance[1] in response to questions, instead of giving an intelligible answer. When words are used, if at all intelligible we may feel that we can somehow find a clue to get at the meaning, but when an inarticulate utterance is given we are quite at a loss how to deal with it, unless we are fortified with some previous knowledge such as I have at some length attempted to give to my readers.

Of all the Zen masters who used to give exclamatory utterance, the most noted ones are Ummon and Rinzai, the former for his 'Kwan!' and the latter for his 'Kwatz!' At the end of one summer sojourn Suigan (Ts'ui-yen) made the following remark: 'Since the beginning of this summer sojourn I have talked much; see if my eyebrows are still there.' This refers to the tradition that when a man makes false statements concerning the Dharma of Buddhism he will lose all the hair on his face. As Suigan gave many sermons during the summer for the edification of his pupils, while no amount of talk can ever explain what the truth is, his eyebrows and beard might perhaps by this time have disappeared altogether. This, as far as its literary meaning is concerned, is the idea of his remark whatever Zen may be concealed underneath.

Hofuku (Pao-fu), one of the masters, said, 'One who turns into a highwayman has a treacherous heart.' Chōkei (Ch'ang-ch'ing), another master, remarked, 'How thickly they are growing!' Ummon, one of the greatest masters towards the end of the T'ang dynasty, exclaimed, 'Kwan!' *Kwan* literally means the gate on a frontier pass where travellers and their baggage are inspected. In this case, however, the term does not mean anything of the sort; it is

[1] Does this not remind us of an old mystic who defined God as an unutterable sigh?

simply 'Kwan!', an exclamatory utterance which does not allow any analytical or intellectual interpretation. Secchō, the original compiler of the *Hekigan*, comments on this, 'He is like one who, besides losing his money, is incriminated,' while Hakuin has this to say, 'Even an angry fist does not strike a smiling face.' Something like this is the only comment we can make on such an utterance as Ummon's. When we try anything approaching a conceptual interpretation on the subject we shall be 'ten thousand miles away beyond the clouds', as the Chinese would say.

While Rinzai is regarded as the author of 'Kwatz!' (*hê*), we have an earlier record of it; for Baso, successor to Nangaku (Nan-yüeh), and an epoch-maker in the history of Zen, uttered 'Kwatz!' to his disciple, Hyakujo (Pai-chang), when the latter came up to the master for a second time to be instructed in Zen. This 'Kwatz!' is said to have deafened Hyakujo's ear for the following three days. But it was principally due to Rinzai that this particular cry was most effectively and systematically made use of and later came to be one of the special features of the Rinzai Zen in distinction to the other schools. In fact, the cry came to be so abused by his followers that he had to make the following remark: 'You are all so given up to learning my cry (*hê*), but I want to ask you this: Suppose one man comes out from the eastern hall and another from the western hall, and suppose both give out the "Kwatz!" simultaneously; and yet I say to you that subject and predicate are clearly discernible in this. But how will you discern them? If you are unable to discern them, you are forbidden hereafter to imitate my cry.'

Rinzai distinguishes four kinds of 'Kwatz!' The first, according to him, is like the sacred sword of Vajrarāja; the second is like the golden-haired lion squatting on the ground; the third is like the sounding rod or the grass used as a decoy; and the fourth is the one that does not at all function as a 'Kwatz!'

Rinzai once asked his disciple, Rakuho (Lê-p'u), 'One man has been using a stick and another resorting to the

"Kwatz!" Which of them do you think is the more intimate to the truth?' Answered the disciple, 'Neither of
them!' 'What is the most intimate then?' Rakuho cried out,
'Kwatz!' Whereupon Rinzai struck him. This swinging of a
stick was the most favourite method of Tokusan and stands
generally contrasted to the crying utterance of Rinzai; but
here the stick is used by Rinzai and the latter's speciality
is taken up in a most telling manner by his disciple Rakuho.

Besides these 'skilful contrivances' (*upāya-kauśalya*) so far
enumerated under seven headings, there are a few more
'contrivances', though I am not going to be very exhaustive
here on the subject.

One of them is 'silence'. Vimalakīrti was silent when
Mañjuśrī asked him as to the doctrine of non-duality, and
his silence was later commented upon by a master as
'deafening like thunder'. A monk asked Basho Yesei
(Pa-chiao Hui-ch'ing) to show him the 'original face'
without the aid of any intermediary conception, and the
master, keeping his seat, remained silent. When Shifuku
(Tzŭ-fu) was asked as to a word befitting the understanding of the inquirer, he did not utter a word, he simply
kept silent. Bunki (Wên-hsi) of Koshu (Hang-chou) was
a disciple of Kyōzan (Yang-shan); he was asked by a
monk, 'What is the self?' but he remained silent. As the
monk did not know what to make of it, he asked again, to
which the master replied, 'When the sky is clouded, the
moon cannot shine out.' A monk asked Sozan (Ts'ao-shan),
'How is the silence inexpressible to be revealed?' 'I do not
reveal it here.' 'Where would you reveal it?' 'At midnight
last night,' said the master, 'I lost three pennies by my
bed.'

Sometimes the masters sit quiet, 'for some little while'
(*liang-chiu*), either in response to a question or when in the
pulpit. This *liang-chiu* does not always merely indicate the
passage of time, as we can see in the following cases: A
monk came to Shuzan (Shou-shan) and asked, 'Please play
me a tune on a stringless harp.' The master was quiet for

some little while, and said, 'Do you hear it?' 'No, I do not hear it.' 'Why,' said the master, 'did you not ask louder?' A monk asked Hofuku (Pao-fu), 'I am told that when one wants to know the path of the uncreate, one should know the source of it. What is the source, sir?' Hofuku was silent for a while, and then asked his attendant, 'What did the monk ask me now?' When that monk repeated the question, the master ejected him, exclaiming, 'I am not deaf!'

Next, we may mention the method of counter-questioning, wherein questions are not answered by plain statements but by counter-questionings. In Zen, generally speaking, a question is not a question in its ordinary sense—that is, it is not simply asked for information—and therefore it is natural that what ordinarily corresponds to an answer is not an answer at all. Some Zen authority enumerates eighteen different kinds of questions, against which we may distinguish eighteen corresponding answers. Thus a counter-question itself is in its way an illuminating answer. A monk requested Jimyo (Tzŭ-ming) to 'set forth the idea of Dharma's coming from the West', and the master said, 'When did you come?' When Rasan Dokan (Lo-shan Tao-hsien) was asked, 'Who is the master of the triple world?' he said, 'Do you understand how to eat rice?' Tenryu (T'ien-lung), the teacher of Gutei, was hailed by a monk who asked him, 'How are we released from the triple world?' He retorted, 'Where are you this very moment?' A monk asked Jōshu, 'What would you say when a man is without an inch of cloth on him?' 'What did you say he has not on him?' 'An inch of cloth on him, sir.' 'Very fine this, not to have an inch of cloth!' responded the master.

When we go on like this, there may be no end to this way of treating the various 'contrivances' devised by the Zen masters for the benefits of their truth-thirsty pupils. Let me conclude this section by quoting two more cases in which a kind of reasoning in a circle is employed, but from another point of view we may detect here a trace of absolute monism in which all differences are effaced. Whether the

Zen masters agree with this view, however, remains to be seen; for while the absolute identity of [meum et tuum] is asserted, facts of individualization are not ignored either.

A monk asked Daizui (Tai-sui), 'What is my [pupil's] Self?' 'That is my [master's] Self', answered the master. 'How is it that my Self is your Self?' The ultimate dictum was, 'That is your Self.' To understand this in a logical fashion, put 'ignorant', or 'confused', or 'human' in place of 'my [pupil's] Self', and in place of 'your [master's] Self' put 'enlightened', or 'Buddha's', or 'divine', and we may have a glimpse into what was going on in the mind of Daizui. But without his last remark, 'That is your Self', the whole affair may resolve into a form of pantheistic philosophy. In the case of Sansho Yenen (San-shêng Hui-jên) and Kyozan Yejaku (Yang-shan Hui-chi), the thought of Daizui is more concretely presented. Yejaku asked Yenen, 'What is your name?' and Yenen replied, 'My name is Yejaku'. Yejaku protested, 'Yejaku is my name.' Thereupon said Yenen, 'My name is Yenen,' which brought out a hearty laugh from Yejaku. These dialogues remind one of the famous Hindu saying, '*Tat tvam asi!*', but the difference between this and 'My name is Yejaku' is that between Vedanta philosophy and Zen Buddhism, or that between Indian idealism and Chinese realism or practicalness. The latter does not generalize, nor does it speculate on a higher plane which has no hold on life as we live it.

According to the philosophy of the Kegon (Avataṁsaka) school of Buddhism, there is a spiritual world where one particular object holds within itself all other particular objects merged, instead of all particular objects being absorbed in the Great All. Thus in this world it so happens that when you lift a bunch of flowers or point at a piece of brick, the whole world in its multitudinosity is seen reflected here. If so, the Zen masters may be said to be moving also in this mystic realm which reveals its secrets at the moment of supreme enlightenment (*anuttara-samyak-saṁbodhi*).

VIII

We now come to the most characteristic feature of Zen Buddhism, by which it is distinguished not only from all the other Buddhist schools, but from all forms of mysticism that are ever known to us. So far the truth of Zen has been expressed through words, articulate or otherwise, however enigmatic they may superficially appear: but now the masters appeal to a more direct method instead of verbal medium. In fact, the truth of Zen is the truth of life, and life means to live, to move, to act, not merely to reflect. Is it not the most natural thing for Zen, therefore, that its development should be towards acting or rather living its truth instead of demonstrating or illustrating it in words; that is to say, with ideas? In the actual living of life there is no logic, for life is superior to logic. We imagine logic influences life, but in reality man is not a rational creature so much as we make him out; of course he reasons, but he does not act according to the result of his reasoning pure and simple. There is something stronger than ratiocination. We may call it impulse, or instinct, or, more comprehensively, will. Where this will acts there is Zen, but if I am asked whether Zen is a philosophy of will, I rather hesitate to give an affirmative answer. Zen is to be explained, if at all explained it should be, rather dynamically than statically. When I raise the hand thus, there is Zen. But when I assert that I have raised the hand, Zen is no more there. Nor is there any Zen when I assume the existence of somewhat that may be named will or anything else. Not that the assertion or assumption is wrong, but that the thing known as Zen is three thousand miles away, as they say. An assertion is Zen only when it is in itself an act and does not refer to anything that is asserted in it. In the finger pointed at the moon there is no Zen, but when the pointing finger itself is considered, altogether independent of any external references, there is Zen.

Life delineates itself on the canvas called time; and time never repeats: once gone, forever gone; and so is an act: once done, it is never undone. Life is a *sumiye*-painting, which must be executed once and for all time and without hesitation, without intellection, and no corrections are permissible or possible. Life is not like an oil-painting, which can be rubbed out and done over time and again until the artist is satisfied. With a *sumiye*-painting, any brush stroke painted over a second time results in a smudge; the life has left it. All corrections show when the ink dries. So is life. We can never retract what we have once committed to deeds; nay, what has once passed through consciousness can never be rubbed out. Zen therefore ought to be caught while the thing is going on, neither before nor after. It is an act of one instant. When Dharma was leaving China, as the legend has it, he asked his disciples what was their understanding of Zen, and one of them who happened to be a nun, replied, 'It is like Ānanda's looking into the kingdom of Akshobhya Buddha, it is seen once and has never been repeated.' This fleeting, unrepeatable, and ungraspable character of life is delineated graphically by Zen masters who have compared it to lightning or spark produced by the percussion of stones: *shan tien kuang, chi shih huo* is the phrase.

The idea of direct method appealed to by the masters is to get hold of this fleeting life as it flees and not after it has flown. While it is fleeing, there is no time to recall memory or to build ideas. No reasoning avails here. Language may be used, but this has been associated too long with ideation, and has lost directness or being by itself. As soon as words are used, they express meaning, reasoning; they represent something not belonging to themselves; they have no direct connection with life, except being a faint echo or image of something that is no longer here. This is the reason why the masters often avoid such expressions or statements as are intelligible in any logical way. Their aim is to have the pupil's attention concentrated in the thing itself which he wishes to grasp and not in anything that is in the remotest possible connection liable to disturb him. Therefore when we attempt to find meaning in dhāraṇīs or exclamations or a nonsensical string of sounds taken as such, we are far away from the truth of Zen. We must penetrate into the mind itself as the spring of life, from which all these words are produced. The swinging of a stick, the crying of a 'Kwatz!', or the kicking of a ball must be understood in this sense; that is, as the directest demonstration of life—no, even as life itself. The direct method is thus not always the violent assertion of life-force, but a gentle movement of the body, the responding to a call, the listening to a murmuring stream, or to a singing bird, or any of our most ordinary everyday assertions of life.

Reiun (Ling-yün) was asked, 'How were things *before* the appearance of the Buddha in the world?' He raised his hossu. 'How were things *after* the appearance of the Buddha?' He again raised the hossu. This raising of the hossu was quite a favourite method with many masters to demonstrate the truth of Zen. As I stated elsewhere, the hossu and the staff were the religious insignias of the master, and it was natural that they would be in much display when the monks approached with questions. One day Ōbaku Kiun (Huang-po Hsi-yün) ascended the pulpit, and as soon as monks were gathered, the master took up his staff and drove them all out. When they were about all out, he called them, and they turned their heads back. The master said, 'The moon looks like a bow, less rain and more wind.' The staff was thus wielded effectively by the masters, but who would ever have thought of a cane being made an instrument of illustrating the most profound truth of religion?

Jōshu was the readiest master for pithy retorts and his 'Sayings' (*Goroku*) is filled with them, but he was also an adept at the direct method. When he was in his pulpit one day, a monk came out of the rank and made bows to him. Without waiting, however, for further movements on the part of the monk, Jōshu folded his hands and a parting salutation was given. Hyakujo Isei's (Pai-chang

Wei-chêng's) way was somewhat different. He said to the monks, 'You open the farm for me and I will talk to you about the great principle [of Zen].' When the monks finished attending to the farm and came back to the master to discourse on the great principle, he merely extended his open arms and said nothing.

A monk came to Yenkwan An, the National Teacher, and wanted to know what was the original body of Vairochana Buddha. The Teacher told him to pass the pitcher, which he did. The Teacher then said, 'Put it back where you got it.' The monk faithfully obeyed, but not being told what was the original body of the Buddha, he proposed the question once more, 'Who is the Buddha?' Answered the master, 'Long gone is he!' In this case the direct method was practised more by the monk himself under the direction of the master, but unfortunately the pupil's spiritual condition was not ripe enough to grasp the meaning of his own 'direct method', and alas, let go 'the old Buddha!' Something similar to this case may be found in the following one:

Sekisō (Shih-shuang) asked Yenchi (Yüan-chih), who was a disciple of Yakusan (Yüeh-shan), 'If some one after your death asked me about the ultimate fact, what should I say to him?' The master gave no answer, but instead called up the boy attendant, who at once responded. He said, 'Fill up the pitcher', and remained quiet for some little while. He now asked Sekisō, 'What did you ask me before?' Sekisō restated the question, whereupon the master rose from his seat and left the room.

As some Zen masters remarked, Zen is our 'ordinary mindedness'; that is to say, there is in Zen nothing supernatural or unusual or highly speculative that transcends our everyday life. When you feel sleepy, you retire; when you are hungry, you eat, just as much as the fowls of the air and the lilies of the field, taking 'no thought for your life, what ye shall eat, or what ye shall drink; nor yet for your body, what ye shall put on'. This is the spirit of Zen. Hence no specially didactic or dialectical instruction in the study of Zen except such as is given below by Dōgo.

Ryutan Sōshin (Lung-t'an Sui-hsin) was a disciple of Tenno Dōgo (Tao-wu). He served the master as one of his personal attendants. He was with him for some time, when one day he said to the master, 'Since I came to you, I have not at all been instructed in the study of mind.' Replied the master, 'Ever since you came to me, I have always been pointing to you how to study mind.' 'In what way, sir?' 'When you brought me a cup of tea, did I not accept it? When you served me with food, did I not partake of it? When you made bows to me, did I not return them? When did I ever neglect in giving you instructions?' Ryutan kept his head hanging for some time, when the master told him, 'If you want to see, see directly into it; but when you try to think about it, it is altogether missed.'

Dōgo Yenchi (Tao-wu Yüan-chih) and Ungan Donjo (Yün-yen Tan-shêng) were standing by the master Yakusan (Yüeh-shan) as attendants, when Yakusan remarked: 'Where our intellect cannot reach, I verily tell you to avoid talking about it; when you do, horns will grow on you. O Yenchi, what will you say to this?' Yenchi thereupon rose from his place and left the room. Ungan asked the master, 'How is it, sir, that Brother Chi does not answer you?' 'My back aches today,' said Yakusan. 'You'd better go to Yenchi himself, for he understands.' Ungan came to his brother monk and inquired thus. 'O Brother Senior, why did you not answer our master just now?' 'You'd better go back to the master himself and ask,' was all that poor Ungan could get out of his senior brother.

There was another favourite movement often practised by Zen masters, which was to call out to the questioner or somebody else. One case of this has already been given somewhere else in another connection. The following are the typical and classical ones. Chu, the National Teacher, called out to his attendant monk three times, to which the latter responded regularly. Said the Teacher, 'I thought I was not fair to you, but it was you that were not fair to me.'[1] This calling and responding took place also three times between Mayoku (Ma-ku) and Ryosui (Liang-sui), which at last made the latter exclaim, 'O this stupid fellow!'

This trick of calling out and responding was frequently practised, as is seen in the following cases: A high government dignitary called upon Ungo Dōyō (Yün-chü Tao-ying) and asked, 'I am told that the World-Honoured One had a secret phrase and Mahākāśyapa did not keep it hidden; what was the secret phrase?' The master called out, 'O honoured officer!' and the officer responded. 'Do you understand?' demanded the master. 'No, Reverend Sir!' was his natural answer. 'If you do not understand, there is the secret phrase: if you understand, there is Mahākāśyapa in full revelation.'

Haikyu (P'ai-hsiu) was a local governor in Shinan (Hsin-an) before he was appointed a state minister. He once visited a Buddhist monastery in his district. While going around in the premises of the monastery, he came across a fine fresco painting and asked the accompanying priests whose portrait this was. 'He was one of the high priests,' they answered. The governor now turned towards them and questioned, 'Here is his portrait, but where is the high priest himself?' They all did not know how to answer

[1] A monk asked Hsüan-sha, 'What is the idea of the National Teacher's calling out to his attendant?' Said Hsüan-sha, 'The attendant knows well.' Yün-chü Hsi commented on this: 'Does the attendant really know, or does he not? If we say he does, why does the National Teacher say, "It is you that are not fair to me"? But if the attendant knows not, how about Hsüan-sha's assertion? What would be our judgment of the case?'

Hsüan-chiao Cheng said to a monk, 'What is the point the attendant understands?' Replied the monk, 'If he did not understand, he would never have responded.' Hsüan-chiao said, 'You seem to understand some.'

A monk asked Fa-yen, 'What is the idea of the National Teacher's calling out to his attendant?' Fa-yen said, 'You go away now, and come back some other time.' Remarked Yün-chü, 'When Fa-yen says this, does he really know what the National Teacher's idea is? or does he not?'

A monk approached Chao-chou with the same question, to which he replied, 'It is like writing characters in the dark: while the characters are not properly formed, their outlines are plainly traceable.'

him. He then further asked if there were any Zen monks about here. They replied, 'We have recently a newcomer in this monastery, he does some menial work for us and looks very much like a Zen monk.' He was then brought in the presence of the governor, who at once said to him, 'I have one question in which I wish to be enlightened, but the gentlemen here grudge the answer. May I ask you to give me a word for them?' 'I humbly wish you to ask,' politely requested the monk. The officer repeated the first question, whereupon the monk loudly and clearly called out, 'O Haikyu!' Haikyu responded at once, 'Here, sir!' 'Where is the high priest now?' cross-questioned the monk. This opened the governor's eye to the sense of the monk's counter-question, in which he could now read the solution of his first query.

The case between Yisan (Wei-shan) and Kyōzan (Yang-shan) was more intellectual and to that extent more intelligible than this mere calling and responding. Kyōzan was the chief disciple of Yisan, and one of the peculiar features of this school was to demonstrate the truth of Zen concordantly both by the master and disciple. They once went out picking tea-leaves. The master said to Kyōzan, 'Picking tea-leaves all day, I hear only your voice and do not see your body; manifest your original body and let me see it.' Kyōzan shook the tea-plant. Said Yisan, 'You have only got its function, you have not got the substance.' Kyōzan said, 'Master, how with you then?' The master was quiet for a while, whereupon the disciple said, 'O master, you have got only the substance, you have not got the function.' 'You will be spared of my twenty blows,' concluded the master. In Buddhist ontology three conceptions are distinguished, as was referred to previously: substance or body, appearance, and function or activity. 'Body' or *bhāva* corresponds to the idea of mass or being, 'appearance' (*lakshaṇa*) to that of form, and 'function' (*kṛitya*) to that of force. Every reality is regarded by Buddhist philosophers as analysable into these three notions. Sometimes, however, the second conception, 'appearance', is absorbed in that of 'being', or

'body'. Without functioning no objects exist, but functioning cannot take place without something functioning. The
two ideas, according to Buddhist philosophers, are thus
inseparable for our understanding of the universe. But
Yisan and Kyōzan were not metaphysicians and would not
argue on the subject. The one shook the tree and the other
stood still. We cannot say that there is Zen in this standing
and shaking, as we may interpret them philosophically,
but we may glean something of Zen in their remarks on
'body' and 'function' together with their direct method.

So far the direct method has not been of any violent
character as to involve a bodily injury or nervous shock,
but the masters had no qualms if they thought necessary
to shake the pupils roughly. Rinzai for one was noted for
the directness and incisiveness of his dealings; the point of
his sword cut through the heart of the opponent. The monk
Jō (Ting) was one of his disciples, and when he asked the
master what the fundamental principle of Buddhism was
Rinzai came down from his straw chair, and taking hold of
the monk slapped him with the palm of his hand, and let
him go. Jō stood still without knowing what to make of the
whole procedure, when a bystanding monk blamed him for
not bowing to the master. While doing so, Jō all of a sudden
awoke to the truth of Zen. Later, when he was passing over
a bridge, he happened to meet a party of three Buddhist
scholars, one of whom asked Jō: 'The river of Zen is deep,
and its bottom must be sounded. What does this mean?' Jō,
disciple of Rinzai, at once seized the questioner and was at
the point of throwing him over the bridge, when his two
friends interceded and asked Jō's merciful treatment of the
offender. Jō released the scholar, saying, 'If not for the inter-
cession of his friends I would at once let him sound the
bottom of the river himself.' With these people Zen was no
joke, no mere play of ideas; it was, on the contrary, a most
serious thing on which they would stake their lives.

Rinzai was a disciple of Ōbaku (Huang-po), but while
under the master he did not get any special instruction on
Zen; for whenever he asked him as to the fundamental

truth of Buddhism, he was struck by Ōbaku. But it was these blows that opened Rinzai's eyes to the ultimate truth of Zen and made him exclaim, 'After all, there is not much in the Buddhism of Ōbaku!' In China and in Korea what little of Zen is left mostly belongs to the school of Rinzai. In Japan alone the Sōtō branch is flourishing as much as the Rinzai. The rigour and vitality of Zen Buddhism that is still present in the Rinzai school of Japan comes from the three blows of Ōbaku so mercifully dealt out to his poor disciple. There is in fact more truth in a blow or a kick than in the verbosity of logical discourse. At any rate the Zen masters were in dead earnest whenever the demonstration of Zen was demanded. See the following instance.

When Tō-Impo (Têng Yin-fêng) was pushing a cart, he happened to see his master Baso stretching his legs a little too far out in the roadway. He said, 'Will you please draw your legs in?' Replied the master, 'A thing once stretched out will never be contracted.' 'If so,' said Tō, 'a thing once pushed will never be retracted.' His cart went right over the master's legs, which were thus hurt. Later Baso went up to the Preaching Hall, where he carried an axe and said to the monks gathered, 'Let the one who wounded the old master's legs a while ago come out of the congregation.' Tō came forth and stretched his neck ready to receive the axe, but the master, instead of chopping the disciple's head off, quietly set the axe down.

Tō-Impo was ready to give up his life to reassert the truth of his deed through which the master got hurt. Mimicry or simulation was rampant everywhere, and therefore Baso wanted to ascertain the genuineness of Tō's understanding of Zen. When the thing is at stake, the masters do not hesitate to sacrifice anything. In the case of Nansen, a kitten was done away with: Kyōzan broke a mirror in pieces; a woman follower of Zen burned up a whole house; and another woman threw her baby into a river. This latter was an extreme case and perhaps the only one of the kind ever recorded in the history of Zen. As to minor cases such as mentioned above, they are plentiful and considered almost matters of course with Zen masters.

IX

While I have not attempted to be very exhaustive in describing all the different methods of demonstration, or rather realization, of the truth of Zen resorted to by the masters of various schools, the statements so far made in regard to them may suffice to give us at least a glimpse into some of the peculiar features of Zen Buddhism. Whatever explanations may be given by critics or scholars to the philosophy of Zen, we must first of all acquire a new point of view of looking at things, which is altogether beyond our ordinary sphere of consciousness. Rather, this new view-point is gained when we reach the ultimate limits of our understanding, within which we think we are always bound and unable to break through. Most people stop at these limits and are easily persuaded that they cannot go any further. But there are some whose mental vision is able to penetrate this veil of contrasts and contradictions. They gain it abruptly. They beat the wall in utter despair, and lo, it unexpectedly gives way and there opens an entirely new world. Things hitherto regarded as prosaic and ordinary, and even binding, are now arranged in quite a novel scheme. The old world of the senses has vanished, and something entirely new has come to take its place. We seem to be in the same objective surrounds, but subjectively we are rejuvenated, we are born again.

Wu Tao-tzŭ, or Godoshi, was one of the greatest painters of China, and lived in the reign of the Emperor Hsuan-tsung, of the T'ang dynasty. His last painting, according to legend, was a landscape commissioned by the Emperor for one of the walls of his palace. The artist concealed the complete work with a curtain till the Emperor's arrival, then drawing it aside exposed his vast picture. The Emperor gazed with admiration on a marvellous scene: forests, and great mountains, and clouds in immense distances of sky, and men upon the hills, and birds in flight. 'Look,' said the painter, 'in the cave at the foot of this mountain dwells a spirit.' He clapped his hands; the door at the cave's entrance flew open. 'The interior is beautiful beyond words,' he continued; 'permit me to show the way.' So saying, he passed within; the gate closed after him; and before the astonished Emperor could speak or move, all had faded to white wall before his eyes, with not a trace of the artist's brush remaining. Wu Tao-tzŭ was seen no more.

The artist has disappeared, and the whole scene has been wiped out; but from this nothingness there arises a new spiritual world, abiding in which the Zen masters perform all kinds of antics, assert all kinds of absurdities, and yet they are in perfect accord with the nature of things in which a world moves on stripped of all its falsehoods, conventions, simulations, and intellectual obliquities. Unless one gets into this world of realities, the truth of Zen will be eternally a sealed book. This is what I mean by acquiring a new point of view independent of logic and discursive understanding.

Emerson expresses the same view in his own characteristic manner: 'Foremost among these activities (that is, mathematical combination, great power of abstraction, the transmutings of the imagination, even versatility, and concentration) are the somersaults, spells, and resurrections, wrought by the imagination. When this wakes, a man seems to multiply ten times or a thousand times his force. It opens the delicious sense of indeterminate size, and inspires an audacious mental habit. We are as elastic as the gas of gunpowder, and a sentence in a book, or a word dropped in conversation, sets free our fancy, and instantly our heads are bathed with galaxies, and our feet tread the floor of the pit. And this benefit is real, because we are entitled to these enlargements, and, once having passed the bounds, shall never again be quite the miserable pedants we were.'

Here is a good illustration of the difference between a

'miserable pedant' and one who has 'passed the bounds'. There was a monk called Gensoku (Hsüan-tsê), who was one of the chief officials of the monastery under the Zen master Hōgen (Fa-yen), of the early tenth century. He never came to the master to make inquiries about Zen, so the master one day asked him why he did not come. The chief official answered, 'When I was under Seiho (Chi'ng-fêng) I got an idea as to the truth of Zen.' 'What is your understanding then?' demanded the master. 'When I asked my master who was the Buddha, he said, Ping-ting T'ung-tzŭ comes for fire.' 'It is a fine answer,' said Hōgen, 'but probably you misunderstand it. Let me see how you take the meaning of it.' 'Well,' explained the official, 'Ping-ting is the god of fire; when he himself comes for fire, it is like myself, who, being a Buddha from the very beginning, wants to know who the Buddha is. No questioning is then needed, as I am already the Buddha himself.' 'There!' exclaimed the master. 'Just as I thought! You are completely off.' Soku, the chief official, got highly offended because his view was not countenanced and left the monastery. Hōgen said, 'If he comes back he may be saved; if not, he is lost.' Soku after going some distance reflected that a master of five hundred monks as Hōgen was would not chide him without cause, and returned to the old master and expressed his desire to be instructed in Zen. Hōgen said, 'You ask me and I will answer.' 'Who is the Buddha?' —the question came from the lips of the now penitent monk. 'Ping-ting T'ung-tzŭ comes for fire.' This made his eyes open to the truth of Zen quite different from what he formerly understood of it. He was now no more a second-hand 'pedant' but a living creative soul. I need not repeat that Zen refuses to be explained, but that it is to be lived. Without this all talk is nothing but an idea, woefully inane and miserably unsatisfactory.

Below is another story illustrating the peculiarity of Zen understanding as distinguished from our ordinary intellectual understandings, which are based on ideas and representations. The same phrase is repeated here as in the preceding case, and as far as its literal meaning goes, we have no reason to suppose its producing different effects on the mind of the recipient. But as I said elsewhere, Zen is the opening of one's own inner consciousness occasioned by some external incidental happening which may be of purely physical nature, but may invoke some mental operation. This opening is therefore something we as out-siders, not belonging to the inner life of the individual con-cerned, have no means to judge beforehand; we know only when it is opened; but the masters seem to know when this opening is going to take place and how it is to be brought about from their own experience. Students of the psychology of Zen will here find an interesting problem to investigate.

Suigan Kashin (Ts'ui-yen K'ê-chên) was a disciple of Jimyo (T'zu-ming, 986–1040), who was one of the greatest Sung masters and under whom the Rinzai school of Zen was divided into two branches, Woryu (Huang-lung) and Yōgi (Yang-ch'i). Kashin was quite proud of being one of the disciples of the master; he was not yet really a master himself, but he thought he was. When he had a talk with another of Jimyo's disciples he was found out and laughed at. When they were having a walk together one day they discussed Zen. His friend picked up a piece of a broken tile and putting it on a flat rock, said, 'If you can say a word at this juncture I will grant your really being Jimyo's dis-ciple.' Kashin wavered, looked this way and that, trying to make some answer. His friend was impatient, and broke out, 'Hesitating and wavering you have not yet penetrated through illusion, you have never yet even dreamt as to what the true insight of Zen is.' Kashin was thoroughly ashamed of himself. He at once returned to the master, who severely reproached him, saying that he came before the termination of the summer session, which was against the regulations. Full of tears, he explained how he was taken to task by his fellow-monk and that it was the reason why he was here even against the monastery rules. The master abruptly asked him, 'What is the fundamental principle of Buddhism?' Replied Kashin:

'No clouds are gathering over the mountain peaks,
And how serenely the moon is reflected on the waves!'

The master's eyes flashed with indignation, and he
thundered: 'Shame on you! To have such a view for an
old-seasoned man like you! How can you expect to be
delivered from birth-and-death?' Kashin earnestly implored to be instructed. Said the master, 'You ask me.'
Thereupon he repeated the master's first question, 'What is
the fundamental principle of Buddhism?' The master
roared:

'No clouds are gathering over the mountain peaks,
And how serenely the moon is reflected on the waves!'

This opened Kashin's eye, and another man was he after
that.

Let me conclude with a sermon from Goso (Wu-tsu), of
whom mention has already been made:
'If people ask me what Zen is like I will say that it is like
learning the art of burglary. The son of a burglar saw his
father growing older and thought: "If he is unable to carry
out his profession, who will be the bread-winner of this
family, except myself? I must learn the trade." He inti-
mated the idea to his father, who approved of it. One night
the father took the son to a big house, broke through the
fence, entered the house, and opening one of the large chests,
told the son to go in and pick out the clothings. As soon as
he got into it the lid was dropped and the lock securely
applied. The father now came out to the courtyard, and
loudly knocking at the door woke up the whole family,
whereas he himself quietly slipped away by the former hole
in the fence. The residents got excited and lighted candles,
but found that the burglars had already gone. The son, who
remained all the time in the chest securely confined, thought
of his cruel father. He was greatly mortified, when a fine
idea flashed upon him. He made a noise which sounded

like the gnawing of a rat. The family told the maid to take a candle and examine the chest. When the lid was unlocked, out came the prisoner, who blew out the light, pushed away the maid, and fled. The people ran after him. Noticing a well by the road, he picked up a large stone and threw it into the water. The pursuers all gathered around the well trying to find the burglar drowning himself in the dark hole. In the meantime he was safely back in his father's house. He blamed him very much for his narrow escape. Said the father: "Be not offended, my son. Just tell me how you got off." When the son told him all about his adventures the father remarked, "There you are, you have learned the art!" '

THE MEDITATION HALL, AND THE
IDEALS OF THE MONKISH DISCIPLINE

I

To get a glimpse into the practical and disciplinary side of Zen, we have to study the institution known as the Meditation Hall. It is an educational system quite peculiar to the Zen sect. Most of the main monasteries belonging to this sect are provided with Meditation Halls, and in the life of the Zen monk more than anywhere else we are reminded of that of the Buddhist Brotherhood (*Saṁgha*) in India. This system was founded by the Chinese Zen master, Hyakujo (Pai-chang, 720–814), more than one thousand years ago. Until his time the monks used to live in monasteries belonging to the Vinaya sect, which were governed by a spirit not quite in accordance with the principles of Zen. As the latter grew more and more flourishing and its followers kept on increasing in number and in influence, there was need for its own institution, exclusively devoted to the promotion of its objects. According to Hyakujo, the Zen monasteries were to be neither Hīnayānistic nor Mahāyānistic, but they were to unite the disciplinary methods of both schools in a new and original manner, best suited to the realization of the Zen ideals, as they were conceived by the masters of the earlier days.

The original book compiled by Hyakujo giving detailed regulations of the Zen monastery was lost. The one we have now was compiled during the Yuan dynasty from the actual life in the monastery at the time, which was then supposed to be a faithful continuation of the old institution, though naturally with some modifications and transformations due to historical exigencies. This book was compiled under the auspices of the reigning Emperor Shud, and is known as 'The Imperial Edition of the Regulations in the Zen Monastery'. In Japan the Zen monasteries have never been established on such a grand scale as in China, and as a result all the regulations as detailed in the Imperial Edition were not practised. But their spirit and all that was applicable to Japanese life and conditions were adopted. The ideals of Zen life were never lost sight of anywhere. And before I proceed further I wish to speak briefly of one of such ideals set before the eyes of all Zen students, for it is really the most important and noteworthy feature in the monastery life of Zen.

It is indeed this that distinguishes Zen from the other Buddhist schools originated in China, and is to be considered most characteristically Zen, and at the same time animating its long history. By this I mean the notion of work or service. Hyakujo left a famous saying which was the guiding principle of his life, and is pre-eminently the spirit of the Meditation Hall. It is this: 'No work, no eating.' When he was thought by his devoted disciples too old to work in the garden, which was his daily occupation besides lecturing and educating the monks in Zen, they hid all his garden implements, as he would not listen to their repeated oral remonstrances. He then refused to eat, saying, 'No work, no eating.'

At all the Meditation Halls work is thus considered a vital element in the life of a monk. It is altogether a practical one, and chiefly consists in manual labour, such as sweeping, cleaning, cooking, fuel-gathering, tilling the farm, or going about begging in the villages far and near. No work is considered beneath their dignity, and a perfect feeling of brotherhood and democracy prevails among them. However hard, or mean from the ordinary point of view, a work may be, they will not shun it. They believe in the sanctity of manual labour. They keep themselves busy in every way they can; they are no idlers as some of the so-called monks or mendicants are, physically at least, as in India, for instance.

We can see in this sanctification of work the practical

attitude of the Chinese mind well reflected. When I said that Zen was the Chinese interpretation of the doctrine of Enlightenment, the Zen conception of work did not essentially or theoretically enter into my conclusion. But from the practical point of view work is such an integral part of the Zen life now that the one cannot be conceived as independent of the other. In India the monks are mendicants; when they meditate they retire into the quiet corner from worldly cares; and inasmuch as they are supported economically by their secular devotees, they do not propose to work in any menial employment such as Chinese and Japanese Zen monks are used to. What saved Zen Buddhism from deteriorating into quietism or mere intellectual gymnastics, which was more or less the fate befalling other schools of Buddhism, was surely due to the gospel of work. Apart from its psychological value, it proved an efficient agency in preserving the health and sanity of Zen Buddhism throughout its long history of growth.

Whatever may be this historical importance of work, Hyakujo must have had a profound knowledge of human psychology when he made work the ruling spirit of the monastery life. His idea of 'No work, no eating,'[1] did not necessarily originate from an economic or ethical valuation of life. His sole motive was not that nobody deserved his daily bread if he did not earn it with the sweat of his face. True, there is a virtue in not eating the bread of idleness, and there have been so many Buddhists since the early days of Buddhism who thought it a most disgraceful thing to be living on other's earnings and savings, that Hyakujo's object, while it might have been unconsciously conceived, was more psychological in spite of his open declaration, 'No work, no eating.' It was to save his monks from a mental inactivity or an unbalanced development of mind which too often results from the meditative habit of the monkish life.

[1] Literally, 'A day [of] no work [is] a day [of] no eating.' cf. II Thessalonians iii, 10: 'If any would not work, neither should he eat.' It is noteworthy that St. Francis of Assisi made this the first rule of his Brotherhood.

When the muscles are not exercised for the execution of spiritual truths, or when the mind and body are not put to practical test, the severance generally issues in inimical results. As the philosophy of Zen is to transcend the dualistic conception of flesh and spirit, its practical application will naturally be, dualistically speaking, to make the nerves and muscles the most ready and absolutely obedient servants of the mind, and not to make us say that the spirit is truly ready but the flesh is weak. Whatever religious truths of this latter statement, psychologically it comes from the lack of a ready channel between mind and muscles. Unless the hands are habitually trained to do the work of the brain, the blood ceases to circulate evenly all over the body, it grows congested somewhere, especially in the brain. The result will be not only an unsound condition of the body in general, but a state of mental torpidity or drowsiness in which ideas are presented as if they were wafting clouds. One is wide awake and yet the mind is filled with the wildest dreams and visions which are not at all related to realities of life. Fantasies are fatal to Zen, and those who practise Zen considering it a form of meditation are too apt to be visited upon by this insidious enemy. Hyakujo's insistence upon manual work has saved Zen from falling into the pitfalls of antinomianism as well as a hallucinatory mode of mind.

Apart from these psychological considerations, there is a moral reason which ought not to escape attention in our estimate of Hyakujo's wisdom in instituting work as a vital part of Zen life. For the soundness of ideas must be tested finally by their practical application. When they fail in this —that is, when they cannot be carried out in everyday life producing lasting harmony and satisfaction and giving real benefit to all concerned—to oneself as well as to others— no ideas can be said to be sound and practical. While physical force is no standard to judge the value of ideas, the latter, however logically consistent, have no reality when they are not joined to life. Especially in Zen, abstract ideas that do not convince one in practical living are of no value whatever. Conviction must be gained through experience and not through abstraction, which means that conviction has no really solid basis, except when it can be tested in our acting efficient life. Moral assertion or 'bearing witness' ought to be over and above an intellectual judgment; that is to say, the truth must be the product of one's living experiences. An idle reverie is not their business, the Zen followers will insist. They, of course, sit quiet and practice 'zazen';[1] for they want to reflect on whatever lessons they have gained while working. But as they are against chewing the cud all the time, they put in action whatever reflections they have made during hours of quiet-sitting and test their validity in the vital field of practicality. It is my strong conviction that if Zen did not put faith in acting its ideas, the institution would have long before this sunk into a mere somniferous and trance-inducing system, so that all the treasure thoughtfully hoarded by the master in China and Japan would have been cast away as heaps of rotten stuff.

Perhaps unwittingly supported by these reasons, the value of work or service has been regarded by all Zen followers as one of their religious ideals. No doubt the idea was greatly enforced by the characteristic industry and practicalness of the Chinese people by whom Zen was mainly elaborated. The fact is that if there is any one thing that is most emphatically insisted upon by the Zen masters as the practical expression of their faith, it is serving others, doing work for others; not ostentatiously, indeed, but secretly without making others know of it. Says Eckhart,

---

[1] *Tso-ch'an* is one of those compound Buddhist terms made of Sanskrit and Chinese. *Tso* is Chinese meaning 'to sit', while *ch'an* stands for *dhyāna* or *jhāna*. The full transliteration of the term is *ch'anna*, but for brevity's sake the first character alone has been in use. The combination of *tso-ch'an* comes from the fact that dhyāna is always practised by sitting cross-legged. This posture has been considered by the Indians the best way of sitting for a long while in meditation. In it, according to some Japanese physicians, the centre of gravitation rests firmly in the lower regions of the body, and when the head is relieved of an unusual congestion of blood the whole system will work in perfect order and the mind be put in suitable mood to take in the truth of Zen.

'What a man takes in by contemplation he must pour out in love.' Zen would say, 'pour it out in work', meaning by work the active and concrete realization of love. Tauler made spinning and shoe-making and other homely duties gifts of the Holy Ghost; Brother Lawrence made cooking sacremantal; George Herbert wrote:

'Who sweeps a room as to thy laws
Makes that and the action fine.'

These are all expressive of the spirit of Zen, as far as its practical side is concerned. Mystics are thus all practical men; they are far from being visionaries whose souls are too absorbed in things unearthly or of the other-world to be concerned with their daily life. The common notion that mystics are dreamers and star-gazers ought to be corrected, as it has no foundation in facts. Indeed, psychologically there is a most intimate and profound relationship between a practical turn of mind and a certain type of mysticism; the relationship is not merely conceptual or metaphysical. If mysticism is true its truth must be a practical one, verifying itself in every act of ours, and, most decidedly, not a logical one, to be true only in our dialectics. Sings a Zen poet known as Hokoji:[1]

'How wondrously supernatural,
And how miraculous this!
I draw water, and I carry fuel!'

---

[1] He was the noted Confucian disciple of Baso (Ma-tsu), and his wife and daughter were also devoted Zen followers. When he thought the time had come for him to pass away, he told his daughter to watch the course of the sun and let him know when it was midday. The daughter hurriedly came back and told the father that the sun had already passed the meridian and was about to be eclipsed. Ho came out, and while he was watching the said eclipse, she went in, took her father's own seat, and passed away in meditation. When the father saw his daughter already in Nirvāṇa, he said, 'What a quick-witted girl she is?' Ho himself passed away some days later.

II

The Meditation Hall (Zendō in Japanese and Ch'an T'ang in Chinese), as it is built in Japan, is generally a rectangular building of various size according to the number of monks to be accommodated. One at Engakuji,[1] Kamakura, was about 36 feet by 65 feet. The floors, about eight feet wide and three feet high, are raised along the longer sides of the building, and an empty space is left in the middle throughout the entire length of the Hall. This space is used for practising an exercise known as 'kinhin' (*ching hsing*), which means literally 'sūtra-walking'. The space allotted to each monk on the *tatami* floor does not exceed one mat, three by six feet, where he sits, meditates, and sleeps at night. The bedding for each is never more than one large wadded quilt, summer or winter. He has no regular pillow except that which is temporarily made up by himself out of his own private possessions. These latter, however, are next to nothing: for they are *kesa* (*kashāya* in Sanskrit) and *koromo* (priestly robe), a few books, a razor, and a set of bowls, all of which are put up in a box about thirteen by ten by three and a half inches large. In travelling this box is carried in front supported with a sash about the neck. The entire property thus moves with the owner. 'One dress and one bowl, under a tree and on a stone' was the graphical description of the monkish life in India. Compared with this, the modern Zen monk must be said to be abundantly supplied. Still, his wants are reduced to a minimum, and no one can fail to lead a simple, perhaps the simplest, life if he models his after that of the Zen monk.

The desire to possess is considered by Buddhism to be one of the worst passions mortals are apt to be obsessed with. What, in fact, causes so much misery in the world is

[1] This historical temple was unfortunately destroyed by the earthquake of 1923, with many other buildings.

due to a strong impulse of acquisitiveness. As power is desired, the strong always tyrannize over the weak: as wealth is coveted, the rich and poor are always crossing their swords of bitter enmity. International wars rage, social unrest ever goes on, unless the impulse to have and hold is completely uprooted. Cannot a society be reorganized upon an entirely different basis from what we have been used to seeing from the beginning of history? Cannot we ever hope to stop the amassing of wealth and the wielding of power merely from the desire for individual or national aggrandizement? Despairing of the utter irrationality of human affairs, the Buddhist monks have gone to the other extreme and cut themselves off even from reasonable and perfectly innocent enjoyments of life. However, the Zen ideal of putting up the monk's belongings in a tiny box a little larger than a foot square and three inches high is their mute protest, though so far ineffective, against the present order of society.

In this connection it will be of interest to read the admonition left by Daitō the National Teacher (1282–1337) to his disciples. He was the founder of Daitōkuji, Kyoto, in 1326, and is said to have spent about one-third of his life, which was not a very long one, among the lowest layers of society under the Gojo bridge, begging his food, doing all kinds of menial work, and despised by the so-called respectable people of the world. He did not care for the magnificence of a prosperous and highly honoured temple life led by most Buddhist priests of those days, nor did he think much of those pious and sanctimonious deeds that only testify to the superficiality of their religious life. He was for the plainest living and the highest thinking. The admonition reads:

'O you, monks, who are here in this mountain monastery, remember that you are gathered for the sake of the religion and not for the sake of clothes and food. As long as you have shoulders [that is, the body] you shall have clothes to wear, and as long as you have a mouth you shall have food to eat.

Be ever mindful, throughout the twelve hours of the day, to apply yourselves to the study of the Unthinkable. Time passes like an arrow; never let your minds be disturbed by worldly cares. Ever, ever be on the look-out. After my wandering away, some of you may have fine temples in prosperous conditions, towers and halls and holy books all decorated in gold and silver, and devotees may noisily crowd into the grounds; some may pass hours in reading Sūtras and reciting dharāṇīs, and, sitting long in contemplation, may not give themselves up to sleep; they may, eating once a day and observing the fast-days, and throughout the six periods of the day, practise all the religious deeds.

'Even when they are thus devoted to the cause, if their thoughts are not really dwelling on the mysterious and intransmissible Way of the Buddhas and Fathers, they may yet come to ignore the law of moral causation, ending in a complete downfall of the true religion. Such all belong to the family of evil spirits; however long my departure from the world may be, they are not to be called my descendants. Let, however, there be just one individual, who may be living in the wilderness in a hut thatched with one bundle of straw and passing his days by eating the roots of wild vegetables cooked in a pot with broken legs; but if he single-mindedly applies himself to the study of his own [spiritual] affairs, he is the very one who has a daily interview with me and knows to be grateful for his life. Who should ever despise such a one? O monks, be diligent, be diligent.'[1]

In India the Buddhist monks never eat in the afternoon. They properly eat only once a day, as their breakfast is no breakfast in the sense that an English or American breakfast is. So the Zen monks, too, are not supposed to have any meal in the evening. But the climatic necessity in China and Japan could not be ignored, and they have an evening meal

---

[1] In those monasteries which are connected in some way with the author of this admonition, it is read or rather chanted before a lecture or *Teisho* begins.

after a fashion; but to ease their conscience it is called 'medicinal food' (*yüeh-shih*). The breakfast, which is taken very early in the morning, while it is still dark, consists of rice gruel and pickled vegetables (*tsukemono*).

The principal meal at 10 a.m. is rice (or rice mixed with barley), vegetable soup, and pickles. In the afternoon, at four, they have only what is left of the dinner—no special cooking is done. Unless they are invited out or given an extra treatment at the house of some generous patrons, their meals are such as above described, year in, year out. Poverty and simplicity is their motto.

One ought not, however, to consider asceticism the ideal life of Zen. So far as the ultimate signification of Zen is concerned, it is neither asceticism nor any other ethical system. If it appears to advocate either the doctrine of suppression or that of detachment, the supposed fact is merely on the surface; for Zen as a school of Buddhism more or less inherits the odium of a Hindu discipline. The central idea, however, of the monkish life is not to waste, but to make the best possible use of things as they are given us, which is also the spirit of Buddhism in general. In truth the intellect, imagination, and all other mental faculties as well as the physical objects surrounding us, our own bodies not excepted, are given us for the unfolding and enhancing of the highest powers possessed by us as spiritual entities and not merely for the gratification of our individual whims or desires, which are sure to conflict with and injure the interests and rights asserted by others. These are some of the inner ideas underlying the simplicity and poverty of the monkish life.

III

As there is something to be regarded as peculiarly Zen in the table manners of the monks, some description of them will be given here.

At meal-times a gong is struck, and the monks come out

of the Meditation Hall in procession carrying their own bowls to the dining-room. The low tables are laid there all bare. They sit when the leader rings the bell. The bowls are set—which, by the way, are made of wood or paper and well lacquered. A set consists of four or five dishes, one inside the other. As they are arranging the dishes and the waiting monks go around to serve the soup and rice, the *Prajñā-pāramitā-hṛidaya-sūtra*[1] is recited, followed by the 'Five Meditations' on eating, which are: 'First, of what worth am I? Whence is this offering? Secondly, accepting this offering, I must reflect on the deficiency of my virtue. Thirdly, to guard over my own heart, to keep myself away from faults such as covetousness, etc.—this is the essential thing. Fourthly, this food is taken as good medicine in order to keep the body in a healthy condition. Fifthly, to ensure spiritual attainment this food is accepted.' After these 'Meditations' they continue to think about the essence of Buddhism, 'The first mouthful is to cut off all evils; the second mouthful is to practice every good; the third mouthful is to save all sentient beings so that everybody will finally attain to Buddhahood.'

They are now ready to take up their chop-sticks, but before they actually partake of the sumptuous dinner, the demons or spirits living somewhere in the triple world are remembered; and each monk taking out about seven grains from his own bowl, offers them to those unseen, saying, 'O you, demons and other spiritual beings, I now offer this to you, and may this food fill up the ten quarters of the world and all the demons and other spiritual beings be fed therewith.'

[1] I must not forget to mention that after the reading of the *Hṛidaya Sūtra* the following names of the Buddhas and others are invoked: 1. Vairocana-Buddha in his immaculate Body of the Law; 2. Vairocana-Buddha in his perfect Body of Bliss; 3. Śākyamuni-Buddha in his infinite manifestations as Body of Transformation; 4. Maitreya-Buddha, who is to come in some future time; 5. All the Buddhas past, present, and future in the ten quarters of the world; 6. The great holy Bodhisattva Mañjuśrī; 7. The great morally perfect Bodhisattva Samantabhadra; 8. The great compassionate Bodhisattva Avalokiteśvara; 9. All the venerable Bodhisattva-mahāsattvas; and 10. Mahaprajñāpāramitā.

While eating quietude prevails. The dishes are handled noiselessly, no word is uttered, no conversation goes on. Eating is a serious affair with them. When a second bowl of rice is wanted, the monk folds his hands before him. The monk-waiter notices it, comes round with the rice receptacle called *ohachi*, and sits before the hungry one. The latter takes up his bowl and lightly passes his hand around the bottom before it is handed to the waiter. He means by this to take off whatever dirt that may have attached itself to the bowl and that is likely to soil the hand of the serving monk. While the bowl is filled, the eater keeps his hands folded. If he does not want so much, he gently rubs the hands against each other, which means 'Enough, thank you.'

Nothing is to be left when the meal is finished. The monks eat up all that is served them, 'gathering up of the fragments that remain'. This is their religion. After a fourth helping of rice, the meal generally comes to an end. The leader claps the wooden blocks and the serving monks bring hot water. Each diner fills the largest bowl with it, and in it all the smaller dishes are neatly washed, and wiped with a piece of cloth which each monk carries. Now a wooden pail goes around to receive the slops.[1] Each monk gathers up his dishes and wraps them up once more, saying, 'I have now finished eating and my physical body is well nourished: I feel as if my will-power would shake the ten quarters of the world and dominate over the past, present, and future: turning both the cause and the effect over to the general welfare of all beings, may we all unfailingly gain in powers miraculous!' The tables are now empty as before except those rice grains offered to the spiritual beings at the beginning of the meal. The wooden blocks are clapped, thanks are given, and the monks leave the room in orderly procession as they came in.

[1] When the slop-basin goes around, spiritual beings are again remembered: 'This water in which my bowls were washed tastes like nectar from heaven. I now offer this to the numerous spirits of the world: may they all be filled and satisfied! Oṁ ma-ku-ra-sai (in Pekingese, *mo-hsui-lo-hsi*) svāhā!'

Their industry is proverbial. When the day is not set for study at home, they are generally seen, soon after breakfast, about half past five in summer and about half past six in winter, out in the monastery grounds, or in the neighbouring villages for begging, or tilling the farm attached to the Zendō. They keep the monastery, inside as well as outside, in perfect order. When we sometimes say, 'This is like a Zen monastery,' it means that the place is kept in the neatest possible order. When begging they go miles away. Commonly, attached to a Zendō there are some patrons whose houses the monks regularly visit and get a supply of rice or vegetables. We often see them along the country road pulling a cart loaded with pumpkins or potatoes. They work as hard as ordinary labourers. They sometimes go to the woods to gather kindlings or fuel. They know something of agriculture, too. As they have to support themselves in these ways, they are at once farmers, labourers, and skilled workmen. For they often build their own Meditation Hall under the direction of an architect.

These monks are a self-governing body. They have their own cooks, proctors, managers, sextons, masters of ceremony, etc. In the days of Hyakujo there seem to have been ten such offices, though the details are not now known, due to the loss of his Regulations. While the master or teacher of a Zendō is its soul, he is not directly concerned with its government. This is left to the senior members of the community, whose characters have been tested through many years of discipline. When the principles of Zen are discussed, one may marvel at their deep and subtle metaphysics, if there is any, and imagine what a serious, pale-faced, head-drooping, and world-forgetting group of thinkers these monks are. But in their actual life they are, after all, common mortals engaged in menial work, but they are cheerful, cracking jokes, willing to help one another, and despising no work which is usually considered low and not worthy of an educated hand. The spirit of Hyakujo is ever manifest among them.

It was not only the monks that worked but the master himself shared their labour. This was according to Hyakujo to co-operate in and equalize the work among all concerned without distinction of rank. Therefore the master together with his disciples tilled the farm, planted trees, weeded the garden, picked tea-leaves, and was engaged in all other kinds of manual work. Making use of such opportunities, he gave them practical lessons in the study of Zen, and the disciples, too, did not fail to appreciate his instructions.

When Jōshu was sweeping the courtyard a monk asked him, 'How does a speck of dust come into this holy ground?' To this Jōshu answered, 'Here comes another!' On another occasion, when the master was found again sweeping the ground, Liu, minister of state, paid a visit to the temple and said to the master gardener, 'How is it that a great wise man like you has to sweep off the dust?' 'It comes from the outside,'[1] replied Jōshu.

When Nansen was working outdoors with his monks, Jōshu, who was told to watch over a fire, suddenly cried out: 'Fire! Fire!' The alarm made all the monks rush back to the dormitory hall. Seeing this, Jōshu closed the gate and declared, 'If you could say a word the doors would be opened.' The monks did not know what to say. Nansen, the master, however, threw the key into the hall through a window. Thereupon Jōshu flung open the gate.

While working on the farm a monk happened to cut an earth-worm in twain with his spade, whereupon he asked the master Chōsa (Chang-sha Ch'ên), 'The earth-worm is cut in twain and both parts are still wriggling: in which of them is the Buddha-nature present?' The master said, 'Have no illusion!' But the monk insisted, 'I cannot help this wriggling, sir.' 'Don't you see that fire and air elements

[1] This question of dust reminds one of Berkeley's remark, 'We have just raised a dust and then complain we cannot see.'

have not yet been dispersed?' When Shiko (Tzŭ-hu) and Shōkō (Shêng-kuang) were out gardening, a similar thing happened, and Shōkō asked the master concerning the real life of the earth-worm. Without answering him, the master took up the rake, first struck the one end of the worm, then the other, and finally the space between the two. He then threw down the rake and went away.

One day Ōbaku was weeding with a hoe, and seeing Rinzai without one, asked, 'How is it that you do not carry any hoe?' Answered Rinzai, 'Somebody has carried it away, sir.' Thereupon, Ōbaku told him to come forward as he wanted to discuss the matter with him. Rinzai stepped forward. Said Ōbaku, lifting his hoe, 'Only this, but all the world's unable to hold it up.' Rinzai took the hoe away from the master and lifted it up, saying, 'How is it that it is now in my own hands?' Ōbaku remarked, 'Here is a man doing a great piece of work today!' He then returned to his own room.

Another day, observing Rinzai resting on a hoe, Ōbaku said to him, 'Are you tired?' Rinzai replied, 'I have not even lifted my hoe, and how should I be tired?' Ōbaku then struck him, who, however, snatching the stick away from the master, pushed him down. Ōbaku called out to the Yino (*karmadāna*) to help him up from the ground. The Yino responded to the call and helped up the master, saying, 'Why do you permit this crazy fellow's rudeness?' As soon as the master was again on his feet, he struck the Yino. Rinzai then began to dig the earth and made this announcement, 'In other places they cremate, but here you will all be buried alive.'

The story of Isan and Kyōzan, while they were out picking tea-leaves, has already been told in one of the preceding essays. Zen history, indeed, abounds with such incidents as here referred to, showing how the masters try to discipline their pupils on every possible occasion. The events of daily life, manifestly trivial on the surface, thus handled by the masters, grow full of signification. At any rate all these *mondō* most eloquently illustrate the whole trend of the monastery life in olden days, where the spirit of work and service was so thoroughly and harmoniously blended with the high thinking on matters deeply spiritual.

V

The monks thus develop their faculties all round. They receive no literary—that is, formal—education, which is gained mostly from books and abstract instruction. But their discipline and knowledge are practical and efficient; for the basic principle of the Zendō life is 'learning by doing'. They despise the so-called soft education, which is like those predigested foods meant for the convalescent. When a lioness gives birth to her cubs, it is proverbially believed that after three days she will push them down over a deep precipice and see if they can climb up to her. Those that fail to come out of this trial are not taken care of any more. Whether this is true or not, something like that is aimed at by the Zen master, who will treat the monks with every manner of seeming unkindness. The monks have not enough clothes to put on, not enough food to indulge in, not enough time to sleep, and, to cap these, they have plenty of work to do, menial as well as spiritual.

The outer needs and the inward aspirations, if they work on harmoniously and ideally, will finally end in producing fine characters well trained in Zen as well as in the real things of life. This unique system of education, which is still going on at every Zendō, is not so well known among the laity even in this country. And then the merciless tides of modern commercialism leave no corner uninvaded, and before long the solitary island of Zen may be found buried, as everything else, under the waves of sordid materialism. The monks themselves are beginning not to understand the great spirit of the successive masters. Though there are some things in the monastic education which may be improved, its highly religious and reverential feeling must be preserved if Zen is at all to live for many years yet to come.

Theoretically, the philosophy of Zen transcends the whole range of discursive understanding, and is not bound by rules of antithesis. But this is very slippery ground, and there are many who fail to walk erect. When they stumble, the result is sometimes disastrous. Like some of the medieval mystics, the Zen students may turn into libertines, losing all control over themselves. History is a witness to this, and psychology can readily explain the process of such degeneration. Therefore, says a Zen master, 'Let one's ideal rise as high as the crown of Vairochana (the highest divinity), while his life may be so full of humility as to make him prostrate before a baby's feet.' Which is to say, 'If any man desire to be first the same shall be last of all, and servant of all.' Therefore, the monastery life is minutely regulated and all the details are enforced in strict obedience to the spirit already referred to. Humility, poverty, and inner sanctification—these ideals of Zen are what saves Zen from sinking into the level of the medieval antinomians. Thus we can see how the Zendō discipline plays a great part in the teachings of Zen and their practical application to our daily life.

When Tanka (Tan-hsia T'ien-jan, 738–824) of the T'ang dynasty stopped at Yerinji of the Capital, it was so severely cold that he finally took one of the Buddha-images enshrined there and made a fire with it in order to warm himself. The keeper of the shrine, seeing this, was greatly exercised.

'How dare you burn up my wooden Buddha?'

Said Tanka, who looked as if searching for something with his stick in the ashes, 'I am gathering the holy śarīras[1] in the burnt ashes.'

'How,' said the keeper, 'could you get śarīras by burning a wooden Buddha?'

'If there are no śarīras to be found in it, may I have the remaining two Buddhas for my fire?' retorted Tanka.

[1] *She-li* is some indestructible substance, generally in pebble-form, found in the body of a saint when it is cremated.

The shrine-keeper later lost his eye-brows for remonstrating against the apparent impiety of Tanka, while the Buddha's wrath never was visited upon the latter.

Though one may doubt its historical occurrence, this is a notable story, and all the Zen masters agree as to the higher spiritual attainment of the Buddha-desecrating Tanka. When later a monk asked a master about Tanka's idea of burning a Buddha's statue, said the master:

'When cold we sit around the hearth with burning fire.'

'Was he then at fault or not?'

'When hot, we go to the bamboo grove by the stream,' was the answer.

I cannot help quoting another comment on the story, as this is one of the most significant subjects in the study of Zen. When Suibi Mugaku (T'sui-wei Wu-hsiao), a disciple of Tanka, was making offerings to the Arhats, probably carved in wood, a monk came up and asked, 'Tanka burned a wooden Buddha and how is it that you make offerings to the Arhats?' The master said, 'Even when it was burned, it could not be burned up; and as to my making offerings, just leave me alone as I please.' 'When these offerings are made to the Arhats, would they come to receive them, or not?' 'Do you eat everyday, or not?' the master demanded. As the monk remained silent, the master declared, 'Intelligent ones are hard to meet!'

Whatever the merit of Tanka from the purely Zen point of view, there is no doubt that such deeds as his are to be regarded as highly sacrilegious and to be avoided by all pious Buddhists. Those who have not yet gained a thorough understanding of Zen may go all lengths to commit every manner of crime and excess, even in the name of Zen. For this reason the regulations of the monastery are very rigid that pride of heart may depart and the cup of humility be drunk to the dregs.

When Shukō (Chu-hung) of the Ming dynasty was writing a book on the ten laudable deeds of a monk, one of those high-spirited, self-assertive fellows came to him, saying, 'What is the use of writing such a book when in

Zen there is not even an atom of thing to be called laudable or not?' The writer answered, 'The five aggregates (*skandha*) are entangling, and the four elements (*mahābhūta*) grow rampant, and how can you say there are no evils?' The monk still insisted, 'The four elements are ultimately all empty and the five aggregates have no reality whatever.' Shukō, giving him a slap on his face, said, 'So many are mere learned ones; you are not the real thing yet; give me another answer.' But the monk made no answer and went off filled with angry feelings. 'There,' said the master smilingly, 'why don't you wipe the dirt off your own face?' In the study of Zen the power of an all-illuminating insight must go hand in hand with a deep sense of humility and meekness of heart.

Let me cite, as one instance of teaching humility, the experience which a new monk-applicant is first made to go through when he first approaches the Meditation Hall. The applicant may come duly equipped with certificates of his qualifications and with his monkish paraphernalia consisting of such articles as are already mentioned, but the Zendō authorities will not admit him at once into their company. Generally, some formal excuse will be found: they may tell him that their establishment is not rich enough to take in another monk, or that the Hall is already too full. If the applicant quietly retires with this, there will be no place for him anywhere, not only in that particular Zendō which was his first choice but in any other Zendō throughout the land. For he will meet a similar refusal everywhere. If he wants to study Zen at all, he ought not to be discouraged by any such excuse as that.

The persistent applicant will now seat himself at the entrance porch, and, putting his head down on the box which he carries in front of him, calmly wait there. Sometimes a strong morning or evening sun shines right over the recumbent monk on the porch, but he keeps on in this attitude without stirring. When the dinner-hour comes he asks to be admitted and fed. This is granted, for no Buddhist monasteries will refuse food and lodging to a travelling monk. After eating, however, the novice goes out again on the porch, and continues his petition for admittance. No attention will be paid to him until the evening, when he asks for lodging. This being granted as before, he takes off his travelling sandals, washes his feet, and is ushered into a room reserved for such purposes. But most frequently he finds no bedding there, for a Zen monk is supposed to pass his night in deep meditation. He sits upright all night, evidently absorbed in the contemplation of a 'koan'.[1] In the following morning he goes out as on the previous day to the entrance hall and resumes the same posture as before expressive of an urgent desire to be admitted. This may go on three or five or sometimes even seven days. The patience and humility of the new applicant are tried thus hard until finally he will be taken in by the authorities, who, apparently moved by his earnestness and perseverance, will try somehow to accommodate him.

This procedure is growing somewhat a formal affair, but in olden days when things were not yet settled into a mere routine, the applicant monk had quite a hard time, for he would actually be driven out of the monastery by force. We read in the biographies of the old masters of still harder treatments which were mercilessly dealt out to them.

The Meditation Hall is regulated with militaristic severity and precision to cultivate such virtues as humility, obedience, simplicity, and earnestness in the monkish hearts that are ever prone to follow indiscriminately the extraordinary examples of the old masters, or that are liable to put in practice in a crude and undigested manner the high doctrines of a Śūnyatā philosophy such as is expounded in the Prajñā-pāramitā class of Mahāyāna literature. A

---

[1] *Kung-an* is a question of theme given to the student for solution. It literally means 'public document', and, according to a Zen scholar, it is so called because it serves as such in testing the genuineness of enlightenment a student claims to have attained. The term has been in use since the early days of Zen Beddhism in the T'ang dynasty. The so-called 'cases' or 'dialogues' (*mondō*) are generally used as koans. A special chapter devoted to the subject will be found in the second series of the Essays.

partial glimpse of such life we have already gained in the description of the table manners as above.

VI

There is a period in the monastic life exclusively set apart for mental discipline, and not interrupted by any manual labour except such as is absolutely needed. It is known as great 'Sesshin' (*Chê-hsin*)[1] and lasts a week, taking place once a month during the seasons called the 'Summer Sojourn' and the 'Winter Sojourn'. The summer sojourn begins in April and ends in August, while the winter one begins in October and ends in February. 'Sesshin' means 'collecting or concentrating the mind'. While this period is lasting the monks are confined at the Zendō, get up earlier than usual, and sit further into the night. There is a kind of lecture every day during the period. Text-books are used, the most popular of which are the *Hekiganshu* and *Rinzairoku*, the two being considered the most fundamental books of the Rinzai school. The *Rinzairoku* is a collection of sermons and sayings of the founder of the Rinzai Zen sect. The *Hekiganshu*, as has been noted elsewhere, is a collection of one hundred Zen 'cases' or 'themes' with critical annotations and poetical comments. It goes without saying that there are many other books used for the occasion. To an ordinary reader, such books generally are a sort of *obscurum per obscurius*. After listening to a series of lectures he is left in the lurch as ever. Not necessarily that they are too abstruse, but that the reader is still wanting in insight into the truth of Zen.

The lecture is a solemn affair. Its beginning is an-

---

[1] I cannot tell how early this 'Sesshin' originated in the history of the Zendō. It is not in Hyakujo's Regulations, and did not start in China, but in Japan probably after Hakuin. The Sojourn period generally being a 'stay-at-home' season, the monks do not travel, but practise 'Sesshin' and devote themselves to the study of Zen; but in the week specially set up as such, the study is pursued with the utmost vigour.

nounced by a bell, which stops ringing as soon as the master appears in the hall where what is known as 'Teisho'[1] takes place. While the master is offering incense to the Buddha and to his departed master, the monks recite a short dhāraṇī-sūtra called *Daihiju*,[2] which means 'the dhāraṇī of great compassion'. Being a Chinese transliteration of the Sanskrit original, mere recitation of the Sūtra does not give any intelligent sense. Probably the sense is not essential in this case; the assurance is sufficient that it contains something auspicious and conducive to spiritual welfare. What is more significant is the way in which it is recited. Its monotone, punctuated with a wooden time-keeper known as 'mokugyo' (Wooden Fish), prepares the mind of the audience for the coming event. After the Dhāraṇī, which is recited three times, the monks read in chorus generally the exhortatory sermon left by the founder of the monastery. In some places nowadays Hakuin's 'Song of Zazen' is often chanted. The following are translations of Hakuin and of Musō Kokushi,[3] whose last exhortatory sermon is one of the most popular.

Musō Kokushi's Exhortatory Sermon

I have three kinds of disciples: those who, vigorously shaking off all entangling circumstances, and with single-ness of thought apply themselves to the study of their own

---

[1] That is, *ti-ch'ang*. *Tei* means 'to carry in hand', 'to show forth', or 'manifest', and *sho* 'to recite'. Thus by a Teisho the old master is revived before the congregation and his discourses are more or less vividly presented to view. It is not merely explaining or commenting on the text.

[2] Dhāraṇī is a Sanskrit term which comes from the root *dhṛi*, meaning 'to hold'. In Buddhist phraseology, it is a collection, sometimes short, sometimes long, of exclamatory sentences which are not translated into other languages. It is not therefore at all intelligible when it is read by the monks as it is done in the Chinese and Japanese monasteries. But it is supposed to 'hold' in it in some mysterious way something that is most meritorious and has the power to keep evil ones away. Later, dhāraṇīs and mantrams have grown confused with one another.

[3] The founder of Tenryuji, Kyoto. He is known as 'Teacher of Seven Emperors' (1274–1361).

[spiritual] affairs, are of the first class. Those who are not so single-minded in the study, but, scattering their attention, are fond of book-learning, are of the second. Those who, covering their own spiritual brightness, are only occupied with the dribblings of the Buddhas and Fathers, are called the lowest. As to those minds that are intoxicated by secular literature and engaged in establishing themselves as men of letters are simply laymen with shaven heads, they do not belong even to the lowest. As regards those who think only of indulging in food and sleep and give themselves up to indolence—could such be called members of the Black Robe? They are truly, as were designated by an old master, clothes-racks and rice-bags. Inasmuch as they are not monks, they ought not to be permitted to call themselves my disciples and enter the monastery and sub-temples as well; even a temporary sojourn is to be prohibited, not to speak of their application as student-monks. When an old man like myself speaks thus, you may think he is lacking in all-embracing love, but the main thing is to let them know of their own faults, and, reforming themselves, to become growing plants in the patriarchal gardens.

HAKUIN'S SONG OF MEDITATION

All sentient beings are from the very beginning the Budd-
    has:
It is like ice and water;
Apart from water no ice can exist.
Outside sentient beings, where do we seek the Buddhas?
Not knowing how near the Truth is,
People seek it far away,—what a pity!
They are like him who, in the midst of water,
Cries in thirst so imploringly;
They are like the son of a rich man
Who wandered away among the poor.
The reason why we transmigrate through the six worlds

336

Is because we are lost in the darkness of ignorance;
Going astray further and further in the darkness,
When are we able to get away from birth-and-death?

As regards the Meditation practised in the Mahāyāna,
We have no words to praise it fully.
The Virtues of Perfection such as charity and morality,
And the invocation of the Buddha's name, confession, and
　　ascetic discipline,
And many other good deeds of merit,—
All these issue from the practice of Meditation.
Even those who have practised it first for one sitting
Will see all their evil karma wiped clean;
Nowhere will they find the evil paths,
But the Pure Land will be near at hand.
With a reverential heart, let them to this Truth
Listen even for once,
And let them praise it, and gladly embrace it,
And they will surely be blessed most infinitely.

For such as, reflecting within themselves,
Testify to the truth of Self-nature,
To the truth that Self-nature is no-nature,
They have really gone beyond the ken of sophistry.
For them opens the gate of the oneness of cause and effect,
And straight runs the path of non-duality and non-trinity.
Abiding with the Not-particular in particulars,
Whether going or returning, they remain for ever un-
　　moved;
Taking hold of the Not-thought in thoughts,
In every act of theirs they hear the voice of the truth.
How boundless the sky of Samādhi unfettered!
How transparent the perfect moon-light of the Fourfold
　　Wisdom!
At that moment what do they lack?
As the Truth eternally calm reveals itself to them,
This very earth is the Lotus Land of Purity,
And this body is the body of the Buddha.

The lecture lasts about an hour. It is quite different from
an ordinary lecture on a religious subject. Nothing is explained, no arguments are set forward, no apologetics, no
reasonings. The master is supposed simply to reproduce in
words what is treated in the text-book before him. When
the lecture ends, the Four Great Vows are repeated
three times, and the monks retire to their quarters. The
Vows are:

'How innumerable sentient beings are, I vow to save
them all;

How inexhaustible our evil passions are, I vow to exterminate them;

How immeasurable the holy doctrines are, I vow to
study them;

How inaccessible the path of Buddhas is, I vow to attain
it.'

VII

During the 'sesshin', they have besides lectures what is
known as 'sanzen',[1] To do 'sanzen' is to go to the master
and present one's views on a koan for his critical examination. In those days when a special 'sesshin' is not going on,
'sanzen' will probably take place twice a day, but during
the period of thought-collection—which is the meaning of
'sesshin'—the monk has to see the master four or five times
a day. This seeing the master does not take place openly,[2]
the monk is required to come up individually to the
master's room, where the interview goes on in a most
formal and solemn manner. When the monk is about to

[1] *San-ch'an* literally means 'to attend or study Zen'. As it is popularly
used now in Japan, it has, besides its general meaning, the special one as
is referred to in the text.

[2] Formerly, this was an open affair, and all the *mondō* (askings and
answerings) took place before the whole congregation, as is stated in the
Regulations of Hyakujo. But, later, undesirable results followed, such as
mere formalism, imitations, and other empty nonsenses. In modern Zen,
therefore, all sanzen is private, except on formal occasions.

cross the threshold of the master's room, he makes three bows, prostrating himself on the floor. He now enters the room keeping his hands folded, palm to palm, before the chest, and when he comes near the master he sits down and makes another bow. Once in the room, all worldly convention is disregarded. If absolutely necessary from the Zen point of view, blows may be exchanged. To make manifest the truth of Zen with all sincerity of heart is the sole consideration here, and everything else receives only a subordinate attention. Hence this elaborate formalism. The presentation over, the monk retires in the same way as before. One 'sanzen' for over thirty monks will occupy more than one hour and a half, and this is the time of the utmost tension for the master, too. To have this four or five times a day must be a kind of ordeal for the master himself, if he is not of robust health.

An absolute confidence is placed in the master as far as his understanding of Zen goes. But if the monk has sufficient reason to doubt the master's ability, he may settle it personally with him at the time of sanzen. This presentation of views, therefore, is no idle play for either of the parties concerned. It is indeed a most serious affair, and because it is so the discipline of Zen has a great moral value outside its philosophy. How serious this is may be guessed from the famous interview between the venerable Shōju and Hakuin, father of modern Zen in Japan.

One summer evening when Hakuin presented his view to the old master, who was cooling himself on the veranda, the master said, 'Stuff and nonsense.' Hakuin echoed, loudly and rather satirically, 'Stuff and nonsense!' Thereupon the master seized him, struck him several times, and finally pushed him off the veranda. It was soon after the rainy weather, and poor Hakuin rolled in the mud and water. Having recovered himself after a while, he came up and reverentially bowed to the teacher, who then remarked again, 'O you, denizen of the dark cavern!'

Another day Hakuin thought that the master did not know how deep his knowledge of Zen was and decided to have a settlement with him anyhow. As soon as the time came Hakuin entered the master's room and exhausted all his ingenuity in contest with him, making his mind up not to give way an inch of ground this time. The master was furious, and finally taking hold of Hakuin gave him several slaps and let him go over the porch again. He fell several feet at the foot of the stone wall, where he remained for a while almost senseless. The master looked down and heartily laughed at the poor fellow. This brought Hakuin back to consciousness. He came up again all in perspiration. The master, however, did not release him yet and stigmatized him as ever with, 'O you, denizen of the dark cavern!'

Hakuin grew desperate and thought of leaving the old master altogether. When one day he was going about begging in the village, a certain accident[1] made him all of a sudden open his mental eye to the truth of Zen, hitherto completely shut off from him. His joy knew no bounds and he came back in a most exalted state of mind. Before he crossed the front gate, the master recognized him and beckoned to him, saying, 'What good news have you brought home today? Come right in, quick, quick!' Hakuin told him all about what he had been through that day. The master tenderly stroked him on the back and said, 'You have it now, you have it now.' After this, Hakuin was never called names.

Such was the training the father of modern Japanese Zen had to go through. How terrible the old Shōju was when he pushed Hakuin down the stone wall! But how motherly when the disciple, after so much ill-treatment,

[1] While thus going around, he came to a house where an old woman refused to give him any rice; he kept on standing in front of it, however, looking as if nothing were said to him. His mind was so intensely concentrated on the subject which concerned him most at the time. The woman got angry, because she thought he was altogether ignoring her and trying to have his own way. She struck him with a big broom with which she was sweeping and told him to depart right at once. The heavy broom smashed his large monkish hat and knocked him down on the ground. He was lying there for a while, and when he came to his senses again everything became to him clear and transparent.

340

finally came out triumphantly! There is nothing lukewarm
in Zen. If it is lukewarm, it is not Zen. It expects one to
penetrate into the very depths of truth, and the truth can
never be grasped until one comes back to one's native
nakedness shorn of all trumperies, intellectual or otherwise. Each slap dealt by Shōju stripped Hakuin of his
insincerities. We are all living under so many casings which
really have nothing to do with our inmost self. To reach the
latter, therefore, and to gain the real knowledge of ourselves, the Zen masters resort to methods seemingly inhuman. In this case, however, there must be absolute
faith in the truth of Zen and in the master's perfect understanding of it. The lack of this faith will also mean the same
in one's own spiritual possibilities. So exclaims Rinzai: 'O
you, men of little faith! How can you ever expect to fathom
the depths of the ocean of Zen?'

VIII

In the life of the Zendō there is no fixed period of
graduation as in a school education. With some, graduation may not take place even after his twenty years' board-
ing there. But with ordinary abilities and a large amount of
perseverance and indefatigability, one is able to probe into
every intricacy of the teachings of Zen within a space of
ten years.

To practise the principle of Zen, however, in every
moment of life—that is, to grow fully saturated in the spirit
of Zen—is another question. One life may be too short for
it, for it is said that even Śākyamuni and Maitreya themselves are yet in the midst of self-training.

To be a perfectly qualified master, a mere understanding
of the truth of Zen is not sufficient. One must go through a
period which is known as 'the long maturing of the sacred
womb'. The term must have originally come from Taoism;
and in Zen nowadays it means, broadly speaking, living a

life harmonious with the understanding. Under the direction of a master, a monk may finally attain to a thorough knowledge of all the mysteries of Zen; but this is more or less intellectual, though in the highest possible sense. The monk's life, in and out, must grow in perfect unison with this attainment. To do this a further training is necessary, for what he has gained at Zendō is after all the pointing of the direction where his utmost efforts have to be put forth. But it is not at all imperative now to remain in the Zendō. On the contrary, his intellectual attainments must be further put on trial by coming into actual contact with the world. There are no prescribed rules for this 'maturing'. Each one acts on his own discretion in the accidental circumstances in which he may find himself. He may retire into the mountains and live as a solitary hermit, or he may come out into the 'market' and be an active participant in all the affairs of the world. The sixth patriarch is said to have been living among the mountaineers for fifteen years after he left the fifth patriarch. He was quite unknown in the world until he came out to a lecture by Inshu (Yin-tsung).

Chu, the National Teacher of Nan-yang, spent forty years in Nanyang and did not show himself out in the capital. But his holy life became known far and near, and at the urgent request of the Emperor he finally left his hut. Isan (Wei-shan) spent several years in the wilderness, living on nuts and befriending monkeys and deer. However, he was found out and big monasteries were built about his anchorage, he became master of 1,500 monks. Kwanzan, the founder of Myōshinji, Kyoto, retired in Mino Province, and worked as day-labourer for the villagers. Nobody recognized him until one day an accident brought out his identity and the court insisted on his founding a monastery in the capital.[1] Hakuin became the keeper of a deserted temple in Suruga which was his sole heritage in the world. We can picture to ourselves the scene of its dilapidations

---

[1] As to the life of his teacher, Daitō, reference was made to it elsewhere.

when we read this: 'There were no roofs and the stars shone through at night. Nor was there any floor. It was necessary to have a rain-hat and to put on a pair of high *getas* when anything was going on while raining in the main part of the temple. All the property attached to it was in the hands of the creditors, and the priestly belongings were mortgaged to the merchants.'—This was the beginning of Hakuin's career.

There are many other notable ones; the history of Zen abounds with such instances. The idea, however, is not to practise asceticism, it is the 'maturing', as they have properly designated, of one's moral character. Many serpents and adders are waiting at the porch, and if one fails to trample them down effectively they raise their heads again and the whole edifice of moral culture built up in vision may collapse even in one day. Antinomianism is also the pitfall for Zen followers against which a constant vigil is needed. Hence this 'maturing'.

IX

In some respects, no doubt, this kind of education prevailing at the Zendō is behind the times. But its guiding principles such as simplification of life, not wasting a moment idly, self-independence, and what they call 'secret virtue', are sound for all ages. Especially this latter is one of the most characteristic features of Zen discipline. 'Secret virtue' means practising goodness without any thought of recognition, neither by others nor by oneself. The Christians may call this the doing of 'Thy Will'. A child is drowning, and I get into the water, and it is saved. What was to be done was done. Nothing more is thought of it. I walk away and never turn back. A cloud passes, and the sky is as blue and as broad as ever. Zen calls it a 'deed without merit', and compares it to a man's work who tried to fill up a well with snow.

This is the psychological aspect of 'secret virtue'. When it is religiously considered, it is to regard and use the world reverentially and gratefully, feeling as if one were carrying on one's shoulders all the sins of the world. An old woman asked Jōshu, 'I belong to the sex that is hindered in five ways from attaining Buddhahood; and how can I ever be delivered from them?' Answered the master, 'O let all other people be born in heaven and let me, this humble self, alone continue suffering in this ocean of pain!' This is the spirit of the true Zen student. There is another story illustrating the same spirit of long-suffering. The district of Jōshu where this Zen master's monastery was situated, and where he got his popular title, was noted for the fine stone bridge. A monk one day came up to the master and asked, 'We hear so much of the splendid stone bridge of Jōshu, but I see here nothing but a miserable old rustic log bridge.' Jōshu retorted, 'You just see the rustic log bridge, and fail to see the stone bridge of Jōshu.' 'What is the stone bridge then?' 'Horses go over it, asses go over it,' was Jōshu's reply.

This seems to be but a trivial talk about a bridge, but considered from the inner way of looking at such cases, there is a great deal of truth touching the centre of one's spiritual life. We may inquire what kind of bridge is represented here. Was Jōshu speaking only of a stone bridge in his monastery premises, which was strong enough for all kinds of passengers over it? Let each one of us reflect within himself and see if he is in possession of one bridge over which pass not only horses and asses, men and women, carts heavy and light, but the whole world with its insanities and morbidities, and which is not only thus passed over but quite frequently trampled down and even cursed— a bridge which suffers all these treatments, good as well as despised, patiently and uncomplainingly. Was Jōshu referring to this kind of bridge? In any event we can read something of the sort in the cases above cited.

But this Zen spirit of self-suffering ought not to be understood in the Christian sense that man must spend all his time in prayer and mortification for the absolution of sin. For a Zen monk has no desire to be absolved from sin; this is too selfish an idea, and Zen is free from egotism. The Zen monk wishes to save the world from the misery of sin, and as to his own sin he lets it take care of itself, as he knows it is not a thing inherent in his nature. For this reason it is possible for him to be one of those who are described as 'they that weep as though they wept not; and they that rejoice as though they rejoiced not; and they that buy as though they possessed not; and they that use this world as not abusing it.'

Says Christ, 'When thou doest alms, let not thy left hand know what they right hand doeth; that thine alms may be in secret.' This is a 'secret virtue' of Buddhism. But when he goes on to say that 'thy Father who seeth in secret shall recompense thee', there we see a deep cleavage between Buddhism and Christianity. So long as there is any thought of anybody, whether he be God or Devil, knowing of your doings, Zen would say, 'You are not yet one of us.' Deeds that are accompanied by such thought are not 'meritless deeds', but full of tracks and shadows. If a Spirit is tracing you, he will in no time get hold of you and make you account for what you have done. The perfect garment shows no seams, inside and outside; it is one complete piece and nobody can tell where the work began and how it was woven. In Zen, therefore, there ought not to be left any trace of consciousness after the doing of alms, much less the thought of recompense even by God. The Zen ideal is to be 'the wind that bloweth where it listeth, and the sound of which we hear but cannot tell whence it cometh and whither it goeth'.

Lieh-tzŭ, the Chinese philosopher, described this frame of mind in a figurative manner as follows: 'I allowed my mind without restraint to think of whatever it pleased and my mouth to talk about whatever it pleased; I then forgot whether the "this and not-this" was mine or other's, whether the gain and loss was mine or other's: nor did I know whether Lao-shang-shin was my teacher, and whether Pai-kao was my friend. In and out, I was thoroughly transformed; and then it was that the eye became like the ear, and the ear like the nose, and the nose like the mouth; and there was nothing that was not identified. The mind was concentrated, and the form dissolved, and the bones and flesh all thawed away: I did not know where my form was supported, where my feet were treading; I just moved along with the wind, east and west, like a leaf of a tree detached from the stem, I was not conscious whether I was riding on the wind or the wind riding on me.'[1]

X

As I stated before, Zen followers do not approve of Christians, even Christian mystics being too conscious of God, who is the creator and supporter of all life and all being. Their attitude towards the Buddha and Zen is that of Lieh-tzŭ on the wind; a complete identification of the self with the object of thought is what is aimed at by the disciples of Jōshu, Ummon, and other leaders of Zen. This is the reason why they are all loth to hear the word Buddha or Zen mentioned in their discourse, not because indeed they are anti-Buddhist, but because they have so thoroughly assimilated Buddhism in their being. Listen to the gentle remonstrance given by Hōyen, of Gosozan, to his disciple Yengo:

[1] The wind is probably one of the best imageries to get us into the idea of non-attachment or Śūnyatā philosophy. The New Testament has at least one allusion to it when it says 'The wind bloweth as it listeth', and here we see the Chinese mystics making use of the wind to depict their inner consciousness of absolute identity, which is also the Buddhist notion of the void. Now compare the following passage from Echkart: Darum ruft die Braue auch weiter: 'Weiche von mir, mein Geliebter, weiche von mir': 'Alles, was irgend der Darstellung fähig ist, das halte ich nicht fur Gott. Und so flieche ich vor Gott, Gottes wegen!'—'Ei, wo ist dann der Seele Bleiben?'—'Auf den Fittichen der Winde!' (Büttner, *Meister Eckeharts Schriften und Predigten*, Erster Band, p. 189) 'So flieche ich vor Gott, Gottes wegen!' reminds us of a Zen master who said, 'I hate even to hear the name of the Buddha.' From the Zen point of view, 'Gottes wegen' may better be left out.

Goso said, 'You are all right, but you have a trivial fault.' Yengo asked two or three times what that fault was. Said the master at last, 'You have altogether too much of Zen.' 'Why,' protested the disciple, 'if one is studying Zen at all, don't you think it the most natural thing for one to be talking of it? Why do you dislike it?' Replied Goso, 'When it is like an ordinary everyday conversation, it is somewhat better.' A monk happened to be there with them, who asked, 'Why do you specially hate talking about Zen?' 'Because it turns one's stomach,' was the master's verdict.

Rinzai's way of expressing himself in regard to this point is quite violent and revolutionary. And if we were not acquainted with the methods of Zen teachings, such passages as are quoted below would surely make our teeth chatter and our hair stand on end. The reader may think the author is simply horrible, but we all know well how earnestly he feels about the falsehoods of the world and how unflinchingly he pushes himself forward through its confusion worse confounded. His hands may be compared to Jehovah's in trying to destroy the idols and causing the images to cease. Read the following, for instance, in which Rinzai endeavours to strip one's spirit off its last raiment of falsehood:

'O you, followers of Truth, if you wish to obtain an orthodox understanding [of Zen], do not be deceived by others. Inwardly or outwardly, if you encounter any obstacles, lay them low right away. If you encounter the Buddha, slay him: if you encounter the Patriarch, slay him; if you encounter the Arhat or the parent or the relative, slay them all without hesitation: for this is the only way to deliverance. Do not get yourselves entangled with any object, but stand above, pass on, and be free. As I see those so-called followers of Truth all over the country, there are none who come to me free and independent of objects. In dealing with them, I strike them down any way they come. If they rely on the strength of their arms, I cut them right off; if they rely on their eloquence, I make them shut themselves up; if they rely on the sharpness of their eyes, I will hit them blind. There are indeed so far none who have presented themselves before me all alone, all free, all unique. They are invariably found caught by the idle tricks of the old masters. I have really nothing to give you; all that I can do is to cure you of the diseases and deliver you from bondage.

'O you, followers of Truth, show yourselves here independent of all objects, I want to weigh the matter with you. For the last five or ten years I have waited in vain for such, and there are no such yet. They are all ghostly existences, ignominious gnomes haunting the woods or bamboo-groves, they are elfish spirits of the wilderness. They are madly biting into all heaps of filth. O you, mole-eyed, why are you wasting all the pious donations of the devout! Do you think you deserve the name of a monk, when you are still entertaining such a mistaken idea [of Zen]? I tell you, no Buddhas, no holy teachings, no discipling, no testifying! What do you seek in a neighbour's house? O you, mole-eyed! You are putting another head over your own! What do you lack in yourselves? O you, followers of Truth, what you are making use of at this very moment is none other than what makes a Patriarch or a Buddha. But you do not believe me, and seek it outwardly. Do not commit yourselves to an error. There are no realities outside, nor is there anything inside you may lay your hands on. You stick to the literal meaning of what I speak to you, but how far better it is to have all your hankerings stopped, and be doing nothing whatever!' etc., etc.

This was the way Rinzai wanted to wipe out all trace of God-consciousness in the mind of a truth-seeker. How he wields Thor-like his thunder-bolt of harangue!

XI

The state of mind in which all traces of conceptual consciousness are wiped out is called by the Christian mystics poverty, and Tauler's definition is 'Absolute poverty is thine when thou canst not remember whether anybody has ever owed thee or been indebted to thee for anything; just as all things will be forgotten by thee in the last journey of death.'

The Zen masters are more poetic and positive in their expression of the feeling of poverty; they do not make a direct reference to things worldly. Sings Mumon (Wumên):

'Hundreds of spring flowers; the autumnal moon;
A refreshing summer breeze; winter snow:
Free thy mind of all idle thoughts,
And for thee how enjoyable every season is!'

Or according to Shuan (Shou-an):

'At Nantai I sit quietly with an incense burning,
One day of rapture, all things are forgotten,
Not that mind is stopped and thoughts are put away,
But that there is really nothing to disturb my serenity.'

This is not to convey the idea that he is idly sitting and doing nothing particularly; or that he has nothing else to do but to enjoy the cherry-blossoms fragrant in the morning sun, or the lonely moon white and silvery; he may be in the midst of work, teaching pupils, reading the Sūtras, sweeping and farming as all the masters have done, and yet his own mind is filled with transcendental happiness and quietude. He is living in God, as Christians may say. All hankerings of the heart have departed, there are no idle thoughts clogging the flow of life-activity, and thus he is empty and poverty-stricken. As he is poverty-stricken, he knows how to enjoy the 'spring flowers' and the 'autumnal moon'. When worldly riches are amassed in his heart, there is no room left there for such celestial enjoyments. The Zen masters are wont to speak positively about their contentment and unworldly riches. Instead of saying that they are empty-handed, they talk of the natural sufficiency of things about them. Yōgi (Yang-ch'i), however, refers to his deserted habitation where he found himself to be residing as keeper. One day he ascended the lecturing chair in the Hall and began to recite his own verse:

'My dwelling is now here at Yōgi; the walls and roof, how weather-beaten!
The whole floor is covered white with snow crystal,
Shivering down the neck, I am filled with thoughts.'

After a pause he added the fourth line:

'How I recall the ancient masters whose habitat was no better than the shade of a tree!'

Kyōgen (Hsiang-yen) is more direct apparently in his allusion to poverty:

'My last year's poverty was not poverty enough,
My poverty this year is poverty indeed;
In my poverty last year there was room for a gimlet's point,
But this year even the gimlet is gone.'

Later, a master called Koboku Gen (K'u-mu Yüan) commented on this song of poverty by Kyōgen in the following verse:

' "Neither a gimlet's point nor the room for it" some sing; but this is not yet real poverty:
As long as one is conscious of having nothing, there still remains the guardian of poverty.
I am lately poverty-stricken in all conscience,
For from the very beginning I do not see even the one that is poor.'

Ummon was not poverty-stricken, but lean and emaciated; for when a monk asked him what were the special features of his school, the master answered, 'My skin is dry and my bones are sticking out.' Corpulence and opulence have never been associated with spirituality, at least in the East. As a matter of fact, they are not inconsistent ideas; but the amassing of wealth under our economic conditions has always resulted in producing characters that do not go very well with our ideals of saintliness. Perhaps our too emphatic protest against materialism has done this. Thus not to have anything, even wisdom and virtue, has been made the object of Buddhist life, though this does not mean that it despises them. In despising there is in a large measure something impure, not thoroughly purgated; as true Bodhisattvas are even above purity and virtuousness, how much more so they would be above such petty weaknesses of human being! When the Buddhists are thus cleansed of all these, they will truly be poverty-stricken and thin and transparent.

The aim of Zen discipline is to attain to the state of 'non-attainment' (*cittaṁ nopalabhyate*) as is technically expressed. All knowledge is an acquisition and accumulation, whereas Zen proposes to deprive one of all one's possessions. The spirit is to make one poor and humble—thoroughly cleansed of inner impurities. Learning, on the contrary, makes one rich and arrogant. Because learning is earning, the more learned, the richer, and therefore 'in much wisdom is much grief; and he that increaseth knowledge increaseth sorrow'. It is, after all, 'vanity and a striving after wind'. Zen will heartily endorse this too. Says Lao-tzŭ, 'Scholars gain everyday while the Taoists lose everyday.'[1] The consummation of this kind of loss is 'non-attainment', which is poverty. Poverty in another word is emptiness, śūnyatā. When the spirit is all purged of its filth accumulated from time

---

[1] The full passage is: 'He who seeks learnedness gets daily enriched. He who seeks the Tao is daily made poor. He is made poorer and poorer until he arrives at non-action (*wu-wei*). With non-action, there is nothing that he cannot achieve.' (Chapter xlviii.)

immemorial, it stands naked, with no raiments, with no trappings. It is now empty, free, genuine, assuming its native authority. And there is a joy in this, not that kind of joy which is liable to be upset by its counterpart, grief, but an absolute joy which is 'the gift of God', which makes a man 'enjoy good in all his labour', and from which nothing can be taken, to which nothing can be put, but which shall stay for ever. Non-attainment, therefore, in Zen is positive conception, and not merely privative. The Buddhist modes of thinking are sometimes different from those of the West, and Christian readers are often taken aback at the idea of emptiness and at the too unconditioned assertion of idealism. Singularly, however, all the mystics, Buddhist or no, agree in their idea of poverty being the end of their spiritual development.

In Christianity we seem to be too conscious of God, though we say that in Him we live and move and have our being. Zen wants to have even this last trace of God-consciousness, if possible, obliterated. That is why Zen followers advise us not to linger even where the Buddha is and to pass quickly away where he is not. All the training of the monk in the Zendō, in theory as well as in practice, is based on the notion of 'meritless deed'. Poetically, this idea is expressed as follows:

'The bamboo shadows are sweeping the stairs,
 But no dust is stirred:
 The moonlight penetrates deep in the bottom of the pool,
 But no trace is left in the water.'

When this is expressed in the more Indian and technical terms of the *Laṅkāvatāra-sūtra*, it is as follows:

'Habit-energy is not separated from mind, nor is it together with mind; though enveloped in habit-energy, mind has no marks of difference.

'Habit-energy, which is like a soiled garment produced by manovijñāna, keeps mind from shining forth, though mind itself is a robe of the utmost purity.

'I state that the ālaya is like empty space, which is neither existent nor non-existent; for the ālaya has nothing to do with being or no-being.

'Through the transformation of manovijñāna, mind is cleansed of foulness; it is enlightened as it now thoroughly understands all things: this I preach.'[1]

XII

The monastery life is not all working and sitting quiet meditating on the '*koan*'. There is something of intellectual life, in the form of lecturing, as has already been referred to. Anciently, however, there was no regular 'sesshin', and all the lecturing or giving sermons to the congregation was carried out on the feast days, memorial days, or on other auspicious occasions such as receiving visitors, honourably discharging the officials, or completing given pieces of work. Every available opportunity was thus used intellectually to enlighten earnest seekers of the truth. These discourses, sermons, exhortations, and short, pithy remarks so characteristic of Zen are recorded in its literature, the bulk of which indeed consists of nothing but these. While claiming to be above letters, Zen is filled with them, almost over-filled. Before giving some of such sermons, let me digress and say a few words about the Chinese language as the vehicle of Zen philosophy.

To my mind the Chinese language is pre-eminently adapted for Zen; it is probably the best medium of expression for Zen as long as its literary side alone is thought of. Being

---

[1] Na vāsanair bhidyate cit na cittaṁ vāsanaiḥ saha,
  Abhinnalakshanaṁ cittaṁ vāsanaiḥ pariveshtitaṁ.
  Malavad vāsanā yasya manovijñāna-sambhāvā,
  Pata-śuklopamaṁ cittaṁ vāsanair na virājate.
  Yathā na bhāvo nābhāvo gaganaṁ kathyate mayā,
  Ālayam hi tathā kāya bhāvābhāva-vivarjitaṁ.
  Manovijñāna vyāvṛittaṁ cittaṁ kālushya varjitam,
  Sarvadharmāvabodhena cittaṁ buddhaṁ vadāmyaham.
                                      The Laṅkāvatāra, p. 296.

monosyllabic, the language is terse and vigorous, and a single word is made to convey so much meaning in it. While vagueness of sense is perhaps an unavoidable shortcoming accompanying those advantages, Zen knows how to avail itself of it, and the very vagueness of the language becomes a most powerful weapon in the hand of the master. He is far from wanting to be obscure and misleading, but a well-chosen monosyllable grows when it falls from his lips into a most pregnant word loaded with the whole system of Zen. Ummon is regarded as the foremost adept in this direction. To show how extremely laconic were his sayings, the following are quoted:

When he was asked what was the sword of Ummon, he replied, 'Hung!'

'What is the one straight passage to Ummon?'

'Most intimate!'

'Which one of the Trikāya [Three Bodies of Buddha] is it that will sermonize?' 'To the point!'

'I understand this is said by all the old masters, that when you know [the truth], all the karma-hindrances are empty from the beginning; but if you do not, you have to pay all the debts back. I wonder if the second patriarch knew this or not.' Replied the master, 'Most certainly!'

'What is the eye of the true Dharma?' 'Everywhere!'

'When one commits patricide, or matricide, one goes to the Buddha to confess the sin; when, however, one murders a Buddha or Patriarch, where should one go for confession?' 'Exposed!'

'What is the Tao [path, way, or truth]?' 'Walk on!'

'How is it that without the parent's consent one cannot be ordained?' 'How shallow!' 'I cannot understand.' 'How deep!'

'What kind of phrase is it that does not cast any shadow?' 'Revealed!'

'How do you have an eye in a question?'[1] 'Blind.'

---

[1] Not an ordinary question asking enlightenment, but one that has a point in it showing some understanding on the part of the inquirer. All those questions already quoted must not be taken in their superficial or

Just one monosyllable, and the difficulties are disposed of. The Zen master has generally nothing to do with circumlocution; if anyone is a direct and plain speaker he is the directest in hitting the point and the plainest in expressing his thoughts without any encumbering appendages. To these purposes the Chinese language is eminently suited. Brevity and forcefulness are its specific qualities, for each single syllable is a word and sometimes even makes a complete sentence. A string of a few nouns with no verbs or with no connectives is often sufficient to express a complex thought. Chinese literature is naturally full of trenchant epigrams and pregnant aphorisms. The words are unwieldy and disconnected: when they are put together, they are like so many pieces of rock with nothing cementing them to one another. They do not present themselves as organic. Each link in the chain has a separate independent existence. But as each syllable is pronounced the whole effect is irresistible. Chinese is a mystic language *par excellence*.

As terseness and directness is the life of Zen, its literature is full of idiomatic and colloquial expressions. The Chinese, as you all know, being such partisans to classic formalism, scholars and philosophers did not know how to express themselves but in elegant and highly polished style. And consequently all that is left to us in ancient Chinese literature is this classicism; nothing of popular and colloquial lore has come down to posterity. Whatever we have of the latter from the T'ang and the Sung dynasties is to be sought in the writings of the Zen masters. It is an irony of fate that those who so despised the use of letters as con-

literary sense. They are generally metaphors. For instance, when one asks about a phrase having no shadow, he does not mean any ordinary ensemble of words known grammatically as such, but an absolute proposition whose verity is so beyond a shadow of doubt that every rational being will at once recognize as true on hearing it. Again, when reference is made to murdering a parent or a Buddha, it has really nothing to do with such horrible crimes, but as we have in Rinzai's sermon elsewhere, the murdering is transcending the relativity of a phenomenal world. Ultimately, therefore, this question amounts to the same thing as asking 'Where is the one to be reduced, when the many are reduced to the one?'

veyors of truth and directly appealed to the understanding of an intuitive faculty became the bearers and transmitters of ancient popular idioms and expressions which were thrown away by the classical writers as unworthy and vulgar from the main body of literature. The reason, however, is plain. The Buddha preached in the vernacular language of the people; so did Christ. The Greek or Sanskrit (or even Pāli) texts are all later elaboration when the faith began to grow stale, and scholasticism had the chance to assert itself. Then the living religion turned into an intellectual system and had to be translated into a highly but artificially polished, and therefore more or less stilted, formalism. This has been what Zen most emphatically opposed from the very beginning, and the consequence was naturally that the language it chose was that which most appealed to the people in general; that is, to their hearts open for a new living light.

The Zen masters, whenever they could, avoided the technical nomenclature of Buddhist philosophy; not only did they discuss such subjects as appealed to a plain man, but they made use of his everyday language, which was the vehicle appreciated by the masses and at the same time most expressive of the central ideas of Zen. Thus Zen literature became a unique repository of ancient wisdom. In Japan, too, when Hakuin modernized Zen he utilized profusely slangy phrases, colloquialisms, and even popular songs. This neological tendency of Zen is inevitable, seeing that it is creative and refuses to express itself in the worn-out, lifeless language of scholars and stylists. As the result even learned students of Chinese literature these days are unable to understand the Zen writings, and their spiritual meanings as well. Thus has Zen literature come to constitute a unique class of literary work in China, standing all by itself outside the main bulk of classical literature.

As I said elsewhere, Zen became truly the product of the Chinese mind by thus creating a unique influence in the history of Chinese culture. As long as Indian influence predominated, Zen could not be free from the speculative abstraction of Buddhist philosophy, which meant that Zen was not Zen in its specialized sense. Some scholars think that there is no Zen in the so-called primitive Buddhism and that the Buddha was not at all the author of Zen. But we must all remember that such critics are entirely ignoring the fact that religion, when transplanted, adapts itself to the genius of the people among whom it is introduced, and that unless it does so it gradually dies out, proving that there was no life-giving soul in that religion. Zen has claimed from the beginning of its history in China that it is transmitting the spirit and not the letter of the Buddha, by which we understand that Zen, independent of traditional Buddhist philosophy including its terminology and modes of thinking, wove out its own garment from within just as the silkworm weaves its own cocoon. Therefore the outer garment of Zen is original, befitting itself wonderfully well, and there are no patchings on it, nor any seams, either: Zen is truly the traditional celestial robe.

XIII

Before closing I must not forget to give some of the sermons by the masters which are recorded chiefly in *The Record of the Transmission of the Lamp*, as well as in the 'Sayings'.

Jōshu says: 'This thing is like holding up a transparent crystal in your hand. When a stranger comes it reflects him as such; when a native Chinese comes it reflects him as such. I pick up a blade of grass and make it work as a golden-bodied one[1] sixteen feet high. I again take hold of a golden-bodied one sixteen feet high and make him act as a blade of grass. The Buddha is what constitutes human

[1] This means Buddha, who is supposed by Buddhists to have been the owner of a golden-coloured body, sixteen feet in height.

desires and human desires are no other than Buddhahood.'
A monk asked:[1]

'For whom are the Buddha's desires roused?'

'His desires are roused for all sentient beings.'

'How does he get rid of them, then?'

'What is the use of getting rid of them?' answered the master.

On another occasion he said, 'Kāśyapa handed [the Law] over to Ānanda, and can you tell me to whom Bodhidharma handed it over?'

A monk interposed, 'How is it that we read about the second patriarch's getting its marrow from Dharma?'[2]

'Don't disparage the second patriarch,' Jōshu continued: 'Dharma claims that the one who was outside got the skin and the inside one got the bone; but can you tell me what the inmost one gets?'

A monk said, 'But don't we all know that there was one who got the marrow?'

Retorted the master: 'He has just got the skin. Here in my place I do not allow even to talk of the marrow.'

'What is the marrow, then?'

'If you ask me thus, even the skin you have not traced.'

'How grand then you are!' said the monk. 'Is this not your absolute position, sir?'

'Do you know there is one who will not accept you?'

'If you say so, there must be one who will take another position.'

'Who is such another?' demanded the master.

'Who is not such another?' retorted the monk.

'I will let you talk all you like.'

The sermons are generally of this nature, short, and to outsiders unintelligible or almost nonsensical. But, according to Zen, all these remarks are the plainest and most straightforward exposition of the truth. When the

---

[1] Generally after a sermon the monks come out and ask various questions bearing on the subject of the sermon, though frequently indifferent ones are asked too.

[2] See the article on the 'History of Zen Buddhism', p. 163 et seq.

formal logical modes of thinking are not resorted to, and yet the master is asked to express himself what he understands in his inmost heart, there are no other ways but to speak in a manner so enigmatic and so symbolic as to stagger the uninitiated. However, the masters themselves are right in earnest, and if you attach even the remotest notion of reproach to their remarks, thirty blows will be instantly on your head.

The next are from Ummon.

Ummon ascended the platform and said: 'O you, venerable monks! Don't get confused in thought. Heaven is heaven, earth is earth, mountains are mountains, water is water, monks are monks, laymen are laymen.' He paused for a while, and continued, 'Bring me out here that hill of Ansan and let me see!'

Another time he said, 'Bodhisattva Vasudeva turned without any reason into a staff.' So saying he drew a line on the ground with his own staff, and resumed, 'All the Buddhas as numberless as sands are here talking all kinds of nonsense.' He then left the Hall.

One day when he came out in the Hall as usual to give a sermon, a monk walked out of the congregation and made bows to him, saying, 'I beg you to answer.' Ummon called out aloud, 'O monks!' The monks all turned towards the master, who then came down from the seat.

Another day when he was silent in his seat for a while, a monk came out and made bows to him; said the master, 'Why so late?' The monk made a response, whereupon the master remarked, 'O you, good-for-nothing simpleton'!

Sometimes his sermon would be quite disparaging to the founder of his own faith; for he said, 'Iśvara, great lord of heaven, and the old Śākyamuni are in the middle of the courtyard, discoursing on Buddhism; are they not noisy?'

At another time he said:

'All the talk so far I have had—what is it all about, anyway? Today, again not being able to help myself, I am here to talk to you once more. In this wide universe is there anything that comes up against you, or puts you in bondage?

If there is ever a thing as small as the point of a pin lying in your way or obstructing your passage, get it out for me! What is it that you call a Buddha or a Patriarch? What are they that are known as mountains, rivers, the earth, sun, moon, or stars? What are they that you call the four elements and the five aggregates? I speak thus, but it is no more than the talk of an old woman from a remote village. If I suddenly happen to meet a monk thoroughly trained in this matter, he will, on learning what I have been talking to you, carry me off the feet and throw me down the steps. And for this would he be blamed? Whatever this may be, for what reason is it so? Don't be carried away by my talk and try to make nonsensical remarks. Unless you are the fellow who has really gone through with the whole thing, you will never do. When you are caught unawares by such an old man as myself, you will at once lose your way and break your legs. And for that, am I to be at all blamed? This being so, is there any one among you who wants to know a thing or two about the doctrine of our school? Come out and let me answer you. After this you may get a turning and be free to go out in the world, east or west.'

A monk came out and was at the point of asking a question when the master hit his mouth with the staff, and descended from the seat.

One day when Ummon was coming up to the Lecture Hall he heard the bell, whereupon he said, 'In such a wide, wide world, why do we put our monkish robes on when the bell goes like this?'

Another time he simply said, 'Don't you try to add frost over snow; take good care of yourselves, good-bye'; and went out.

'Lo, and behold, the Buddha Hall has run into the monks' quarters.' Later his own remark was, 'They are beating the drum at Lafu (Lo-fu), and a dance is going on at Shōju (Shao-chou).'

Ummon seated himself in a chair before the congregation, there was a pause for a while, and he remarked, 'Raining so long, and not a day has the sun shone.'

Another time, 'Lo, and behold! No life's left!' So saying, he acted as if he were falling. Then he asked: 'Do you understand? If not, ask this staff to enlighten you.'

As soon as Yōgi (Yang-ch'ih), a great master of the eleventh century under the Sung dynasty, got seated in his chair, he laughed loudly, 'Ha, ha, ha!' and said: 'What is this? Go back to your dormitory hall and each have a cup of tea.'

One day Yōgi ascended the seat, and the monks were all assembled. The master, before uttering a word, threw his staff away and came right down, jumping from the chair. The monks were about to disperse, when he called out, 'O monks!' The latter turned back, whereupon said the master, 'Take my staff in, O monks!' This said, the master went off.

Yakusan (Yüeh-shan, 751–834) gave no sermons for some little time and the chief secretary came up to him asking for one. The master said, 'Beat the drum then.' As soon as the congregation was ready to listen to him he went back to his own room. The secretary followed him and said, 'You gave consent to give them a sermon, and how is it that you uttered not a word?' Said the master, 'The Sūtras are explained by the Sūtra specialists, and the Śastras by the Śastra specialists; why, then, do you wonder at me? [Am I not a Zen master?]'

One day Goso (Fa-yen) entered the Hall and seated himself in the chair. He looked one way over the shoulder and then the other. Finally, he held out his staff high in his hand and said, 'Only one foot long!' And without further comment he descended.

The foregoing selections from Ummon and Jōshu and others will be sufficient to acquaint the reader with what kind of sermons have been carried on in the monastery for the intellectual or super-intellectual consumption of the monks. They are generally short. The masters do not waste much time in explaining Zen, not only because it is beyond the ken of human discursive understanding, but because such explanations are not productive of any practical and lasting benefits for the spiritual edification of the monks. The masters' remarks are, therefore, necessarily laconic; sometimes they do not even attempt to make any wordy discussion or statement, but just raising the staff, or shaking the hossu, or uttering a cry, or reciting a verse, is all that the congregation gets from the master. Some, however, seem to have their own favourite way of demonstrating the truth of Zen; for instance, Rinzai is famous for his 'Kwatsu' (*hê* in Chinese), Tokusan for his flourishing staff, Gutei for his lifting up a finger, Hima for a bifurcate stick, Kwasan for beating a drum, and so on.[1] It is wonderful to observe what a variety of methods have sprung up, so extraordinary, so ingenious, and so original, and all in order to make the monks realize the same truth, whose infinite aspects as manifested in the world may be comprehended by various individuals, each according to his own capacity and opportunity.

Taking it all in all, Zen is emphatically a matter of personal experience; if anything can be called radically empirical, it is Zen. No amount of reading, no amount of teaching, and no amount of contemplation will ever make one a Zen master. Life itself must be grasped in the midst of its flow; to stop it for examination and analysis is to kill it, leaving its cold corpse to be embraced. Therefore, everything in the Meditation Hall and every detail of its disciplinary curriculum is so arranged as to bring this idea into the most efficient prominence. The unique position maintained by the Zen sect among other Mahāyāna schools in Japan and China throughout the history of Buddhism in the Far East is no doubt due to the institution known as the Meditation Hall or Zendō.

[1] For detail see 'Practical Methods of Zen Instruction'.

THE TEN COW-HERDING PICTURES

The attainment of Buddhahood or the realization of Enlightenment is what is aimed at by all pious Buddhists, though not necessarily during this one earthly life; and Zen, as one of the Mahāyāna schools, also teaches that all our efforts must be directed towards this supreme end. While most of the other schools distinguish so many steps of spiritual development and insist on one's going through all the grades successively in order to reach the consummation of the Buddhist discipline, Zen ignores all these, and boldly declares that when one sees into the inmost nature of one's own being, one instantly becomes a Buddha, and that there is no necessity of climbing up each rung of perfection through eternal cycles of transmigration. This has been one of the most characteristic tenets of Zen ever since the coming east of Bodhidharma in the sixth century. 'See into thy own nature and be a Buddha' has thus grown the watchword of the Sect. And this 'seeing' was not the outcome of much learning or speculation, nor was it due to the grace of the supreme Buddha conferred upon his ascetic followers; but it grew out of the special training of the mind prescribed by the Zen masters. This being so, Zen could not very well recognize any form of gradation in the attainment of Buddhahood. The 'seeing into one's nature' was an instant act. There could not be any process in it which would permit scales or steps of development.

But in point of fact, where the time-element rules supreme, this was not necessarily the case. So long as our relative minds are made to comprehend one thing after another by degrees and in succession and not all at once and simultaneously, it is impossible not to speak of some kind of progress. Even Zen as something possible of demonstration in one way or another must be subjected to the limitations of time. That is to say, there are, after all, grades of development in its study; and some must be said to have more deeply, more penetratingly realized the truth of Zen. In itself the truth may transcend all form of limitation, but when it is to be realized in the human mind, its psychological laws are to be observed. The 'seeing into thy nature' must admit degrees of clearness. Transcendentally we are all Buddhas just as we are, ignorant and sinful if you like; but when we come down to this practical life, pure idealism has to give way to a more particular and palpable form of activity. This side of Zen is known as its 'constructive' aspect, in contradistinction to its 'all-sweeping' aspect. And here Zen fully recognizes degrees of spiritual development among its followers, as the truth reveals itself gradually in their minds until the 'seeing into one's nature' is perfected.

Technically speaking, Zen belongs to the group of Buddhist doctrines known as 'discrete' or 'discontinuous' or 'abrupt' (*tun* in Chinese), in opposition to 'continuous' or 'gradual' (*chien*)[1]; and naturally the opening of the mind, according to Zen, comes upon one as a matter of discrete or sudden happening and not as the result of a gradual, continuous development whose every step can be traced and analysed. The coming of satori is not like the rising of the sun gradually bringing things to light, but it is like the freezing of water, which takes place abruptly. There is no middle or twilight condition before the mind is opened to the truth, in which there prevails a sort of neutral zone, or a state of intellectual indifference. As we have already observed in several instances of satori, the transition from ignorance to enlightenment is so abrupt, the common cur, as it were, suddenly turns into a golden-haired lion. Zen is an ultra-discrete wing of Buddhism. But this holds true only when the truth of Zen itself is considered, apart from its relation to the human mind in which it is disclosed. Inasmuch as the truth is true only when it is considered in the

[1] Cf. also 'History of Zen Buddhism', where reference is made to the Northern and Southern school of Zen under the fifth patriarch in China.

light it gives to the mind and cannot be thought of at all independent of the latter, we may speak of its gradual and progressive realization in us. The psychological laws exist here as elsewhere. Therefore when Bodhidharma was ready to leave China he said that Dōfuku got the skin, the nun Sōji got the flesh, and Dōiku the bone, while Yeka had the marrow (or essence) of Zen.

Nangaku, who succeeded the sixth patriarch, had six accomplished disciples, but their attainments differed in depth. He compared them with various parts of the body, and said: 'You all have testified to my body, but each has grasped a part of it. The one who has my eyebrows is the master of manners; the second, who has my eyes, knows how to look around; the third, who has my ears, understands how to listen to reasoning; the fourth, who has my nose, is well versed in the act of breathing; the fifth, who has my tongue, is a great arguer; and finally, the one who has my mind knows the past and the present. This gradation was impossible if 'seeing into one's nature' alone was considered; for the seeing is one indivisible act, allowing no stages of transition. It is, however, no contradiction of the principle of satori, as we have repeatedly asserted, to say that in fact there is a progressive realization in the seeing, leading one deeper and deeper into the truth of Zen, finally culminating in one's complete identification with it.

Lieh-tzǔ, the Chinese philosopher of Taoism, describes in the following passage certain marked stages of development in the practice of Tao:

'The teacher of Lieh-tzǔ was Lao-shang-shih, and his friend Pai-kao-tzǔ. When Lieh-tzǔ was well advanced in the teachings of these two philosophers, he came home riding on the wind. Yin-shêng heard of this and came to Lieh-tzǔ to be instructed. Yin-shêng neglected his own household for several months. He never lost opportunities to ask the master to instruct him in the arts [of riding on the wind]; he asked ten times, and was refused each time.

Yin-shêng grew impatient and wanted to depart. Lieh-tzǔ
did not urge him to stay. For several months Yin-shêng kept
himself away from the master, but did not feel any easier
in his mind. He came over to Lieh-tzǔ again. Asked the
master, "Why this constant coming back and forth?"
Yin-shêng replied, "The other day, I, Chang Tai, wished
to be instructed by you, but you refused to teach me, which
naturally I did not like. I feel, however, no grudge against
you now, hence my presence here again."

' "I thought the other time," said the master, "you
understood it all. But seeing now what a commonplace
mortal you are, I will tell you what I have learned under
the master. Sit down and listen! It was three years after
I went to my master Lao-shang and my friend Pai-kao
that my mind began to cease thinking of right and wrong,
and my tongue talking of gain and loss, whereby he
favoured me with just a glance. At the end of five years
my mind again began to think of right and wrong, and my
tongue to talk about gain and loss. Then for the first time
the master relaxed his expression and gave me a smile. At
the end of seven years I just let my mind think of whatever
it pleased, and there was no more question of right and
wrong, I just let my tongue talk of whatever it pleased, and
there was no more question of gain and loss. Then for the
first time the master beckoned me to sit beside him. At the
end of nine years, just letting my mind think of whatever it
pleased and letting my tongue talk of whatever it pleased,
I was not conscious whether I or anybody else was in the
right or wrong, whether I or anybody else gained or lost;
nor was I aware of the old master's being my teacher or the
young Pai-kao's being my friend. Both inwardly and outwardly I was advanced. It was then that the eye was like
the ear, and the ear like the nose, and the nose like the
mouth; for they were all one and the same. The mind was
in rapture, the form dissolved, and the bones and flesh all
thawed away; and I did not know how the frame supported
itself and what the feet were treading upon. I gave myself
away to the wind, eastward or westward, like leaves of a

tree or like a dry chaff. Was the wind riding on me? or was I riding on the wind? I did not know either way.

' "Your stay with the master has not covered much space of time, and you are already feeling grudge against him. The air will not hold even a fragment of your body, nor will the earth support one member of yours. How then could you ever think of treading on empty space and riding the wind?"

'Yin-shêng was much ashamed and kept quiet for some time, not uttering even a word.'

The Christian and Mahommedan mystics also mark the stages of spiritual development. Some Sufis describe the 'seven valleys'[1] to traverse in order to reach the court of Simburgh, where the mystic 'birds' find themselves gloriously effaced and yet fully reflected in the Awful Presence of themselves. The 'seven valleys' are: 1. The Valley of Search; 2. The Valley of Love, which has no limits; 3. The Valley of Knowledge; 4. The Valley of Independence; 5. The Valley of Unity, pure and simple; 6. The Valley of Amazement; and 7. The Valley of Poverty and Annihilation, beyond which there is no advance. According to St. Teresa, there are four degrees of mystic life: Meditation, Quiet, a numberless intermediate degree, and the Orison of Unity; while Hugo of St. Victor has also his own four degrees: Meditation, Soliloquy, Consideration, and Rapture. There are other Christian mystics having their own three or four steps of 'ardent love' or of 'contemplation'.[2]

Professor R. A. Nicholson gives in his *Studies in Islamic Mysticism* a translation of Ibnu 'I-Fárid's 'The Poem of the Mystic's Progress' (*Tá'iyya*), parts of which at least are such exact counterparts of Buddhist mysticism as to make us think that the Persian poet is simply echoing the Zen sentiment. Whenever we come across such a piece of mystic literature, we cannot help being struck with the

---

[1] According to Fariduddin Attar, A.D. 1119–1229, of Khorassan, Persia. Cf. Claud Field's *Mystics and Saints of Islam*, p. 123 et seq.

[2] Underhill—*Mysticism*, p. 369.

inmost harmony of thought and feeling resonant in the depths of human soul, regardless of its outward accidental differences. The verses 326 and 327 of the *Tá'iyya* read:

'From "I am She" I mounted to where is no "to", and I perfumed [phenomenal] existence by my returning:

'And [I returned] from "I am I" for the sake of an esoteric wisdom and external laws which were instituted that I might call [the people to God].'

The passage as it stands here is not very intelligible, but read the translator's comments which throw so much light on the way the Persian thought flows:

'Three stages of Oneness (*ittihád*) are distinguished here: 1. "I am She", i.e. union (*jam'*) without real separation (*tafriqa*), although the appearance of separation is maintained. This was the stage in which al-Halláj said *"Ana 'l-Haqq"*, "I am God". 2. "I am I", i.e. pure union without any trace of separation (individuality). This stage is technically known as the "intoxication of union" (*sukru 'l-jam'*). 3. The "sobriety of union" (*sahwu 'l-jam'*), i.e. the stage in which the mystic returns from the pure oneness of the second stage to plurality in oneness and to separation in union and to the Law in the Truth, so that while continuing to be united with God he serves Him as a slave serves his lord and manifests the Divine Life in its perfection to mankind.

' "Where is no 'to' ", i.e. the stage of "I am I", beyond which no advance is possible except by means of retrogression. In this stage the mystic is entirely absorbed in the undifferentiated oneness of God. Only after he had "returned", i.e. entered upon the third stage (plurality in oneness), can he communicate to his fellows some perfume (hint) of the experience through which he has passed. "An esoteric wisdom", i.e. the Divine providence manifested by means of the religious law. By returning to consciousness, the "united" mystic is enabled to fulfil the law and to act as a spiritual director.'

When this is compared with the progress of the Zen

mystic, as is pictorially illustrated and poetically commented in the following pages, we feel that the comments were written expressly for Zen Buddhism.

During the Sung dynasty a Zen teacher called Seikyo illustrated stages of spiritual progress by a gradual purification or whitening of the cow until she herself disappears. But the pictures, six in number, are lost now.[1] Those that are still in existence, illustrating the end of Zen discipline in a more thorough and consistent manner, come from the ingenious brush of Kakuan, a monk belonging to the Rinzai school. His are, in fact, a revision and perfection of those of his predecessor. The pictures are ten in number, and each has a short introduction in prose, followed by a commentary verse, both of which are translated below. There were some other masters who composed stanzas on the same subjects using the rhymes of the first commentator, and some of them are found in the popular edition of 'The Ten Cow-herding Pictures'.

The cow has been worshipped by the Indians from very early periods of their history. The allusions are found in various connections in the Buddhist scriptures. In a Hinayana Sutra entitled 'On the Herding of Cattle',[2] eleven ways of properly attending them are described. In a similar manner a monk ought to observe eleven things properly in order to become a good Buddhist; and if he

[1] Since this book went to press I have come across an old edition of the spiritual cow-herding pictures, which end with an empty circle corresponding to the eighth of the present series. Is this the work of Seikyo as referred to in Kakuan's Preface? The cow is shown to be whitening here gradually with the progress of discipline.

[2] See also a Sūtra in the Anguttara Āgama bearing the same title which is evidently another translation of the same text. Also compare 'The Herdsman, I', in *The First Fifty Discourses of Gotama the Buddha*, Vol. II, by Bhikkhu Sīlācāra. (Leipzig, 1913.) This is a partial translation of the Majjhima Nikāya of the Pāli Tripitaka. The eleven items as enumerated in the Chinese version are just a little differently given. Essentially, of course, they are the same in both texts. A Buddhist dictionary called *Daizo Hossu* gives reference on the subject to the great Mahāyāna work of Nāgārjuna, the *Mahāprajñāpāramitā-Sūtra*, but so far I have not been able to identify the passage.

fails to do so, just like the cow-herd who neglects his duties, he will be condemned. The eleven ways of properly attending cattle are: 1. To know the colours; 2. To know the signs; 3. Brushing; 4. Dressing the wounds; 5. Making smoke; 6. Walking the right path; 7. Tenderly feeling for them; 8. Fording the streams; 9. Pasturing; 10. Milking; 11. Selecting. Some of the items cited here are not quite intelligible.

In the *Saddharma-puṇḍarīka Sūtra*, chapter iii., 'A Parable', the Buddha gives the famous parable of three carts— bullock-carts, goat-carts, and deer-carts—which a man promises to give to his children if they come out of a house on fire. The finest of the carts is the one drawn by bullocks or cows (*goratha*), which represents the vehicle for the Bodhisattvas, the greatest and most magnificent of all vehicles, leading them directly to the attainment of supreme enlightenment. The cart is described thus in the Sūtra: 'Made of seven precious substances, provided with benches, hung with a multitude of small bells, lofty, adorned with rare and wonderful jewels, embellished with jewel wreaths, decorated with garlands of flowers, carpeted with cotton mattresses and woollen coverlets, covered with white cloth and silk, having on both sides rosy cushions, yoked with white, very fair and fleet bullocks, led by a multitude of men.'

Thus reference came to be made quite frequently in Zen literature to the 'white cow on the open-air square of the village', or to the cow in general. For instance, Tai-an of Fu-chou asked Pai-chang, 'I wish to know about the Buddha; what is he?' Answered Pai-chang, 'It is like seeking for an ox while you are yourself on it.' 'What shall I do after I know?' 'It is like going home riding on it.' 'How do I look after it all the time in order to be in accordance with [the Dharma]?' The master then told him, 'You should behave like a cow-herd, who, carrying a staff, sees to it that his cattle won't wander away into somebody else's rice-fields.'

'The Ten Cow-herding Pictures' showing the upward

steps of spiritual training is doubtless another such instance, more elaborate and systematized than the one just cited.

THE TEN STAGES OF SPIRITUAL COW-HERDING [1]

I

Looking for the Cow. She has never gone astray, so what is the use of searching for her? We are not on intimate terms with her, because we have contrived against our inmost nature. She is lost, for we have ourselves been led out of the way through the deluding senses. The home is growing farther away, and byways and crossways are ever confusing. Desire for gain and fear of loss burn like fire, ideas of right and wrong shoot up like a phalanx.

Alone in the wilderness, lost in the jungle, he is searching, searching!
The swelling waters, far-away mountains, and unending path;
Exhausted and in despair, he knows not where to go,
He only hears the evening cicadas singing in the maple-woods.

II

Seeing the Traces of the Cow. By the aid of the Sūtras and by inquiring into the doctrines he has come to understand something; he has found the traces. He now knows that things, however multitudinous, are of one substance, and that the objective world is a reflection of the self. Yet he is unable to distinguish what is good from what is not; his

[1] The ten pictures reproduced between pages 192 and 193 were specially prepared for the author by Reverend Seisetsu Seki, Abbot of Tenryuji, Kyoto, which is one of the principal historical Zen monasteries in Japan.

mind is still confused as to truth and falsehood. As he has not yet entered the gate, he is provisionally said to have noticed the traces.

By the water, under the trees, scattered are the traces of the
	lost:
Fragrant woods are growing thick—did he find the way?
However remote, over the hills and far away, the cow may
	wander,
Her nose reaches the heavens and none can conceal it.

III

Seeing the Cow. He finds the way through the sound; he sees into the origin of things, and all his senses are in harmonious order. In all his activities it is manifestly present. It is like the salt in water and the glue in colour. [It is there, though not separably distinguishable.] When the eye is properly directed, he will find that it is no other thing than himself.

Yonder perching on a branch a nightingale sings cheer-
	fully;
The sun is warm, the soothing breeze blows through the
	willows green on the bank;
The cow is there all by herself, nowhere is there room to hide
	herself;
The splendid head decorated with stately horns, what
	painter can reproduce her?

IV

Catching the Cow. After getting lost long in the wilderness, he has at last found the cow and laid hand on her. But owing to the overwhelming pressure of the objective world, the cow is found hard to keep under control. She constantly longs for sweet grasses. The wild nature is still unruly, and altogether refuses to be broken in. If he wishes to have her completely in subjection, he ought to use the whip freely.

With the energy of his whole soul, he has at last taken hold
    of the cow:
But how wild her will, ungovernable her power!
At times she struts up a plateau,
When lo! she is lost in a misty, impenetrable mountain-
    pass.

V

Herding the Cow. When a thought moves, another follows, and then another—there is thus awakened an endless train of thoughts. Through enlightenment all this turns into truth; but falsehood asserts itself when confusion prevails. Things oppress us not because of an objective world, but because of a self-deceiving mind. Do not get the nose-string loose; hold it tight, and allow yourself no indulgence.

Never let yourself be separated from the whip and the
    tether,
Lest she should wander away into a world of defilement:
When she is properly tended, she will grow pure and docile,
Even without chain, nothing binding, she will by herself
    follow you.

VI

Coming Home on the Cow's Back. The struggle is over; he is no more concerned with gain and loss. He hums a rustic tune of the woodman, he sings simple songs of the village-boy. Saddling himself on the cow's back, his eyes are fixed on things not of the earth, earthy. Even if he is called to, he will not turn his head; however enticed, he will no more be kept back.

Riding the cow he leisurely wends his way home:
Enveloped in the evening mist, how tunefully the flute vanishes away!
Singing a ditty, beating time, his heart is filled with a joy indescribable!
That he is now one of those who know, need it be told?

VII

The Cow Forgotten, Leaving the Man Alone. Things are one and the cow is symbolic. When you know that what you need is not the snare or set-net but the hare or fish, it is like gold separated from the dross, it is like the moon rising out of the clouds. The one ray of light serene and penetrating shines even before days of creation.

Riding on the cow he is at last back in his home,
Where lo! there is no more the cow, and how serenely he sits all alone!
Though the red sun is held up in the sky, he seems to be still quietly asleep;
Under a straw-thatched roof are his whip and rope idly lying beside him.

VIII

The Cow and the Man Both Gone out of Sight. All confusion is set aside, and serenity alone prevails; even the idea of holiness does not obtain. He does not linger about where the Buddha is, and as to where there is no Buddha he speedily passes on. When there exists no form of dualism, even a thousand-eyed one fails to detect a loophole. A holiness before which birds offer flowers is but a farce.[1]

All is empty, the whip, the rope, the man, and the cow:
Who has ever surveyed the vastness of heaven?
Over the furnace burning ablaze, not a flake of snow can fall:
When this state of things obtains, manifest is the spirit of the ancient master.

IX

Returning to the Origin, Back to the Source. From the very beginning, pure and immaculate, he has never been affected by defilement. He calmly watches the growth and decay of things with form, while himself abiding in the immovable serenity of non-assertion. When he does not identify himself with magic-like transformations, what has he to do with artificialities of self-discipline? The water flows blue, the mountain towers green. Sitting alone, he observes things undergoing changes.

To return to the Origin, to be back at the Source—already a false step this!
Far better it is to stay home, blind and deaf, straightway and without much ado.
Sitting within the hut he takes no cognizance of things outside,
Behold the water flowing on—whither nobody knows; and those flowers red and fresh—for whom are they?

---

[1] It will be interesting to note what a mystic philosopher would say about this: 'A man shall become truly poor and as free from his creature will as he was when he was born. And I say to you, by the eternal truth, that as long as ye desire to fulfil the will of God, and have any desire after eternity and God; so long are ye not truly poor. He alone hath true spiritual poverty who wills nothing, knows nothing, desires nothing.'— From Eckhart as quoted by Inge in *Light, Life, and Love*.

X

Entering the City with Bliss-bestowing Hands. His humble
cottage door is closed, and the wisest know him not. No
glimpes of his inner life are to be caught; for he goes on his
own way without following the steps of the ancient sages.
Carrying a gourd he goes out into the market; leaning
against a stick he comes home. He is found in company
with wine-bibbers and butchers; he and they are all converted into Buddhas.

Barechested and barefooted, he comes out into the market-
    place;
Daubed with mud and ashes, how broadly he smiles!
There is no need for the miraculous power of the gods,
For he touches, and lo! the dead trees come into full bloom.

INDEX